HEALTH CARE ETHICS

Critical Issues for the 21st Century

FOURTH EDITION

Edited by

Eileen E. Morrison, EdD, MPH, LPC, CHES

Professor, School of Health Administration
Texas State University, San Marcos
San Marcos, Texas

Beth Furlong, PhD, JD, RN

Associate Professor Emerita, Center for Health Policy and Ethics
Creighton University
Omaha, Nebraska

JONES & BARTLETT
LEARNING

World Headquarters
Jones & Bartlett Learning
5 Wall Street
Burlington, MA 01803
978-443-5000
info@jblearning.com
www.jblearning.com

Jones & Bartlett Learning books and products are available through most bookstores and online booksellers. To contact Jones & Bartlett Learning directly, call 800-832-0034, fax 978-443-8000, or visit our website, www.jblearning.com.

Substantial discounts on bulk quantities of Jones & Bartlett Learning publications are available to corporations, professional associations, and other qualified organizations. For details and specific discount information, contact the special sales department at Jones & Bartlett Learning via the above contact information or send an email to specialsales@jblearning.com.

Production Credits

VP, Product Management: David D. Cella
Director of Product Management: Michael Brown
Product Specialist: Danielle Bessette
Production Manager: Carolyn Rogers Pershouse
Vendor Manager: Molly Hogue
Senior Marketing Manager: Sophie Fleck Teague
Manufacturing and Inventory Control Supervisor: Amy Bacus
Composition: codeMantra U.S. LLC
Project Management: codeMantra U.S. LLC
Cover Design: Kristin E. Parker
Rights & Media Specialist: Robert Boder
Media Development Editor: Shannon Sheehan
Cover Image: © nixki/Shutterstock; © Dutourdumonde Photography/Shutterstock.
Printing and Binding: Edwards Brothers Malloy
Cover Printing: Edwards Brothers Malloy

Library of Congress Cataloging-in-Publication Data
Names: Morrison, Eileen E., editor. | Furlong, Elizabeth, editor.
Title: Health care ethics: critical issues for the 21st century / edited by
    Eileen Morrison, Beth Furlong.
Other titles: Health care ethics (Morrison)
Description: Fourth edition. | Burlington, Massachusetts: Jones & Bartlett Learning, [2019] |
Includes bibliographical references and index.
Identifiers: LCCN 2017043204 | ISBN 9781284124910 (pbk.: alk. paper)
Subjects: | MESH: Bioethical Issues | Delivery of Health Care—ethics | Ethics, Clinical
Classification: LCC R724 | NLM WB 60 | DDC 174.2—dc23
LC record available at https://lccn.loc.gov/2017043204

6048

Printed in the United States of America
22 21 20 19 18   10 9 8 7 6 5 4 3 2 1

Writing is always a collaboration. While writers have unique ways of seeing the world, they are influenced by their experiences, research, and education. Therefore, I dedicate this edition of Health Care Ethics: Critical Issues for the 21st Century *to all those who contributed to chapters in this work and those who supported me through its creation. First, there is my immediate family, Grant, Kate, Emery Aidan, and Morrigan Leigh, who listened and encouraged. There are also colleagues, relatives, and friends who provided feedback and a lift of spirit when I needed it. Finally, there is my publisher, Michael Brown; my coeditor, Beth Furlong; and my Jones & Bartlett Learning editor, Danielle Bessette. They each added much to the quality and integrity of this work.*

–Eileen E. Morrison

Mentors facilitate one's journey. My gratitude goes to Dr. Amy Haddad and colleagues at Creighton University's Center for Health Policy and Ethics. I value the ever-present support of my husband, Robert Ramaley. Furthering the ethics education of others with this book is possible because of the collegiality and support of my coeditor, Dr. Eileen Morrison. It has been a professional pleasure to work with her.

–Beth Furlong

Contents

Contributors

Omolola Adepoju, PhD, MPH
Assistant Professor
School of Health Administration
College of Health Professions
Texas State University
San Marcos, TX

Karen J. Bawel-Brinkley, RN, PhD
Professor
School of Nursing
San Jose State University
San Jose, CA

Sidney Callahan, PhD
Distinguished Scholar
The Hastings Center
Garrison, NY

Kimberly A. Contreraz, BSN, MSN, FNP, ACHPN
Director of Palliative Care
St. Vincent Anderson Regional Hospital
Anderson, IN

Dexter R. Freeman, DSW, LCSW
Director
Master of Social Work Program
Army Medical Department Center & School
Army-Fayetteville State University
Houston, TX

Janet Gardner-Ray, EdD
CEO
Country Home Healthcare, Inc.
Charlottesville, IN

Glenn C. Graber
Professor Emeritus
Department of Philosophy
The University of Tennessee
Knoxville, TN

Nicholas King, PhD
Assistant Professor
Biomedical Ethics Unit
McGill University Faculty of Medicine
Montreal, QC, Canada

Scott Kruse, MBA, MSIT, MHA, PhD, FACHE, CPHIMS, CSSGB, Security+, MCSE
Assistant Professor and Graduate Programs
   Director
School of Health Administration
College of Health Professions
Texas State University
San Marcos, TX

Christian Lieneck, PhD, FACMPE, FACHE, FAHM
Associate Professor
School of Health Administration
College of Health Professions
Texas State University
San Marcos, TX

Richard L. O'Brien, MD
University Professor Emeritus
Creighton University
Omaha, NB

Robert W. Sandstrom, PT, PhD
Professor and Faculty Associate
School of Pharmacy and Health Professions
Creighton University
Omaha, NB

Jim Summers, PhD
Professor Emeritus
School of Health Administration
College of Health Professions
Texas State University
San Marcos, TX

Carole Warshaw, MD
Director
National Center on Domestic Violence,
   Trauma & Mental Health
Chicago, IL

Michael P. West, EdD, FACHE
Executive Director
University of Texas Arlington-Fort Worth
   Campus
Fort Worth, TX

About the Editors

Eileen E. Morrison is a professor in the School of Health Administration at Texas State University, San Marcos, Texas, USA. Her educational background includes a doctorate from Vanderbilt University, Nashville, Tennessee, USA, and a master of public health degree from the University of Tennessee, Knoxville, Tennessee, USA. In addition, she holds an associate degree in logotherapy and a clinical degree in dental hygiene.

Dr. Morrison has taught graduate and undergraduate courses in ethics and provided workshops to professionals, including those in medicine, nursing, clinical laboratory services, health information, and dentistry. She has also authored articles and chapters on ethics for a variety of publications. In addition, she is the author of *Ethics in Health Administration:* *A Practical Approach for Decision Makers* (3rd ed.), published by Jones & Bartlett Learning, and a children's book called *The Adventures of Emery the Candy Man.*

Beth Furlong is an associate professor emerita and adjunct faculty in the Center for Health Policy and Ethics at Creighton University, Omaha, Nebraska, USA. Her academic background includes a diploma, BSN, and MS in nursing, an MA and PhD in political science, and a JD. Dr. Furlong has taught graduate ethics courses and provided continuing education unit (CEU) workshops for nurses on ethics issues. Her publications are in the areas of health policy, vulnerable populations, and ethics.

Preface

The history of health care is filled with change. For example, providers and systems have embraced changes that lead to cures for disease, new ways to care for patients, regulation, and funding. However, during the creation of this fourth edition of *Health Care Ethics: Critical Issues for the 21st Century*, the healthcare system has been in change overload. It must address changes from technology, the emphasis on patient-centered care, and fiscal challenges. It is also trying to address the truly unknown. For example, legislators continue to consider the appeal of the Patient Protection and Affordable Care Act of 2010, while others are debating its repair. Since healthcare funding, programs, and regulations are linked to this legislation, the healthcare system will continue to engage in multilayers of contingency planning for survival and service.

Readers will also notice changes in this edition as its authors consider the implications of change with respect to their content areas. However, the fourth edition still reflects the organizational model that was used in previous editions. Therefore, the Greek temple image remains its organizational framework as a model for addressing ethics issues in health care (see Figure FM.1).

Like all buildings, this temple needs a firm foundation and ethics theory and principles serve this purpose. It also makes sense if one is going to be able to analyze the ethical

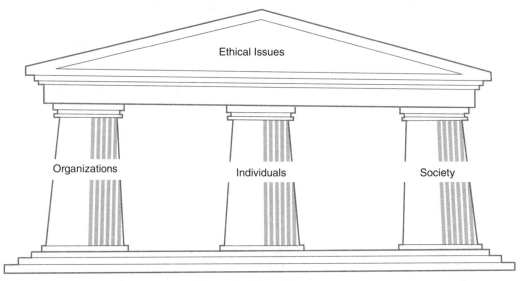

FIGURE FM.1 Healthcare Ethics Organizational Model.

implications of an issue. An appropriate analogy would be that a surgeon cannot be successful unless he or she understands human anatomy. Likewise, a student who wishes to analyze the ethics of a particular issue in health care must have knowledge of theories and principles of ethics. Dr. Summers provides a strong foundation for applying ethics in the chapters "Theory of Healthcare Ethics" and "Principles of Healthcare Ethics" of this edition.

The three main pillars of the temple model illustrate sections to organize the ethics issues faced in healthcare situations. Note that the center pillar represents individuals who are called patients in the healthcare system. This is because the healthcare system would not function unless there are patients who need care. The remaining two pillars represent issues relevant to healthcare organizations and society and reflect challenges to the future of healthcare organizations and their ability to care for patients.

Given the current environment in the healthcare system, the potential for chapters and their content was extensive. The challenge for the writers was to select example of topics that represent ethics challenges for the future and avoid a non-readable tome. While it was not possible to address each potential issue, topics were updated and expanded within a 16-chapter format. For example, under the "Critical Issues for Individuals" section, attention was given to the most vulnerable patients. Therefore, there are chapters related to the moral status of embryos and infants and reproductive technology. To address patients at the other end of the life continuum, major revisions were made to the discussion of aging patients and the ethics of their care. The other pillars of healthcare organizations and society also include major revisions of existing chapters. New chapters that reflect current ethics issues in today's environment have also been added. For example, there are chapters on the ethics of health information management and the ethics of epidemics.

Health care is truly in the epoch of change, but ethics will always matter. Even experts in ethics and health care cannot predict the future of health care with absolute certainty. However, this does not mean that ethics should not be part of making decisions amid a challenging environment. In fact, the ethics of what we do maybe even more important because health care is always held to a higher standard, even when it must meet unknown challenges.

However, Morrison and Furlong are optimistic that students will continue to ask themselves, "Is this the best ethical decision to make?" and "How do I know that this it is the best?" as they progress through their careers. Patients, healthcare organizations, and the community rely on their answers so that health care can be patient-centered, cost-effective, and fiscally responsible. What a challenging combination to face in the epoch of change!

PART I

Foundations in Theory

Change is not new, but it appears to be the theme of the current era of health care. The Patient Protection and Affordable Care Act (ACA 2010) became a law in 2010 and created major changes in the health care system. Regardless of the outcome of its status, healthcare organizations will be expected to provide patient-centered care that complies with legislation, uses qualified and compassionate professionals, and is conducted with fiscal responsibility. In addition, the foundation of health care must also be centered in ethical policies and action.

To address necessary ethics-based decisions amid an environment of consistent change, you must have a foundation in ethics theory and principles. While some think that ethics is just about "doing the right thing," in an epoch of change, one must justify decisions. In addition, the professionals employed in healthcare settings have ethics guidelines and duties encoded in their practices. Of course, patients expect healthcare providers and facilities to be concerned about their best interests, which include ethical behavior and practices. How can you justify your decisions in the practice or administration with an ethics rationale? The first section of this new edition of *Health Care Ethics: Critical Issues for the 21st Century* begins with two chapters that will provide this foundation.

The foundation in ethics theory and principles provided in the chapters "Theory of Healthcare Ethics" and "Principles of Healthcare Ethics" give you practical tools for analyzing ethics-related issues. In the chapter "Theory of Healthcare Ethics," Dr. Summers presents a well-researched overview of the theories commonly used in healthcare ethics. He includes a model that illustrates the position of ethics in philosophy. Following that, he discusses theories that indirectly relate to healthcare, such as authority-based ethics, egoism, and ethical relativism. Then, he provides a thorough analysis of theories that are most commonly applied in healthcare practice. These include natural law, deontology, utilitarianism, and virtue ethics. In his discussions, he uses several examples to improve understanding concerning the application of these theories in professional practice.

In the chapter "Principles of Healthcare Ethics," Summers continues his scholarly discussion of ethics by presenting the most commonly used ethics principles in health care. These principles are nonmaleficence, beneficence, autonomy, and justice. Because justice is the most complex of the four, he provides additional definitions of types of justice and includes information for making decisions about justice in healthcare practice. At the end of the chapter, Summers also presents a decision-making model called the *reflective equilibrium model*. This model demonstrates the application of ethics theory and principles in the practice of making clinical and business decisions.

You can apply the information given in these two chapters to your understanding of the remaining chapters in this edition. You will find that having a solid grounding in theory and principles will allow you to have greater clarity in making ethics-based decisions in your own area of health care. Certainly, as Summers suggests, principles and theory should be an important part of your ethical decision-making throughout your practice of health care.

CHAPTER 1
Theory of Healthcare Ethics

Jim Summers

▶ Introduction

In this chapter, Dr. Summers provides a scholarly review of the main theories that apply to the ethics of healthcare situations. Why is knowledge of theory important to busy healthcare professionals? In this time of great change and challenge within the healthcare system, there is a need to apply ethics in all types of decision-making. To make this application successfully, one needs a foundation in ethics, in addition to data and evidence-based management tools, including those offered by advanced technologies. An understanding of ethics theory gives you the ability to make and defend ethics-based decisions that support both fiscal responsibilities and patient-centered care. While these kinds of decisions are difficult, without a foundation in ethics theory, they might prove impossible. Therefore, this chapter and the one that follows, on the principles of ethics, will serve as your ethics theory toolbox.

▶ Ethics and Health Care

From the earliest days of philosophy in ancient Greece, people have sought to apply reason in determining the right course of action for a particular situation and in explaining why it is right. Such discourse is the topic of normative ethics. In the 21st century, issues resulting from technological advances in medicine will provide challenges that will necessitate reasoning about the right course of action. In addition, healthcare resource allocations will become more vexing as new diseases threaten, global climate change continues apace, and ever more people around the world find their lives increasingly desperate. In the Patient Protection and Affordable Care Act of 2010 (ACA 2010) era, managers of healthcare organizations will find the resources to carry out their charge increasingly constrained by multiple levels of change, differences in payment structures, and labor shortages. A foundation in ethics theory and ethical decision-making tools can assist healthcare leaders in assessing the choices that they must make in these vexing circumstances.

With the current emphasis on patient-centered care, knowledge of ethics can also be valuable when working with healthcare professionals, patients and their families, and policy makers. In this sense, ethical understanding, particularly of alternative views, becomes a form of cultural competence.[1] However, this chapter is limited to a discussion of normative ethics and meta-ethics. *Normative ethics* is the study of what is right and wrong; *metaethics* is the study of ethical concepts. Normative ethics examines ethics theories and their application to various disciplines, such as health care. In health care, ethical concepts derived from normative theories, such as autonomy, beneficence, justice, and nonmaleficence, often guide decision-making.[2]

As one might suspect, when normative ethics seeks to determine the moral views or rules that are appropriate or correct and to explain why they are correct, major disagreements in interpretation often result. These disagreements influence the application of views in many areas of moral inquiry, including health care, business, warfare, environmental protection, sports, and engineering. **FIGURE 1.1** lists the most common normative ethics theories to be considered in this chapter. Although no single theory has generated consensus in the ethics community, there is no cause for despair.

The best way to interpret these various ethics theories, some of which overlap, is to use the analogy of a toolbox.

Each of these theories provides tools that can assist with decision-making. One advantage of the toolbox approach is that you will not find it necessary to choose one ethics theory over another for all situations. You can choose the best theory for a task, according to the requirements of your role and the circumstances. Trained philosophers will find flaws with this approach, but the practical advantages will suffice to overcome these critiques.

All of the theories presented have a value in the toolbox, although like any tools, some are more valuable than others. For example, I can argue that virtue ethics has much value for healthcare applications. Before explaining why this chapter has chosen to present particular theories, a quick overview is in order.

- *Authority-based theories* can be faith-based, such as Christian, Muslim, Jewish, Hindu, or Buddhist ethics. They can also be purely ideological, such as those based on the writings of Karl Marx (1818–1883) or on capitalism. Essentially, authority-based theories determine the right thing to do on the basis of what an authority has said. In some cultures, the authority is simply "that is what the elders taught me" or "that is what we have always done." The job of the ethicist is to determine what that authority would decree for the situation at hand.

- *Natural law theory*, as considered here, uses the tradition of St. Thomas Aquinas (1224–1274) as the starting point of interpretation. The key idea behind natural law is that nature has order both rationally and in accordance with God's wisdom or providence. The right thing to do is that which is in accord with the providentially ordered nature of the world. In health care, natural law theories are important because of the influence of the Roman Catholic Church and the extent to which the Church draws on Aquinas as an early writer in the field of ethics.

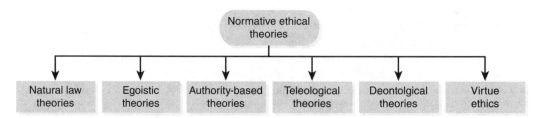

FIGURE 1.1 Normative ethics theories.

Several important debates, such as those surrounding abortion, euthanasia, and social justice, draw on concepts with roots in natural law theory.

- *Teleological theories* consider the ethics of a decision to be dependent on the consequences of the action. Thus, these theories are called *consequentialism*. The basic idea is to maximize the good of a situation. The originators of one such theory, Jeremy Bentham (1748–1832) and John Stuart Mill (1806–1873), called this maximization of good *utility*; thus, the name of their theory is *utilitarianism*.

- *Deontological theories* find their origins in the work of Immanuel Kant (1724–1804). The term *deon* is from Greek and means "duty." Thus, deontology could be called the science of determining our duties. Most authors place Kant in extreme opposition to consequentialism, because he argued that the consequences themselves are not relevant in determining what is right. Thus, doing the right thing might not always lead to an increase in the good.[3] More contemporary deontologists, including John Rawls (1921–2007) and Robert Nozick (1938–2002), reached antithetical conclusions about what our duties might be.

- *Virtue ethics* has the longest tenure among all of these views, except for authority-based theories. Its roots can be traced to Plato (427–347 BCE) and Aristotle (384–322 BCE). The key idea behind virtue ethics is to find the proper end for humans and then to seek that end. In this sense, people seek their perfection or excellence. Virtue ethics comes into play as people seek to live virtuous lives, developing their potential for excellence to the best of their abilities. Thus, virtue ethics addresses issues any thinking person should consider, such as "What sort of person should I be?" and "How should we live together?" Virtue ethics can contribute to several of the other theories in a positive way, particularly in the understanding of professional ethics and in the training necessary to produce ethical professionals.

- *Egoistic theories* argue that what is right is that which maximizes a person's self-interest. Such theories are of considerable interest in contemporary society because of their relationship to capitalism. However, the ethical approach of all healthcare professions is to put the interests of the patient above the practitioner's personal interests. Even when patients are not directly involved, such as with healthcare managers, the role is a *fiduciary relationship*, meaning that patients can trust that their interests come before those of the practitioners. Egoistic theories are at odds with the value systems of nearly all healthcare practitioners.

▶ Ethical Relativism

Before exploring any of these ethics theory tools in depth, it is first necessary to confront the relativist argument, which denies that ethics really means anything. Those who deal with ethical issues, whether in everyday life or in practice, will inevitably hear the phrase "It is all relative." Given that the purpose of this text is to help healthcare professionals deal with real-world ethical issues, it is important to determine what this phrase means and what the appropriate course of action is. Philosophers have not developed a satisfactory ethics theory that covers every situation. In fact, they are expert at finding flaws in any theory; thus, no theory will be infallible. In addition, different cultures and different groups have varying opinions about what is right and wrong and how to behave in certain situations.[4]

Does the fact that people's views differ mean that any view is acceptable? This appears to be the meaning of such statements as "It is all relative." In that sense, deciding that something is right or wrong, or good or bad, has no more significance than choices of style or culinary preferences. Thus, ethical decision-making and practice is a matter of aesthetics or preferences, with no foundation on which to ground it. This view makes a normative claim that there is no real right, wrong, good, or bad.

One could equally say that there is no truth in science, because scientists disagree about the facts and can prove nothing, only falsify it by experiment.[5] However, the intrinsic lack of final certainty in the empirical sciences does not render them simply subjective. As one commentator on the rapid changes in scientific knowledge put it, these changes reveal "the extraordinary intellectual and imaginative yields that a self-critical, self-evaluating, self-testing, experimental search for understanding can generate over time."[6] Why should we expect any less of ethics?

Sometimes, there is a claim made that because there are many perspectives, there cannot be a universal truth about ethics. Therefore, we are essentially on our own. Hugh LaFollette argued that the lack of an agreed-upon standard or the inability to generalize an ethics theory does not render ethical reasoning valueless.[7] Rather, the purpose of ethics theories is to help people decide the right course of action when faced with troubling decisions. Some ethics theories work better in some situations than in others. The theories themselves provide standards, akin to grammar and spelling rules, as to making decisions and supporting them with a particular theory.

Thus, even though ethics might not produce the final answers, we still must make decisions. Ethics theories and principles are tools to help us in that necessary endeavor. The lack of absoluteness in ethics theory also does not eliminate rationality. Often, we simply must apply our rationality without knowing whether we are correct. The better our understanding is of ethics, the more likely it is that the decision we reach will be appropriate. The ability to reach the appropriate decision is especially important in the field of health care, where our decisions affect the health, well-being, and even the lives of our patients.

▶ Ethics Theories

Let us begin to examine the tools in the toolbox, not only knowing that we are fallible, but also knowing that we are rational.[8] The first tool has little application to healthcare ethics; however, it is widely believed and therefore needs to be addressed. It involves the idea of egoism in ethics.

Egoism

Egoism operates from the premise that people either should (a normative claim) seek to advance solely their self-interests or (psychologically) this is actually what people do. The normative version, *ethical egoism*, sets as its goal the benefit, pleasure, or greatest good of the self alone.[9] In modern times, the writings of Ayn Rand[10] and her theory of *objectivism*[11] have popularized the idea of ethical egoism. For example, Rand said, "The pursuit of his own rational self-interest and of his own happiness is the highest moral purpose of his life."[12] This is a normative statement and a reasonable description of ethical egoism.

Although this theory has importance to the larger study of ethics, it is less important in healthcare ethics because the healing ethic itself requires a sublimation of self-interests to those of the patient. A healthcare professional who fails to do this is essentially not a healthcare professional. No codes of ethics in the healthcare professions declare the interests of the person in the professional role to be superior to those of the patient.

Healthcare professionals who do not understand the need to sublimate their own interests to those of the patient or their role have not yet become true healthcare professionals. An understanding of the need to sublimate one's own interests for the sake of the patient is essential in providing patient-centered care, which has become a key emphasis in healthcare delivery.

Although occasionally healthcare professionals do not put the patient's best interests first, it is not a goal of the profession to put one's self ahead of the client or patient. A realist might complain, "Yet this is the way most people behave!" Although that may be true, the fact that many people engage in a particular kind of behavior does not make it into an ethics theory. Ethical egoism constitutes more of an ethical problem than anything else. Most people who think of an ethics theory consider it something that is binding on people. However, ethical egoism is not binding on anyone else beyond self-interest. It is not binding on all (i.e., normative) and, thus, does not meet the criteria of a true ethics theory but is simply a description of human behavior. Indeed, to care for someone else above your self-interest, as required by codes of ethics in health care, is antithetical to the human behavior of truly pursuing only your self-interest. Later, we shall see how Rawls uses the idea that people pursue their self-interests to develop a theory of a just society in which solidarity seems to be the outcome, as opposed to the extreme individualism ethical egoism typically suggests.

Authority-Based Ethics Theories

Most teaching of ethics ignores religion-based ethics theories, much to the chagrin of those with deep religious convictions. A major problem with these theories is determining which authority is the correct one. Authority-based approaches, whether based on a religion, the traditions or elders of a culture, or an ideology, such as communism or capitalism, have flaws relative to the criteria needed to qualify as a normative ethics theory. Each of the authority-based approaches, to be an ethics theory, must claim to be normative relative to everyone. Because many of these authority-based approaches conflict, there is no way to sort them out other than by an appeal to reason. Not only do we have the problem of sorting through the

ethical approaches, but also arguments inevitably arise concerning the religion itself and its truth claims. If two religions both claim to be inerrant, it is difficult to find a way to agree on which of the opposing inerrant authorities is correct.

In spite of the philosophical issues arising from the use of religion in healthcare ethics, it is important for healthcare providers to understand the role of religions and spirituality in healthcare delivery. For example, all religions provide explanations of the cause or the meaning of disease and suffering. Many theologies also encourage believers to take steps to remove or ameliorate causes of disease and suffering. Over the millennia, some of these religions have even formalized their positions by becoming involved with healthcare delivery by providing inpatient and hospital care.

In addition, patients often have religious views that help them understand and cope with their conditions. Understanding a person's faith can help the clinician and health administrator provide health care that is more patient-focused.[13] For some patients, an ethical issue may arise if their faith or lack of faith is neither recognized nor respected. This failure to address or respect the faith needs of patients also conflicts with the tenets of patient-centered care.

Beyond direct patient care, a second reason to understand the authority-based philosophies common in the healthcare environment is their effect on healthcare policy. The role of authority-based ethical positions appears to be gaining importance in the 21st century. Effective working within the health policy arena, whether at the institutional, local, regional, state, federal, or international level, requires an understanding of the influence of the religious views of those involved in the debates and negotiations. This knowledge can only serve to strengthen your ability to reason with them. In other words, it is important to understand the "common" morality of those engaged in the debate. The greater the diversity in beliefs and reasoning, the more important the need for understanding what those beliefs and reasoning might be.

Religion also plays an important role in the creation of healthcare policy, because religions have provided a multiplicity of philosophical answers to questions about the nature and truth of the world. They also provide guidance on that how we should act in the world. They explain what is right or wrong and why it is right or wrong. They also help people define their identities, roles in the world, and relationships to one another. In addition, religions help us understand the nature of the world and our place in it.

Thus, as a tool, understanding authority-based philosophical systems has value because it can help in the treatment of patients. It also increases your understanding regarding the positions of persons who may be involved in debates over healthcare issues, such as resource allocations, or clinical issues such as abortion. In addition, it is important to understand authority-based philosophical systems relative to yourself. As a healthcare professional, your role requires that you do not impose your religious views on patients. At the same time, it is not part of the role for you to accept the imposition of another's religious values, even those of a patient.

These complex issues relate to professional ethics and are not part of the scope of this chapter. However, it does seem incumbent on all healthcare professionals to evaluate their own faith and to recognize the extent to which they might impose it on others. From the earliest tradition of Hippocrates, the charge was to heal the illness and the patient. More recently, the Declaration of Geneva from the World Medical Association stated that members of the medical profession would agree to the following statement: "I will not permit considerations of age, disease or disability, creed, ethnic origin, gender, nationality, political affiliation, race, sexual orientation, social standing or any other factor to intervene between my duty and my patient."[14] In addition, patient-centered care requires that healthcare professionals avoid judging patients

and treat them as individuals with a caring and concerned manner. Let us now turn our attention to the oldest non-authority-based ethics theory—virtue ethics.

Virtue Ethics

Virtue ethics traces its roots most especially to Aristotle (384–322 BCE). Aristotle sought to explain the highest good for humans. Bringing the potential of that good to actualization requires significant character development. This concept of character development falls into the area of virtue ethics because its goal is the development of those virtues in the person and the populace.

Aristotle's ethics derived from both his physics and his metaphysics. He viewed everything in existence as moving from potentiality to actuality. This is an organic view of the world, in the sense that an acorn seeks to become an oak tree. Thus, your full actuality is potentially within you. As your highest good, your potential actuality is already inherent because it is part of your nature; it only needs development, nurture, and perfecting. This idea is still part of the common morality.

Finding Our Highest Good

Just what did Aristotle conclude was our final cause or our highest good? The term Aristotle uses for this is *eudaimonia*. The typical translation is "happiness." However, this translation is inadequate, and many scholars have suggested enhancements. Many writers prefer to use the translation "flourishing." Because any organic entity can flourish, such as a cactus, so the term is not an adequate synonym.

The major complaint about translating *eudaimonia* as "happiness" is that our modern view of happiness would render it subjective. No one can know whether you are happy or you aren't; you are the final arbiter. Aristotle thought *eudaimonia* applied only to humans because it required rationality that goes beyond mere happiness. In addition, Aristotle's *eudaimonia* includes a strong moral component that is lacking from our modern understanding of happiness. In this sense, "happiness" would necessarily include doing the right thing, that is, being virtuous. Others could readily judge whether you were living a virtuous or "happy" life by observing your actions.

For Aristotle, happiness is not a disposition, as in "he is a happy sort." *Eudaimonia* is an activity. Indeed, children and other animals unable to engage self-consciously in rational and virtuous activities cannot yet be in the state translated as Aristotle's "happy."[15] Because it is commonplace to describe children as being "happy," this is clearly not an adequate translation. Given these translation problems, I shall use the term *eudaimonia* rather than its translations of "happiness" or "flourishing." Essentially, you can understand *eudaimonia* best as a perfection of character nurtured by engaging in virtuous acts over a life of experience.

The most important element of *eudaimonia* is the consideration of what it takes to be a person of good character. Such a person seeks to develop excellence in himself or herself. Because Aristotle recognized the essential social and political nature of humans, developing individual excellence would also have to include consideration of how we should live together.

Developing a Professional as a Person of Character

Consider what it takes to develop a competent and ethical healthcare professional. The process involves a course of study at an accredited university taught by persons with credentials and experience in the field. It also includes various field experiences, such as clerkships, internships, and residencies or clinical experiences with patients. Part of the education includes coming to an understanding of what behaviors are appropriate for the role, which is the definition of *professional socialization*.

For all healthcare professions, the educational process includes a substantial dose of the healing ethic by specific instruction or by observation of role models. The most fundamental idea behind this healing ethic teaches healthcare professionals to sublimate their self-interests to the needs of the patient. This education also includes recognition of the idea that the healing ethic means first doing no harm and second that whatever actions are done should provide a benefit.[16]

An Example of Professional Socialization: The Character of a Physician

The goal of professional education and socialization is to produce healthcare professionals of high character. Many professional ethics codes describe the character traits that define high character, or what could be called virtues.[17] For example, the 2016 American Medical Association statement of the principles of medical ethics notes that the principles are "standards of conduct which define the essentials of honorable behavior for the physician."[18] Essentially, the principles define the appropriate character traits or virtues for a physician.

Relative to virtue ethics, these traits or virtues combine to create not only a good physician but also a person of good character. Like Aristotle's person of virtue, engaging in the activities of *eudaimonia* produces practical wisdom. "Moral virtue comes about as a result of habit."[19] The virtues come into being in us because "we are adapted by nature to receive them, and they are made perfect by habit."[20]

Not only is practice required, but the moral component is essential, too. Good physicians are not merely technically competent; they are persons of good character. How do we know this? Their actions coalesce to reveal integrity in all levels of their practice. In addition, a physician or any other person of good character does not undertake to do what is right simply to appear ethical. In a modern sense, the properly socialized physicians have internalized the ethical expectations of their profession. To do the right thing is part of their identities.[21]

To use Aristotle's term, physicians have become persons of practical wisdom. In describing practical wisdom, Aristotle says the following:

> [I]t is thought to be the mark of a man of practical wisdom to be able to deliberate well about what is good and expedient for himself, not in some particular respect, e.g. about what sorts of things conduce to health or to strength, but about what sorts of things conduce to the good life in general.[22]

The mere fact that inculcation of such character traits is so important in all healthcare professions indicates that these ancient teachings are part of the common morality, or at least the professional morality of healthcare professions. In short, persons of virtue nurture *eudaimonia* because they believe it is the right way to live and that "[w]ith the presence of practical wisdom [they] will be given all the virtues."[23] Good physicians are living excellent lives; perfecting themselves is part of their self-identities.[24] These persons will act on the ethics principles that form the core of their identification of themselves with their role. In health care, these principles function as virtues.

Principles of Biomedical Ethics as Virtues

Beauchamp and Childress have popularized what they call the principles of biomedical ethics in a textbook of the same name that has gone through seven editions from 1978 to 2013.[25] The following list provides brief definitions of these principles:

- *Autonomy* is the ability to decide for oneself. The word derives from the Greek words for "self" (*auto*) and "rule" (*nomos*). Autonomy means that people are free to make their own decisions. The failure to respect the personhood of others, making decisions for them without their consent, is *paternalism*.
- *Beneficence* is from the Latin root *bene*, meaning "to do well." More specifically, it derives from the Latin word *benefacere*, meaning "to do a kindness, provide a benefit." It is the practice of doing the good thing. Health care has clearly valued beneficence from its early Hippocratic origins. It is the second part of the dictum "First do no harm, benefit only." As an active beneficence, professionalism requires healthcare practitioners to put patients' interests before their own. When combined with beneficence, healthcare professionals hold dear the virtue *of altruism*.
- *Nonmaleficence* derives from the Latin word *mal*, meaning "bad." A *malevolent* person wishes ill of someone. Thus, nonmaleficence means to *not* do wrong toward another.
- *Justice* is a concept with a vast history and multiple interpretations. The etymology is Latin and suggests more than just fairness. The words *just* and *justice* include elements of righteousness ("She is a just person."), equity ("He received his just due."), and lawfulness ("She was brought to justice.").[26] A just person is fair, lawful, reasonable, correct, and honest.[27] Most writers in ethics discuss two kinds of justice, distributive and procedural. *Distributive justice* determines the proper sharing of property and of burdens and benefits. *Procedural justice* determines the proper application of the rules in the hearing of a case.

These concepts are foundational principles of healthcare ethics.[28] A person having these virtues as part of his or her character structure, self-definition, and actions is considered a person of good character. In healthcare terms, such a person would be walking the talk of the healing ethic and would be a person of practical wisdom.

Elitism

A person who seeks to nurture *eudaimonia* through his or her actions achieves this goal after long practice of Aristotle's practical wisdom. In applying practical wisdom, the person has learned to live well, exemplifying what we would call a person of virtue or integrity, a good person. Such a person often sets the standard for the right action in a particular situation. Thus, virtue ethics has the problem of being elitist. Owing to his view of the hierarchical nature of reality, Aristotle thought that some people were simply not capable of maximizing their potential to reach the highest good.[29]

Aristotle noted the difficulty in encouraging many to a character of virtue, a life of nobility and goodness.[30] Aristotle believed that living in fear, living by emotions, and pursuing pleasures are the motivations for most people. They lack even a conception of the noble and truly pleasant, having never known it. Aristotle seemed to despair that once these bad traits have long been in place, they are impossible to remove. He concluded, "We must be content if, when all the influences by which we are thought to be good are present, we get some tincture of virtue."[31] The person of practical wisdom becomes the standard for ethical decision-making. This leads to an understanding of how virtue ethics can facilitate the management of ethical conflicts.

Balancing Obligations from the Virtue Ethics Perspective

Because different principles of ethics or different virtues conflict, it is not possible to practice in the healthcare professions for long without encountering some kind of ethical dilemma. Some treatments involve harm (we are to do no harm) yet provide a benefit (benefit only). An experienced healthcare professional must be able to explain the relative benefits and risks of such treatments and gain the cooperation of the patient for the treatments.

Sometimes, one principle alone might create conflict. For example, physicians must know how to tell the truth to patients. Even though information can be regarded as therapy, information delivered at the wrong time or in the wrong way can be devastating. Information not delivered at the right time or never delivered at all could mean that the physician is not being honest and is guilty of paternalism. Learning how to deal with these issues effectively takes experience (practical wisdom) and theoretical knowledge.

A major component of the patient–clinician relationship is the patients' trust that their caregivers have their best interests at heart and that they are competent. If patients perceive caregivers as persons of integrity, virtue, or practical wisdom, their confidence in their caregivers will increase. That increase in patients' confidence has documented effects on enhancing the placebo effect.[32] How caregivers communicate, and even how they carry themselves, will do much to influence these perceptions.[33] A caregiver who knows how to do these things is a person of practical wisdom, at least when it comes to medical practice.

Caregivers with practical wisdom, which, by necessity, includes being of good character, or virtuous, will also be able to make appropriate decisions about the means to ends. This has significant implications for healthcare ethics. When faced with ethical challenges in medical care, such caregivers will have the practical wisdom to know how to weigh the various issues and concerns and form a conclusion. Because wise and good people can, and do, come to different conclusions about an ethically appropriate choice of action, persons of practical wisdom should consult with one another.

Healthcare organizations have sought to institutionalize this approach by using ethics committees. Those with practical wisdom in health care are far ahead of most professionals in having a decades-long tradition of ethics committees, ethics consultations, and institutional review boards. The key here is that persons of good character, pursuing virtuous ends, are much more likely to make an appropriate choice than those without such experience or such character. These choices would appear to refute one of the usual criticisms levied against virtue ethics—that there is no clear way to resolve disputes when those who have practical wisdom disagree about the correct course of action. Mechanisms such as ethics committees lead the deliberators to make a decision, even though it may not be unanimous.

Virtue ethics thus leads to the conclusion that within health care at least, the probability is good that persons socialized to put the patient's interests first will come up with the ethically correct ranking of options. They will also respect the patient's wishes, even if they do not agree with those wishes.

Of course, this depiction makes the situation sound much better than it is. Persons well trained in the healing ethic take unethical actions. Is that a fault of the education or the person? Aristotle would fault the person. In Aristotle's view, some people, by nature, are unable to control their passions, their desires, and their emotions. Others are unable to act rationally. Some are just wicked.[34] Yes, the theory results in a form of elitism. However, it seems fair to say that health care has a major advantage over many other fields in that it has a strong educational and socialization process for developing the right character. In a sense, the purpose of the educational process is to develop a cadre of elite professionals. In doing so, they should become persons of high character.

Ethics Theories and Professional Roles

Knowledge of virtue ethics offers one further advantage. Persons of practical wisdom should be better prepared to know when to use a particular ethics theory, depending on the role in which they find themselves. Again, take physicians as an example. Although physicians have a primary obligation to their patients, it is not their only role. Consider the following physician roles, none of which involves patients directly: conducting scientific studies; negotiating with vendors selling equipment and supplies; and hiring, firing, and supervising employees. In addition, physicians might be negotiating with third-party payers, lobbying on behalf of health policy issues, and conducting peer reviews of other physicians. They might also be involved in the management of healthcare organizations and be part of various advisory and regulatory agency boards. Many other non-patient-related tasks could be listed, such as working with community groups or serving as faculty, as needed.

Some of the ethics theories work better in certain roles than others. How do physicians choose the appropriate theory? The socialization process seeks to develop caregivers who are persons seeking the highest good, at least in health care. This foundational process should develop persons of integrity and practical wisdom who can manage the inevitable ethical dilemmas and make the best ethical decisions in any role. They can apply reason to the situation and make the best-possible decision within their respective role.

Natural Law

The theory of natural law owes a great debt to Aristotle. Natural law also is important to Roman Catholic theology, given its origins with Aquinas. Many texts on ethics and medical ethics leave out natural law or give it short shrift. Some authors consider the theory a version of moderate deontology,[35] defining deontology as simply any view that defines the right thing to do as dependent on something other than consequences. Thus, there is consequentialism and everything else. In the realm of healthcare ethics, such an approach appears overly limiting. As a tool in the ethics theory toolbox, there are a number of good reasons to know natural law theory. Even if philosophically one can reduce this theory to another, natural law is sufficiently definitive and important to consider on its own merits.[36]

One key to understanding natural law is its assumption that nature is rational and orderly. This theory goes back to the ancient Greeks, who believed that the cosmos was essentially unchanging in its order. Aristotle certainly believed this.[37] This is now a statement of physics—a statement about the nature of the world—rather than a statement about ethics.

Natural Law's Relationship to Aristotle, St. Thomas Aquinas, and the Catholic Church

Aquinas's beliefs gained prominence in the Catholic Church at the Council of Trent (1545–1563). In 1879, Pope Leo XIII declared Thomism (Aquinas's theology) to be eternally valid.[38] Nearly all writers recognize Aquinas as setting the standard for natural law theory, just as Aristotle serves as the standard-bearer for virtue ethics.[39] Aquinas developed his theory in his work titled *Summa Theologica*, meaning "the highest theology." Aquinas structured the work in the form of a series of questions, which he answered.[40]

The Thomistic conception of *natural law* proceeds as follows: "All things subject to Divine providence are ruled and measured by the eternal law" (ST IaIIae 91, 2). "The rational creature is subject to Divine providence in the most excellent way . . . . Wherefore it has a share of the Eternal Reason, whereby it has a natural inclination to its proper act and end: and this participation of the eternal law in the rational creature is called the natural law" (ST IaIIae 91, 2). This establishes that natural law is given by God and thus authoritative over all humans. Not only can we know the law, but also as rational and moral creatures, we can violate it.

Recall Aristotle's concept of practical wisdom; Aquinas used the same concept. In fact, he called Aristotle "the philosopher" and cited

him as frequently as Scripture. One can find the importance of practical reason, how it works, its similarity to Aristotle's conception of it, and the most concise statement of what the natural law compels in Aquinas's writings.

The first principle of practical reason is one founded on the notion of good, namely that good is that which all things seek. Hence, the first precept of law is that good is to be done and pursued and evil is to be avoided. All other precepts of the natural law are based upon this: whatever the practical reason naturally apprehends as man's good (or evil) belongs to the precepts of the natural law as something to be done or avoided (ST IaIIae 94, 2).

Unfortunately, some have stopped at this quote and simply say that natural law means to "do the good and avoid the evil."[41] Because this lacks clarity about what the good might be or about any decision rule by which to decide what to do when goods conflict or when rankings are required, this statement alone does not constitute an ethics theory. It sells the theory short.[42]

Aquinas also drew on Aristotle's idea of potentiality moving to actuality and states that in the realm of what is good, "all desire their own perfection" (ST Ia 5, 1). Again, following Aristotle's lead, Aquinas noted that when it comes to practical reason, the rules might be clear but their application might not be. In short, the details make the principle more difficult to apply (ST IaIIae 94, 4).

Aquinas then offered an excellent example that shows the difficulty at hand. Everyone would agree that in general, "goods entrusted to another should be restored to their owner" (ST IaIIae 94, 4). However, Aquinas noted that "it may happen in a particular case that it would be injurious, and therefore unreasonable, to restore goods held in trust; for instance, if they are claimed for the purpose of fighting against one's country. And this principle will be found to fail the more, according as we descend further into detail" (ST IaIIae 94, 4). Taking this practical wisdom approach even further, he generalized that "the greater the number of conditions added, the greater the number of ways in which the principle may fail" (ST IaIIae 94, 4).

Aquinas even went so far as to note that although all are governed by the natural law, all might not know it or act upon it: "In some the reason is perverted by passion, or evil habit, or an evil disposition of nature" (ST IaIIae 94, 4).[43] So what are we to do? In seeking a principle to determine what is good and what is bad, it is not difficult to find specific behaviors listed by Aquinas. However, an excellent philosophical overview of natural law by Michael Murphy concluded that there are no obvious master principles but only examples of flawed acts.[44] The *Catholic Encyclopedia* suggested a number of things that would be wrong or right under the dictum to always do good and avoid harm. However, there was nothing about how to resolve conflicts among these requirements.[45] This seems to add a quandary. All decisions are specific, and the details will change, so are there any decision rules?

At this point, scholars disagree on exactly how Aquinas resolved the quandary, and we do not need to follow them in those debates. However, there is still a need for a decision principle when there are disputes regarding which of the various actions to take. There are two such principles, and the one most closely associated with natural law theory is that of the double effect.

Principle of Double Effect

The first principle that proposes to distinguish between a good and an evil is the *theory of double effect*. Derived from *Summa Theologica*, the principle has four key points:

- The act must be good, or at least morally neutral, independent of its consequences.
- The agent intends only the good effects, not the bad effect.
- The bad effect must not be a means to the good effect. If the good effect were to be the causal result of the bad effect, the agent would intend the bad effect in pursuit of the good effect.
- The good effect must outweigh the bad effect.[46]

The theory of double effect has use in medical ethics when dealing with abortion, euthanasia, and other decisions where there is a conflict between a good and an evil. For example, under this view, abortion is an evil, but saving the life of a mother is a good. Under this view, euthanasia is an evil, but relieving pain by the use of morphine is a good. If the person dies and the death was not intended, then is it acceptable? Major issues arise in the application of the theory concerning how to determine a person's intent. We know that not everyone is a person of practical wisdom who only has a good intent. However, how would we know the intent in a particular case?[47]

At the policy-making level, is it acceptable to cut taxes for the rich at the expense of the poor? What good comes of it? Because there are few rich and many poor, does the good of the rich count more than the good lost by the poor? Note that the further we delve into these types of questions, the more important consequences seem to become, until natural law becomes a form of consequentialism, perhaps rule consequentialism.[48] It is not necessary to resolve these disputes here, because the purpose is to understand the theories for the purposes of making appropriate decisions in health care. Relative to that end, a second decision rule for natural law is available.

Entitlement to Maximize Your Potential

The key to understanding this proposed decision rule relates to metaphysics: "Ethics especially is impossible without metaphysics, since it is according to the metaphysical view we take of the world that ethics shapes itself."[49] The Thomistic ethic draws heavily on the Aristotelian metaphysics that describes the world as a hierarchy of being, with all entities in it striving to reach their own complete state of actualization of their potential. This means that it is part of the natural order for all entities to strive to maximize their potential. To deny something its ability to actualize its potential is to violate its very nature. Such a violation causes harm to the entity and would be a violation of its nature and of the natural law to avoid harm. Thus, natural law proscribes any activities that would violate an entity's potential.[50] Concerns about termination of potential, at least for rational creatures, are evident in several contemporary healthcare issues.

Many religions and social activists place considerable emphasis on social and political factors that prevent humans from actualizing their potential. These groups often are at the forefront of social justice movements addressing poverty, ignorance, unhealthy living conditions, and slave-like working conditions. Clearly, healthcare professionals need to understand natural law theory when working with patients who believe in its tenets and with those who advocate social justice. This might include those who are working to improve public health, social conditions, or human rights. Now let us look at another common ethics theory, deontology.

Deontology

The derivation of *deontology* comes from the Greek word *deon*, which means "duty." Thus, deontology is concerned with behaving ethically by meeting our duties. The ethics theory of deontology originates with the German philosopher Kant (1724–1804).[51] Although Kant's influence on deontology is significant, many other thinkers are part of the deontological tradition as well.[52] Nonetheless, just as we relied on Aristotle for virtue ethics and on Aquinas for natural law, Kant sets the standard for deontology. Following the review of Kant, we shall examine some of the more contemporary advocates of deontological theories.

Kant's Metaphysics and Epistemology Grounded His Ethics

Kant is most well-known for his work in metaphysics and epistemology, the *Critique of Pure Reason*,[53] but he also did groundbreaking work in ethics. Kant's writings on ethics appear in several different volumes, with titles such as *Groundwork of the Metaphysics of Morals*[54] and *Critique of Practical Reason*[55] among others.

The concept of honoring commitments clearly did not start with Kant, but his approach to the issue led to the identification of his ethics theory with deontology. Kant's work in metaphysics and epistemology had a significant influence on this approach and his ethical views. As seen with Aristotle and Aquinas, a complete understanding of ethics often includes a view about the nature of the world and how we know it—in other words, the disciplines of metaphysics and epistemology. Kant concluded that the belief that perception represented the world was incorrect, or at least incomplete. Instead, the structure of consciousness processes sense data through the means of categories of thought and two forms of intuition, space and time.

Of these categories of thought, the one that relates most directly to ethics is causality. All experiences are subject to causation, which in Kant's view undermines free will. In the Newtonian world of his time, it was widely believed that if you could completely know the behavior of all the matter in existence, you could predict the future behavior of anything material. This did not pose a problem for most people at this time because of the earlier dividing of mind and matter by Rene Descartes (1595–1650). Like most people, Kant found free will to be essential for ethics. If one's every act is determined, how can one be held responsible for one's choices?

At the same time, Kant's reasoning inexorably led him to conclude that we cannot know what the world is like in and of itself. It is beyond knowing, because we cannot experience anything without use of the categories and forms of intuition. Kant, thus, divided the realm of being into the *phenomenal world* of experience and the *noumenal world*. We can think about the noumenal world, but we cannot directly experience it. Thus, we have "an unavoidable ignorance of things in themselves and all that we can theoretically *know* are mere appearances" (B xxix).[56] Relative to ethics, it should be clear from Kant's perspective that the metaphysical issue of whether free will is possible is foundational.[57]

Kant argued that knowledge of the sensible world was insufficient for knowing the moral law.[58] Yet he also argued that free will makes ethics possible. Free will is the precondition of ethics. If all things are determined by natural causes, then our supposed ethical choices are specious, an illusion. Humans, as a natural phenomenon, are determined by natural laws; causality applies to all natural phenomena. However, the self, in and of itself (the soul), is free from these laws.[59]

Kant recognized that this puts morality beyond the pale of empirical science, and indeed, the question about free will is beyond such testing. However, Kant believed that he left a "crack in the door" that is wide enough to allow for morality. He did this by arguing that the concept of freedom, although not knowable in a scientific way, is something we can think about without contradiction: "Morality does not, indeed, require that freedom should be understood, but only that it should not contradict itself, and so should at least allow of being thought" (B xxix).[60] In this sense, Kant redefined humans as participating in two kinds of reality, the phenomenal and the noumenal. According to Kant, "There is no contradiction in supposing that one and the same will is, in the appearance, that is, in its visible acts, necessarily subject to the law of nature, and so far *not free*, while yet, as belonging to a thing in itself, is not subject to that law, and is therefore *free*" (B xxviii).[61]

Freedom of the Will

Like Aristotle and Aquinas, Kant certainly thought good character was laudable. However, he was concerned that the properties that constitute good character, without a good will to correct them, could lead to bad outcomes. For example, we can misuse courage and perseverance without the direction of a good will.[62] Kant went so far as to argue that one should act on the duty of obligation to the moral law regardless of any relationship that might have an outcome such as *eudaimonia*: "A good will is good not because of what it performs or effects, not by its aptness for the attainment of some proposed end, but simply by virtue of its volition, that is, it is good in and of itself" (AK 4:394).[63] In other words, a good will is good because it wills properly. Thus, Kant set a high standard. Some of his language even suggests that the true test of a good will is whether the person continues to act out of duty and reverence for the moral law, even when doing so has no personal benefit and might "involve many a disappointment to the ends of inclination" (AK 4:396).[64]

Reason, Autonomy, the Moral Law, and the Will

Kant was distinctive relative to his predecessors in seeking to ground our duties in a self-governing will. This is an appeal to reason itself being autonomous, meaning that we are free to choose. If we choose according to reason, we shall conform to the moral law: "If reason completely determined the will, the action would without exception take place according to the rule" (AK 5:20).[65] One can see the extremely prominent principle of autonomy coming into play here.

Typically, an autonomous agent is one who makes his or her own rules and is responsible for his or her actions.[66] To violate that autonomy is to violate a person's innermost selfhood, something Kant developed as one form of the categorical imperative. Thus, one does not seek the foundation of ethics in the development of a person of good character seeking to actualize his or her intrinsic nature in order to seek the end of *eudaimonia*. Instead, the subject matter of ethics is not character but, rather, the nature and content of the principles that determine a rational will. Free will is determined by moral principles that cohere with the categorical imperative. This abstruse approach, for many, simply disconnects the moral law and free will from real life.

The idea of autonomy here is not the view that individuals make their own laws. It means that the laws that bind you in some sense derive from your own making, your own fundamental nature as a self.[67] For Kant, the will is free in the sense that you choose to be bound by these principles of reason. You freely choose to bind yourself to the constraints of the categorical imperative and the dictates of reason.

The requirement of the duty to obey the moral law to express a good will brings the notion of intent into the discussion. Why a person acts in such a way as to conform to the moral law is an important component of ethical evaluation in the Kantian scheme. Let us turn to what Kant saw as rational principles that would ground ethics or the moral law.

Kant attempted to discover the rational principle that would ground all other ethical judgments. He called this principle the categorical imperative. The *categorical imperative* is not so much a rule as a criterion for determining what ethics principles meet the test of reason.[68] The imperative would have to be categorical rather than hypothetical, or conditional, because true morality should not depend on individual likes and dislikes or on abilities and opportunities. These are historical "accidents." Any ultimate principle of ethics must transcend them in order to meet the conditions of fairness. We shall later see how Rawls used similar ideas in developing his concept of a veil of ignorance. Kant developed

several formulations of the categorical imperative. The most commonly presented ones follow:[69]

- "Always act in such a way that you can also will that the maxim of your action should become a universal law" (AK 4:421).[70] This principle often is caricatured as the *Golden Rule: Do unto others as you would have them do unto you.*[71] This does not capture the full meaning of what Kant had in mind and may, indeed, miss the essence of his teachings, as he specifically disavowed that this was his intended meaning (AK 4:430).[72]

- "Act so that you treat humanity, both in your own person and in that of another, always as an end and never merely as a means" (AK 4:429).[73] Kant spoke of the good society as a place that was a kingdom of ends (AK 4:433–434).[74]

The Categorical Imperative as a Formal Decision Criterion

Although Kant believed that these two statements of the categorical imperative were formally equivalent, the first illustrates the need to apply moral principles universally. That a principle be logically consistent was important to Kant. This principle of universal application is also what allowed ethical egoism to be dismissed as something humans do when making decisions but not as something that is an ethics theory. The second formulation points to making the radical distinction between things and persons and emphasizes the necessity of respect for persons.

Kant's theory evaluates morality by examining the nature of actions and the will of agents rather than goals achieved. You have done the right thing when you act out of your obligation to the moral law, not simply because you act in accordance with it. Note the fundamental importance of intent as compared with any concern with outcomes. One reason for the emphasis on duties in Kant's deontology is that we are praised or blamed for actions within our control, and that includes our willing, not our achieving.

Kant did care about the outcomes of our actions, but he thought that as far as the moral evaluation of actions was concerned, consequences did not matter. As Kant pointed out, this total removal of consequences "is strange enough and has no parallel in the remainder of practical knowledge" (AK 5:31).[75] Let us now look at the second version of the categorical imperative, which is foundational in healthcare ethics.

The Categorical Imperative as Respect for Persons

The second version of the categorical imperative emphasizes respect for persons. According to Kant, you should "[s]o act as to treat humanity, whither in thine own person or in that of any other, in every case as an end withal, never as means only" (AK 4:429).[76] People, unlike things, ought never to be merely used. Their value is never a means to our ends; they are ends in themselves. Of course, a person might be useful as a means, but you must always treat that person with respect.

Kant held this view because of his belief that people are rational and that this bestows them with absolute worth: our "rational nature exists as an end in itself" (AK 4:428).[77] This makes people unique in the natural world. In this sense, it is our duty to give every person consideration, respect, and dignity. Individual human rights are acknowledged and inviolable in a deontological system. The major emphasis on autonomy in health care springs from these considerations and others like them. Although most people who defend autonomy and treat people as ends and not merely as means do not use these formalistic Kantian reasons, this principle of autonomy is foundational in healthcare ethics. It is part of health care's common morality.

The Categorical Imperative and the Golden Rule

According to the categorical imperative, if the maxim or the rule governing an action is not capable of being a universal law, then it is unacceptable. Note that universalizability is not the same as universality. Kant's point is not that we would all agree on some rule. Instead, we must logically be able to accept that it could be universal. This is why the concept seems very much like the Golden Rule.[78] If you cannot will that everyone should follow the same rule, your rule is not a moral one. As indicated earlier, many think Kant's first formulation of the categorical imperative implies or even is a restatement of the Golden Rule. However, Kant specifically repudiates the Golden Rule interpretation (AK 4:430, note 13).[79]

Kant saw the justification for the Golden Rule in terms of consequences and fairness. If it is fair for me to do something, then it should be fair for everyone. Alternatively, in consequential terms, we typically hear officials, merchants, managers, and parents, when they are considering exceptions to policy, say, "If I do X for you, I have to do X for everyone." If one made exceptions for each individual, then the consequences would be unfair for others.[80]

Kant wanted to get beyond such issues. He wanted to know whether a person performed an act out of duty to moral law and thus expressed a good will. He stipulated that the moral agent acting solely out of a good will should ignore empirical considerations such as consequences, fairness, inclinations, and preferences. For Kant, an act carried out from an inclination, no matter how noble, is not an act of morality (AK 4:398). Indeed, he went so far as to say that the less we benefit from acting on the moral law, the more sublime and dignified it is (AK 4:425).[81]

Acts have moral worth if the person acts solely from duty to the moral law, absent any emotional inclinations or tangible benefits. This sets up the difficult standard that we can only know whether persons are morally worthy or obeying the moral law when there is nothing in it for them. Their actions would be opposed to their desires, inclinations, and even their self-interests. Taking such an extreme position essentially disconnected Kant from the real world in which people live and make ethical judgments.

Virtue Ethics and Kant's Moral Law

Although likely controversial, it seems, for purposes of healthcare ethics, that the best way to make sense of Kant is to conceive of the person of a good will in a manner akin to Aristotle's virtue ethics. Thus, to make Kantian deontology useful, you could say that a person of a good will also is a person of practical wisdom, as described by Aristotle. Does this inclusion of Aristotle reject Kant's work? No, but a critical analysis and comparison to virtue ethics are warranted.

Although Kant's theory suffers from disconnection from any normal motivational structure in human life, it still has applications in healthcare ethics.[82] The deontological theory emphasizes the attention to duty found in all codes of ethics in health care. Kant put into sharp relief the ethical idea that it is wrong for people to claim they can follow a principle or maxim that suits their interests but would not want others to do the same. Most important for health care is the recognition of human dignity and autonomy. To use people solely as a means to an end, whether as teaching material in medical schools, prisoners in research experiments, or slaves, is fundamentally a violation of all beings.

Deontology poses two problems that lead many to reject it. First, the statement of categorical imperatives, maxims, duties, rules, or commandments yields only absolutes. Kant really had only one absolute—you must act solely on the basis of a good will. You must have a reverence for, and an obligation to, the moral law formalized by the categorical imperative. However, the lack of prescriptive content leaves many unsatisfied. Actions either pass or fail, with no allowance for a "gray area." Virtue ethics handles the gray areas by depending on the wisdom of the person of practical wisdom. This is one reason virtue ethics as an ethical tool enables us to handle the problems of healthcare ethics more robustly.

The inability to make distinctions between lesser evils or greater goods is the other problem. We face moral dilemmas when duties come into conflict and there is no mechanism for resolving them. Kant, with his limited description of only one ethical duty (to obey the moral law), could claim to escape this problem within his philosophy. He used the radical view that such decisions are outside the bounds of morality if based on inclinations or consequences. Defining the real world of ethics in this radical way does not help much when faced with decisions that involve your inclinations and the weighing of consequences. Even if you have, as Kant seemed to think, only one duty, it is a formal one, and its various manifestations could conflict.

Virtue ethics and natural law theory face this problem of conflicting duties as well. For example, whereas abortion is clearly wrong under natural law theory, the outcomes of unwanted children, starving children, child abuse, malnutrition, etc., also have a moral bearing. Duties also conflict in healthcare situations. For example, if I tell the truth in some situation, it may lead to someone getting hurt, whereas a lie could have prevented it. However, my duty is both not to lie and not to do things that cause harm to others. Therefore, any decision violates a duty. Pure deontology theory does not allow for a theoretically satisfying means to rank conflicting duties. However, most duty-driven people will not be so literal with the Kantian version of deontology that they are unable to rank conflicting duties. Virtue ethics offers guidance for people using practical wisdom with available tools such as considered judgments, common morality, ethics theories, and ethics principles.

Of the theories presented so far, virtue ethics offers a much more useful and helpful approach in achieving ethical processes and ethical outcomes in the realm of health care. Virtue ethics is more interested in the development of ethical persons than in the development of maxims and imperatives. The normal understanding of the Golden Rule works perfectly well in ethical decision-making within the framework of virtue ethics, even if Kant himself disavowed it.

The policy implications for deontology are significant because of the emphasis on duty and the training of most healthcare professionals in the duties incumbent upon them. The emphasis on duty leads most clinicians to consider themselves deontologists. However, most would balk at the pure Kantian version of duty and would more readily assent to the duties experienced by a person of practical wisdom. Duty-driven clinical staff can walk into a meeting and know in advance what the right thing to do is: maximize the benefit to their patients. This is their duty, and their professional code of ethics codifies this duty. If they had to rank their duties, it would be patients first, their profession second, other clinical professionals third, with maybe their employing organization a distant fourth.

Having such a clear sense of their duties makes it easy for clinicians to talk about their obligations to patient care. In contrast, healthcare administrators and officials who make policy have a more difficult ethical chore. They must balance competing claims among many groups, and their loyalty is not simply to one group. Administrators represent the organization, whereas clinicians represent individual patients. The ethical obligations of administrators are much more complex; if the organization fails, the clinicians will not be able to help the patients. Let us now look at two deontologists whose theories have a more practical influence on the issues involved in healthcare policy decisions. Their theories are important

because of the need to allocate burdens and benefits such as access to health care that is of high quality and that is not delivered in a way that denies us other social goods because of its high costs.

Non-Kantian Versions of Deontology: John Rawls and Robert Nozick

This section presents two influential and relatively recent theorists from the deontological tradition. Rawls and Nozick have different ideas of what is right. They argue that by following their principles of what is right, a more just society will result. Of course, as philosophers do, they disagree over not only what is right but also what is just. These two thinkers have influenced the debate on the provision of health care in our nation, including the recent healthcare reforms.

John Rawls (1921–2002)

Rawls's *A Theory of Justice*, published in 1971, is considered a seminal text. Knowledge of his ideas is part of the common morality of most policy makers, even if many expressly reject those ideas. The basic idea behind Rawls's theory of justice is "justice as fairness."[83] Rawls limits his plan to a theory of justice that would apply to a society where the rule of law is respected.[84] People in such a society will differ with regard to their goals and their views of what counts as just. Yet, they recognize agreed-upon methods to arbitrate disputes so that they are capable of continued functioning within society. In other words, a disappointment or a disagreement does not lead to violence or rebellion. Rawls identified himself as being in the tradition of social contract theorists and, as a deontologist, even a Kantian. Rawls said that his theory is essentially deontological because it is not consequentialist.[85]

The idea of a social contract as the origin of society goes back to Thomas Hobbes

(1588–1679), John Locke (1632–1704), David Hume (1711–1776), and Jean Jacques Rousseau (1712–1778). All of these thinkers conceived of the beginnings of civil society as a compact or contract made among consenting adults to give up certain things in order to achieve others, such as order, harmony, trade, security, and protection. They agreed about the idea of a hypothetical situation that could be altered by persons acting to obtain some rights and privileges in exchange for others without the use of coercion. Rawls used a similar hypothetical situation and called it the original position, in which rational people are behind a veil of ignorance relative to their personal circumstances. The decisions about the principles of a just society that they select when they know nothing about their circumstances are what Rawls described as the principles of a just society.

Rawls emphasized that people seek to protect and maximize their self-interests. He argued that fundamental to that goal is liberty. He further argued—his most controversial point—that to have a just society requires an infrastructure and a system of rights that protect the minority and those who have fared less well in life's "lottery" than others. The key to his theory is the situation in which bargaining takes place about the nature of society and includes what those who are bargaining know about their society and themselves. Rawls called this the original position.

The Original Position and the Veil of Ignorance

In explaining the original position, Rawls took as rational the ethical egoist's position that everyone would want to maximize his or her personal self-interest. However, while negotiating the most just society for yourself, you are asked to voluntarily draw a veil of ignorance over yourself. This veil of ignorance is, from a personal perspective, absolute. You know nothing about yourself at all. You do not know your station in life, your preferences, your motivational structure, your willingness to take risk, your age, your health, your socioeconomics, your intelligence, your demographics—nothing.[86] In one fell swoop you have lost all the reasons for protecting your particular advantages or for hedging your bets to protect you from your disadvantages. You know you want to be in the best-possible circumstances when the veil of ignorance is lifted and you leave the original position.[87] Not knowing exactly what to protect, we are then inexorably forced to the kind of considerations that are common in medical ethics when treating patients about whom we lack information of any useful sort.

It is not unusual in healthcare settings to have patients who are in need of treatment but are unable to communicate their wishes. We know nothing of their families, their station in life, etc. Often, we cannot find anyone to speak for them, and they cannot speak for themselves. We have no clue about what they would have wanted. Normal notions of informed consent, durable power of attorney, and substituted judgment fall away as tools for us. We are forced back onto the position of deciding what to do for such persons on the basis of the idea of what a rational person would want in such circumstances. This position is sometimes called the best interests standard.[88] We could say that persons with such a complete inability to speak for their own interests are in the original position. In this situation, this original position, they are all truly equal because we know nothing of their circumstances.[89]

Now, although we are behind this veil of ignorance relative to our personal circumstances, we nonetheless have a considerable amount of knowledge about other things. Rawls allowed those who are behind the veil of ignorance to know general laws pertaining to political affairs and economic theory and to know something of human psychology.[90] Indeed, he assumed that the parties will "possess all general information"[91] but no information about their own particulars. Thus, they have no way of calculating the probability that they will be in a certain position as a result of their choices. Only by such extreme means did Rawls believe that one can ensure the fairness of the result. It is a hypothetical thought experiment that, he argued, guarantees that whatever principles are chosen will be just.

In his view, everyone should get an equal share of the burdens and benefits, unless there is a material reason to discriminate. If our job is to come up with a set of principles that will decide what these material reasons are, then we should carry out our job with the least bias. If we go back to the ideal of justice as blind, we see that the blindfold has become a veil of ignorance. Rawls did not at all advocate that we would seek an equalitarian outcome. He assumed that we are persons who want to maximize our self-interests, but he did not assume concepts such as benevolence or even nonmaleficence.[92] Once we determine the principles of a just society, then we can use them to develop material reasons to discriminate in the distribution of burdens and benefits.

Two Basic Principles of Justice

The first principle of justice meets with little objection, but the second inspires considerable debate. Rawls ordered these principles serially, in that liberties in the first principle cannot be rationally traded for favorable inequalities described in the second principle.[93] The prioritizing of liberty above other principles of justice was how Rawls distinguished himself from consequentialists. Their perspective, according to Rawls, is that there is only one principle: the greatest good for the greatest number.[94]

Rawls described the first principle of justice as follows: "[E]ach person is to have an equal right to the most extensive basic liberty compatible with a similar liberty for others."[95] This type of right is similar to the liberties protected in the U.S. Bill of Rights and can be called a process right. He described these rights as follows:[96]

- Political liberty (the right to vote and to be eligible for public office)

- Freedom from arbitrary arrest and seizure (which goes back to *habeas corpus*)
- Freedom of the person, along with the right to hold (personal) property
- Freedom of speech and assembly
- Liberty of conscience and freedom of thought

Rawls took a controversial position relative to the distribution of inequalities of office, income, wealth, and goods. He called this the "difference" principle.[97] In this second principle of justice, social and economic inequalities are appropriate if they are arranged such that the inequalities actually help out the least fortunate persons in society. In addition, the inequalities should be connected to positions, offices, or jobs in society that everyone has an equal opportunity to attain.[98] The inequalities that Rawls saw as permissible are (i) inequalities in the distribution of income and wealth and (ii) inequalities set up by institutions that use differences in authority and responsibility or chains of command. Rawls also said that society cannot justify a decrease in liberty by an increase in social and economic advantages. In this sense, liberty is the most important of the principles.

A classic example of how Rawls's principles might apply relates to physicians. Physicians often command superior incomes and social status, which are clearly inequalities. This circumstance requires an explanation. Once everybody is out of the original position and back in the real world, the hope is that anybody can become a doctor if he or she has the talent.[99] Suppose a person decides that he or she wants to become a physician. However, obtaining the education needed to actually become a physician requires an inequality: less fortunate people help pay for this education with their taxes. In the just society envisioned by Rawls, the person desiring the education would have to compensate the less fortunate in some way once he or she became a physician. The physician is free to keep the wealth, or at least some of it. But because gains in wealth are allowed only if they benefit the least advantaged along the way, the physician would never escape an obligation to help the less fortunate.

Some Concerns with Rawls's Theory

According to the difference principle, inequalities may be justified but only if they are to the advantage of the least well off. Rawls considered it "common sense" that all parties be happy with such a principle.[100] Rawls also stated that "the combination of mutual disinterest and the veil of ignorance achieves the same purpose as benevolence."[101] However, it is not difficult to imagine that many would voice concerns over forced beneficence and the government mechanisms and taxing schemes that would be needed to identify what counts as a natural gift or talent and is therefore unearned.

Consider the relatively bitter discussion of reparations to the descendants of slaves.[102] Recall the still active debates over affirmative action or over how to treat illegal immigrants or their American-citizen children. Many if not most of the wealthy would also be unlikely to assent to the thought experiment of putting on a veil of ignorance, because they would not accept the forced benevolence that the difference principle imposes. Simply put, many are less interested in justice than in keeping their advantages for themselves and their children. Thus, Rawls's position, although just, runs into human nature.

Some might argue that because Rawls was running up against human nature, his theory should be dismissed. Rawls addressed such arguments. He was perfectly aware of the imperfections of the real world outside the veil of ignorance; that is why he invented the thought experiment. The fact that the distribution of burdens and benefits by nature is unequal is not an excuse. "Occasionally this reflection is offered as an excuse for ignoring injustice, as if the refusal to acquiesce in injustice is on a par with being unable to accept death."[103] Rawls

believed that "the natural distribution is neither just nor unjust."[104] As Rawls stated, "[T]hese are simply natural facts. What is just and unjust is the way that institutions deal with these facts."[105] Thus, it is up to us to decide the principles of a just society and to take steps to create that society.

Rawls conceded that one might affirm his or her contract approach but eschew the difference principle, or vice versa.[106] To understand Rawls's theory and its application, we need to examine his most famous opponent, Nozick, the philosophical defender of libertarianism. Nozick accepted neither the contract approach of the original position nor the difference principle.

Robert Nozick (1938–2002) and Libertarianism

Nozick and Rawls both worked in the Department of Philosophy at Harvard University at the same time, but their philosophies disagreed considerably. However, both described themselves as coming from the deontological tradition relative to ethics theory in that they rejected consequentialism. Nozick's first, and most famous book, *Anarchy, State, and Utopia* (1974), was an attack on Rawls's work that focused on the extensive state envisioned as necessary to bring about Rawls's ends.[107]

In the healthcare field, Nozick's work in political theory helps provide the theoretical underpinnings to the debate that argued that there are no positive rights to health care, nor should there be any.[108] On the other side, Rawls's difference principle can be used to argue for health care as a component of the primary social goods.[109] Thus, Rawls and his followers represent the liberal tradition that the government should step in to help people disadvantaged in life's lottery, while Nozick and his followers represent the conservative tradition that if you want something you should obtain it yourself.

Like Rawls, Nozick claimed roots in Kant. However, Nozick focused on the second formulation of the categorical imperative. You may recall that Kant said, "So act as to treat humanity, whither in thine own person or in that of any other, in every case as an end withal, never as means only" (AK 4:429).[110] Nozick drew on this formulation, earlier described as the emphasis on autonomy. In the first sentence of the book, he stated his approach clearly: "Individuals have rights, and there are things no person or group may do to them (without violating their rights)."[111] He said that this imperative puts a constraint upon how others may be used. He stated that this version of autonomy can "express the inviolability of others."[112]

Nozick argued that Kant, in his categorical imperative, did not simply say we should *minimize* the use of humanity as a means. Rather, he said we should treat others as ends in every case, never as means only.[113] The word "only" leaves the meaning of this statement open to alternate interpretations that would suggest that minimization is all anyone could really mean in the actual world. In Nozick's view, people obviously are means to ends. If people are means to ends, then how is it possible to treat them only as ends?

Nozick also said that if we take his view of Kant and the inviolability of persons seriously, then we misspeak when we say that someone must make a sacrifice for the social good. He argued that there is no social entity to whom we can make a sacrifice; there are only other persons. Social entities are simply abstractions. "Using one of these people for the benefit of others uses him and benefits others. Nothing more . . . Talk of an overall social good covers this up."[114] To use a person in this way is to fail to respect him or her as a separate person: "No one is entitled to force this [sacrifice] upon him—least of all a state or government."[115]

Nozick also objected to Rawls's difference principle. He opposed the forced redistribution of benefits and burdens so that the less fortunate are made better off as the price for the more fortunate being more fortunate: Holdings to which people are entitled may not be seized, even to provide equality of opportunity for others. In the absence of magic wands, the remaining means toward equality of opportunity is to convince each person to choose to devote some of his or her holdings to achieving it.[116]

Simply put, if you do not like what you have, take steps to get more. If you want people to help others, convince them to do it. Is this justice? Are we really being just if we tell people who are severely disadvantaged to choose to improve themselves?

Rawls would hold that such outcomes are arbitrary—not just—in that they are based on the natural lottery, over which we have no control. The veil of ignorance is intended to get us to think about the principles of justice that would follow if we did not know our personal circumstances. For Rawls, what is just is what persons in that original position would choose.[117] The principles that result are the distributive justice principles of a just society. Nozick claimed that theories like Rawls's could be defeated by voluntary agreements. Indeed, he opposed the use of the term "distributive justice" because it implied a central distribution authority. This is not the reality of free adults, so he preferred the term "holdings" and talked of how they are acquired and transferred.[118] Nonetheless, he was unable to escape completely from the long tradition of the term "distributive justice" and continued to use it. He specified three conditions that meet the requirements of distributive justice:[119]

- "A person who acquires a holding in accordance with the principle of justice in acquisition is entitled to that holding."[120]
- If a person is entitled to the holding and transfers the holding, the person to whom it is transferred is now entitled to it.
- No one is entitled to anything except by gaining a holding from a previously unheld state (principle 1) or obtaining it from such a person by voluntary transfer.

An interesting outcome of Nozick's reliance on these three principles is that it is unnecessary to argue that anyone deserves the outcome that results.[121] Nozick, thus, rejected the basic idea of distributive justice; the principle is that everyone should get an equal share unless there is a material reason to discriminate. He complained that any reason to discriminate results in an inappropriate end state or patterned outcome.[122] What was appropriate was the three principles that he enunciated relative to historical entitlement and then subsequent transfers of holdings.

Most puzzling, at the end of his chapter on distributive justice, Nozick did take up what should be done to rectify the problems of historical injustice. Justice prevails only in following the three principles that described proper acquisition and transfer. If these are followed, there is no injustice in the resultant outcomes, whatever they are. "If, however, these principles are violated, the principle of rectification comes into play."[123] He then allowed that a specified (he used the term "patterned") outcome might be appropriate to rectify the past injustice. Nozick provided the following view of how this could be done: "A *rough* rule of thumb for rectifying injustices might seem to be the following: organize society so as to maximize the position of whatever groups end up least well-off in the society."[124]

This remarkable statement by the champion of libertarians sounded very like the difference principle.[125] However, it left out Rawls's idea that the better off can be better off but only if the less well off benefit as well. In Nozick's formulation, it seems we have moved back to equalitarianism because our only interest, when tasked to correct injustice, is maximizing the position of the least well off. The only possible outcome of this logic must be a leveling or rising of everyone to the average.

Because what happened historically is what counts as justice, it would be hard to find a significant case in which the original holdings were justly gained. For example, when Thomas Jefferson made the Louisiana Purchase, it was certainly a great surprise to the Native Americans, who had been living there for thousands of years, that they had no ownership rights in their land. This loss of ownership rights ended up being true for them no matter how much labor they had mixed in with the land.[126]

As a libertarian, Nozick's principles resonate loudly with those who emphasize the free market and a meritocracy. Typically, these will be the same people who resist calls for allocation of resources to healthcare needs, especially if this is done by taxation.

The extent to which these libertarian views are part of the common morality has a great influence on healthcare policy.

At this point we have examined all but one of the major ethics theories. Let us now examine the ethics theory that describes how most administrators work: consequentialism.[127]

Consequentialism

Consequentialist moral theories evaluate the morality of actions in terms of progress toward a goal or end. The consequences of the action are what matter, not their intent. This is in contrast to previously noted theories (e.g., deontology, virtue ethics, and natural law) that consider intent. Consequentialism is sometimes called *teleology*, using the Greek term *telos*, which refers to "ends." Thus, one finds that the goal of consequentialism is often stated as the greatest good for the greatest number. Consequentialism has several versions, the best known of which is utilitarianism. *Utilitarianism* defines morality in terms of the maximization of the net utility expected for all parties affected by a decision or action. For the purposes of discussion, *consequentialism* and *utilitarianism* are used here as synonyms.

For the consequentialist, the person's intentions are irrelevant to the ethical evaluation of whether the deed is right or wrong. Outcomes are all that matter. The consequentialist will agree that intentions do matter, but only to the evaluation of a person's character, not to the evaluation of the morality of his or her acts. In natural law, virtue ethics, and deontology, part of the ethical assessment concerns the person's intention. The consequentialist would say that intention simply confuses two issues: (i) whether the act itself is leading to good or bad outcomes and (ii) whether the person carrying out the act should be praised for it or not praised. Consequentialists consider the second issue to be independent of moral consideration relative to the act. It is relevant only to the evaluation of the person's moral character. Of course, to leave out intentions completely seems to violate a deep sense of our understanding about what it means to be ethical. Most people find something wrong with saying an act is ethical if it happened by accident.

Types of Consequentialism

The two major types of consequentialism are as follows:[128]

- *Classical utilitarianism (or act consequentialism)*. Each act is considered on the basis of its net benefit. This version of utilitarianism has received the most criticism and is not supported by modern ethicists. Nonetheless, it makes a convenient target for those who dislike consequentialism. For example, determining the consequences of something is often an exceedingly data-intensive undertaking, and the data may be lacking. The facts regarding the consequences are also themselves in debate. Imagine the difficulty if an administrator had to make decisions on the basis of the consequences of each employee's actions rather than a standard or rule.
- *Rule consequentialism*. The decision maker develops rules that will have the greatest net benefit.[129] The development of rules to guide conduct is similar to the actions of administrators who develop policies. This rule version of consequentialism includes two subspecies, negative consequentialism and preference consequentialism.

In organizational healthcare settings, policy-making is an important component of providing patient-centered care and meeting organizational needs. Consequentialism is often used as a basis for decision-making. For example, one could readily see that the creation of a diversity policy is justified by rule consequentialism. Lawmakers and administrators who develop health policies at the national level also use consequential arguments to justify decisions, such as requirements to provide indigent care or emergency services. To better understand the use of consequentialism, we first must examine classical utilitarianism and consider rule utilitarianism.

Classical Utilitarianism

Classical utilitarians spoke of maximization of pleasure or happiness. Classical utilitarianism is most often associated with the British philosopher Mill (1806–1873). He developed the theory from a pleasure-maximizing version put forward by his mentor Bentham (1748–1832). As clearly stated by Mill, the basic principle of utilitarianism is that actions are right to the degree that they tend to promote the greatest good for the greatest number.[130]

Of course, it is unclear what constitutes "the greatest good." For Bentham, it was simply the tendency to augment or diminish happiness or pleasure. Bentham, being a hedonist in theory, did not try to make distinctions about whether one form of pleasure or happiness was better than another.

For Mill, not all pleasures were equally worthy. He defined "the good" in terms of well-being and distinguished, both quantitatively and qualitatively, between various forms of pleasure.[131] Mill is closer to the virtue theory idea of *eudaimonia* as a goal in that he specified qualitative distinctions rather than simply adding up units of happiness or pleasure.[132] Indeed, Mill said that one is duty-bound to perform some acts, even if they do not maximize utility.[133]

A defining characteristic of any type of consequentialism is that the evaluation of whether an outcome is good or bad should be, in some sense, measurable, or that the outcome should be within the realm of predictability. Thus, in the realm of consequentialism, ethics theory attempts to become objective, seeking a foundation that is akin to the sciences. This principle is enshrined in the world of commerce, trade, management, and administration as the *cost–benefit analysis approach.*

As a theory, consequentialism is not as closely tied to its founder as are the previous three theories discussed. Thus, rather than probing the depths of Mill's writing, a more free-ranging approach is used, and the section presents various versions of consequentialism that are in play today. This approach will avoid the considerable controversies surrounding what Mill meant by his theories.[134] It presents tools derived from consequentialism tools that are useful to persons dealing with issues in healthcare ethics.

Relative to what consequentialism means, Bentham insisted that "the greatest number" included all who were affected by the action in question, with "each to count as one, and no one as more than one."[135] Likewise, in Bentham's version of the theory, the various intrinsic goods that counted as utility would have an equal value, such that one unit of happiness for you is not worth more than one unit of happiness for me. Quite clearly, to talk about "units of happiness" is far-fetched, and indeed, that is one of the criticisms of the theory.[136] However, numerous correctives to the theory have been advanced over the years, and some of these are helpful.

Unlike deontology and natural law with their conflicting absolutes, consequentialism of any form allows for degrees of right and wrong. If the consequences can be predicted and their utility calculated, then in such situations, the choice between actions is clear-cut: always choose those actions that have the greatest utility. For this reason, the theory has had great appeal in economic and business circles. However, in healthcare decision-making, the economic view of utility is not fully satisfactory. For example, how do you compute the suffering of someone whose spouse has become disabled? Although attorneys do calculate the monetary value of life years lost when there is an injury, whether monetary settlements can really compensate for a lost livelihood or a broken future is debatable.

In spite of this objection, administrators of healthcare organizations, including managers, must often think in terms of the aggregate when evaluating their decisions. Persons taking the tack of a deontologist and trying to fulfill their duty can readily say that their obligation is to the patient. Administrators have to consider patients in the aggregate, the organization, the larger community, and their employees in their decision-making. Their divided duties and obligations are part of their job descriptions, as opposed to the single obligation to the patient that clinicians enjoy. Administrators also are trained to consider their decisions in terms of maximization—the best outcome for the resources expended is the greatest good.[137] They would say that utilitarianism assists them in obtaining the "biggest bang for the buck." Of course, in administration, as in ethics, problems arise:

- It is not always clear what the outcome of an action will be, nor is it always possible to determine those affected by it.
- The calculation required to determine the right decision is both complicated and time-consuming.
- Because the greatest good for the greatest number is described in aggregate terms, the good might be achieved under conditions that are harmful to some so long as that harm is balanced by a greater good. This leads to the attack that consequentialism means "the end justifies the means."[138]

The theory fails to acknowledge that individual rights could be violated for the sake of the greatest good, which is sometimes called the "tyranny of the majority." Indeed, the murder of an innocent person would seem to be condoned if it served the greater number. The complaint is that consequentialism ignores the existence of basic rights and ethics principles such as autonomy and beneficence. The fact that Mill would categorically deny this by saying some acts are wrong regardless of the consequences appears to be a violation of his own stated philosophy. Of course, we are not seeking doctrinal purity but useful tools to help us in healthcare ethics.

Finally, who has the time to run endless computations every time a decision is needed? "Analysis paralysis" would be the predicted outcome, which would not maximize any version of utility. In any case, because of these problems, few philosophers today subscribe to act consequentialism.[139] The proposed improvement to several of these problems is rule consequentialism.

Rule Consequentialism

The idea behind rule consequentialism is that one evaluates behavior by rules that would lead to the greatest good for the greatest number. At this point, the theory begins to tie in more clearly to virtue ethics and to the person who has achieved practical wisdom. It takes a person of some experience to know how to develop rules that will likely lead to the greatest good for the greatest number. Healthcare administrators and government officials would call these rules *policies*.

Once there is a policy, presumably developed by an evaluation of its likely outcomes, then the person who needs to make a decision refers to the applicable policy. Indeed, a person of practical wisdom might well conclude that long-term utility is undermined by acts of injustice. He or she would then develop a policy that recognizes and respects autonomy. Rule utilitarianism would thus use the utility principle to justify rules establishing human rights and the universal prohibition of certain harms. Such rules would codify the wisdom of experience and preclude the need for constant calculation.

Thus, rule consequentialism looks like the same activity in which healthcare administrators

and policy makers engage when they make policies and procedures. A policy is a general statement meant to cover any number of situations. The person creating it makes the decision that following the policy is the best way to achieve the organization's goals. The person then uses procedures as the means to carry out the created policies. Healthcare administrators and government officials have been using this process for a long time. Overall, it works well, even though rules or policies do not work fairly in every situation.

Indeed, the failure of the rules to fit every situation is one of the reasons to have humans in charge instead of machines. At this point, the inclusion of a person of practical wisdom, from the virtue ethics tradition, comes into play. Administrators or clinicians (persons of practical wisdom) can decide whether the special circumstances warrant making an exception to the rule when they need to make judgments. If so, they could modify the rule to consider the special circumstances. In this way, fairness is preserved.

These exceptions might be justified by material reasons such as need, merit, potential, and past achievement. The manager or policy maker will also have to recognize, and be willing to accept, that sometimes the enforcement of a rule will lead to unfair outcomes. However, the principle is still sound and much better than the chaos of trying to evaluate the probable consequences of a situation each time a decision is required.[140]

Rule consequentialism can also incorporate the goals of negative consequentialism. The idea behind *negative consequentialism* is that the alleviation of suffering is more important than the maximization of pleasure. Further, to have the alleviation of suffering as a goal incorporates into the goal the protection of the powerless, the weak, and the worse off. Thus, from a social policy point of view, rules that operate as safety nets can accomplish this goal. Allowing access to emergency treatment regardless of the ability to pay is an obvious healthcare example. Now let us look at the last version of consequentialism, *preference consequentialism.*

Preference Consequentialism

Preference consequentialism argues that the good is the fulfillment of preferences and the bad is frustration of desires or preferences. People, in this sense, are not seen as having preferences for pleasure or happiness per se; their preferences are left to them. Thus, autonomy becomes a bedrock value.

How can someone know another person's preferences when making decisions that involve that person? To answer this question, health care has developed clearly enunciated procedures in the area of informed consent. One can speak of *substituted judgment* when one knows the preferences of a person who is now incompetent.[141] In case the person has not communicated his or her preferences, we are forced to fall back on what is called the "best interests standard," or, more commonly, the "reasonable person standard." What would a reasonable person want in the circumstances at hand?[142]

Healthcare ethicists have done well in discerning what the preferences are of an individual who has become incompetent. However, policy-making decisions have an impact on large groups of people, most of whom will be personally unknown to the decision makers. Development of tools to ascertain the preferences of a large aggregate of individuals is a much different task.[143] The direction that seems to occur is that the decision maker applies the "reasonable person standard" to the aggregate. However, considerable evidence suggests that such a standard may fall short of meeting a specific person's actual preferences, whether it is what a reasonable person would want or wouldn't want.[144] Simply put, the preferences that humans have are so diverse and changeable that it might not make sense to use them as a standard for maximization. Thus, although this preference standard may work at the individual level, it seems to have less value as a policy statement to use in the aggregate. When one institutionalizes the reasonable person standard as a rule, its implementation might run roughshod over individual preferences that are "unreasonable."

Evaluation of Consequentialism

One of the most common criticisms of consequentialism is that it appears to allow some to suffer if the net outcome is an improvement for a greater number. This argument is specious. The theory presumes respect for autonomy by the very statement that the good sought is the greatest good for the greatest number. Although consequentialists might talk about utility, the good in mind has to include respect for the personhood of others as a minimum requirement. If respect for the other is not presupposed, then it seems the theory would really devolve into a form of egoism. Thus, respect for the wants, preferences, hopes, and choices of others must be implicit for the theory to remain intact. A lack of this foundational component would mean that the theory really does boil down to the ends justifying the means, as noted earlier. However, such a view is off base relative to the intent of the theory.

Mill stated this quite clearly in his classic essay "On Liberty": "The only freedom which deserves the name is that of pursuing our own good in our own way, so long as we do not attempt to deprive others of theirs, or impede their efforts to obtain it."[145] It is difficult to think of a more obvious reference to respect for the autonomy of others and their liberty to pursue it. Some argue that this meant that Mill was really a deontologist. However, such arguments seem arcane, academic, and irrelevant to our purposes. Thus, I consider it a compliment to Mill that he recognized the need to temper his "greatest good for the greatest number" with respect for basic principles of autonomy and freedom.

▶ Ethics Theories and Their Value to Healthcare Professionals

Over thousands of years, no ethics principle or theory has survived criticism by trained philosophers without serious flaws emerging. Nonetheless, in the changing healthcare environment, professionals cannot throw up their hands because flaws exist. They must make decisions based on reason. In making decisions, professionals must often choose a course that some will not support.[146] They also understand the need for choosing among the theories to address the circumstances at hand.[147] This is why practical wisdom, from the virtue ethics tradition, serves as the best model and is the model that various healthcare professions choose. In the case of physicians, this tradition goes back millennia. For other healthcare professions, the development of a sense of professionalism, and for production of persons of practical wisdom, has been much shorter.[148]

Clinicians and healthcare administrators will use their practical wisdom to advance the interests of specific patients, patients in the aggregate, the community, and the organization by drawing on the necessary principles and theories. For the administrator, having rules that tend to provide the greatest good for the greatest number over the long term functions as a guiding principle in the same way that duties do for the clinician. Both the clinician and the administrator can also come to the table with ideas about what is appropriate to do in a given situation. In this case, the clinician may have the emotional upper hand because most people respond better to appeals based on helping a specific individual rather than protecting a policy. Nonetheless, the administrator is well equipped by understanding the proper role of rules or policies.

People in the policy-making arena can enhance their evaluation of the behaviors or motivations of various stakeholders if they determine the ethical system these stakeholders are likely to be using. For example, clinicians are likely to take a deontological approach because their training makes their primary duty to the individual patient. They will not be as concerned with the external consequences of a decision (e.g., costs, inconvenience to the family) as they are with whether they are doing the right thing for the patient's medical care. For clinicians, the right thing is that which allows them to meet their duty and therefore support their sense of upholding the integrity of the profession. In other words, they want to sustain their sense of themselves as virtuous persons. They want to be viewed as persons of practical wisdom who do the right thing for their patients. The right thing includes not only meeting their duty but also evaluating the consequences of their decisions for patients and their families.

Healthcare administrators are in a more difficult position because they have obligations to many stakeholders, not just to the individual patient. These obligations are often unequal and conflicting. Their best strategy may be to recognize that they lack the luxury of having obligations that are pure and easily defined. Instead, they have to think of multiple and conflicting stakeholders and try to develop a solution that will generate the greatest good for the greatest number. All the while, they must respect the principles of autonomy, justice, beneficence, and nonmaleficence.[149] In their experience, the rules they adhere to have had these positive results; therefore, they suggest them in current cases. It is clear that the ethical challenge for a healthcare administrator is more difficult than for those working from a strictly clinical perspective.

▶ Summary

This chapter clarifies that no one ethics theory is sufficient for all healthcare decisions. However, a review of the principle features of the main ethics theories used in health care provides a toolbox for decision-making. After a brief explanation of authority-based ethics, virtue ethics is described as something common in the socialization of healthcare professionals. Next, the chapter provides a discussion of the features and use of natural law theory. It also includes two prominent ethics theories used in health care: utilitarianism and deontology. Finally, the merits of considering virtue ethics as a healthcare professional are discussed.

The 21st century promises challenging healthcare ethical issues for individuals, organizations, and society. It is a time of rapid change, fiscal challenge, and technology expansion within the field of health care. Therefore, a deeper understanding of and the ability to apply ethics theory will be even more necessary for appropriate responses to these challenges. It is important to remember that ethics theory did not develop in a vacuum. Each theorist studied the works of his or her predecessors and provided his or her own wisdom. Similarly, these theories form the basis for the main ethics principles used in healthcare practice and decision-making. You will find a discussion of these principles in the chapter "Principles of Healthcare Ethics." In addition, subsequent chapters will apply both theories and principles to current and future healthcare challenges.

▶ Questions for Discussion

1. If ethics theories are so complicated, why should one bother developing a professional theory of ethics?
2. Is virtue ethics the best model for persons who work in healthcare professions?
3. Why is deontology still important in contemporary healthcare practice? How can you use the categorical imperative to make decisions in today's healthcare practice?
4. How does utilitarianism affect healthcare decision-making? Will this theory be used more frequently in the era of the ACA 2010?
5. How does Rawls's theory connect to the changes in the current healthcare system? How would Nozick argue against Rawls's theory in this context?

▶ Notes

1. For a good overview of the value of cultural competence in health care, see J. R. Betancourt et al., *Cultural Competence in Health Care: Emerging Frameworks and Practical Approaches* (New York: The Commonwealth Fund, 2002).
2. T. L. Beauchamp and J. F. Childress, *Principles of Biomedical Ethics*, 7th ed. (New York: Oxford University Press). Beauchamp and Childress popularized these four concepts, starting with the first edition of their text in 1979. The concepts, or "principles," as these authors call them, appear later in this chapter. The authors consider these principles more valuable than the theories. For purposes of clinical medical ethics, this ordering may be appropriate. It seems less suitable for the more general category of healthcare ethics, which includes policy-making well beyond the bedside.
3. Some authors distinguish deontology from consequentialism solely by the fact that it places total or some limits on the relevance of the consequences in the deliberations. See T. A. Mappes and J. S. Zembaty, eds., *Biomedical Ethics*, 2nd ed. (New York: McGraw Hill, 1981), 4.

4. R. Benedict, "A Defense of Moral Relativism," *Journal of General Psychology* 10 (1934): 59–82. Written by a leading figure in 20th-century anthropology, this work is one of the most influential contemporary defenses of ethical relativism. Numerous anthologies, including C. Sommers and F. Sommers, eds., *Everyday Life*, 3rd ed. (San Diego, CA: Harcourt, Brace and Jovanovich, 1992), include reprints of this work.

5. See K. Popper, *The Logic of Scientific Discovery* (New York, NY: Basic Books, 1959) for the defense of falsifiability as a criterion of scientific knowledge.

6. V. Klingenborg, "On the Recentness of What We Know." *New York Times*, August 9, 2006, http://nytimes.com/2006/08/09/opinion/09talkingpoints.html.

7. H. LaFollettee, "The Truth in Relativism," *Journal of Social Philosophy* (1991): 146–54.

8. The lack of certainty and infallibility disturbs many. See M. J. Slick, "Ethical Relativism," Christian Apologetics and Research Ministry, 2003, http://www.carm.org/relativism/ethical.htm. This organization renounced relativism. According to this group, reliance on Scripture improves this messy process.

9. In an introductory chapter, a complete account is not possible. However, for an extensive bibliography, see L. M. Hinman, "A Survey of Selected Internet Resources on Ethical Egoism," Ethics Updates, http://ethics.sandiego.edu/theories/Egoism/index.asp.

10. See, for example, A. Rand, *Virtue of Selfishness* (New York, NY: Signet, 1964).

11. The Ayn Rand Institute website recommends L. Peikoff, *Objectivism: The Philosophy of Ayn Rand* (London: Meridian, 1993).

12. A. Rand, *Introducing Objectivism* (Irvine, CA: Ayn Rand Institute, 1992).

13. The spiritual dimension is one of the nine elements of the patient-centered care model championed by the Planetree model. See S. B. Frampton et al., Putting *Patients First: Designing and Practicing Patient Centered Care* (San Francisco, CA: Jossey-Bass, 2003). See also the Duke University Center for Spirituality, Theology, and Health, http://www.spiritualityandhealth.duke.edu/. This site contains an extensive reference to the literature in this area.

14. World Medical Association, "The Declaration of Geneva," originally adopted in 1948 and most recently amended in 2006, http://www.wma.net/en/30publications/10policies/g1/.

15. Following tradition, the citations for references used to locate classical passages are by the name of the work and the particular line number. See *Nicomachean Ethics*, Bk. I, Chap. 9, 1099b32–1100a5. The actual edition used is R. McKeon, *Basic works of Aristotle* (New York: Random House, 1971).

16. Very substantial arguments arise over just what *harm* and *benefit* mean, but those are not necessary to consider here. The exact words noted do not occur in the Hippocratic Corpus. However, *Of the Epidemics* (Bk. I, sect. II, pt. 5, http://classics.mit.edu/Hippocrates/epideics.html, an online collection of the Hippocratic Corpus) states it clearly: "The physician must . . . have two special objects in view with regard to disease, namely, to do good or to do no harm."

17. There is considerable debate about the definition of virtues, including which ones are important. I shall have to leave that discussion aside and simply hope the reader has an ordinary conception of what a virtue is.

18. See American Medical Association, *Principles of Medical Ethics* (Chicago: American Medical Association, 2001),

www.ama-assn.org/ama/pub/category/2512.html.

19. *Nicomachean Ethics*, Bk. I, Chap. 2, 1103a17.

20. Ibid., Bk. I, Chap. 2, 1103a25.

21. The following material on honesty was inspired by R. Hursthouse, "Virtue Ethics," *Stanford Encyclopedia of Philosophy*, 2007, http://plato.stanford.edu/entries/ethics-virtue/. I have rewritten it to fit healthcare professionals from its original, more general appeal.

22. *Nicomachean Ethics*, Bk. 6, Chap. 13, 1140a–b.

23. Ibid., Bk. 6, Chap. 13, 1145a2–3.

24. This seeking of self-perfection has a major influence in Western culture, extending from the Greeks into the Roman Stoics and then into Christianity. In some interpretations, Islamic *jihad* means a similar struggle with the self, a striving for spiritual self-perfection. Muslims knew of Aristotle's teachings far in advance of Christendom. After the decline of Rome, Aristotle's work was lost in the West. However, in the 9th century, Arab scholars introduced Aristotle to Islam, and Muslim theology, philosophy, and natural science all took on an Aristotelian cast. After the Crusades, Arab and Jewish scholars reintroduced Aristotelian thought in the West. The correct interpretation of *jihad* is a matter of considerable debate and is not a topic here.

25. Beauchamp and Childress, *Principles of Biomedical Ethics*, 7th ed.

26. "Justice," in *The Concise Oxford Dictionary of English Etymology*, ed. T. F. Hoad (New York: Oxford University Press, 1996), www.oxfordreference.com/views/ENTRY.html?subview=Main&entry=t27.e8229.

27. For example, a teacher might say, "Your response did the subject justice," meaning that it was right and that it was a more than merely adequate response; it was good. Or one might say, "The person showed the justice of his claim," meaning it was a proper and correct claim.

28. Beauchamp and Childress, *Principles of Biomedical Ethics*, 7th ed.

29. Aristotle thought slavery was OK because some persons could comprehend the rational principle but not possess it. They acted from instinct (*Politics*, Bk. II, Chap. 5). Aristotle described barbarians as brutish, along with people of vice (*Nicomachean Ethics*, Bk. VII, Chap. 1, 1145a30 and Chap. 5, 1148al5–30). By nature, some people should rule and others should be ruled. He thought Greeks should rule barbarians, "for by nature what is barbarian and what is slave are the same" (*Politics* Bk. I, Chap. 2, 1252b8). Women were inferior by nature to men as well: "The relationship between the male and the female is by nature such that the male is higher, the female lower, that the male rules and the female is ruled" (*Politics*, Bk I, Chap. 4, 1254b12–14). The hierarchy of being and value had significant importance politically for millennia, and continues to do so today. Obviously, metaphysics influences our lives. The common morality has changed relative to many of these views.

30. *Nicomachean Ethics*, Bk. X, Chap. 9, 1179b5–10.

31. Ibid., Bk. X, Chap. 9, 1179b18. The other sentiments are written directly preceding this line. A tincture of something seems to suggest that it is not quite the real thing, although it could do some good. So many various definitions of the term *tincture* exist that it is difficult to get a precise understanding of the meaning of the phrase.

32. See B. Justice, *Who Gets Sick: How Beliefs, Moods, and Thoughts Affect Your Health*, 2nd ed. (Houston: Peak Press, 2000). This book reviews the scientific

literature on the subject and provides an excellent introduction to the field.

33. In the realm of healthcare management, providing cues to quality to assure patients that the services are appropriate is part of the management of the dimensions of quality. See V. A. Zeithaml et al., *Services Marketing*, 4th ed. (New York: McGraw Hill, 2006). See also Frampton, Gilpin, and Charmel, *Putting Patients First.*

34. Some of these issues are discussed in *Nicomachean Ethics*, Bk. VII, Chaps. 1–10, 1145a15–1154b30.

35. Mappes and Zembaty, *Biomedical Ethics*, 2nd ed., 7. The brush that paints all ethical theories as either more or less consequentialist seems much too wide.

36. For an extremely informative philosophical overview of natural law theory in general and Aquinas's version of it in particular, including an excellent defense of how natural law does not neatly fall into either deontology or consequentialism, see M. Murphy, "The Natural Law Tradition in Ethics," *Stanford Encyclopedia of Philosophy*, 2002, http://plato.stanford.edu/archives/win2002/entries/natural-law-ethics. Accessed November 28, 2011.

37. On how the heavens have never changed in their orderly cycles, see *On the Heavens*, Bk. I, Chap. 3, 270b10–17.

38. See G. Kemerling, "Thomas Aquinas," PhilosophyPages.com, 2011, www.philosophypages.com/ph/aqui.htm. Accessed November 28, 2011.

39. For more modern writers in the field of natural law, see, in alphabetical order, T. D. J. Chappell, *Understanding Human Goods* (Edinburgh: Edinburgh University Press, 1995); J. Finnis, *Aquinas: Moral, Political, and Legal Theory* (Oxford: Oxford University Press, 1998); P. Foot, *Natural Goodness* (Oxford: Oxford University Press, 2000); J. E. Hare, *God's Call* (Grand Rapids, MI:

Eerdmans, 2001); M. Moore, "Good without God," in *Natural Law, Liberalism and Morality*, ed. R. P. George (Oxford: Oxford University Press, 1996); and M. C. Murphy, *Natural Law and Practical Rationality* (Cambridge: Cambridge University Press, 2001).

40. St. Thomas Aquinas, *Summa Theologica*. The entire work (Benziger Bros. edition, 1947, trans. Fathers of the English Dominican Province) is available online at the Christian Classics Ethereal Library. The online index can be found at http://www.ccel.org/ccel/aquinas/summa.toc.html. Question 94 is found at http://www.ccel.Org/a/aquinas/summa/FS/FS094.html#FSQ94OUTP1. The standard reference format for something in *Summa Theologica* is, for example, ST IaIIae 94, 4. This is interpreted to mean that the citation comes from the first part of the second part of *Summa Theologica*, question 94, article 4.

41. B. B. Longest Jr. and K. Darr, *Managing Health Service Organizations*, 6th ed. (Baltimore: Health Professions Press, 2014); K. Darr, *Ethics in Health Services Administration*, 5th ed. (Baltimore, MD: Health Professions Press, 2014), 19.

42. For a better account within the healthcare literature, see J. W. Carlson, "Natural Law Theory," in *Biomedical Ethics*, 2nd ed., eds. T. A. Mappes and J. S. Zembaty (New York: McGraw Hill, 1981), 37–43, and M. C. Brannigan and J. A. Boss, *Healthcare Ethics in a Diverse Society* (Mountain View: Mayfield Publishing, 2001), 23–25.

43. This also contradicts some commentators, who say that it assumes all rational beings will agree on the content of the natural law. For this error, see Brannigan and Boss, *Healthcare Ethics in a Diverse Society.*

44. M. Murphy, "The Natural Law Tradition in Ethics," *Stanford Encyclopedia*

of *Philosophy*, 2002, http://plato
.stanford.edu/archives/win2002
/entries/natural-law-ethics.

45. V. Cathrein, "Ethics," *Catholic Encyclopedia Online*, ed. K. Knight, 2003, http://
www.newadvent.org/cathen/05556a
.htm.

46. See Beauchamp and Childress, *Principles of Biomedical Ethics*, 7th ed., 164.

47. To go further into such controversies,
see, as examples, P. J. Cataldo, "The
Principle of the Double Effect," *Ethics & Medics* 20 (March 1995): 1–3;
B. Ashley and K. O'Rourke, *Healthcare Ethics: A Theological Analysis*, 4th
ed. (Washington, DC: Georgetown
University Press, 1997), 191–95; and
D. B. Marquis, "Four Versions of Double Effect," *Journal of Medicine and Philosophy* 16 (1991): 515–44.

48. A similar insight was noted by Beau-
champ and Childress, *Principles of
Biomedical Ethics*, 7th ed. (New York:
Oxford University Press, 2013), 357.

49. Cathrein, "Ethics."

50. This theory does not appear to protect
nonhuman animals, plants, dammed
rivers, strip-mined mountains, and the
like. Given their lack of rationality, the
fact that they are not made in the image
of God, their lower level in the hierarchy of being, and their being a means
to our ends, their potential would matter less. In the Aristotelian scheme,
only angels were between humans and
the unmoved mover, or God. Later,
Descartes, although not favored by
either Catholics or Protestants in his
time, made a fundamental distinction
between mind and matter. Only humans
were believed to be endowed with mind
capacity. *Mind* easily translated into concepts such as *soul*. Thus, the rest of the
natural world, being without mind or
soul, did not require us to worry about
whether its potential would be circum-
scribed by our actions upon it.

51. Most of Kant's works appear to be available free online at http://oll.libertyfund
.org/Intros/Kant.php, along with works
of many other authors. I do not know
whether the translations are those most
accepted by scholars.

52. Although in near complete disagreement about the substance of their
respective views, Rawls and Nozick are
considered deontologists. Their views
are essential to understanding current
political debates.

53. I. Kant, *The Critique of Practical Reason*, trans. L. W. Beck (Indianapolis, IN:
Bobbs-Merrill, 1956).

54. I. Kant, *The Moral Law*, trans. H. J. Pat-
ton (London: Hutchinson University
Press, 1948).

55. Kant, *Critique of Practical Reason*.

56. I. Kant, *Critique of Pure Reason*, trans.
N. K. Smith (New York: St. Martin's
Press, 1965), p. 29. The "B xxix" refers
to the standard paging of the work. The
"B" indicates that this passage is in the
Critique's second edition only.

57. There is vast literature on the issues
involved in whether free will exists.
Different flavors of determinism are
discussed, and there are different perspectives on what it means to say that
someone acts freely. Although these
issues are important, they simply cannot
be broached here. For a good overview
of the issues and the approaches taken
by various religions, as well as various
thinkers, see W. K. Frankena, *Ethics:
Foundations of Philosophy Series* (Englewood Cliffs, NJ: Prentice Hall, 1963),
54–62, and T. O'Conner, "Free Will,"
Stanford Encyclopedia of Philosophy,
2005, http://plato.stanford.edu/entries
/freewill/. Accessed November 28, 2011.

58. What the moral law is will be taken up
with the discussion of the categorical
imperative.

59. Kant, *Critique of Pure Reason*, 26–29
(B xxv–B xxx).

60. Ibid., 29.

61. Ibid., 28. If you find this argument hard to follow, you are not alone. It takes a considerable study of philosophy to understand the argument, which, by no means, suggests you would agree with it.

62. I. Kant, "Fundamental Principles of the Metaphysics of Morals," trans. T. K Abbott, in *Basic Writings of Kant*, ed. A. L. Wood (New York: Modern Library, 2001), 151.

63. Ibid., 152.

64. Ibid., 154–55.

65. I. Kant, *Foundations of the Metaphysics of Morals*, trans. L. W. Black (Indianapolis, IN: Bobbs-Merrill, 1959). The "AK 20" is the conventional page numbering used in Kant scholarship, locating this quote within the 22 volumes in the Preussische Akademie edition. Different pagination is used when referring to the *Critique of Pure Reason*.

66. Beauchamp and Childress, *Principles of Biomedical Ethics*, 7th ed., 101–41, provide a good discussion of autonomy in the context of medical ethics. E. E. Morrison, *Ethics in Health Administration: A Practical Approach for Decision Makers*, 3rd ed. (Burlington, MA: Jones & Bartlett Learning, 2016), 31–71, provides a discussion tailored to healthcare managers.

67. R. Johnson, "Kant's Moral Philosophy," *Stanford Encyclopedia of Philosophy*, February 26, 2004, http://plato.stanford.edu/archives/spr2004/entries/kant-moral/. Accessed November 28, 2011.

68. Beauchamp and Childress, *Principles of Biomedical Ethics*, 7th ed., 361–67, provide a useful summary of these issues.

69. Kant posits a third version of the categorical imperative, "The Idea of the Will of Every Rational Being as a Universally Legislative Will" (AK 4:431). See Kant, "Fundamental Principles of the Metaphysics of Morals," 188. However, since this seems to restate the emphasis on autonomy found in the second version, I shall not take up analysis of it separately.

70. Kant, "Fundamental Principles of the Metaphysics of Morals," 178.

71. For a sampling of sources stating or suggesting that Kant's categorical imperative is the Golden Rule, see Longest Jr. and Darr, *Managing Health Service Organizations*, 5th ed., 103; Darr, *Ethics in Health Services Administration*, 5th ed.; Brannigan and Boss, *Healthcare Ethics in a Diverse Society*, 29; J. O. Hertzler, "On Golden Rules," *International Journal of Ethics* 44, no. 4 (1934): 418–36; S. B. Thomas, "Jesus and Kant, a Problem in Reconciling Two Different Points of View," *Mind* 79, no. 314 (April 1970): 188–99; P. Weiss, "The Golden Rule," *Journal of Philosophy* 38, no. 16 (July 31, 1941): 421–30; and J. E. Walter, "Kant's Moral Theology," *Harvard Theological Review* 10, no. 3 (July 1917): 272–95, esp. 293. Those who write about ethics without having philosophical training are even more likely to make this mistake. A website on engineering ethics simply indicates that the categorical imperative is the Golden Rule; see http://www.engr.psu.edu/ethics/theories.asp. I have even made the error myself in discussing ethical theories in the healthcare literature. See the following examples, which were part of a column on healthcare ethics: J. Summers, "Managers Face Conflicting Values," *Journal of Health Care Material Management* 7, no. 5 (July 1989): 89–90; J. Summers, "Determining Your Duties," *Journal of Health Care Material Management* 7, no. 3 (April 1989): 80–81; and J. Summers, "Ethical Theories: An Introduction," *Journal of Health Care Material Management* 7, no. 1 (January 1989): 56–57. The fact that something looks like something else does not make it that something else.

72. The disavowal occurs in a footnote in Kant, "Fundamental Principles of the Metaphysics of Morals," 187, note 13. To the normal reader, the footnote would not clearly indicate that it references the Golden Rule, because Kant cited it in Latin, and none of the terms resemble the English version of the Golden Rule.

73. Kant, "Fundamental Principles of the Metaphysics of Morals," 186.

74. Ibid., 190–91.

75. Kant, *Foundations of the Metaphysics of Morals*, 31.

76. Kant, "Fundamental Principles of the Metaphysics of Morals," 186.

77. Ibid., 186.

78. For a good history of the Golden Rule, including versions that precede the Christian formulation of Matthew 7:12, see J. O. Hertzler, "On Golden Rules," *International Journal of Ethics* 44, no. 4 (July 1934): 418–36.

79. Kant, "Fundamental Principles of the Metaphysics of Morals," 187, note 13.

80. Ibid., 156.

81. Ibid., 183.

82. Some of the ideas in this section were drawn from F. Feldman, "Kant's Ethical Theory," in *Biomedical Ethics*, eds. T. A. Mappes and J. S. Zembaty (New York: McGraw-Hill, 1981), 26–37, esp. 36–37.

83. J. Rawls, *A Theory of Justice* (Cambridge, MA: Harvard University Press, 1971), 11.

84. Ibid., 4–5.

85. Ibid., 30.

86. Ibid., 136–37.

87. Ibid., 142–43.

88. Beauchamp and Childress, *Principles of Biomedical Ethics*, 7th ed., 126–27.

89. Rawls, *Theory of Justice*, 17–19.

90. Ibid., 137–38.

91. Ibid., 142.

92. Ibid., 17.

93. Ibid., 43, 61.

94. Ibid., 43–44.

95. Ibid., 60.

96. Ibid., 61.

97. Ibid., 75–83.

98. Ibid., 60–61, 75–83, and elsewhere.

99. For purposes of the argument, we have to leave aside the real issue that equal opportunity is simply not available to large swaths of the population whether they have the talent to be a physician or they don't.

100. Rawls, *Theory of Justice*, 104.

101. Ibid., 148.

102. For two of many articles favoring reparation to descendants of slaves, see D. T. Osabu-Kle, "The African Reparation Cry: Rationale, Estimate, Prospects, and Strategies," *Journal of Black Studies* 30, no. 3 (2000): 331–50, and W. William Darity Jr. and D. Frank, "The Economics of Reparations," *American Economic Review* 93, no. 2 (2003): 326–29. For an article showing public opinion about such reparations, see M. R. Michelson, "The Black Reparations Movement: Public Opinion and Congressional Policy Making," *Journal of Black Studies* 32, no. 5 (2002): 574–87.

103. Rawls, *Theory of Justice*, 102.

104. Ibid.

105. Ibid.

106. Ibid., 15.

107. R. Nozick, *Anarchy, State and Utopia* (New York: Basic Books 1974), xi.

108. E. Feser, "Robert Nozick," *Internet Encyclopedia of Philosophy*, 2006, http://www.iep.utm.edu/n/nozick.htm. Accessed December 9, 2006.

109. Rawls, *Theory of Justice*, 62, 92–93.

110. Kant, "Fundamental Principles of the Metaphysics of Morals," 186.

111. Nozick, *Anarchy, State and Utopia*, ix.

112. Ibid., 32.

113. Ibid.

114. Ibid., 33.

115. Ibid.

116. Ibid., 235.

117. Rawls, *Theory of Justice*, 42.

118. Nozick, *Anarchy, State and Utopia*, 149–150.
119. Ibid., 151.
120. Ibid.
121. Ibid., 156–160, 217.
122. Ibid., 156–57.
123. Ibid., 230.
124. Ibid., 231.
125. Such statements made truly hard-core libertarians turn against Nozick. See M. N. Rothbard, *The Ethics of Liberty* (New York: New York University Press, 1998), esp. section 29, "Robert Nozick and the Immaculate Conception of the State." For other criticisms of Nozick cited by Rothbard in the libertarians' own journal, see R. E. Barnett, "Whither Anarchy? Has Robert Nozick Justified the State?" *Journal of Libertarian Studies* 1 (Winter 1977): 15–21; R. A. Childs Jr., "The Invisible Hand Strikes Back," *Journal of Libertarian Studies* 1 (Winter 1977): 23–33; J. T. Sanders, "The Free Market Model Versus Government: A Reply to Nozick," *Journal of Libertarian Studies* 1 (Winter 1977): 35–44; J. Paul, "Nozick, Anarchism and Procedural Rights," *Journal of Libertarian Studies* 1, no. 4 (Fall 1977): 33–40; and J. D. Davidson, "Note on *Anarchy, State, and Utopia*," *Journal of Libertarian Studies* 1, no. 4 (Fall 1977): 341–48. The website for the journal is http://www.mises.org /jlsdisplay.asp.
126. The same is true in recent times. The Bushmen of the Kalahari in southern Africa, after living in the area for 35,000 years as hunter-gatherers, were ejected from the land as having no tenure rights. See E. M. Thomas, *The Old Way: A Story of the First People* (New York: Sarah Crichton Books, Farrar Straus Giroux, 2006), Chap. 20, esp. 294–95.
127. Healthcare administrators do have a fiduciary duty to the organization and its patients. Such duties include the duties of care and loyalty created when a person undertakes to act for the benefit of another with whom he or she has a relationship implying confidence and trust and creating the expectation that he or she will act with a high degree of good faith.
128. For a good overview of these views and a critical review as well, see A. Gandjour and K. W. Lauterbach, "Utilitarian Theories Reconsidered: Common Misconceptions, More Recent Developments, and Health Policy Implications," *Health Care Analysis* 11, no. 3 (September 2003): 229–44. A different source lists 10 versions of consequentialism; see W. Sinnott-Armstrong, "Consequentialism," *Stanford Encyclopedia of Philosophy*, 2011, http://plato.stanford. edu/entries/consequentialism/. At least three versions of rule consequentialism are described; see B. Hooker, "Rule Consequentialism," *Stanford Encyclopedia of Philosophy*, 2008, http://plato.stanford. edu/entries/consequentialism-rule.
129. Deontology can also be divided into rule deontology and act deontology, although I did not find the distinction useful here. See Frankena, *Ethics*: 21–25.
130. J. S. Mill, *Utilitarianism* (1863), Chap. II, para. 2, http://www.utilitarianism .com/mill1.htm. Accessed November 29, 2011. Owing to the many printed versions, I am citing this work by reference to chapter and paragraph.
131. Ibid., Chap. II, para. 2. Accessed November 29, 2011.
132. *Eudaimonia*, as previously discussed, is human happiness that necessarily includes pursuit of the good for humans as humans.
133. See D. Lyons, "Mill's Theory of Morality," *Nous* 10, no. 2 (April 1976): 101–20, esp. 103–4. He draws this conclusion from Mill's discussion of duty and punishment in *Utilitarianism*, Chap. V, para. 14–15, where Mill finds that punishment is necessary for persons not

fulfilling their duties, without regard to any specific calculation of consequences. The fact that this begins to sound like deontology we leave unchallenged.

134. For example, Lyons, "Mill's Theory of Morality," 101–20, notes the considerable debate over whether Mill was an act utilitarian or a rule utilitarian and whether considerations other than utility entered into his decision calculus. Lyons cites considerable sources on both sides of the debate.

135. Discussed by S. Gosepath in "Equality," *Stanford Encyclopedia of Philosophy*, 2007, http://plato.stanford.edu/entries/equality/.

136. For an extremely well-written, even witty, analysis of this difficulty, see M. Sagoff, "Should Preferences Count?" *Land Economics* 70, no. 2 (May 1994): 127–44. For an abstruse and technical paper reaching essentially similar conclusions, see D. M. Hausman, "The Impossibility of Interpersonal Utility Comparisons," *Mind* 104, no. 415 (July 1995): 473–90.

137. See J. Summers, "Managers Face Conflicting Values," *Journal of Health Care Material Management* 7, no. 5 (May–June 1989); J. Summers, "Clinicians and Managers: Different Ethical Approaches to Honoring Commitments," *Journal of Health Care Material Management* 7, no. 4 (May–June 1989): 62–63; J. Summers, "Determining Your Duties," *Journal of Health Care Material Management* 7, no. 3 (April 1989): 80–81; and J. Summers, "Duty and Moral Obligations," *Journal of Health Care Material Management* 7, no. 2 (February–March 1989): 80–83.

138. One of the common texts used for teaching healthcare administrators the principles of management includes a section on ethics. Although much of the section is on point and the overall text is excellent, the discussion of consequentialism does not even mention that the typical understanding is "the greatest good for the greatest number" but, instead, simply says "a summary statement that describes utilitarian theory is 'the end justifies the means.'" See Longest Jr. and Darr, *Managing Health Service Organizations*, 7th ed. The author of the statement, Kurt Darr, had previously written *Ethics in Health Services Administration*, 5th ed. In that text, he mentioned the idea of "the greatest good for the greatest number" along with "the end justifying the means" but thought both attributable to utilitarians, although not to be "applied without qualification" (p. 17). He did not discuss those qualifications. Unfortunately, many healthcare administrators, only exposed to the more general management theory book, will never know about the greatest good for the greatest number. They would likely perceive consequentialism as inherently allowing an evil to seek a good. For one of many other examples of misunderstanding consequentialism, many of the sites making the claim that utilitarianism means the end justifies the means are religious sites. For an example of a business misreading of Mill's consequentialism, see R. Scruton, "Thoroughly Modern Mill," *Wall Street Journal*, May 19, 2006, A10, http://online.wsj.com/article_email/SB114800167750457376-lMyQjAxMDE2NDI4MjAyMDIxWj.html.

139. B. Hooker, "Rule Consequentialism," *Stanford Encyclopedia of Philosophy*, 2008, http://plato.stanford.edu/entries/consequentialism-rule. Accessed November 29, 2011. Hooker provides the reasons for this rejection and cites a large body of scholarship to support his contention. See also E. Millgram, "What's the Use of Utility?" *Philosophy*

and Public Affairs 29, no. 2 (Spring 2000): 113–36, esp. 126.

140. A criticism in the philosophical literature is that revision of the rule to deal with exceptions leads inevitably back to act consequentialism. See Hooker, "Rule Consequentialism." Practical experience as a manager and an educator of managers suggests that any manager worth his or her salt learned long ago not to let this happen.

141. Beauchamp and Childress, *Principles of Biomedical Ethics*, 7th ed., 227, discuss the substituted judgment approach and find it lacking. They promote the phrase "pure autonomy standard" (pp. 227–228) for what I understand as the substituted judgment approach. Their change in terminology is not used in the healthcare literature as a replacement for "substituted judgment."

142. See Morrison, *Ethics in Health Administration*, 3rd ed., 32–36, and Beauchamp and Childress, *Principles of Biomedical Ethics*, 7th ed., 126.

143. In political decision-making, we fall back on the idea of having an elected person who represents us. These representatives collect information about what their constituents think in a number of ways. In the organizational setting, the entire discipline of market research can be involved in this process. However, these information-gathering methods are seldom quick or inexpensive.

144. See Sagoff, "Should Preferences Count?", and Hausman, "The Impossibility of Interpersonal Utility Comparisons."

145. Mill, *On Liberty*, Chap. I, para. 13.

146. I refer the reader to P. Tillich, *The Courage to Be* (New Haven: Yale University Press, 1952) for helpful thoughts on coping with difficult quandaries about the meaning of life and difficult choices in life.

147. See Longest Jr. and Darr, *Managing Health Service Organizations*, 5th ed. The authors stress the balancing and eclectic nature of the work of the manager in drawing on ethical theories and principles. See also Brannigan and Boss, *Healthcare Ethics in a Diverse Society*, 28, for a similar view.

148. For example, the professional society of healthcare managers, the American College of Healthcare Executives, traces its origins to 1933. The organization was founded to develop the profession of healthcare managers. See http://www.ache.org/CARSVCS/wesbury_fellowship.cfm. Many other healthcare professions are even more recent in origin.

149. See J. Summers, "Doing Good and Doing Well: Ethics, Professionalism and Success," *Hospital and Health Services Administration* 29, no. 2 (March–April 1984): 84–100, for an early discussion in the healthcare literature about the integration of these values and approaches.

CHAPTER 2
Principles of Healthcare Ethics

Jim Summers

▶ Introduction

T he chapter "Theory of Healthcare Ethics" of *Health Care Ethics: Critical Issues for the 21st Century* provided an overview of the major ethics theories and gave examples of how these theories apply to the practice of health care. In the changing Patient Protection and Affordable Care Act of 2010 (ACA 2010) era, knowledge of theories of ethics is especially important for appropriate patient and organizational decision-making. However, a foundation in ethics theory is not sufficient for day-to-day practice. Theories form the basis of the principles of ethics that provide a rationale for action in healthcare practice. This chapter includes the most commonly used principles (justice, autonomy, nonmaleficence, and beneficence) and presents information about their application. In addition, the chapter presents a model for decision-making that applies knowledge of both theories and principles of ethics.

▶ Nonmaleficence

If we go back to the basic understanding of the Hippocratic ethical teaching, we arrive at the dictum of "First do no harm, benefit only." The principle of *nonmaleficence* relates to the first part of this teaching and means "to do no harm." In healthcare ethics, there is no debate over whether we want to avoid doing harm to patients, professional staff, or the community. However, the debate occurs when we consider the meaning of the word *harm*. The following ethics theories come into play here:

- A consequentialist would say that harm is that which prevents the good or leads to less good or utility than other choices.
- A natural law ethicist would say that harm is that which is opposed to our rational natures, that which circumscribes or limits our potential.

- A deontologist would say that harm is that which prevents us from carrying out our duty or that which is opposed to the formal conditions of the moral law.
- A virtue ethicist, a person of practical wisdom, would find that harm is that which is immoderate, that which leads us away from manifesting our proper ends as humans.
- An ethical egoist would define harm as that which was opposed to his or her self-interest.

What Is Harm in the Clinical Setting?

In the clinical setting, harm is that which worsens the condition of the patient. However, deciding what *harm* or *worsen* means is no simple matter. Much of health care involves pain, discomfort, inconvenience, expense, and perhaps even disfigurement and disability. Using the natural law theory of double effect, we justify harm to patients because there is a greater good. A consequentialist would say that the greater good, the greater utility, occurs from accepting the pain or dismemberment as part of the cost to get the benefit the healthcare procedures promise. The due care standard to provide the most appropriate treatment with the least pain and suffering sounds almost like a deontological principle.[1]

Most healthcare professionals consider harm to mean physical harm because the long history of healing has focused primarily on overcoming bodily disorders. However, harm can occur in other ways. For example, healthcare managers can cause harm by failing to supervise effectively. The result may be inadequate staff or a lack of equipment that is maintained or kept up to date. Either of these can lead to adverse patient outcomes. Harm also comes from strategic decisions that lead to major financial losses and jeopardize the ability of the organization to continue. From a community standpoint, making a decision to dispose of hazardous materials without taking proper precautions puts the community at risk. In another example, healthcare policy makers can cause harm to the community by changing eligibility requirements that lead to patient populations being unable to afford or access the care they need. The ways in which harm can occur are infinite.

Harm as Negligence

Given the vast number of ways in which harm can occur, healthcare professionals have developed numerous protocols to protect patients, families, the organizations, the community, and themselves. Failure to engage in these protocols is an act of omission as opposed to directly doing harm, which is an act of commission. A substantial body of law and ethical understanding supports the view that such a failure is *negligence* (omission). Negligence occurs when the person has not exercised the due diligence expected of someone in his or her role and level of responsibility.

Healthcare financial managers, other administrators, and clinicians also face a number of laws to ensure that they are not engaging in fraud and abuse, which also cause harm. For example, failure to follow the expectations of good financial management is essentially *malfeasance*. This term is close to *maleficence* and represents neglect of fiscal responsibility and actions that conflict with policy or the law. Medical professionals are subject to a similar concept called *malpractice*. Part of the education of all healthcare professionals concerns what it takes to avoid doing harm in avoiding malpractice. To ensure the best patient care with the least amount of harm, the practice of due diligence is included in the education and practice of healthcare professionals.

Part of the education and development of a healthcare professional is the creation of persons of integrity who consider it a violation of self to put those who trust in them at risk. These professionals work to avoid this violation and are persons of practical wisdom. They have achieved *eudaimonia* in their professions and in their lives. They also have the ability to meet with other health professionals and discuss the action needed in a complex ethical situation. It is an understanding of the healthcare community that persons who assume the role of healthcare professionals share a common understanding of the mission, vision, and values of health care. They are also able to reason together, even if they arrive at their conclusions by different ethics theories and principles. This shared value of "First do no harm, benefit only" provides a foundation that is often lacking in ethical disputes outside of health care.

Harm as a Violation of Autonomy

An exceedingly large number of issues come to the surface as soon as you begin to address, in a thoughtful way, the issue of what harm is. For example, quality-of-life issues come into play. If a person elects not to receive a treatment because of a loss of life quality, then many people believe that imposing the treatment on that person is wrong. This would violate the principle of autonomy and evidence paternalism. In contrast, think of the situation in which a healthcare professional does not fully educate a patient about treatment options or dissuades the patient from using a certain treatment because of cost or a lack of insurance. While this action may save money for the insurance company or the facility, it does not respect the full autonomy of the patient. Regardless of circumstances, if one applies the principle of autonomy, persons own their lives.

Autonomy is also an issue if the person is incompetent. In this situation, the ethical approach is to determine whether one knows the person's wishes from the time when he or she was competent and, if so, follows them. This practice is termed *substituted judgment*. If the person's wishes are unknown, then the healthcare professional uses an approach called the *best interest* or *reasonable person decision*. The basis for this approach is the assumption that a reasonable person would choose what is in his or her best interest.

▶ Beneficence

The other part of the Hippocratic ethical dictum is "benefit only." The principle of beneficence addresses this dictum. The *bene* is the Latin term for "well" or "good."

Beneficence and a Higher Moral Burden

Beneficence involves more than just avoiding doing harm. It represents a level of altruism that is absent from simply refraining from harm. The ethics principle of having to engage in altruistic or beneficent acts means that we are morally obligated to take positive and direct steps to help others. Relative to the ethics theories, the underlying principle of consequentialism, the greatest good for the greatest number, is itself a statement of beneficence.[2] Early writers in the consequentialist tradition argued for the theory because of their belief that human nature was benevolent.[3]

Because beneficence is a fundamental principle of healthcare ethics, ethical egoism (i.e., the belief that our primary obligation is to ourselves and that selfishness is a virtue) is not logically connected to health care. This is true because the motivation for most people who want to be healthcare professionals is helping people. Health care also is different in terms of common morality. In the larger society, people are not seen as negligent or deficient when they fail to perform beneficent acts. However, in health care, everyone involved in the provision of care, including clinicians, administrators, and support personnel, are expected to act with beneficence.

For example, acts of kindness and courtesy not expected by typical strangers are required of healthcare workers. For example, failure to open a door to help someone in a wheelchair may be discourteous in most settings or perhaps even rude. However, if healthcare personnel take this action, it is unprofessional and may result in disciplinary action. Acting with kindness, compassion, and understanding, even under extremely stressful circumstances, is part of the description of professionalism in health care. In addition, active beneficence requires the ability to see every patient as a unique person who has worth. It also requires a balance between beneficence and clinical decision-making for the best patient care. Such a balance is often difficult, especially in times of great change and challenge.[4] Despite its challenges, beneficence is part of the common morality of health care.

Nonmaleficence and Beneficence Are Insufficient Principles

Historically, the main problem that emerged from emphasis on nonmaleficence and beneficence is that in most healthcare situations, the physician was the person who defined "harm" and "good." Historically, most people were ignorant of what the physician was doing or talking about or why he or she prescribed certain treatments. Thus, the physician defined the patient's self-interest and carried it out. When the person who is receiving a benefit or avoiding harm has little or no say in the matter, that person receives paternalistic treatment. The term *paternalism* comes from the Latin *pater,* which means "father." Paternalism, by definition, means that one treats the patient as one would treat a child.[5] While the concept of paternalism is still part of health care today, changes such as the ACA 2010 and Internet access to healthcare information affect the patient–provider relationship. Patients increasingly assert their desire to make decisions for themselves and see themselves as partners in their own care. Thus, we have to move beyond nonmaleficence and beneficence to include the principle of autonomy.

▶ Autonomy

If a health professional makes a decision for a patient from the "First do no harm, benefit only" perspective without involving the patient in the decision, then the patient's autonomy has been violated. Even if the professional's entire intent is to put the patient's interests before his or her own, leaving the patient out of decisions violates the patient's "self." While the motivation may be beneficence, the patient may not experience this action as one of kindness or compassion. Taking the appropriate action for patient decision-making requires an understanding of the principle of autonomy and its application in clinical and administrative decisions.

Autonomy and the Kantian Deontological Tradition

Autonomy as a concept means that the person is self-ruling. The term *auto* is from Greek and means "self." The rest of the term comes from the Greek *nomos,* which means "rule" or "law." Thus, one can understand autonomy as self-rule.[6] Underlying the concept of autonomy is the idea that we are to respect others for who they are. This view is honored in the medical tradition as far back as the Hippocratic writings. Therefore, the duty of the physician is to treat people's illnesses, not to judge them for why they are ill. It might be necessary for the physician to try to get patients to change what they are doing or who they are, but that is part of the treatment, not a character judgment.

Autonomy in Health Care

In the healthcare setting, it is often unclear whether the patient does or does not possess the conditions required for autonomy. Two important conditions must be met for autonomy:

- Are patients competent to make decisions for themselves?
- Are patients free of coercion in making decisions?

These questions reflect the idea that autonomy implies the freedom to choose. Typically, people have an understanding of what it means to be competent and be able to make choices on their own behalf. However, that is not all there is to competence and autonomy.

A competent person also needs to be free of coercion. Coercion could mean he or she is trying to please someone—parents, children, or care providers—and thus is hiding his or her real choices. In health care, coercion that might prevent free choice occurs in many ways. Providers often encounter patients whose choices are compromised or coerced. For example, an abused spouse may not feel free to discuss the causes of injuries. A raped daughter may avoid discussion of a sexually transmitted disease. Drug abusers may hide their condition for fear of job loss.

An interesting approach to competence is the idea of specific competence as opposed to general competence.[7] Competence can be understood as the ability to complete a task. This may mean you are able to do and understand some things but not others. For example, a person with a transient ischemic attack might be unable to balance a checkbook. However, that same person might be able to understand the consequences of medical procedures and thus might assent to them or might not. This is an example of specific competence. A person may be intermittently competent because of his or her medical condition. Thus, the person is competent to assent to treatment right now but was not so 2 hours previously and might be unable to do so 2 hours in the future. Given the complexity of defining competence and the need to respect the autonomy of patients, clinicians must serve as gatekeepers for decision-making based on their ability to determine a patient's competence for decision-making. Fortunately, there are tools and standards to assist with this gate-keeping role.[8]

At this point, we have examined the importance of nonmaleficence, beneficence, and autonomy as principles of healthcare ethics. Application of these principles is essential to providing high standards of patient care and to the function of mission-based healthcare organizations. The community assumes that these three principles are a given in all healthcare organizations. However, consistently practicing them is often challenging, especially in a complex, ever-changing healthcare environment.

The last of the four principles of ethics, justice, often tests the healthcare system in both patient and organizational ways. This last section examines the theory and application principle of justice in today's healthcare environment. It provides a foundation for understanding the need to practice justice and the difficulties in defining and practicing this principle.

▶ Theories of Justice

In general, to know something is unjust is to have a good reason to think it is morally wrong. However, we must be able to decide whether that action is truly morally wrong. Therefore, we can ask questions like "What kinds of facts make an act unjust rather than simply wrong in general?"

People use the term *injustice* to mean that they are unfairly treated. Injustice in this sense occurs when patients with similar cases do not receive similar treatment. Following Aristotle, many believe that healthcare professionals are required, as a formal principle of justice, to treat similar cases alike except where there is some relevant or material difference in the cases. The equity requirement in this 2400-year-old principle is critical.

Justice usually comes in two major categories, procedural and distributive. *Procedural justice* asks, "Were fair procedures in place, and were those procedures followed?" *Distributive justice* is concerned with the allocation of resources. In some cases, both of these justice issues will be in play at the same time. Both of these justice principles start from the idea that in the distribution of burdens and benefits, the allocation should be equal unless there is a material reason to discriminate.

Procedural Justice

Procedural justice can be defined as *due process*. For example, in the legal system, we speak of being equal before the law as part of procedural justice. In the legal sense, then, procedural justice or due process means that when you get your turn, you receive the same treatment as everyone else. One can apply this concept to health care. For example, when you were waiting to see your primary care physician, did you receive the same attention care as the person who preceded you? Or as procedural injustice, were others seen before you without any clear medical reason?

Procedural injustices occur in patient care, but they are more common when dealing with healthcare employees. For example, if a healthcare administrator has to terminate a few employees because of economic considerations, are the procedures for determining who will go applied without bias? In such cases, the issue is not so much whether what happened was in itself just or fair but whether the method used followed the stated procedures. No one would claim that it is fair to terminate good employees with long careers of service who have done nothing wrong. However, if economic circumstances dictate that employees must be terminated, the procedural justice question of whether there were standards and procedures for making the selections and whether the decision maker followed those standards and procedures correctly emerges.

Failures of due process or procedural justice can also occur in the health policy arena, and policy makers should carefully watch for these failures. For example, at a public hearing concerning a health program that is controversial within the community it is attempting to serve, the chair allows each speaker 3 minutes to present his or her comments. You will not think it justice if some speakers are allowed 10 minutes, whereas others are constrained to 3 or told to sit down after only 1 minute. You would also not think it just to only allow speakers who agree with the committee to have a voice.

The concept of distributive justice is also important for maintaining an ethics-based healthcare system. Because of its importance, it merits its own section and a discussion of principles and issues. This information should assist healthcare professionals and others in the difficult task of providing justice related to resources.

Distributive Justice

The concept of distributive justice relates to determining what is fair when decision makers are determining how to divide burdens and benefits.[9] The Kaiser Family Foundation data suggest that there are distributive justice issues related to the extent of the resource allocation disparity in healthcare demand and spending.[10] For example, in the United States, the average cost of health care in 2010 was $8402 per person and totaled over $2.6 trillion dollars. The United States also spends more money on health care than any other developed nation. In addition, an estimated 20% of the total healthcare costs expenditures are caused by waste and fraud. Is this fair?

When it comes to distributive justice on the national level, many questions emerge: Why is health care so expensive in the United States as opposed to other countries? Does the amount of expenditure mean that Americans are healthier than anyone else on earth? Are there less expensive ways to achieve healthcare goals? Will the changes created in the changing ACA era provide better health care for more people and reduce the cost of care overall? Such questions continue to be debated. However, for our discussion, the point is to understand the difficulty of distributing the burdens of healthcare costs, while seeking the holy grail of affordability, availability, and quality all at the same time.

To understand distributive justice, you must first understand that resource allocation issues occur at all levels. For example, a physician has to decide how much time to spend with each patient. Busy nurses have to decide how quickly to respond to a call button relative to the task in which they are currently engaged. Nurse managers have to effectively allocate too few nurses to too many patients.

Justice issues also exist for health administrators whose duties include hiring employees. In trying to be just in providing compensation, they must decide the best method to use to increase salaries. Should the increase be across the board or by merit or seniority? If by merit, then who decides which employees deserve a pay raise, and is the method fair? The latter question is one of procedural justice.

In the bigger picture, organizational leaders have to decide whether to spend scarce money on capital improvements on buildings and equipment, new employees, current employees, new services, or advertising or whether to save the money. In health care, allocation of scarce resources can be a matter of life and death. Those who must allocate funds often face difficult decisions related to distribution. For example, in Texas, persons with acquired immunodeficiency syndrome (AIDS) and human immunodeficiency virus (HIV) infection pleaded at a Texas Department of Health public hearing that funding not be cut. On the line was a drug assistance program facing budget cuts. At that time, the drugs for treating AIDS and HIV cost $12,000 per year, and the state was considering only allowing coverage if income levels did not exceed $12,400. If a person with AIDS or HIV made $13,000 a year, he or she would have only $1000 on which to live. In addressing this issue, patients with HIV or AIDS told the panel members to look them in the eye so they would know who they were killing. Hearing attendees promised "not to slip quietly into their graves."[11]

Regardless of the outcome of that policy decision, the emotional consequences, coupled with necessary fiscal decisions, highlight the need for the reflective equilibrium in making decisions about distributive justice. Reflective equilibrium is discussed later in this chapter. To be knowledgeable about why decisions are made with respect to distributive justice, one must explore issues related to these types of decisions.

Material Reasons to Discriminate

The basic principle of distributive justice is that each person should get an equal share of the burdens and benefits unless there is a material reason to discriminate. What are the reasons to discriminate?[12] One can summarize the multiple reasons to discriminate for material reasons in two different concepts: the person deserves it or the person needs it. Society believes that those who work hard and do well deserve their success. That is the common moral thinking in the United States. In contrast, a person who breaks the law and hurts people deserves punishment. This common moral thinking is often held by healthcare professionals and organizations. However, it also includes a more complex element—need. The following list includes the most common candidates for material reasons for health care to discriminate, all of which are subsets of need or being deserving:

- Deserving or worthy of merit includes one's contribution or results and effort.
- It also includes the needs of individuals or groups, such as the following:
  - Circumstances characterized as misfortune
  - Disabilities of a physical or mental nature or, more generally, unequal natural endowments
  - A person's special talents or abilities
  - The opportunities a person might have or might lose
  - Past discrimination against a group that is perceived as having negative effects in the present
  - Structural social problems perceived as restricting opportunity or even motivation.

In the larger society, there is also a need to discriminate on the basis of material need. One of society's views of distributive justice is that you get what you deserve or merit. Your results or contributions are what count the most in getting what you deserve. The most common form of getting what you deserve comes from the market. Therefore, if you are good at what you do, the market rewards you. If you are not, the market does not reward you, or even punishes you. For example, a physician who sees the most patients should be the one with the higher income. In addition, healthcare administrators who meet revenue or productivity goals should get higher pay than their peers who fail to do so.

In the larger society, effort matters, too. Many people seek rewards based on their effort, and often, this effort is rewarded by our institutions or culture. In some cases, we cannot determine whether the results that did or did not occur were within the person's control. However, we can observe their effort, and it translates into rewards. Thus, the healthcare administrator, who supervises the more complex healthcare system, receives more pay than a department manager. Researchers in biomedicine might work long and hard without necessarily getting the results they seek, yet they receive compensation for their expertise and labor.

Many people are willing to assist a person whom they perceive as putting forth effort and give up on a person who is not. This applies to healthcare treatments as well. For example, patients who follow "doctor's orders" and do not ask too many questions are viewed as working hard to solve their health problems. They will likely elicit more support and effort from the clinical team. These situations are common in the management of chronic diseases and in behavioral health. What of the reasons to discriminate on the basis of need?

Discrimination on the Basis of Need

It is exceedingly difficult to put an upper limit on the concept of need. For example, the classic World Health Organization (WHO) definition of *health* is "a state of complete physical, mental, and social well-being and not merely the absence of disease or infirmity."[13] This definition sets up a model of need that is theoretically impossible to meet. However, some approaches are more useful than others. These include the following:

Need based on misfortune. In health care, the common morality is to discriminate for or against patients on the basis of their need for care. For example, persons with emergencies are treated first, no matter how long one has waited in line. Persons in accidents, regardless of whose fault it is, are seen as having experienced a misfortune. Victims of natural disasters generally are perceived the same way. However, many of the conditions we treat in healthcare organizations are not owing to an infection, a bad series of decisions, or a natural disaster. People may suffer from genetic defects that vastly restrict their functioning. Others have reduced abilities in physical or mental capacity. One can consider these conditions a form of misfortune.

Even in the healthy population, significant disparities exist between people as to physical and mental ability, including factors such as motivation. For example, one could consider a person's special talents or abilities as a potential area for discrimination. Although we normally do not think of discriminating in favor of someone because of special talents or abilities, it does occur. In health care, the clinical team may make more efforts to help someone with a special talent. For example, each Olympic athlete competing in Rio, Brazil, had a primary physician, who worked with the athlete during his or her preparation for the games. In addition, the U.S. Olympic Committee had 80 medical professionals to care for the athletes. There was also a full-service clinic to address the needs of athletes' coaches and staff. The average American certainly does not have this type of access to care. However, it was determined that the abilities of these elite athletes and their representation of the United States merit discrimination based on their special talents.[14]

From a healthcare organization's viewpoint, administrators make hiring and promotion decisions on perceived ability, speculating that past performance will be a guide to future performance. In that sense, the criteria for hiring are a mix of something the candidate for employment has done and a gamble that he or she will continue to perform well. Policy decisions sometimes are made this way as well, such as when awarding a contract or a grant or funding a program. Decisions on rewards or funding are based on the appearance that those involved have the ability to accomplish necessary goals of the policy makers or organizations.

Children and the elderly also receive special consideration based on abilities or talents. For example, the argument for spending money on children's health care ties into the idea of their future abilities. This echoes the natural law argument to maximize potential. Many clinical workers will go to great lengths to help a child become whole because the child has so much life yet to live. Advocates for the disabled and the elderly also are concerned with ability. They worry that the reduced potential and ability of the elderly can lead to discrimination and thus loss of opportunity.[15]

Need based on past discrimination. Other forms of need might include redress of past injustices to social groups, which overlaps with the need to provide opportunities and prevent the loss of ability.

In the United States, this thinking led to the Civil Rights Act of 1965 and affirmative action laws. It could also be argued that past discrimination means that the protected groups deserve special dispensations. Clearly, the opportunities of many persons in those groups were restricted. Many special talents went undeveloped because the conditions included in discrimination. In health care, we have seen the nation respond to special groups and their needs by the development of entire healthcare systems for them. For example, the creation of the Veterans Health Administration was in response to the needs of those who served the country. In addition, the Indian Health Service was created to provide care to a limited and specific group that experienced discrimination on many levels.

For some disadvantaged groups, the effects of adverse discrimination have led to access and structural problems that prevent some of the members from taking advantage of available opportunities. These burdens, such as poverty, poor educational and housing systems, and poor transportation systems, often contribute to the difficulties experienced by some individuals. Regardless of the root cause of problems, one knows that structural burdens have adverse health consequences.

Many people who claim to have a need also say they have a right to our services. The debate about whether health care is a right or a privilege is still part of the national discussion today. Let us look at the concept of rights, because they are intertwined with the concept of justice.

Distributive Justice and Rights

The efforts toward addressing changes in the ACA 2010 and other healthcare reforms continue the debate over whether access to health care is a right or a purchased commodity. Much of the language in the debate is confusing because there are many types of rights. One thing is clear: to claim a right means that a person believes there is some legal reason that he or she is entitled to something or that there is at the least a moral claim supported by ethics principles and theories. Categories of rights range from ideal rights to legal rights. When a person claims that something is a right, the typical reaction of the other party is to consider the basis of the claim. Is it a legal one? Is it moral? Alternatively, is it not a right but simply a wish or a statement of a preference?

Ways of Categorizing Rights

FIGURE 2.1 provides a visual reference for the types of rights and their relationships. One can find all the rights within the circle of ideal rights, which are rights we wish we had. All of the rights within the larger circle are subsets of the ideal right. Rights that are partially within one or more other circles are rights that share common characteristics with their shared circles. For example, natural rights include elements of substance rights and negative rights. Some of the substance rights and negative rights have become legal rights. A positive right is a certain type of thing or social good to which you have a legal right. All positive rights are a subset of legal rights.

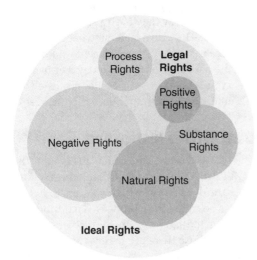

FIGURE 2.1 Types of rights and their relationships.

The size of the circle also indicates the relative importance of each type of right within the common morality of the United States. For example, in the United States, the common morality puts more emphasis on negative rights than on substance rights. Some other nations place a greater emphasis on collective welfare as opposed to individual opportunity. In these cases, the substance rights category would be larger, and more of it would fit inside the legal rights circle.

The list of rights here is by no means exhaustive. The following discussion of the types of rights in Figure 2.1 provides a synopsis of the issues involved.

Major literature exists on the topic of rights and includes others that are not part of Figure 2.1.[16] The best of all rights, from the point of view of the claimant, are enforceable and legal rights.

Legal and Positive Rights

Margaret Mahoney notes that positive rights used to be called "social goods," which society may or may not provide. The change to calling them "rights" was part of a rhetorical technique to give them a greater sense of legitimacy for the public.[17] A *legal right* means that someone has a legal obligation to fulfill your right, whatever it happens to be. A *positive right* is a narrow example of a legal right, because it is a specific social good. For this reason, it is shown in Figure 2.1 as a circle completely within the set of legal rights. These rights are written into law and are described as *entitlements*. However, a legal right can include more than simply entitlements. For example, the legal system protects the right to due process, but it is not the provision of a good. One could say the same of the legal right to privacy under the Health Insurance Portability and Accountability Act (HIPAA). Thus, like due process, a right to privacy is not a positive right, even though it is a legal right.

When rights are under pressure because of budget shortfalls, political pressure to cap government spending, or the like, the real meaning of a legal right is that you can go to court to get it enforced. Legal rights are not as strong as they were once thought to be in protecting the person with the right. For example, you may have a legal right to abortion or to Medicare and Medicaid, but if no one is providing it, your right has little value. Apparently, even the strongest version of a right does not mean that you will be able to exercise whatever rights you have.

Substance Rights

Substance rights may or may not be legal rights. They are rights to a particular thing, such as health care, housing, a minimum wage, welfare, food stamps, safe streets, a clean environment, and the like. In this sense, they are similar to positive rights but not necessarily legal, as with an entitlement. This is somewhat of a nuanced difference, because a substance right might imply that it is a right to something basic needed to maintain life. Nations, such as those in Europe, can be concerned with substance rights and attempt to guarantee an outcome or a basic minimum for their citizens. In those nations, the substance rights became legal rights. The positive legal rights noted earlier for health care also are substance rights, as would be the right in the United States to get treatment at an emergency department regardless of the ability to pay.

Negative Rights

In Figure 2.1, depending on the common morality of the United States, the circle for negative rights is relatively large and extends into the legal rights domain. The terminology used for negative rights comes from the British tradition and essentially means that you have the right to be left alone. You have the right to do anything not strictly forbidden by the law.

Negative rights are clear and enshrine liberty. For example, the Bill of Rights is primarily a list of negative rights, for example, speech and assembly will not be restricted. The Bill of Rights also includes the idea that a state will not enforce a religion. It also reinforces the negative right that allows individuals to have weapons because "a well-regulated militia, being necessary to the security of a free state, [means] the right of the people to keep and bear arms shall not be infringed."[18]

In the realm of health care, one major negative right is that we have the freedom to pursue our lives as we see fit. For example, motorcyclists claim they have a negative right to be free from having to wear protective helmets. Another negative right enshrined in law in some places is the right not to have smokers in your workplace, eating area, or public areas generally. Smokers maintain this is a major affront to their freedom. One person's negative right to be free of smoke is the cancellation of another person's negative right to be free to smoke. Therefore, there are often conflicts about how individuals view these rights and their effect on others.

Other legal protections that ensure you are left alone involve the protections against sexual harassment and hostile work environments. The privacy protections in HIPAA are yet one more legal negative right. An individual's medical information cannot be accessed unless he or she authorizes it or unless there are medically necessary reasons related to his or her care. As in the case of positive substance rights, the costs for those who must honor these rights and take responsibility for ensuring that individuals are free of these hazards can be large.

Process Rights

Given the Bill of Rights, many laws relate to ensuring that due process is followed, at least for most people. As noted in the discussion of the layout of the diagram in Figure 2.1, process rights do overlap with natural rights. In the United States and in most developed nations, process rights also are legal rights.

Natural Rights

Natural rights have a long history. The concept of a natural right means that we should respect attributes that humans have by nature.[19] For Aristotle and St. Thomas Aquinas, these features would be those that best support the achievement of our highest good. The appeals to natural rights within our common morality that are most well-known go back to the Founding Fathers. Drawing heavily on John Locke, Thomas Jefferson proclaimed in the Declaration of Independence, "We hold these truths to be self-evident, that all men are created equal, that they are endowed by their Creator with certain unalienable Rights, that among these are Life, Liberty, and the pursuit of Happiness."[20]

One practical advantage of the natural rights approach to determining a person's rights is that people from very different perspectives use the same language. Thus, even if their views are philosophically inconsistent, they can agree that someone has a natural right. For example, many will say that there exists a natural right to that which is necessary to move toward one's full potential, and health is important to this. To the extent that health care is related to health, one should be able to sustain the argument that morally one has a right to health care. Note that the philosophical reasons for why anyone should be able to develop his or her potential are manifold. However, people of differing religious and philosophic views could agree about having a natural right to develop potential without having to even acknowledge their underlying philosophical differences. Thus, simply as a matter of rhetoric, the language of natural rights plays an important role in making right claims within our common morality.

Ideal Rights

An *ideal right* is a statement of a right that is meant to be motivational, a goal to seek. WHO's definition of health and its subsequent claim that everyone has a right to the highest-attainable health falls into this category. Ideal rights serve to guide organizations, communities, and nations to go beyond the minimum concept of human rights and seek to provide higher standards for their patients or constituents.

Reflections on Rights

One element of the reflective equilibrium model (discussed later in this chapter) that comes into play is the weighting of rights. The fact that we have a right seldom means that it trumps all other considerations. Consider the issue of conflicting rights at the policy-making level. Assume there are rights to national security, education for the young, transportation, protection of property rights, and health care. Is one right more important than the others at all times? Probably not, even though sometimes people think that their claim of a right should more important than all the others. In a healthcare example, do the healthcare needs of the old deserve more attention and financial support than those of the young?

What Does Having a Right Mean?

The U.S. Supreme Court has noted that you have no rights unless they are legal rights backed by statute. The fact that a strong moral case can be made is not sufficient. This applies directly to the example healthcare case that follows. Recruiters for the military sold military service to World War II and Korean War veterans by stating that if they put in 20 years or more of service, they could obtain free medical care at Veterans Affairs (VA) hospitals. However, the Pentagon ended those benefits for veterans over age 65 in 1995 because they were eligible for Medicare. However, Medicare is not a complete healthcare system, and it is not free. Further, some veterans over age 65 say they cannot afford the premiums, deductibles, and copayments of supplemental programs.

When the veterans filed suit to stay in the VA program, they learned that a promise by a recruiter does not equal a law on the books. Thus, in one sense, they had a right to something because they were promised it. However, in the strictest sense of the word, they had no rights if a law did not compel their treatment. A review of the laws dating from just after the Civil War found that the Department of Veterans Affairs was treating people without statutory authorization. The Supreme Court ruled 5–4 that although the recruiters had made promises in good faith, there was no contractual obligation. Thus, the federal government had no contractual obligation to the veterans.[21] This ruling is significant because it enshrines the idea that the only rights you have are strictly legal ones. As the nation and the world struggle increasingly with resource allocation issues, concerns about rights and distributive justice will become ever more common.

▶ Reflective Equilibrium as a Decision-Making Model

FIGURE 2.2 depicts the reflective equilibrium model. The middle of the figure shows the basic facts of the situation for a healthcare issue in which there is a need for a decision. In discussions of ethics, those making decisions about who must decide what to do use what are called *considered judgments* as decision-making guides.[22] Another term for such considered judgments is *ethical intuitions*, although the terms are not exactly the same.

A considered judgment implies that a degree of thinking and reasoning occurs before making a decision. To many people, an intuition is simply a feeling, but to ethicists, a moral intuition includes an element of reasoning. In moral reasoning, we test our considered judgments against our feelings, and vice versa. Clearly, the common morality will have a considerable influence on these judgments and intuitions as well.

Intuitions or considered judgments, as understood by ethicists, are essentially moral attitudes or judgments that we feel sure are correct.[23] These are of two types:

- Intuitions or considered judgments about particular cases. For example, letting people stay in the New Orleans Superdome during the Hurricane Katrina incident without doing anything to supply or protect them adequately was not a decent thing to do.
- Judgments regarding general moral rules. For example, people whose lives or property are threatened by a natural disaster should be helped.

Many such considered judgments exist in health care. For example, a person with a

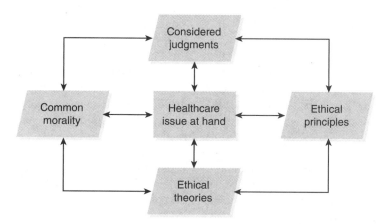

FIGURE 2.2 Reflective equilibrium at work.

medical emergency should receive treatment regardless of his or her ability to pay.

Ethics theory comes into play in examining people's motivations. Some people may believe they act because they have a duty to help others. Others may believe that assisting in a decrease of suffering of others is appropriate and that the more people their decisions can help, the better. Still others might appeal to our basic inclinations as humans to do the right thing or suggest that God or some deity guides our behavior in addressing the problem. When asked to justify their actions and decisions, these same persons might rely on their personal explanations or they might also rely on ethics principles.

As discussed earlier, ethics principles include the advancement of liberty, respect for autonomy, and actions taken out of beneficence to advance welfare. They also include ensuring that following the principle of nonmaleficence, we do nothing to cause harm. We try to do this all fairly by upholding principles of justice. The typical portrayal of the healing ethic, "First do no harm, benefit only," captures at least two of these principles, nonmaleficence and beneficence. The questions become just what to do. In the midst of all the decision-making, the people involved are unlikely to consciously draw on ethics theories or principles. They have internalized these ethical foundations for making decisions and simply make a decision. This is what it means to be a person of practical wisdom, a person exhibiting *eudaimonia*, as described in the chapter "Theory of Healthcare Ethics."

The term *reflective equilibrium* describes this back-and-forth process of coming to a coherent solution. John Rawls described this method,[24] and its hallmark is its lack of dogmatism. The person involved in making the decision revises the decision as new information becomes available. The person may choose to draw on one principle or ethics theory more heavily than he or she did in previous decisions.

Such movement back and forth among competing ethics theories and the quick reweighing of the importance of ethics theories and principles can sometimes look like incoherence or arbitrariness. However, people making healthcare decisions are not as troubled by the requirements of doctrinal purity as they are by the need to come to a decision. They need to have a sound ethical basis to explain the decision, get action on that decision, and get on to the next task. Ethics theories and principles can help them reach those decisions, explain them, and motivate others to act decisively, urgently, or passionately on them.

With this foundation, the outcome is better, assuming the decision was sound. If not, the reflective equilibrium begins again. For this reason, the author chose the toolbox approach to better equip healthcare decision makers with an understanding of the principles and theories of ethics so that they can better decide, better explain, and better motivate. As Beauchamp and Childress put it, disunity, conflict, and moral ambiguity are pervasive features of moral life. Thus, it should be no surprise that untidiness, complexity, and conflict should be part of the process, too.[25]

▶ Summary

The principles of healthcare ethics complete the elements necessary for reflective equilibrium. The primary principles of healthcare ethics are autonomy, beneficence, nonmaleficence, and justice. Justice is, by far, the most complex principle because it includes various conceptions of rights and there is greater dispute about what justice is and how to achieve it. Understanding the various nuances of rights and justice is of considerable importance in making resource allocations at the patient bedside, at the organizational level, or at the health policy level of government.

In using the reflective equilibrium model, a person will have to use reason to pick from among the principles, theories, the common morality, and his or her considered judgments to apply them to the issue at hand. In health care, we have a great advantage over most organizational approaches to dealing with ethical issues. Given the tradition of ethics committees and consultants, a group of persons skilled and experienced in applying the reflective equilibrium is more likely to reach a decision that is reasonable than is a single person. This process will be messy; it will be error-prone. That is the human condition, and there seems to be no way around it.

Ethics is a complex field. Even after thousands of years, humans have yet to develop an ethics theory that will satisfactorily handle all the issues. Nonetheless, some approaches have proven more satisfactory than others and have led to the development of principles. You might ask, "Now what?" Are there any final answers for healthcare issues now and in the future? The answer is no. However, the important role of the study of ethics and ethical issues and the use of the reflective equilibrium model is to keep the inquiry going. The process matters as much, or even more, than the products. Given the current state of profound change within the healthcare system and the need to make changes that are ethically sound, the application of ethics theories and principles is ever more important. Let us hope the changes we face and must make will result in an improvement of our lives and an increase in the good. It is the job of each of us to keep the process going.

▶ Questions for Discussion

1. Why should clinicians have a thorough understanding of the principles of ethics?
2. It is said that you can hire those who will not participate in nonmaleficence, but it is more difficult to ensure beneficence. Why is it difficult to hire for beneficence?
3. Given the changes that are occurring with the ACA 2010, technology, and

other aspects of health care, why will respect for autonomy be more challenging in our future?

4. Justice in health care is more than doing what is fair. What aspects of justice are particularly challenging in healthcare environments?
5. How can you use the reflective equilibrium model to make practical decisions on ethical issues in your practice of health care?

▶ Notes

1. See E. E. Morrison, *Ethics in Health Administration,* 3rd. ed. (Burlington, MA: Jones & Bartlett Learning, 2016), 55.
2. J. J. C. Smart, "Distributive Justice and Utilitarianism," in *Justice and Economic Distribution*, eds. J. Arthur and W. Shaw (Englewood Cliffs, NJ: Prentice Hall, 1979), 103–15, esp. 103. In contrast, Richard Hare, also a consequentialist, specifically disavows that intuitions are a sufficient base for an ethics theory; R. M. Hare, "Justice and Equality," in *Justice and Economic Distribution*, eds. J. Arthur and W. Shaw, 116–31, esp. 117.
3. D. Goleman, "The Roots of Compassion," *New York Times,* December 19, 2006, http://happydays.blogs.nytimes.com/2006/12/19/the-roots-of-compassion/?78ty&emc=ty. The author of the article surveys brain research and finds that humans may be hard-wired to have empathy, compassion, and thus beneficence. T. L. Beauchamp and J. F. Childress, *Principles of Biomedical Ethics,* 7th ed. (New York: Oxford University Press, 2013), point out compassion as a focal virtue in health care on pages 37–39.
4. See Morrison, *Ethics in Health Administration,* 3rd ed., 60.
5. For an insightful discussion of the concept of paternalism, including its effect

on policy and practice, see Beauchamp and Childress, *Principles of Biomedical Ethics*, 7th ed., 214–23.

6. See R. E. Ashcroft et al., eds., *Principles of Health Care Ethics*, 2nd ed. (West Sussex, England: John Wiley & Sons), 12–13.

7. This approach was pioneered by Beauchamp and Childress, *Principles of Biomedical Ethics*, 7th ed., who point out this history on pages 114–20.

8. See Beauchamp and Childress, *Principles of Biomedical Ethics*, 7th ed., 117–20, for examples of standards and tests for incompetence.

9. Robert Nozick, in *Anarchy, State, and Utopia* (New York: Basic Books, 1974), 149–50, argues that the very language of "distribution" implies a central organization deciding who gets what and why. To him this improperly frames the discussion to imply a state and its attendant mechanisms when the problem is the state itself and its inevitable oppression.

10. Kaiser Family Foundation, "Health Care Cost: A Primer 2012 Report," May 2012, http://kff.org/report-section/health-care-costs-a-primer-2012-report/.

11. M. A. Roser, "Don't Cut State Drug Funds, AIDS, HIV Patients Plead," *Austin-American Statesman,* January 17, 2003, B1, B6.

12. J. Arthur and W. Shaw, eds., *Justice and Economic Distribution,* 2nd ed. (New York: Pearson, 1991), were helpful here.

13. World Health Organization, "About WHO," http://www.who.int/about/en/index.html.

14. K. Fiore, "Olympic Doctors Ready to Treat Team USA," MedPage Today (July 24, 2012), http://www.mepagetoday.com/orthopedics/sportsmedicine/33890.

15. For a sampling of complaints, see K. Hausman, "Mentally Ill Workers Rarely Prevail in ADA Discrimination Claims, Survey Finds," *Psychiatric News* 37,

no. 16 (2002): 6. See also M. Weiss, "Study Finds Discrimination against Disabled Patients," ABCNewsHealth.com, http://abcnews.go.com/Health/story?id=2633167&page=1&CMP=OTC-RSSFeeds0312. See also R. Longley, "Disabled Face Discrimination in Rental Attempts," About.com, http://usgovinfo.about.com/od/rightsandfreedoms/a/disablerents.htm.

16. See L. Wenar, "Rights," *Stanford Encyclopedia of Philosophy*, 2015, http://plato.stanford.edu/entries/rights/.

17. M. E. Mahoney, "Medical Rights and the Public Welfare," *Proceedings of the American Philosophical Society* 135, no. 1 (1991): 22–29, especially 23.

18. Second Amendment of the United States Constitution, Legal Information Institute, https://www.law.cornell.edu/wex/second_amendment.

19. Wenar, "Rights," was helpful here. See, especially, section 6.1 on status rights, http://plato.stanford.edu/entries/rights/.

20. Declaration of Independence. See paragraph 2, http://www.ushistory.org/declaration/document/.

21. Associated Press, "Veterans Lose Health Care Suit against Pentagon," *Washington Post,* November 20, 2002, www.americasveterans.org/news/112002.html. For a sample of unhappy commentaries, see M. Marquez, "Government Must Honor Promises from the Past," *Austin-American Statesman,* January 21, 2003: A11.

22. J. Rawls, *A Theory of Justice* (Cambridge, MA: Harvard University Press, 1971), 47–48.

23. Arthur and Shaw, eds., *Justice and Economic Distribution*, 14.

24. Rawls, *Theory of Justice,* esp. 20–21, 48–51.

25. Beauchamp and Childress, *Principles of Biomedical Ethics,* 7th ed., Chap. 10, especially 404–10.

PART II

Critical Issues for Individuals

It is possible to write an entire book on the ethics issues related to individuals as they seek prevention for a disease or its treatment. However, this book represents the survey of ethics issues for individuals, organizations, and society as a whole. Therefore, the authors decided to feature issues related to the most vulnerable individuals who seek care and included chapters relating to the beginning of life and its end in Part II of this edition.

Chapter 3   The chapter "The Moral Status of Gametes and Embryos: Storage and Surrogacy" begins the discussion of ethics and vulnerable populations with the moral status of individuals before their birth. In this chapter, Graber defines the moral community and what it means to be a person. He includes a fascinating table that describes 46 ways to make a baby that reflects the impact of new technologies. This chapter also provides insight into ethics dilemmas associated with the beginnings of moral personhood.

Chapter 4   In the chapter "The Ethical Challenges of the New Reproductive Technologies," Callahan continues the theme by exploring the standards and ethics of the ways that children become part of families. She also provides a thorough discussion of the ethics of reproductive donors, adoptions, and other options to create families. Her discussions also include the effects of these methods on children and families. Using ethics principles such as autonomy, she proposes a standard for addressing collaborative reproductive technology in the future.

Chapter 5   In the chapter "Ethics and Aging in America," Gardner-Ray and Contreraz, address the issues related to the disabled, aging, and those who face the end of their lives. They present legislation that is designed to improve access to needed services for these populations. In addition, the cost of care is addressed as both a fiscal and an ethical issue. Of particular interest for ethics is their section on palliative care for individuals facing the end of life. The practitioner update section stresses the ethics principles of autonomy and social justice as part of the moral duty toward the growing number of aging populations who experience an increasing need for compassionate and effective health care.

CHAPTER 3

The Moral Status of Gametes and Embryos: Storage and Surrogacy

Glenn C. Graber

▶ Introduction

Technology sometimes complicates issues regarding human reproduction by increasing the number of choices available to us. **TABLE 3.1**, which I have whimsically entitled "46 Ways to Make a Baby," illustrates this idea.[1]

Technology has made possible a separation of the role of the genetic mother (who contributes germ cells, perhaps for in vitro fertilization) from that of the gestational mother (in whose uterus the fetus develops). In addition, the social mother (who cares for the child after its birth, perhaps through adoption or foster parenting) might be different from either of these. The roles of genetic and social fathers have always been separable.

Row 37 of the table expresses the situation in which the baby has five parents—or perhaps six if you count the technician who delivers the sperm to the ovum as a sort-of father. In row 38 (male cloning), the source of the enucleated ovum might be different from the gestational mother and the social mother might be still a different woman, or perhaps the genetic father might choose to raise the child in a life partnership with another male, giving the child two male and two female parents.

Who among these four or five or six are *really* the parents of the resulting baby? Who should be given authority to make decisions about whether to continue the pregnancy if complications develop? Who should have a say in decisions about terminating treatment of a newborn if he or she is severely compromised?

Not only are these relationships complex, but they also multiply decision points beyond the traditional possibilities. Until the advent of the birth control pill, no safe way was available to stop the process between fertilization and implantation, because this took place in the inaccessible

TABLE 3.1	46 Ways to Make a Baby								
		Source of Germ Cells		Delivery of Sperm	Site of Fertilization	Site of Gestation	Social Parents		
		♂	♀				♂	♀	
1	Traditional	S♂	S♀	S♂	S♀	S♀	S♂	S♀	1
2	AIH	S♂	S♀	Technician	S♀	S♀	S♂	S♀	2
3	IVF	S♂	S♀	Technician	In vitro	S♀	S♂	S♀	3
4	ICSI	S♂	S♀	Injection	In vitro	S♀	S♂	S♀	4
5	Rent-a-womb	S♂	S♀	Technician	In vitro	Surrogate	S♂	S♀	5
6	Adultery-a	G♂	S♀	G♂	S♀	S♀	?	S♀	6
7	AID	G♂	S♀	Technician	S♀	S♀	S♂	S♀	7
8	AID + IVF	G♂	S♀	Technician	In vitro	S♀	S♂	S♀	8
9	AID + rent-a-womb	G♂	S♀	Technician	In vitro	Surrogate	S♂	S♀	9
10	Adultery-b	S♂	G♀	S♂	G♀	G♀	S♂	?	10
11	Surrogate (AID)	S♂	G♀	Technician	G♀	G♀	S♂	S♀	11
12	Ovum donor	S♂	G♀	Technician	In vitro	S♀	S♂	S♀	12
13	Surrogate (IVF)	S♂	G♀	Technician	In vitro	Surrogate	S♂	S♀	13
14	Fornication	G♂	G♀	G♂	G♀	G♀	?	?	14
15	Bachelor motherhood	G♂	S♀	G♂	S♀	S♀	–	S♀	15
16	#15 + AID	G♂	S♀	Technician	S♀	S♀	–	S♀	16
17	#16 + IVF	G♂	S♀	Technician	In vitro	S♀	–	S♀	17
18	#16 + rent-a-womb	G♂	S♀	Technician	In vitro	Surrogate	–	S♀	18
19	Bachelor fatherhood	S♂	G♀	S♂	G♀	G♀	S♂	–	19
20	#19 + AID	S♂	G♀	Technician	G♀	G♀	S♂	–	20
21	#20 + IVF	S♂	G♀	Technician	In vitro	G♀	S♂	–	21
22	#20 + rent-a-womb	S♂	G♀	Technician	In vitro	Surrogate	S♂	–	22
23	Two mothers	G♂	S♀	G♂	S♀	S♀	–	S♀S♀	23
24	#23 + AID	G♂	S♀	Technician	S♀	S♀	–	S♀S♀	24
25	#24 + IVF	G♂	S♀	Technician	In vitro	S♀	–	S♀S♀	25
26	#24 + rent-a-womb	G♂	S♀	Technician	In vitro	Surrogate	–	S♀S♀	26
27	Adoption—2 moms	G♂	G♀	G♂	G♀	G♀	–	S♀S♀	27
28	Two fathers	S♂	G♀	S♂	G♀	G♀	S♂S♂	–	28
29	#28 + AID	S♂	G♀	Technician	G♀	G♀	S♂S♂	–	29
30	#29 + IVF	S♂	G♀	Technician	In vitro	G♀	S♂S♂	–	30
31	#29 + rent-a-womb	S♂	G♀	Technician	In vitro	Surrogate	S♂S♂	–	31

		Source of Germ Cells		Delivery of Sperm	Site of Fertilization	Site of Gestation	Social Parents		
		♂	♀				♂	♀	
32	Adoption—2 dads	G♂	G♀	G♂	G♀	G♀	S♂S♂	–	32
33	Adoption	G♂	G♀	G♂	G♀	G♀	S♂	S♀	33
34	#33 + AID	G♂	G♀	Technician	G♀	G♀	S♂	S♀	34
35	#34 + IVF	G♂	G♀	Technician	In vitro	G♀	S♂	S♀	35
36	Embryo adoption—IVF	G♂	G♀	Technician	In vitro	S♀	S♂	S♀	36
37	Five parents (or is it 6?)	G♂	G♀	Technician	In vitro	Surrogate	S♂	S♀	37
38	Clone—male E♀	S♂	–	–	In vitro	?	S♂	?	38
39	Clone—female E♀	–	S♀	–	In vitro	?	?	S♀	39
40	Cytoplasmic transfer E♀	S♂	G♀	Technician	In vitro	Surrogate	S♂	E♀	40
41	Twin fission (blastomere separation)	?	?	?	Twin fission	?	?	?	41
42	Embryo transfer	G♂	G♀	G♂	G♀	S♀	S♂	S♀	42
43	GIFT/ZIFT/DOST/IPI	S♂	S♀	Technician	S♀	S♀	S♂	S♀	43
44	LTOT	S♂	S♀	S♂	S♀	S♀	S♂	S♀	44
45	Artificial womb	?	?	Technician	In vitro	Artificial womb	?	?	45
46	Genetic therapy	?	?	?	Germ cell therapy	?	?	?	46

Key to Abbreviations

S♂	=	social father
S♀	=	social mother
?	=	unknown—indicates multiple possibilities
AIH	=	artificial insemination by husband
IVF	=	in vitro fertilization and embryo transfer
E♀	=	source of enucleated ovum [Germ Cell source contributes cell <u>nucleus</u> only. Mitochondrial genes NOT transferred.]
IPI	=	intraperitoneal insemination

GIFT	=	gamete intrafallopian transfer
ZIFT	=	zygote intrafallopian transfer
G♂	=	genetic father (merely)
G♀	=	genetic mother (merely)
–	=	none
AID	=	artificial insemination by donor
ICSI	=	intra-cytoplasmic sperm injection
DOST	=	direct oocyte-sperm transfer
LTOT	=	lower tubal ovum transfer

Sources: Glenn C. Graber, "The Moral Status of Gametes and Embryos: Storage and Surrogacy," in *Health Care Ethics: Critical Issues for the 21st Century*, eds. Eileen E. Morrison (Sudbury, MA: Jones and Bartlett, Publishers, 2009), 61–70; Glenn C. Graber, "The Moral Status of Gametes and Embryos, Storage and Surrogacy," in *Health Care Ethics: Critical Issues*, eds. John Monagle and David C. Thomasma (Gaithersburg, MD: Aspen Systems Corporation, 1997), 8–14; Rem B. Edwards and Glenn C. Graber, eds., *Bioethics* (New York: Harcourt, Brace, Jovanovich, 1988), 635.

regions of the woman's reproductive tract. Now we have ways to access the reproductive tract safely. Microinvasive surgical techniques allow physicians to manipulate ova within the fallopian tubes or the uterus, including assisting a sperm in penetrating the wall of the ovum. These techniques give rise to some of the more exotic possibilities in Table 3.1, such as those in rows 40 through 46. In addition, many of the early steps in the reproductive process can be carried out in the laboratory (e.g., in vitro fertilization, twin fission, and genetic therapy), and we may have to decide at each stage whether to move forward to the next stage as well as with whom to consult about the decision. One dramatic example of this is the practice of removing one cell from a preembryo created through in vitro fertilization to test for genetic anomalies. The results of this test might help the parents decide which preembryo to implant.[2] All these possibilities are ones with which we are not conceptually, emotionally, or ethically prepared to deal. We must sort out myriad questions about the status of the entity at each stage and the relationship of the other parties to this entity.

▶ The Moral Community

I am convinced that if it can be settled at all, the thorny question of the moral status of the materials of human reproduction will be settled by decision rather than by discovery. It is less an ontological question and more a political one (in the broadest sense of the term *political*, referring to the conventions and agreements among the members of a community or a society). Facts about the entities in question may, of course, be relevant to the outcome—but not in anything like the way in which further analysis of the molecular structure of a soil sample retrieved from Mars may furnish evidence for or against the question of whether there is life on that planet.

The issue here is to establish the boundaries of the moral community: *who* counts, morally; who stand to us (i.e., to those of us

in the acknowledged moral community) in a way that requires us to consider them in and of themselves in our decisions and actions. These are boundaries that the community draws for itself, not lines that we discover embedded in the ontological landscape.

This issue transcends the usual divide in ethics theories between teleological and deontological theories.[3] Before teleologists begin to calculate the consequences of their actions, they must determine *whose* welfare is to count; only then can they begin the process of calculating which action is optimal. I have elsewhere[4] distinguished between several characterizations of what I call the "moral reference group" (**TABLE 3.2**).

"Human" designates a biological feature; whereas "person" designates a social role. A *person* is an entity who can enter into certain sorts of social relations with us. A *human* is the genetic offspring of human parents. The movie character E.T. may or may not have been a person, but he certainly was *not* human. A fetus in the womb, immediately before birth, is human but is not, yet, a person because it is not available for social interaction.

Two teleologists with identical theories of value may come up with very different assessments of a given course of action if they approach their welfare calculations from the perspective of different moral reference groups. For example, a thorough-going sexist who refuses to take into account at all the interests of one gender would come to a very different conclusion about the optimal division of household tasks in a typical family from a person who takes the interests of all members of the household into account. More seriously, a personalist would be willing to withdraw life support from a permanently comatose individual (because the capacity for social interaction is no longer present), whereas a humanist might point to the continuing humanity of the individual as a reason for continuing support.

Determination of the moral reference group is also a meta-theoretical issue for deontologism. Kant's categorical imperative, for example, glosses together the moral reference

TABLE 3.2 Moral Reference Groups[4]	
Label	**Scope**
Personalism	Persons and only persons
Humanism	Humans and only humans
Vitalism	All and only living entities
Racism	All and only members of one race
Nationalism	All and only citizens of one nation
Sexism	All and only those of one gender
Universalism	All and only sentient creatures

Data from G. C. Graber, A. D. Beasley, and J. A. Eaddy, Ethical Analysis of Clinical Medicine: A Guide to Self-Evaluation (Baltimore: Urban & Schwarzenberg, 1985), 256–258.

group of personalism with that of humanism when it is phrased to read "Act so that you treat humanity, whether in your own person or in that of another, always as an end and never as a means only."[5] It might be unclear whether this definition applies to persons only or to all humanity; but it is clear, on the one hand, that it does *not* countenance sexism, racism, or nationalism and, on the other hand, that it does not include sentient nonhuman animals in the moral community. Kant was no animal rights advocate.

The debate about animal rights can help illuminate the issues here. Animal rights advocates point out the features of nonhuman animals that are similar to human attributes (especially sentience, including especially the capacity to suffer pain). They accuse us of inconsistency if we uphold moral rules against certain sorts of treatment of humans at the same time that we allow similar treatment of nonhuman animals. I contend that even if successful, this argument is not enough to establish so-called rights in any full-blooded sense or to establish genuine moral standing for nonhuman animals. Even if we are persuaded by these arguments that we have been needlessly cruel in our treatment of animals in food production, research, and other activities, and we resolve to treat them in less cruel and more humane ways in the future, we are still a long way from granting them genuine moral standing or membership in the moral community.

Moral standing goes beyond describing actions as cruel or inhumane. For members of the moral community, another, more serious category of wrong is possible: the wrong of moral affront, indignity, or disrespect. One can show disrespect without being cruel (e.g., through indifference), and one can cause pain (and perhaps even be cruel in a sense) without showing disrespect. For an example of the latter, consider a father who refrains from rescuing his son from a painful situation in the interest of allowing him to experience the natural consequences of a mistake he has made so that he will learn the wrongness of it.

The common element in instances of disrespect or affronts to dignity has to do with the breakdown in an established system of cooperative mutual interaction. Instead of treating you as a peer engaged in a joint enterprise, I fail to acknowledge your interests or concerns and "use" you to further goals of my own. This notion of indignity or disrespect is the core notion in moral standing. If nothing we do to an individual qualifies as an indignity, that individual lacks full moral standing.[6]

Individually, some of us may form such a strong bond with our pets that we admit them to our moral circle, and thus we regard a slight to them as an indignity. However, as a society, we are a long way from having this sort of regard for nonhuman animals generally. The day might come when we do, and we might then look back on our current treatment of nonhuman animals with the same disdain as we hold for the institution of slavery in our nation's past. However, unless and until we reach this sort of general understanding of their status, we cannot say that nonhuman animals are truly admitted into the moral community.

It is difficult to say precisely when (if ever) an established status of moral standing for nonhuman animals will have been achieved. It is not enough for one or two visionaries to treat them in this way and to urge us to follow their example. At the other extreme, it is probably not necessary that each member of the moral community acknowledge their standing. Some (ill-defined) threshold of acceptance would be enough to persuade the moral anthropologist to say that this entity has become a full-fledged member of our moral community.

We can raise questions in this regard as to whether already-born children are currently fully established members of our moral community. Child abuse statutes are on the books throughout our society, but they are not always seriously enforced. Authorities all too often condone gross abuse of children by their parents or caretakers as acceptable discipline or as falling within the domain of the privacy of the family and therefore none of the community's business. If we are still at this stage with regard to children well over a century after the establishment of humane societies to campaign against cruelty to children and animals,[7] it is not surprising that we are uncertain about the moral standing of reproductive materials or of the embryo at various stages of its development.

One aspect of this issue with regard to pre-birth entities faced a concrete political test in November 2011. The state of Mississippi put on the ballot a constitutional amendment that would extend legal protection to the earliest forms of human life. The amendment read as follows:

SECTION 33. Person defined. As used in . . . Article III of the state constitution, "The term 'person' or 'persons' shall include every human being from the moment of fertilization, cloning or the functional equivalent thereof."[8]

If enacted, this amendment would have made illegal all forms of abortion, including those when the mother's life is at stake, as well as any forms of birth control that prevent implantation of the fertilized ovum. Although polls before the voting indicated that the amendment might pass, when they reached the privacy of the voting booth, the citizens of Mississippi defeated the measure resoundingly. Fifty-eight percent voted against the measure; only 42% favored it. Proponents promise to carry this issue to other states and perhaps to introduce it as an amendment to the U.S. Constitution, so we may see this debate on an issue at the heart of our discussion here continue in the years to come.

Technological developments in the reproductive area not only increase the points at which we may (and perhaps must) make decisions but also have an impact on our attitude toward the developing embryo. On the one hand, the use of ultrasonography gives the expectant parent(s) prenatal contact and experience with the embryo. I have heard more than one couple describe the ultrasound images of its fetus *in utero* as "our first baby pictures." In contrast, however, the greater awareness of the uncertainties of pregnancy, which have come to our attention through our diagnostic technologies, has led to what one commentator has called "the tentative pregnancy."[9] Women may not fully acknowledge that they are pregnant (especially to their friends but also attitudinally to themselves) until early ultrasounds, amniocentesis, or both have established that the fetus is free from the sort of significant problems that might lead to miscarriage or to a decision to have an elective abortion.

▶ Making Decisions

How does one make decisions about the separation of roles within the reproductive process that affect the stake of the various parties? It is far from clear. Parents I know who have both one or more children who are genetically theirs (e.g., lines 1–4 on Table 3.1) and one or more who are adopted (e.g., row 33 in Table 3.2) uniformly insist that there is no fundamental difference in their commitment, emotional attachment, or sense of parenthood toward these children. Indeed, after a while, they may have to stop to remember which children are genetically theirs and which are not.

Similarly, when a case was in the news a few years ago about a child who had been switched at birth with another baby some dozen years earlier, I asked many of my friends who have children how they would feel if they were to learn, after many years, that a child they had been caring for was not genetically their child. I could not find anyone who would even begin to countenance the possibility of returning the child they now cared for to his or her genetic parents. They uniformly and emphatically said that they considered the child currently in their household as *their* child.

Yet, infertile couples expend enormous resources and effort in attempts to have a child who is genetically theirs, whereas many adoptable children languish in institutions or foster homes. To these people at this stage of the "career" of parenthood, genetics matters a great deal; to people at a later stage of the career, it seems to matter much less. The child for whom I have cared and established a relationship with is clearly *mine,* no matter whether he or she is genetically mine; the child that I *propose* to care for is less obviously mine merely because I am entrusted to care for her or him. I suggest that identification comes with extended contact with the child and getting to know that child *as a person*. Until that point, the child is, in a way, an abstraction, but I may more nearly identify the abstraction with myself if I am aware of a genetic linkage. All this suggests that genetics, although not to be discounted entirely, is far from fundamental to the long-range bond between child and parent.

The interest of adopted children in learning about their genetic parents raises similar ambiguities. Most (but not all) adopted children report a strong interest in learning about their genetic parentage. However, most also insist that this interest does not interfere with or diminish their emotional ties to the parents who have cared for them since birth (what I call their "social parents" in Table 3.1).

New technologies introduce one more complication. Even if the notion of the zygote or fetus as a *potential* person could be given sense in traditional reproduction, perhaps in terms of the course of development that would occur naturally if nature were left without interference to follow its course, this makes little or no sense in today's world. The natural course of events for a frozen pre-embryo[10] is inertial—it will remain in suspended animation until some intervention occurs to change its status. Little practical difference exists between the potential for personhood of a frozen pre-embryo and that of an individual germ cell. Only one additional laboratory step is required to move the individual sperm or ovum onto the path toward becoming a person (i.e., in vitro fertilization). Only one additional step is required to move the frozen pre-embryo onto the same path (i.e., implantation). Without technical intervention, the potential is nil in both cases.

Several ambiguities cannot help but be reflected in our valuation of the entity in question and in our decision-making about it. A pre-embryo is not the same as a child. In fact, a vast gap exists between the ways we experience and think of these two stages of the reproductive process. The way we think about what constitutes a child also varies on the basis of the time of gestation and the change in status from embryo to fetus to birth.

It is argued by some that the pre-embryo is already genetically individuated and, thus, that it should be accorded the respect due to any human being.[11] However, this overlooks at least two respects in which a pre-embryo falls short of full human status. For one thing, twinning could occur after this stage, so we may have here the protostage of two persons (i.e., identical twins) instead of one individual. Second, the cells at this stage are not yet differentiated in terms of which cell will become one organ and which another; indeed, some of the cells that form part of the unified organism at this point of development will differentiate into placental material and thus will be discarded after the birth of the child. Thus, it flies in the face of genetic fact to insist at this stage that the person who will (perhaps) come into being is present in some inchoate form. Furthermore, the probabilities of carrying the pre-embryo to term are only in the neighborhood of 25%[12], even if implantation occurs, so the odds are decisively against having a child develop from this clump of cells.

At what point in development shall we rule that an embryo or a baby becomes a member of the moral community in her or his own right? **TABLE 3.3** sketches some key candidates for the transition point, together with the underlying philosophical rationale for each. It might not be the case that a bright line comes to be established; instead, I would suggest that an increasing value may be placed on the entity as it develops, culminating finally in a full-fledged sense of dignity or moral personhood after birth.

These sorts of considerations led the Ethics Committee of the American Fertility Society to conclude the following:

> We find a widespread consensus that the pre-embryo is not a person but is to be treated with special respect because it is a genetically unique, living human entity that might become a person. In cases in which transfer to a uterus is possible, special respect is necessary to protect the welfare of the potential offspring. In that case, the pre-embryo deserves respect because it might come into existence as a person. This viewpoint imposes the traditional duty of reasonable prenatal care when actions risk harm to prospective offspring. Research on or intervention with a pre-embryo, followed by transfer, thus creates obligations not to hurt or injure the offspring who might be born after transfer.[13]

Theologian Richard McCormick, who was a member of the committee that wrote this report, puts it somewhat differently (and I think a bit *too* strongly): "I would argue that the preembryo should be treated as a person but that this is a *prima facie* obligation only, albeit a strong one."[14]

The Warnock Commission in the United Kingdom made a similar point about respect for the entity but with a more utilitarian approach to safeguards:

> Though the human embryo is entitled to some added measure of respect beyond that accorded to other animal subjects, that respect cannot be absolute, and must be weighed against the benefits arising from research.[15]

I am convinced that applying this reasoning to the various decisions that might arise will lead to a sensitive and morally serious approach. All the parties affected by choices ought to have some significant voice in decisions, and all parties should take into account the special respect owed to these entities at every stage. In addition, special precautions should be taken if there is a possibility that the entities are to be implanted and allowed to develop.

▶ Surrogacy

Surrogacy contracts ought not to be regarded as indistinguishable from a contract that a woman might enter into to keep some piece of property in trust for a period of time. In addition

TABLE 3.3 Beginning of Moral Personhood[11]	
Transition Point	**Underlying Philosophical Rationale**
Preconception	Transmigration of souls. Reincarnation—the personal identity (soul) exists before and independent of embodiment.
Conception	Identification of personal identity and/or potentiality with genetic integrity.
Conception + 14 days	Past the twinning limit. Assumes that individuation of the soul, identity, or life is established once genetic integrity is firm.
Implantation	Acknowledging the high frequency of spontaneous abortions before this stage; thus, individual identity or potentiality is tied with the *probability* of live birth.
Organ function	The beginning of life is sometimes dated from the initiation of the functioning of certain key organs, such as the heart or the brain. This is an attempt to make the criterion of the beginning of life parallel to the operational criterion of death.
Quickening	The ancient view that the fetus was inert matter until a certain point and then it "came alive." The change was usually ascribed to ensoulment (see the next item).
Ensoulment	Infusion into the fetus of a soul.
Viability	The possibility of independence as the identifying feature of a person.
Birth	Actual independence. Direct relationship as the crucial feature of membership in the moral community.
"Personhood"	Usually correlated with certain landmarks in mental and social development, such as a concept of self. Usually based on an analysis of rights.

Reproduced from G. C. Graber, A. D. Beasley, and J. A. Eaddy, Ethical Analysis of Clinical Medicine: A Guide to Self-Evaluation (Baltimore: Urban & Schwarzenberg, 1985), 197.

to fiduciary duties to the contracting parties, the surrogate mother has special obligations to protect the life that, it is hoped, will result. However, if her life or health were threatened from continuing the pregnancy, it would be unreasonable to expect her to jeopardize her future in order to continue the process. Thus, she would retain her right to elective abortion in this sort of situation. The legal right to elective abortion might remain even if her reasons for ending the pregnancy were less weighty (e.g., the notorious case of pique over a late expense payment by the contracting parties), but ethically we would surely criticize the gestational mother in these cases for failure to show the special respect that is due to the fetus.

Surrogacy arrangements ought to be developed with caution, recognizing that we are not dealing with a mere material possession but rather with an entity that merits special respect and that may well generate intense emotions in the gestational mother, thus making it difficult for her to carry through agreements to give the child up and sever all ties once the child is born. Several notorious court cases have dealt with these matters, but even more common are the hurt feelings of surrogate mothers who had expected to continue to be involved in the child's life after birth. All these issues require a thorough discussion throughout the gestational process, and clear-cut agreements should be negotiated in detail and renegotiated continually as the embryo develops. One court case spoke of the gestational mother in a "rent-a-womb" situation (i.e., row 5 of Table 3.1) as a "genetic stranger" to the child and denied her any continuing contact with the child as a result.[16]

It may be too much to expect the law to be responsive to all these ambiguities, at least immediately, but our ethical judgment is that they need to be taken into account. We are dealing here with issues for which we must stretch our thinking to provide nuanced, sensitive ethical guidance. It would be too heavy-handed to prohibit development of this technology because we do not have a ready set of rules for dealing with its ethical dimensions.

It is simplistic to thrust these decisions into the Procrustean bed of our moral rules for dealing with already-born children. Instead, we must undertake the task of sorting through the complexities and ambiguities of these unprecedented human dilemmas and attempt to reach a consensus on the courses of action that maximize all the values involved. In the best sense, casuistry (resolving moral questions by refining ethics principles) is called for because we have a moral landscape before us that has been heretofore uncharted and must be filled in through the most careful and sensitive analysis of all its features.

▶ Storage

Ethical issues regarding storage of embryonic materials arise at the beginning, the middle, and the end of the process. The special status of the entities can affect each stage of the process. In the beginning stage, it is quite common to retain and store bits of tissue left over from biopsies just in case there might be either a need to refer to them to guide future treatment. This tissue may also be needed in a legal defense or for a possible research purpose. However, these reasons are not weighty enough to justify retaining and storing embryos. Consider pre-embryos that are "left over" from *in vitro* procedures. There must be a significant commitment by the couple whose genetic material is involved to implant them and bring them to term. This commitment should also include the prospective gestational mother and/or the social parents, if they are different from the genetic parents. This is not to say that circumstances that arise might override this commitment, but it ought to be a serious prospect to be considered.

The chief ethical issue in the middle period of storage is the safety of the embryonic material and of the baby, which might result. We need to make serious effort to learn about the risks concerning the methods and duration of storage and to minimize those risks. All parties concerned must keep in mind that these entities have a different status from other biological materials—the well-being of the prospective future child must be a guiding factor in development and use of the technologies of storage.

The special status of the entity should also be considered in determining the end of storage. Storage too long may jeopardize the safety of the prospective baby. Therefore, parents with pre-embryos in storage, who are making decisions about spacing pregnancies, have to take this factor into account. Parents who store pre-embryos for future use and then decide that they do not want additional children also have some moral obligation. They need to consider offering the embryos to other would-be parents whose medical condition precludes their creating their own genetic offspring. Embryo adoption services are becoming more readily available. Absolutists consider it murder to terminate a frozen pre-embryo; those on the other extreme would see it as morally insignificant.

I would argue that it is not an action to be taken lightly, but it is a matter of the morally serious discretion of all the affected parties—genetic, gestational, and social.

▶ Summary

In this chapter, Graber discusses the many reproduction options that will be part of the creation of human beings in the 21st century. Although these options are a tribute to the progress of reproductive technology, they pose serious ethical issues in terms of the moral status of gametes and embryos and the need to identify the boundaries of the moral community. Graber uses ethics theories to show how to define the members of this community.

In addition to complicating the definition of a moral community, reproductive technology also creates ambiguity about how one sees the nature of an embryo. The chapter discusses these issues and presents information about parents' attitudes toward the personhood of children, whether they are their genetic offspring or they aren't. Finally, it points out the gap between the advances of reproductive technology and the moral decisions they will generate. His discussion of surrogacy and the storage of embryos are examples of areas where gaps continue to exist. The 21st century will continue to require courage to travel this moral landscape and map our course though ethical reasoning and discourse.

▶ Questions for Discussion

1. How important is the definition of *moral community* to defining the moral status of gametes and embryos?
2. What elements of deontology apply to making ethical decisions about this topic?
3. How can teleological thinking apply when defining the moral status of gametes and embryos? What special issues do teleologists face in dealing with gametes and embryos?
4. Autonomy seems to be a theme in this chapter. What are the ethical issues relating to autonomy for the surrogate mother?
5. What ethical issues are associated with the storage of embryos? Who should be making the decision about the status of stored embryos?

▶ Additional Readings

American Society for Reproductive Medicine. *Ethical Considerations of Assisted Reproductive Technologies: ASRM Ethics Committee Reports and Statements*, http://www.asrm.org/EthicsReports/.

J. L. Dolgin, "The Law Debates the Family: Reproductive Transformations," *Yale Journal of Law and Feminism* 7 (1995): 37–86.

Genetics and Public Policy Center, Washington, DC, https://jscholarship.library.jhu.edu/handle/1774.2/843, reports on:

■ *Reproductive Genetic Testing: Issues and Options for Policymakers* (2004)
■ *Preimplantation Genetic Diagnosis: A Discussion of Challenges, Concerns, and Preliminary Policy Options Related to the Genetic Testing of Human Embryos* (2004)
■ *IVF, Egg Donation, and Women's Health* (2006)
■ *The Genetic Town Hall: Public Opinion About Research on Genes, Environment, and Health* (2009)

J. Glover, *Ethics of New Reproductive Technologies: The Glover Report to the European Commission* (DeKalb, IL: Northern Illinois University Press, 1989).

Y. Hashiloni-Dolev and N. Weiner, "New Reproductive Technologies, Genetic Counseling and the Standing of the Fetus: Views from Germany and Israel," *Sociology of Health and Illness* 30, no. 7 (2008): 1055–69.

J. M. Humber and R. F. Almeder, eds., *Bioethics and the Fetus: Medical, Moral and Legal Issues* (Totowa, NJ: Humana Press, 1991).

B. Jenning, ed., *Encyclopedia of Bioethics*, 4th ed. (New York: Macmillan Reference USA, 2014). See, especially, the following articles:

■ "Embryo and Fetus"
■ "Genetics and Human Behavior"
■ "Genetics and Human Self-Understanding"
■ "Human Dignity"

- "Maternal–Fetal Relationship"
- "Moral Status"
- "Reproductive Technologies"

B. Steinbock, "Moral Status, Moral Value, and Human Embryos: Implications for Stem Cell Research," in *The Oxford Handbook of Bioethics*, ed. B. Steinbock (Oxford: Oxford University Press, 2007), 416–40.

W. Walters and P. Singer, *Test-Tube Babies: A Guide to Moral Questions, Present Techniques, and Future Possibilities* (New York: Oxford University Press, 1982).

▶ Notes

1. For an earlier version of this chart, see G. C. Graber, "Ethics and Reproduction," in *Bioethics,* eds. R. B. Edwards and G. C. Graber (New York: Harcourt, Brace, Jovanovich, 1988), 635.

2. See PGD, Preimplantation Genetic Diagnosis, http://www.advancedfertility.com/pgd-genetic-testing-embryos.htm.

3. For an explanation of the terms "teleological" and "deontological," see Chapter 1 of this text.

4. G. C. Graber et al., *Ethical Analysis of Clinical Medicine: A Guide to Self-Evaluation* (Baltimore: Urban & Schwarzenberg, 1985), 256–58.

5. I. Kant, *Foundations of the Metaphysics of Morals*, trans. Lewis White Beck (Indianapolis, IN: Bobbs-Merrill, 1959), 47.

6. For a fuller account of this argument, see R. B. Edwards and G. C. Graber, *Bioethics* (New York: Harcourt, Brace, Jovanovich, 1988), 16–18.

7. See https://www.americanhumane.org/about-us/history/.

8. See https://ballotpedia.org/Mississippi_Life_Begins_at_the_Moment_of_Fertilization_Amendment, _Initiative_26_(2011).

9. B. Katz Rothman, *The Tentative Pregnancy: Prenatal Diagnosis and the Future of Motherhood* (New York: Viking/Penguin, 1986).

10. J. Lejeune, *The Concentration Can: When Does Human Life Begin? An Eminent Geneticist Testifies* (San Francisco: Ignatius Press, 1992).

11. Graber et al., *Ethical Analysis of Clinical Medicine*, 197.

12. See https://www.verywell.com/making-sense-of-miscarriage-statistics-2371721.

13. American Fertility Society, "Ethical Considerations of the New Reproductive Technologies," *Fertility and Sterility* 46, no. 3, Suppl. 1 (1986): 35S.

14. R. A. McCormick, "Who or What Is the Preembryo?" *Kennedy Institute of Ethics Journal,* 1 (1991): 13.

15. Warnock, M., *Report of the Committee of Inquiry into Human Fertilisation and Embryology* (London: Her Majesty's Stationery Office, reprinted 1988), 62.

16. Johnson v. Calvert, No. X 63 31 90 (Cal. Super. Ct. Oct. 22, 1990). This way of talking/thinking has an ancient heritage. The Greek scholar Pythagoras, who lived around 530 BCE, argued that hereditary material (which he described as "likeness") was transmitted in the father's sperm and that the mother served merely as a vessel to nourish the developing being. A bit later, in 485 BCE, the playwright Euripides used this logic in the play *Eumenides*, in which a character defended himself against the capital penalty attached to the crime of matricide by arguing that the woman he killed was no more than a stranger who happened to house him before birth. Also see S. Mukherjee, *The Gene: An Intimate History* (New York: Scribner, 2016), 21.

CHAPTER 4

The Ethical Challenges of the New Reproductive Technologies

Sidney Callahan

▶ Introduction

How should we ethically evaluate the new reproductive technologies that treat human infertility? The national debate over this issue continues as the incidence of infertility increases and new techniques become available. Without a consensus about what is morally acceptable, a huge, profitable, and virtually unregulated "baby business" has grown and expanded.[1] At this point in the United States, legal lacunae and regulatory inconsistencies exist amidst contested ethical views.[2] One cause for the confusion arises from the rapidity of technological innovations and the burgeoning market practices serving the growing demand.

Another factor is the existence of large conflicts over the morality of sex and reproduction. Ongoing bitter debates still exist over abortion, stem cell research, the status of embryos, and, to a lesser extent, contraception and sex education in the schools. Lacking societal consensus on the morality of using medical technology to plan, limit, or interrupt pregnancies, we confront difficulties in evaluating the newest assisted reproductive technologies aimed at producing births. To add to the uncertainty, the developed world is experiencing cultural changes in attitudes toward women, children, gender, and the family. These interrelated social and technological changes have produced a pressing need to develop an ethic of responsible reproduction.

My focus here is on some of the newest challenges. How should we ethically assess the innovative array of recent techniques developed to assist reproduction, such as in vitro fertilization (IVF), embryo transplants, egg and sperm donations, and surrogate mothers?

▶ Two Inadequate Approaches to Evaluating Alternative Reproductive Technology

Two inadequate approaches to the ethical assessment of the new alternative reproductive technologies are mirror images of each other in the narrowness of their focus. A conservative approach adopts as a moral requirement an "act analysis," in which the biological integrity of each marital heterosexual act must be preserved without artificial interference. In this view, a married heterosexual couple's act of sexual intercourse and union must always remain open to procreation.[3] Morally, there must not be a separation between marital "love making" and "baby making." This view forbids separation of sexual acts from their procreative potential in order to obtain a contraceptive or reproductive effect; ergo, artificial techniques that separate conceptions from acts of marital intercourse are wrong. This definition also does not support third-party sperm and eggs ever being used for assisted reproduction. The fact that many alternative reproductive technologies do not protect embryonic lives gives further cause for condemnation. Although the use of medical knowledge of human fertility for interventions that increase the probabilities of in vivo conception are approved, achieving procreation through IVF, artificial insemination, cloning, or third-party egg and gestational surrogacy is judged to be unethical.[4]

At the opposite end of the ideological spectrum, another form of act analysis focuses on the private acts of autonomous individuals for reproduction by medical technologies as exercises of procreative liberty and the intrinsic human right to reproduce. One must permit competent adult persons to exercise their reproductive rights at will, without interference. As long as due process and informed consent by these adults are safeguarded through appropriate contracts, they should be free to engage in any safe alternative reproductive technology that can be procured from providers.[5] This permissive stance toward individual-willed choices and the acceptance of market transactions is held to be morally justified on the basis of an individual's right to privacy and autonomy. In this perspective, those who would limit acts of reproductive liberty must bear the burden of proving or demonstrating concrete harm from an innovative practice. Therefore, in effect, almost any alternative reproductive technologies will be ethically acceptable because it is not possible to know long-term negative consequences beforehand.

One can evaluate both of the above approaches to the ethics of using reproductive technologies as too narrow to address the breadth and complexities of the moral challenge posed by these technologies. In a multifaceted, intergenerational, socially critical, and conflicted situation, no single good can be decisive. A reproductive ethic based solely on private liberty or on preserving the biological integrity of each marital act of genital intercourse will hardly be adequate or satisfactory. This is true because humans are both biologically evolved creatures and socially embedded rational persons living within overlapping cycles of familial cultures. Mastery of biological nature through technological interventions is an essential characteristic of the human species.

Religious believers will add that the exercise of reason and technological discovery fulfills the call of the Creator to further human survival, human flourishing, and relief from suffering. Yet either as believers or unbelievers, rational human beings observing their own historical record must acknowledge that innovative technologies can also produce harm.

That the unrestricted use of new technologies has resulted in ecological and ethical disasters is an unfortunate but incontestable truth. In too many cases, such as the invention of lethal weapons of war, the ends were destructive and intended. In other cases, well-meaning innovative technologies have inadvertently produced unforeseen harms. In addition, harms arise from ignoring the ecological and social environment or from failing to foresee that long-term side effects will outweigh immediate advantages. There is a grain of truth in the warning that control of nature by some people can end in producing oppressive control of others. Because technological innovation is rarely value-free or neutral, there must be a prudent and ethical assessment of its consequences. According to a precautionary principle, one should ask those proposing innovations and change to show that no biological or social harms would ensue.

Innovative reproductive technologies are particularly worrisome because the stakes are so high for both individuals and society. New human lives are at risk, and the children conceived and born are nonconsenting third parties who are completely vulnerable to the desires and decisions of adults. In addition, reproduction not only is central to family formation but also carries significant cultural values. Highly intelligent humans are "the self-interpreting animals," who live in sociocultural groups governed by symbolic meanings. Endorsing particular reproductive technologies will have cultural effects beyond fulfilling an individual's private desire to become a parent. Unfortunately, individual human desires, even good desires, may not serve the good of others.

Faced with assisted reproductive technologies, the technological imperative (i.e., what can be done should be done) must not be allowed to govern individual and group reproductive practices and policies. The question is whether certain practices are right, good, and conducive to human flourishing for all the individuals and social groups concerned. One must address complex moral and social concerns as well as technological effectiveness.

▶ A Basis for Developing an Ethical Position

In the case of reproductive technology, one should ground one's ethical position on consideration of what furthers the future good of potential children, their individual parents, their families, and the moral standards of worth of the larger society. What will benefit the various individuals involved as well as the common good? Conflicts will assuredly arise, and priorities and limitations will be enforced. However, it seems right and just that in conflicts of interest, one should give precedence to the good of the potential and newly existing child. This is true because the nascent human life is the most vulnerable party in the reproductive process and cannot give consent. Practically and politically, it is also clear that the physical and psychosocial welfare of a population's children determines the future welfare of the whole society. Because of children's importance, their protection, care, and education are a central moral obligation of humanity, and they are also collectively necessary for survival and social flourishing. The 1989 United Nations Convention on the Rights of the Child[6] recognizes this moral and social truth. Human communities have a moral and social imperative to protect children and to institute practices that will provide for their well-being.

Prudent decision makers respect the biologically built-in social needs that evolution has produced for the successful reproduction of the species, as well as recognize the advantages that scientific knowledge and technological interventions bring. Evolved biological processes, sociocultural norms, and altruistic ideals have served human reproductive success. Parental altruism and protective caretaking are the foundation of group survival. In the human struggle against biological and social dangers, achievements have produced wonderful progress against disease, mortality, and social oppression. Yet, when scientific and social innovation involves unknown risks to vulnerable lives without their informed consent, precautionary principles should prevail. In the pursuit and practice of parenthood, given the intensity of emotional desires mixed in with profit motives and discrepancies in personal power, vigilance and safeguards are necessary. *Do no harm* is the primary moral mandate, always and everywhere.

One ethical justification for taking risks and adopting new assisted reproductive technologies claims that they should be permitted because they are analogous to, and just an extension of, the socially accepted practice of adopting children. Adoption is an ancient and widespread human practice that continues to flourish in modern societies. Evidence abounds that without ties of genetic kinship, one can incorporate children successfully into families by legal adoption. Therefore, why not allow and encourage innovative infertility treatments that break genetic ties and involve collaboration from third parties, such as egg and sperm donors or surrogate mothers? The claim is that the psychological intent and social commitment of parents are the most important and essential characteristics for family success. Therefore, achieving parenthood and founding a family through reproductive technological assistance should, like adoption, be open to infertile heterosexual couples, single parents, and homosexual couples. Moreover, individual children can prove to be resilient and manage to cope with stepfamilies, single-parent families, and other cases where nonbiologically related "fictive kin" step in to rear children.

However, arguing from the example of adoption, "after the fact" crisis management is flawed and hardly justifies initiating or accepting any and all innovative reproductive technologies. Emergency adaptations make for poor standard operating procedures and norms.[7] In the case of adoption, a child already exists and is in need of parental care. Adoption rescues a child in need of a parent through an altruistic and committed action that benefits the child.[8] Regulations are placed on adoption

by law, and there are many social protective measures aimed at preventing abuse. A rescue situation differs greatly from deliberately conceiving a child in order to give it up to others for monetary or other rewards.

Commercial sale or intentional breeding of human beings has been legally and morally unacceptable in Western society since the outlawing of slavery. In the interest of preserving the human dignity inherent in embodied integrity, there has been a prohibition on the purchase of brides, children, sexual intercourse, or bodily organs. Society considers the selling of children for sexual trafficking and pornography as a monstrous abuse. Existing moral norms regarding personal bodily integrity safeguard the moral mandate to treat a human being as an end and not as a means to another's purpose. To fabricate, make to order, or sell a baby to satisfy another individual's reproductive desires for parenthood reduces a human life to a product or material commodity.

Admittedly, no child can consent to its own birth, and a child once born generally would rather exist than not. A person can be grateful for life but also disapprove of his or her means of conception, even wanting to ban such acts in the future. A child conceived through rape or incest could adapt well in a good adoptive family environment, but surely it would be wrong to plan or approve of such conceptions. For example, children of prisoners in Argentina's Dirty War kidnapped at birth could have experienced good family care but feel deeply wronged. It is also no argument for employing an innovative procedure to point out all the failures and family dysfunction that beset children conventionally conceived. Yes, genetically related families can produce suffering, but existing dysfunction hardly justifies risk-taking practices because the outcomes could be no worse. Ethical decisions for employing an alternative reproductive technology should be justified because it will strengthen, rather than threaten, basic operating moral and cultural values. What ethical norms should be proposed and defended?

▶ A Proposed Ethical Standard

With the aim of safeguarding the well-being of the child, individual parents, family structures, and positive moral values of society, one could propose the following ethical standard for the use of alternative reproductive technologies: It is ethically permissible to use an alternative reproductive technology if it makes it possible for a socially adequate, married heterosexual couple to have a child that the couple would normally expect to have but cannot because of infertility. In addition, professionals should use innovative techniques that are medically safe and not harmful to nascent life or to the health and well-being of individual women and men.

Infertility does not seem strictly classifiable as a disease and is never life-threatening. Nor is infertility or childlessness a bar to living a worthwhile, happy life. One does not prove or enhance one's masculinity or femininity by producing a child. However, procreating and founding a family is an important natural good and an expected outcome for a young adult married couple. Infertility can cause intense suffering, and one can aptly view it as a dysfunctional burden. The moral dedication of medicine is to correct human dysfunction and relieve suffering by effective and ethical interventions. Consequently, it can be a great benefit when scientific knowledge and medical technology can assist an infertile couple to fulfill its normally expected reproductive functions.

As in any practice of medicine, the techniques used must be ethically acceptable; they should correct, remedy, and restore without doing harm—to the infertile who suffer, to the child, or to others. Important values of the society at large need to be respected and encouraged. Ethically acceptable assisted reproductive technologies that meet these requirements would include artificial insemination by husband (AIH), IVF of the couple's egg and sperm, or various tubal transfer methods that neither use third-party donors nor deliberately destroy embryonic lives. It seems morally contradictory to destroy human life to create new life. Such a remedial ethical standard for reproductive technology is based on evolved biological and developed sociocultural norms in which the genetic parents, the gestational mother, and the rearing parents are not separate and are adequately prepared to rear the child that results from remedial medical intervention. To this end, potential parents who are to be medically assisted to reproduce should be presently alive and well, be in an appropriate period in their life cycle, and possess average psychological and social resources to care for a potential child.

Helping the severely retarded, the mentally ill, the genetically diseased, the destitute, the aged, or widows with their dead spouses' sperm to have a child they otherwise could not have would be ethically unacceptable. It would also be ethically suspect and medically risky to alter average expectable reproductive conditions by using techniques that intentionally produce multiple births that endanger the health of the prospective children. Such methods also lead to selection and destruction of "excess" embryos in the womb or to the use of genetic screening to obtain a desired gender. (The practices of sex-selective and other forms of abortion, genetic screening, and selection produce a whole range of other ethical problems that are not within the scope of this chapter.)

One can generally acknowledge that the power to intervene in such a crucial matter as the procreation of a new life puts medical professionals and institutions in a fiduciary relationship with the potential child and not just with the adults involved. As causal agents, professionals have an ethical duty not to take serious risks on behalf of nonconsenting others. Agency brings moral responsibility and produces unavoidable moral obligations for professional practitioners. They, like other members of society, have moral obligations to uphold larger social goods and values as well as their duties to individuals in their care. Moreover, the fact that we employ medical resources and professional skills for hugely expensive remedial infertility treatments means that larger questions of distributive justice cannot be ignored. The huge profits that arise from unregulated marketing and innovative infertility services raise other ethical and political concerns.[9] Other developed countries have instituted far more regulation and legal safeguards for use of reproductive technology than the United States, which is often derided as "the Wild West" of reproductive medicine.

The claim that it is a violation of an individual's right to reproduce if infertility treatments are not available to any individual who can pay for them seems wrongheaded. A negative right not to be interfered with (e.g., the right to marry, which itself is not absolute) does not entail a positive right (e.g., that society is obligated to provide a spouse). Moreover, as a society, we have already decided that when child welfare is in the balance, social, legal, and professional interventions and curtailments of liberty are justified. For example, adoption procedures, custodial decisions, and child abuse cases require that professionals make judgments on the fitness of parental capacities. As the frequent cases of child abuse leading to death attest, it is better to err on the side of safety than to take risks with children's lives. Should not medical professionals and clinics be similarly responsible and cautious in carrying out the interventions that will create new children? The emotional desperation of many infertile persons (most often women) can be conducive to abusive but unregulated practices in a multibillion-dollar industry.

Employing third-party donors or different forms of surrogates is not, in this author's judgment, an ethically acceptable use of reproductive technologies. The practice of selling eggs and sperm is equally suspect and belies the meaning of a "donor" as a gift giver. It is possible to variously combine collaborative procedures using procured surrogates or sperm and eggs to produce embryos that may gestate in hired gestational wombs purchased through contract. Such separating and fragmenting of the reproductive process poses social and psychological risks arising from diffusion of responsibility and fragmentation of identity. To understand the problems with third-party donors, we need to consider the evolution of values, goods, and safeguards in the biological and cultural norm of having two heterosexual parents who are the genetic, gestational, and rearing parents of their biological children, who will be cared for over an extended family life cycle.

Many proponents of third-party donors in alternative reproduction—whether for infertile married heterosexuals, single men and women, or homosexual couples—ignore what happens *after* the conception, production, and procurement of a baby. There has been little account taken of the fact that individuals live out their lives within complex familial ecological systems.[10] The assumption seems to be that why and how one gets a baby makes no difference in what happens afterward in the years of childrearing and family life. This might be true when breeding dogs and horses, but it is hardly true of complex-thinking, feeling, imaginative, self-aware humans interested in their origins and narrative destinies in the world. Knowing one's family history and kinship ties can be important in constructing one's self-identity, especially during adolescence. Identifying one's father, mother, and extended kinship group is critical in understanding and finding one's place in the world.

When a young person becomes sexually mature and wishes to marry and procreate, thoughts turn to his or her own progenitors and life story. The difficult challenges of developing into adulthood can become more confusing when collaborative reproduction is the basis for one's birth. In old age too, genetic family relationships become more salient in the arc of a life. Legitimizing and morally sanctioning third-party or collaborative reproductive technology puts at risks the well-being of the child, the parents in families, the donor(s), and important moral goods of our culture.

▶ The Family

The advantages and safeguards for children in having two married heterosexual parents who also are the genetic, gestational, and rearing parents are manifold and becoming more evident in new sociological research.[11] This kind of family produces biological and cultural advantages for its immediate and extended members. From an evolutionary point of view, mammalian *in vivo* reproduction and primate parent–child bonding provide an effective means for the protection, defense, and complex long-term nurture and socialization of offspring. In contrast, there is endangerment of species survival when a species lays eggs that are left floating unprotected in the sea or buried in the sand to take their chances with passing predators.[12]

With the advent of long-living rational animals such as human beings, the basic primate models of parenting were broadened and deepened; they are constituted by committed pair-bonded parenting and extended kinship bonds, such as siblings and grandparents.[13] Two heterosexual parents supported by their respective kin can engage in more arduous parental care taking over an extended period. Grandparents give aid to the third generation, or their children's children. The mated pair who reproduces is also embedded in a larger social network that gives protection and generates the culture that furthers human flourishing. Society bases the foundation of present families on biological realities along with the cultural norms of commitment that produce altruistic bonds and mutual caretaking between the generations.[14]

Slowly the Western cultural family ideal has become less patriarchal as societies recognize the equal moral worth and rights families. Families ensure far more benefits than simply maintaining law, order, and stable continuity. As a man and woman freely choose each other, they make a commitment to share the tasks and joys of life. Bonded by love and a legal contract, they mutually exchange exclusive rights to each other and give each other emotional, sexual, and socioeconomic support. Sexual mating results in children, who concretely embody the marital union and have an equal claim to parental care from father and mother. In addition, the extended families of both parents are important resources for the couple; they can serve as backup caregivers, especially in cases of death or disaster.

No analysis of one procreative act in a marriage can do justice to the social fact that a reproductive couple and its children exist as a unit within an extended family of kin. Siblings, cousins, aunts, uncles, grandparents, and other relatives are important in family life for both practical and psychological reasons. Individual identity is rooted in biologically based descent and cooperative kinship networks within larger social groups. The family is one remaining institution where one is given or ascribed a status by birth; one cannot earn or achieve the provision of unconditional altruistic care. Psychologically and socially, the family provides emotional connections and opportunities for altruism and gives meaningful purpose to life. Those individuals who do not marry or found families of their own still have strong connections to their kin through their families of origin.[15] Human beings exist within familial and social envelopes and must do so to flourish. However, as a human, culturally constructed commitment, why must genes and biology be the basis for the family? Cannot any persons who intend and declare themselves to be a family, be a family?

Although the internalized conscious psychological identification and commitment to be and supportively act like a family is the foundation of human families, one cannot deny the powerful bond created by genetic relationships. Biological kinship ties are important in other primates, and one should not underestimate them in human societies.[16] One working definition of the family is that a family consists of people who share genes. Sociobiologists and evolutionary psychologists emphasize the power of genetic relationships to generate altruism and human bonding automatically.[17] In fact, the willingness of infertile couples to continue the struggle to procreate their own biological child is testimony to the existence of strong innate urges to reproduce oneself genetically with a beloved mate. Even half of a genetic tie may be preferred to none. When an adoption is initiated, the legal system uses the template of genetic kinship ties as a model for legal relationships.

One understands that the genetic parental relation to the offspring of two married persons is the synthesis of two equal genetic heritages, with the child situated within both lineages. Members of both families give support, or one set of kin may by choice or chance become more important. But having two sets of kin provides important social resources or social capital. The child is heir to more than money or property when situated in a clear and biologically rooted kinship community. Siblings and collateral kin take an interest and help their biological relatives who share their genes and progenitors. In old age, younger generations of families take responsibility for caring for their older relatives. Filial piety is an ancient virtue that still has force. The genetic tie is a powerful motivating factor because it is unique, localized, embodied, and an irreversible connection existing through time and space. It cannot be undone changing circumstances and intentional commitments.

The search by adopted children for their biological parents and possible siblings reveals the psychological predisposition of humans to know of their birth origins and history.[18] Social movements toward greater transparency and openness of information regarding biological origins respond to the children's right to know. The children resulting from third-party donations increasingly seek out knowledge of the third-party donors. When there are one or more third-party donors—of sperm, eggs, or embryos—a child is distanced or cut off from either half or all of his or her genetic origins and heritage. If there is secrecy or deception concerning a child's origins, then there are wrongs to the child. The child's biological relatives remain unknown to him or her, and for their part, the grandparents and half-siblings are deprived from knowing their descendant and family member. Because family secrets are difficult to keep and seep into a family's atmosphere, delayed disclosures can produce distrust among those kept ignorant or overtly deceived. Even when a child and his or her relatives know the truth, the identity of the donor (or donors) can become an issue for all concerned. Are there other siblings and relatives out there?

Evolutionary psychology has come to see genetic factors as being increasingly important in mating, parent–child interactions, and childrearing outcomes.[19] When rearing parents and genetic parents differ and the donor is unknown, there is a provocative void. If there is knowledge of the donor and he or she is part of the rearing parents' family or social circle, other potential psychological problems and conflicts may emerge regarding who the real parent is and who has primary rights and responsibilities. When the third-party donor is also the surrogate mother, combining genetic and gestational parenthood, the social and legal problems can be profound. For example, the Whitehead–Stern court struggle indicates the divisive chaos and suffering that is possible in third-party surrogate arrangements and contracts.

In the average expectable situation, two married parents possess an equal genetic investment in the child. The mutual and equal genetic relationship to the child can become a unifying force for the parents. They are irreversibly connected and made kin to each other through the child they have jointly procreated. This new life is the concrete embodiment of their love, commitment, and sexual bonding. A pregnancy with mutual monitoring of the developing child unites the couple and prepares the parents for their joint caretaking enterprise.[20] Each parent shares his or her genetic link with the child with his or her own extended family. A common genetic inheritance produces a family likeness and a sense of belonging. Biological sharing of genes leads to empathy and easy affective attunement for family members. The child's genetic link to the other partner and to each marital partner's own kin can work to strengthen the marital and family bonds.

At the same time, the fact that the child is also a new and unique life formed by a random combination of a couple's genetic heritage gives the child enough difference so that he or she is seen as a separate and unique person. The child possesses what some call an "alien dignity" as an irreplaceable, unique human life that must be recognized.[21] (Cloning one's self or another would be wrong because of its denial of and infringement on a child's possession of a new and unique identity.) Because we are embodied creatures, we build psychological bonds of caring, empathy, and social commitment on the firm foundation of biological ties and bodily identity.

Assisting two parents to have their own biological child through technological interventions without third parties can further the bonding of the couple. Medical treatments and other procedures to remedy infertility can be an arduous process that tests personal commitment to each other and to the potential child. When techniques such as AIH or IVF or tubal ovum transfer are used to correct a couple's infertility, the time and money spent, the shared stress and discomfort, and the cooperative effort required can serve to strengthen the couple's union. Seeking to bear their biological child can focus two persons upon their marital relationship and their mutual contribution to parenthood. The psychological bonding can increase and transcend the stress and unpleasant procedures that intervene in their sexual and social lives. Parents' mutual sacrifices are necessary. When successful, the resulting baby will be a new person in whom there is mutual investment and who is equally related to both parents. Given the equal investment in their child, both parents are equally responsible for childrearing and support.

Unfortunately, in assisted reproduction, the success rates for the arduous and expensive treatments of infertility are low and often disappointing.[22] The advancing age of men and women with infertility conditions is one obstacle; the expense of treatments is another problem. A couple has to be able to withstand frustration and burdens together and not become dangerously obsessed with the quest. Otherwise, the temptation is strong to move to ethically and medically problematic methods offered in unregulated marketplaces. So-called baby hunger can produce emotional pressures that cloud judgment and produce so-called genetically clouded children who will bear the risks.

When employing third-party genetic donors, one parent will have a biological relation to the child, and the other parent will not. True, the nonrelated parent can give consent, but even when consent is free, there is never an equalization of the imbalance. Although there is certainly no question of adultery in such a situation, the psychological intrusion of a third-party donor can have an effect on the couple's union. Even if there is no jealousy or envy, the situation dramatically defines the reproductive inadequacy of one partner, and he or she places reliance on an outsider's genetic heritage and superior reproductive capacity. Asymmetry of biological parental relationships within a family or household has always been problematic, from Cinderella to today's stepparents and reconstituted families.[23] Children who are unrelated to one of their married parents have less positive social outcomes and are in greater danger of abuse.[24] In addition, the most frequently cited cause of divorce in second marriages is the difficulty of dealing with another person's children.[25]

The empathy and irreversible identification and tie that come from a knowledge of shared biological kinship seem to buttress parental authority and commitment. However, in disturbed families under stress, one finds more incest, child abuse, and scapegoating if biological kinship is asymmetrical.[26] Biological ties become psychologically potent just because human persons in families engage in imaginative subjective relations with one another, whether as children or as adults.

Parents' fantasies about a child's past and future make a difference, as all students of child development or family dynamics will attest. For example, identical twins might even be treated differently because parents project different fantasies upon them.[27] In addition, third-party donors and surrogates cannot be counted on to disappear from family consciousness, even if legal contracts can control other ramifications and overt interventions. A child conceived by new forms of collaborative reproduction is part of a biosocial experiment without his or her consent. Although, as noted, no child gives informed consent to conception, a biological child of two parents is begotten and born in the same way as his or her parents. Even if there is no danger of transmitting an unknown genetic disease or causing a physiologic harm to the child, the psychological relationship of the child to his or her parents is at risk by third-party technological innovations. A child confronts the fact that he or she was created and made to order as a contracted product by third-party strangers—for pay. Treating a child like a commodity—something to be fabricated and procured to satisfy the desires of purchasing parents—infringes upon the child's alien dignity as a gift of nature's biological bounty.

As ideals of parenthood have developed, those who seek a child, not as a gift received for its own sake, but to satisfy some personal parental need or desired extrinsic end, are judged ethically lacking in altruism and commitment. Unfortunately, we are still struggling to overcome residual beliefs that see children as a kind of personal property or as an adult entitlement that provides a "life-enhancing experience." Only gradually have we welcomed children as new lives given to their parents in trusted guardianship. Children are now valued as equal in moral worth to adults, despite their dependency and powerlessness. Having a child solely for some selfish purpose has now

become as morally suspect as marrying solely for money or status. In the past, people have wanted children to secure domestic labor, to have caretakers in old age, to increase social power, to prove sexual prowess, or to have someone of their own to possess—or scapegoat.

A person or a couple obsessively driven to procure a child might not be prepared to rear the actual child once born. Being wanted and being well reared are not the same. Parental dreams of the optimal baby or the perfect child, the overinvestment in "gourmet children," also can be psychologically burdensome for a child.[28] Adolescent problems of anorexia, depression, and suicide have been viewed as related to the dynamics of parental overcontrol.[29] A young person must achieve a separate identity in order to interrelate adequately with others and to become autonomous-in-relationship. More ominously, a child whose parents desired him or her for all the wrong reasons may not be accepted if born with problems. Outright rejection of imperfect or non-optimal babies cannot be safely avoided by contracts. There may also be some health risks for IVF children, mainly due to multiple births and prematurity.

In the course of a child's development, psychologists note that thinking and fantasizing about one's origins seem to be inevitable in the search for self-identity. In alternative reproduction, the question "Whose baby am I?" becomes inevitable.[30] "Why was my biological parent not more concerned with what would happen to the new life he or she helped to create?" The need to know about possible half-siblings and other kin might become urgent at some point in development. The first infants conceived from sperm donors have entered young adulthood, and they have started new Internet support groups and blogs to address their issues. Similarly, young adopted adults also search for their biological relatives and support movements for transparency and access to information. One concern is the problem of inadvertent incest, but the main focus is on the issue of achieving identity and integrity.

▶ Donors and the Cultural Ethos

Procuring donors of sperm, eggs, embryos, or gestational wombs is an essential component of collaborative reproduction. Brokers, individuals, and clinics advertise and sell sperm, eggs, and gestating surrogate services in competitive marketing. The multibillion-dollar business has grown as infertility has increased. Reproductive marketing has been clothed in a "gauzy shroud of sentimentality," where misleading terms such as "donors," "surrogate mothers," "family building," or "forever families" are used to describe highly profitable enterprises.[31] Affluent infertile persons shop for sperm, eggs, and womb services in competitive markets with fluctuating prices. Brokers advertise and search for donors to recruit them for a profit; clients shop for the eggs and sperms they want and that they can afford. Donors, too, shop for the best deal.[32]

However, in this burgeoning enterprise, there is still a need for research to examine the effect of the baby business on the donors. Women's physiologic health is one growing concern, as the complicated, arduous process of egg donation has increased the dangers posed by powerful drugs and invasive procedures. In addition, there has been little critical analysis of the morality and psychology of what a donor is doing. When persons are being paid, they are not strictly donors but are selling their genetic and bodily resources. There is an effort to have such transactions assimilated into the model of blood donations or organ donations, but this analogy is misleading.

When young people sell their eggs and sperm, they are selling the unique genetic identity that they received from their own parents and grandparents. This is not like donating a kidney, because sperms and eggs contain the unique information and inherited generative potential that is basic to identity—one's own, and a future other. When an individual treats this inherited gift of unique genetic

identity and generative power as less than personally inviolate, or contracts to sell it, he or she breaks an implicit compact to respect and practice "procreative stewardship."[33] An egg donor is selling the reproductive capacities of the eggs that she inherited from her mother while still in her mother's womb. A gestational surrogate mother sells her reproductive capacities much as one sells bodily sexual function in prostitution. The poor will need money, and the rich can offer to pay.

Occasionally there will not be an exchange of money, and donors or surrogates can consider that their voluntary participation in another's assisted reproduction is an act of unalloyed altruism, perhaps undertaken for a relative or close friend. But this altruism is clearly being directed to fulfill the desires of adult(s), not of the child who will be born. No donation, paid or unpaid, of either sperm or eggs avoids the serious problem in the practice of donation of sperm or eggs by third parties. Such practices counter a basic principle of morality, that is, that you take responsibility for the future consequences of your actions as a causal agent.

Adult persons are held morally responsible for the effects of their words and deeds. In serious matters that bring about powerful effects, such as sex and reproduction, which have irreversible lifetime consequences, we rightly hold competent persons to a high standard of moral and legal responsibility. Specifically, to counteract tendencies toward sexual irresponsibility and child neglect, Western culture has insisted that men and women are accountable for those sexual acts that create new life. Donors, whether male or female, who take part in collaborative reproduction, abdicate their future responsibility for their reproductive acts that will enable the births of their own biological children.

In fact, in most cases, the donor contracts to avoid any future personal interventions. A person is specifically enjoined not to monitor or carry through on what he or she initiates or causes to happen. Instead, sellers hand over control of their generative resources and potency to physicians, brokers, or others, usually strangers. By design and contract, persons abdicate all consequences for their reproductive cooperative actions. Yet, procreative responsibility is a basic demand of the natural responsibility arising from the causal efficacy inherent in the possession of power by rational human agents.[34] Taking part in the procreation of a new life incurs moral obligations and moral claims from the life engendered. It seems doubtful that a legal convention devised to further an innovative technology can undo such obligations. Certainly, contracts cannot undo the unique genetic linkage with biological parents.

Donors who abdicate reproductive responsibility also deprive their own parents of grandparenthood. They also keep other closely related family members from knowing their biological relatives. Future children of the donor, or other children of a surrogate mother, might never know their half-siblings. Disregarding the biological reality of genetic relationships promotes a mistakenly disembodied, fragmented view of how human beings actually function. Moreover, when a woman donates her eggs or gestational capacity or both, there is a grave danger of exploitation, as feminists have warned.[35] The physiologic risks attending the drastic intervention in a woman's reproductive system needed for egg retrieval and surrogacy are considerable.

If the gestational market offers a woman a great deal of money, she might be tempted to sell her bodily resources and suffer the consequences. In addition, poor third-world women can be enticed into the gestational surrogacy market. Middle-class young women with desirable looks and high intelligence quotients (IQs) can command high prices for their eggs; affluent bidders now advertise in college papers. When eggs are commodities sold to the highest bidder, a woman's identity as an integrated whole person is under the threat of reduction to a material supplier of parts.

Similarly, with the sale of sperm, we sanction fragmented integrity and male abdication of responsibility for their biological offspring. Society allows the profit-making commerce in sperm, also complete with competitive advertising, despite social epidemics of male sexual irresponsibility and father-abandonment of children. Many young males think nothing of masturbating and selling their sperm for cash until later in life, when they begin to rear their families.

When there is commercialization of reproduction, governed by contract and the purchase of body parts and functions, familial culture becomes even more fragmented and alienated. There can be endangerment of the great primordial civilizing reality of invested parental commitment, mutual dependency, and irreversibly bonded genetic kinship. There can be a weakening of commitment to support and care for one's own children when we legitimize the isolation of genetic, gestational, and social parentage. Those individuals who disregard the biological and cultural values that have previously evolved in our societies are engaging in a risky experiment with their children and their family lives. Most often, as persons of good intentions, they do everything they can to normalize and fulfill their desired parental roles.

Their argument is that the great good of having children justifies the means employed. Often, they may refrain from deception and even encourage extended familial relations with donors and surrogates. However, in the end, can children comprehend, without anxiety, the fact that men sell their sperm, women market their eggs, and mothers make babies and give them away for money? Nothing could be more risky to human welfare than to enable men and women to distance themselves emotionally from their own bodily being, from their own family heritage, or from their future offspring.

One of the requirements for a responsible ethic of sexuality and reproduction is to acknowledge sexual acts as personal acts involving the whole person. Lust is wrong outside of committed loving relationships because it disregards the whole person in the pursuit of sensual gratification. If money is involved, it causes a person to be reduced to a means to fulfill another's desire, and exploitation follows. So, too, it seems wrong and dangerous to isolate, purchase, and intentionally use a person's reproductive capacities apart from his or her own family existence.

▶ Summary

An approved practice of isolating sexual and reproductive acts from personal responsibility for the outcomes is a form of moral abdication that can only increase existing problems within the culture. Society already faces a challenge to its traditional norms of moral obligation, responsible reproduction, and parental commitments to caretaking. Cultural norms, based on reason and natural evolution, have mandated the unity of genetic, gestational, and rearing parents. A mated and committed pair-bonded couple exists in an acknowledged, extended biological kinship system. Families exist as dynamic intergenerational institutions that are part of the larger society; through procreation and altruistic adoption, families fundamentally enable human health, economic well-being, and emotional flourishing.

In Western societies, scientific knowledge has brought techniques of assisting infertility dysfunctions, but these interventions require ethical assessment. Morally, the parental role is correctly understood as basically an altruistic endeavor: parents procreate and rear children so that these new lives can develop and flourish. From an ethics standpoint, society no longer views children as personal property or as a means to satisfy adult desires, needs, or purposes. When adults make individual reproductive decisions, or groups enact public

policies, the good of the potential child should be the primary consideration. Children will most safely flourish in a society that culturally endorses socially committed, biologically related families upheld by personal moral responsibility in their procreating.

This author has argued for an ethical standard that limits alternative reproductive techniques to those that remedy the infertility of a committed couple in average expectable conditions that can adequately support childcare. To this end, she argues that the unity of genetic, gestational, and rearing parents should remain intact. Collaborative reproduction risks the good of the child, the good of families, the good of donors, and the important norm that agents uphold personal moral responsibility for their reproductive actions. Certain limits should be set on using new technological means for assisted reproduction. As Gandhi wisely said, "Means are ends in the making."[36]

▶ Questions for Discussion

1. According to Callahan's ethical reasoning, why would a business to create "gourmet children" be unethical when the potential parents are able to provide informed consent?

2. What ethical principles apply in a decision to limit the use of current and future reproductive technologies?

3. How is Callahan's position on reproductive technology different from Graber's view in the chapter "The Moral Status of Gametes and Embryos: Storage and Surrogacy"?

4. What ethics theories support Callahan's position in this chapter? What theories would not support it?

5. What ethics principles could be used to support Callahan's position in this chapter? What principles would not support it?

▶ Notes

1. See D. L. Spar, *The Baby Business: How Money, Science, and Politics Drive the Commerce of Conception* (Cambridge, MA: Harvard Business School Press, 2006); D. L. Spar, "The Business of Babies," *Science & Theology News* (July–August 2006): 43–46; and D. L. Spar, "Buying Our Children, Selling Our Souls? The Commodification of Children," *Conscience* 27 (2006): 14–16.

2. See B. Steinbock, *Life before Birth: The Moral and Legal Status of Embryos and Fetuses*, 2nd ed. (Oxford: Oxford University Press, 2011); and E. Marguardt, *The Revolution in Parenthood: The Emerging Global Clash between Adult Rights and Children's Needs* (New York: Institute for American Values, 2006).

3. Congregation for the Doctrine of Faith, *Instruction on Respect for Human Life in Its Origin and on the Dignity of Procreation* (Washington, DC: United States Catholic Conference, 1987).

4. One can find a statement of these principles in Roman Catholic Church teaching: see Congregation for the Doctrine of Faith, *Instruction on Respect for Human Life*. Also see P. Lauritzen, *Pursing Parenthood* (Bloomington, IN: Indiana University Press, 1993).

5. J. A. Robertson, *Children of Choice: Freedom and the New Reproductive Technologies* (Princeton, NJ: Princeton University Press, 1994).

6. See United Nations, "No. 27531 Convention on Rights of the Child Adopted by the General Assembly of the United Nations on 20 November 1989," *United Nations Treaty Series V.1577* (New York: United Nations, 1999). https://treaties.un.org/doc/Publication/UNTS/Volume%201577/v1577.pdf.

7. J. Wallerstein, J. Lewis, and S. Blakeslee, *The Unexpected Legacy of Divorce: A 25-Year Landmark Study* (New York: Hyperion, 2000).

8. M. Stewart Van Leeuwen and G. Miller Wrobel, "The Moral Psychology of Adoption and Family Ties," in *The Morality of Adoption: Social-Psychological, Theological, and Legal Perspectives*, ed. T. P. Jackson (Grand Rapids, MI: William B. Eerdmans, 2005), 3–31.

9. M. Ryan, *Ethics and Economics of Assisted Reproduction: The Cost of Longing* (Washington, DC: Georgetown University Press, 2003). See also D. L. Spar, *The Baby Business*; D. L. Spar, "The Business of Babies," and D. L. Spar, "Buying Our Children, Selling Our Souls?"

10. A classical statement of this process can be found in E. H. Erickson, *Childhood and Society* (New York: Norton, 1950); also see J. Heckhausen, "Psychological Approaches to Human Development," in *The Cambridge Handbook of Age and Ageing*, ed. M. L. Johnson (Cambridge: Cambridge University Press, 2005), 181–89; and R. Martinson and S. A. Martinson, "The Nature of Parenting," in H. Anderson et al., eds., *The Family Handbook* (Louisville, KY: Westminster John Knox Press, 1998), 63–89.

11. Institute for American Values, *Why Marriage Matters: 26 Conclusions from the Social Sciences*, 2nd ed. (New York: Institute for American Values, 2005); Marguardt, *The Revolution in Parenthood*.

12. See J. Altman, "Sociobiological Perspectives on Parenthood," in *Parenthood: A Psychodynamic Perspective* (New York: Guilford Press, 1984); and E. O. Wilson, *Sociobiology* (Cambridge, MA: Harvard University Press, 1975). See also M. Daly and M. Wilson, "Evolutionary Psychology and Marital Conflict: The Relevance of Stepchildren," in *Sex, Power, Conflict: Evolutionary and Feminist Perspectives*, eds. D. M. Buss

and N. M. Malamuth (Oxford: Oxford University Press, 1996), 9–28.

13. The role of the father has been seen as critically important in both the female and the male child's intellectual development, moral development, sex role identity, and future parenting; for a summary of relevant research, see R. D. Parke, *Fathers* (Cambridge, MA: Harvard University Press, 1981), and S. M. H. Hanson and F. W. Bonett, *Dimensions of Fatherhood* (Beverly Hills, CA: Sage, 1985).

14. See K. Gough, "The Origin of the Family," *Journal of Marriage and the Family* (November 1971): 760–68; P. J. Wilson, *Man the Promising Primate: The Conditions of Human Evolution* (New Haven, CT: Yale University Press, 1980); G. P. Murdock, "The University of the Nuclear Family," in *A Modern Introduction to the Family*, eds. N. W. Bell and E. F. Vogel (New York: The Free Press, 1968); and M. J. Bane, *Here to Stay: American Families in the Twentieth Century* (New York: Basic Books, 1976).

15. S. P. Bank and M. D. Kahn, *The Sibling Bond* (New York: Basic Books, 1982); I. Arnet Connidis, "Sibling Ties Across Time: The Middle and Later Years," in *Cambridge Handbook of Age and Aging*, 429–36.

16. Wilson, *Man the Promising Primate*; Daly and Wilson, "Evolutionary Psychology and Marital Conflict."

17. D. S. Browning, "Adoption and the Moral Significance of Kin Altruism," in *The Morality of Adoption*, 52–77.

18. C. Nadelson, "The Absent Parent, Emotional Sequelae," in *Infertility: Medical, Emotional, and Social Considerations*, eds. M. D. Mazor and H. F. Simons (New York: Human Sciences Press, 1984); M. Stewart Van Leeuwen and G. Miller Wrobel, "Moral Psychology of Adoption."

19. Twin studies and the recognition of inherited temperamental traits have followed studies showing a genetic component to alcoholism, manic depression, schizophrenia, antisocial behavior, and IQ. For a popular discussion of the findings concerning schizophrenia and criminal behavior, see S. Mednick, "Crime in the Family Tree," *Psychology Today* 19 (March 1985): 58–61. For a more general discussion by an anthropologist, see M. Konner, *The Tangled Wing: Biological Constraints on the Human Spirit* (New York: Holt, Rinehart & Winston, 1982). See also Daly and Wilson, "Evolutionary Psychology and Marital Conflict."

20. A. Macfarlane, *The Psychology of Childbirth* (Cambridge, MA: Harvard University Press, 1977); M. Greenberg, *The Birth of a Father* (New York: Continuum, 1985).

21. H. Thielcke, *The Ethics of Sex* (New York: Harper & Row, 1964), 32ff. Later analyses of the ethics of having children can be found in J. Blustein, *Parents and Children: The Ethics of the Family* (Oxford: Oxford University Press, 1982); O. O'Neill and W. Ruddick, eds., *Having Children: Philosophical and Legal Reflections on Parenthood* (New York: Oxford University Press, 1979); and S. Callahan, "An Ethical Analysis of Responsible Parenthood," in *Genetic Counseling: Facts, Values, and Norms; Birth Defects*, Original Article Series 15, no. 22 (New York: Alan R. Liss, 1979).

22. Centers for Disease Control and Prevention, American Society for Reproductive Medicine, and Society for Assisted Reproductive Technology, *2003 Assisted Reproductive Technology Success Rates: National Summary and Fertility Clinic Reports* (Atlanta: U.S. Department of Health and Human Services, Centers for Disease Control and Prevention, 2003). See also D. L. Spar, *The Baby*

Business; D. L. Spar, "The Business of Babies"; and D. L. Spar, "Buying Our Children, Selling Our Souls?"

23. Daly and Wilson, "Evolutionary Psychology and Marital Conflict."

24. Institute for American Values, *Why Marriage Matters.*

25. B. Maddox, *The Half Parent: Living with Other People's Children* (New York: M. Evans and Company, 1975); R. Espinoza and Y. Newman, *Stepparenting: With Annotated Bibliography* (Rockville, MD: National Institute of Mental Health, Center for Studies of Child and Family Mental Health, 1979).

26. See "Explaining the Differences between Biological Father and Stepfather Incest," and "Social Factors in the Occurrence of Incestuous Abuse," in *The Secret Trauma: Incest in the Lives of Girls and Women*, ed. D. E. H. Russell (New York: Basic Books, 1986).

27. D. N. Stern, *The Interpersonal World of the Infant: A View from Psychoanalysis and Developmental Psychology* (New York: Basic Books, 1985).

28. See "The Child as Surrogate Self" and "The Child as Status Symbol," in D. Elkind, *The Hurried Child* (Reading, MA: Addison-Wesley, 1981).

29. S. Minuchin, B. L. Rosman, and W. Baker, *Psychosomatic Families: Anorexia Nervosa in Context* (Cambridge, MA: Harvard University Press, 1978).

30. L. Andrews, "Yours, Mine, and Theirs," *Psychology Today* 18 (December 1984): 20–29; Marguardt, *The Revolution in Parenthood.*

31. See Spar's descriptions in D. L. Spar, *The Baby Business*; D. L. Spar, "The Business of Babies"; and D. L. Spar, "Buying Our Children, Selling Our Souls?" See also L. Mundy, *Everything Conceivable: How Assisted Reproduction Is Changing Men, Women, and the World* (New York: Knopf, 2008).

32. Donor 15, "Ova Sale: The Art of the Deal in the Gray Market for Human Eggs," *Reason*, October 2006, www.reason.com/news/show/36867.html.

33. B. Waters, "Adoption, Parentage, and Procreative Stewardship," in *The Morality of Adoption*, 32–51.

34. H. Jonas, *The Imperative of Responsibility: In Search of an Ethics for the Technological Age* (Chicago: University of Chicago Press, 1984).

35. B. Rothman, *The Tentative Pregnancy* (New York: Viking Press, 1986); H. Holmes, B. Hoskins, and M. Gross, *The Custom-Made Child: Women-Centered Perspectives* (Clifton, NJ: Humana Press, 1981); A. M. Jagger, ed., *Living with Contradictions: Controversies in Feminist Social Ethics* (Boulder, CO: Westview Press, 1994); Michelle Goodwin, "Assisted Reproductive Technology and the Double Bind: The Illusory Choice of Motherhood," *Journal of Gender Race & Justice* 3 (2005–2006).

36. M. Gandhi, *The Essential Gandhi: An Anthology of His Writings on His Life, Work and Ideas* (New York: Random House, 1962).

CHAPTER 5

Ethics and Aging in America

Janet Gardner-Ray and Kimberely Contreraz

▶ Introduction

This chapter presents a review of issues concerning access to quality health care for the elderly, more specifically long-term palliative care and the urgent need for changes in the future. The authors of this chapter are Janet Gardner-Ray, an executive in the long-term care industry, and Kimberely Contreraz, a certified palliative care nurse practitioner. Their expertise and experience engendered an understanding and awareness of healthcare services for the aging population that will become more critical, in the near future, given the imminent influx of advanced elderly baby boomers in need of services. They foresee a system in dire need of improvement. Within this system, access to quality health care promises to be both taxing to the Medicare system as well as to healthcare providers who assume responsibility for the quality of care provided within a cost-driven system.

The ethical issues posed by Gardner-Ray and Contreraz are certainly not limited to the elderly population. However, treatment of the elderly speaks loudly of who we are as a nation and ultimately how we treat individuals regardless of age. Therefore, as the authors examine the continuum of healthcare for elder adults, they challenge our thinking to include an ethical foundation to guide future decision-making. In fact, the issue of quality long-term health and palliative care for our older population will loom large on the social, political, and ethical horizon well into the 21st century. Therefore, it is important to understand the current social and political climate as well as the history surrounding elder care before one can adequately address ethical decision-making for the future.

During the last decades of the 20th century, there was increasing evidence of the public's interest in improving access to humane and appropriate health and palliative care services for the elderly in the United States. Opinion polls indicate that a substantial majority of Americans, in all adult age groups, fear the financial, familial, psychological, spiritual, and social consequences of dependence on others as they age. Most Americans favored the general principle of expanding government financing for such care as the principal means of increasing access.[1]

A number of bills that would provide for public funding for elder healthcare were introduced in Congress in the late 1980s and the 1990s. These changes in healthcare policy subsequently lead to the Patient Protection and Affordable Care Act of 2010 (ACA 2010). These healthcare reforms have accrued an estimated annual price tag ranging from $60 billion in the first year to $2 trillion over the next decade for the ACA 2010. Why did health care begin to emerge from the shadows during the 1980s and 1990s? Simply, it was cast into the healthcare arena by the increase in dramatic and aggressive treatments offered by acute care medicine, which allow the eldest elderly to survive longer with chronic illness and disability. Living longer became the single-most cost-driven element in the healthcare industry, given the enormous growth of our older population. For example, the number of those aged 65 and older doubled from 16 million in 1960 to 32 million in 1990. Persons in this age category constitute presently 12.5% of our population, and there is an expectation that they will constitute 71 million, or 20%, in the year 2030.[2]

Another element that precipitated the demand for quality health care was the growing constituency of adult children providing care to elderly parents. These individuals came to understand the importance of quality healthcare services because they were providing direct contact care or arranging for the care of their aged parents. In 1989, over 13 million adults in the United States who had elderly parents or spouses were potential providers of elder care, financial assistance, and emotional support. There were 4.2 million who provided direct care in home settings.[3] Today, the number of adult caregivers has risen to over 10 million, with an estimated cost of $3 trillion in lost wages, pensions, and Social Security benefits as a result of leaving the workforce early.[4]

Despite the underlying needs and hopes of elder caregivers, enactment of a government program to expand access to quality elder care in the immediate future is problematic because of the substantial funds that would be required. Achieving a "balanced budget" is the rhetorical mainstay of contemporary national politics, and containing government expenditures on healthcare costs is one of the major means for balancing the federal and state budgets.

The challenges of ensuring adequate access to quality health care for all who need it are substantial. The number of Americans requiring some form of long-term health care is already large and will grow significantly over the next few decades. Financing such care is already difficult for individuals, their families, and governments. Even with the advent of further healthcare reform, indications are that the prices for services and their aggregate national costs will continue to escalate, whereas there could be a curtailment of the role of governments in paying for the care of an expanded elderly population.

This chapter focuses on issues of healthcare access for older people and the need for access to quality care and long-term palliative care resources during the aging process. First, it provides a definition of palliative care and discusses the growing need for quality long-term palliative care. Second, it discusses issues of access to care. Third, it briefly recounts how proposals to expand public funding for long-term care became the national policy agenda in the early 1990s and then abruptly fell from it. Finally, it presents the political and ethical prospects for improving access to quality elder care in the years ahead.

▶ The Growing Population Needing Care

Long-term care need is defined by being functionally dependent on a long-term basis due to physical or mental limitations or both.

Two broad categories of functional limitations are widely used by clinicians to assess need for care. One category is dependence in basic *activities of daily living* (ADLs): getting in and out of bed, toileting, bathing, dressing, and eating. *ADL-dependent* is the term used for persons who have cognitive impairments and need cueing from someone else to be able to perform their own ADLs. The other category is limitations in *instrumental activities of daily living* (IADLs): taking medications, preparing meals, managing finances, doing light housework and other chores, being able to get in and out of the home, using the telephone, etc. (Professionals use other criteria to assess children and people with mental illness, such as the ability to attend school or problems in behavior.) The range of services needed by those who have difficulty in carrying out their ADLs and IADLs, as well as those services needed by their primary caregivers, is extensive.[5]

In 1982, the U.S. Congress enacted legislation providing funding for hospice care benefits on the basis of a National Hospice Study that was still in progress. The legislation ultimately became part of the Medicare Hospice Benefit and led to the proliferation of hospice care throughout the United States. During the following 30 years, little changed in the hospice arena, with the exception of funding fluctuation and the increase of aging in home programs. However, in the past 20 years, the healthcare industry has seen the rise of palliative care initiatives.[6]

Palliative care initiatives, covered by private health insurance or Medicare, are treatment-driven programs that assist the elderly in managing their chronic illnesses. They are medical treatments specializing in care for the chronically ill, which can be provided at any time during the disease process.[7] These programs provide a continuum care for elderly individuals with an emphasis placed on aging in the home. Palliative care programs begin seeing patients with multiple health issues and comorbidities sometimes years before there is a referral to hospice. These patients are generally suffering with varying degrees of pain and disability. The goal of this form of care is to provide access to a specialty group of support staff that can facilitate the needs of the patients, prevent hospital readmissions, and monitor the elderly in maintaining the greatest amount of independence while managing their chronic illnesses and balancing the need to contain cost, while preserving human dignity.

The majority of palliative care cases are elderly. For example, in 2013, people aged 65 and older constituted 83.4% of palliative care cases, with one-third of those aged 85 or older. Working-age adults accounted for 16.1% of the total and children less than 1%. Moreover, only 22% of the elderly population required long-term care, and 19% of that total was the disabled population, resided in nursing homes and other institutions. Data that are more recent indicate that these percentages are changing, partially as a result of the increase in alternatives in elder care, such as aging-in-place programs.[8]

Although it seems apparent that the number of people needing long-term care will grow substantially in the future, precise predictions regarding the size of that population and its composition are difficult to generate because of many factors. New and improved medical treatments and technological developments could help prevent, delay, and compensate for various types of functional difficulties. Moreover, health-related lifestyle changes and environmental protection measures could markedly reduce rates of disabling diseases and injuries.

Lower death rates from heart disease and stroke, for example, could mean that more people will live longer with disabling conditions and thus enter the pathway of late-onset illnesses such as Alzheimer disease (AD). Similarly, improvements in dealing with the complications of acquired immunodeficiency syndrome (AIDS) could engender longer periods of care for patients with this condition. All of the previous conditions will require early palliative care intervention to assist with the issues of dealing with long-term chronic illness. The earlier healthcare professionals intervene in the chronic disease trajectory, the better the outcome.

Demographic factors might also affect future needs for providing and financing long-term chronic diseases. For instance, cohorts reaching old age in the next several decades will be better educated than their predecessors. Statistics suggest that higher levels of education are associated with lower levels of disability and need for care.[9] Despite this statistic, the ethnic composition of the population will have an effect on the need for long-term care. The ethnic composition by 2030 will be 72% white, 10% African American, 11% Hispanic, and 5% Asian, suggesting the need for increased healthcare services and governmental subsidies for financing. From 1990 to 2050, the proportion of non-white Americans aged 65 and older is projected to more than double, from 9.8% to 21.3%. When they reach old age, these racial minorities might be highly dependent on public subsidies for their long-term health care if present patterns of economic resource distribution among racial and ethnic groups persist throughout the first half of the 21st century. Among persons aged 65 and older who have the lowest household incomes, nearly 40% are racial minorities, and their aggregate net worth is less than one-third that of older white persons.[10] Studies show that health disparities also exist among certain racial and ethnic groups who are disproportionately affected by chronic conditions.[11]

Even though precise projections are difficult, it is clear that there will be enormous increases in the number of disabled older people in the 21st century. When much of the baby boomers—a large cohort of 74 million Americans born between 1946 and 1964—reach the ranks of old age in 2030, the absolute number of people aged 65 and older will have more than doubled, from about 31 million in 1990 to about 71 million. Moreover, the number of people in advanced-old-age ranges will also more than double. Those aged 75 and older will grow from 13 million to 30 million between 1990 and 2030, and those aged 85 and older will increase from 3 million to 8 million.[12]

Rates of disability increase markedly at these advanced ages. One reflection of this is in the most currently available data (from 2004) on rates of nursing home use in different old-age categories. Of the 1.4 million residents of nursing homes, about 4.5% are 65–74 years old. This compares with 3.6% of persons aged 75–84 and 13.9% of persons aged 85 and older.[13] Similarly, disability rates increase in older old-age categories among persons who are not in nursing homes. According to the 2000 U.S. Census Bureau data on the disability of non-institutionalized populations over age 65 (33,346,626 people), almost 42% demonstrated some degree of disability. The most common form was physical disability (28%), with difficulty going outside the home (20%) and sensory disability (14%) in second and third places, respectively.[14]

The tremendous future growth expected in the older population suggests that there will be millions more disabled elderly people in the decades ahead. Whether rates of disability in old age will increase or decline in the future, however, is a matter on which experts disagree, depending on their assumptions and measures. Assuming no changes in age-specific risks of disability, He et al. calculated a 31% increase between 1990 and 2010 in the number of persons aged 65 and older experiencing difficulty with ADLs.[15] Using the same assumption, the Congressional Budget Office projected that the nursing home population will increase by 50% between 1990 and 2010, double by 2030, and triple by 2050.[16] Even those researchers who report a decline in the prevalence of disability at older ages emphasized that there will be large absolute increases in the number of older Americans needing long-term health and palliative care in the decades ahead.

Predicting whether long-term health and palliative care needs among people younger than 65 will increase or decline is more difficult. One of the principal reasons is that reliable data bases for making projections are limited compared to well-developed national and longitudinal sources available regarding the older population. Data collected on a state basis vary widely with respect to state rates for various types of disabilities.[17] Moreover, the numbers involved with respect to various disabling conditions, such as spinal cord injury, cerebral palsy, and mental retardation, are relatively small and much more susceptible to changing conditions.

Yet, experts agree that the number of younger disabled persons has grown in recent years, and this trend might well persist. New technologies and increased access to medical care continue to enable more people to survive injuries and other conditions that were heretofore fatal, and thereby live for many years with ADL limitations. For example, biomedical advances have enabled many more children with developmental disabilities, as well as low-birth-weight infants, to survive much longer than in the past and to extend the years in which they need long-term health and palliative care resources.

▶ Issues of Access

Whether a long-term health and palliative care patient is in a nursing home, living at home, or in another type of residential setting, there are certain aspects of care that such a person desires. An ideal system of services would be amply available, of high quality, provided by well-trained palliative care personnel, easily located and arranged, and readily accessible through private or public funding or both.

The present system, however, is far from ideal. The supply of services is insufficient, service providers lack education and training, and the quality of many services is poor.[18] Moreover, the system is so fragmented that even when high-quality services are sufficiently available, many patients and families do not know about them and require help in defining their service needs and arranging for them to be provided.[19] Underlying each of these problems is the issue of financing. As is the case with most aspects of the U.S. healthcare delivery system, the nature and extent of policies for funding have substantially shaped the characteristics of long-term healthcare services.

The Costs of Care

Aggregate expenditures for long-term health and palliative care are sizable and likely to increase in the decades immediately ahead. The total bill in 1995 was $106.5 billion; of this amount, 73% went to nursing home care and 27% to home- and community-based care.[20] Out-of-pocket payments by individuals and their families accounted for 32.5% of the total. Private insurance benefits paid for 5.5%. Other private funds accounted for 4.6%. Federal, state, and local governments financed the remaining 57.4%. Medicaid paid for 85% of nursing home care.

In 2003, the total bill had risen to $183 billion, while out-of-pocket payments fell to 20% of the total. Paying the costs of long-term care out of pocket can be a catastrophic financial experience for patients and their families. The annual cost of a year's care in a nursing home averages more than $58,000, but it can cost well over $100,000.[21] Although the use of a limited number of services in a home- or other community-based setting is less expensive, using non-institutional care for those patients otherwise appropriately placed in a nursing home is not cheaper.[22]

For a high percentage of older people, the price of long-term care is simply unafford-able. Among persons aged 65 and older, 40% have a pretax income of less than 200% of the poverty threshold—under $10,458 for an indi-vidual and $14,602 for a married couple in which the man is aged 65 or older.[23] The costs of care will undoubtedly grow in the future. Price increases in nursing home and home- and community-based care have consistently exceeded the general rate of inflation. Trends in long-term health and palliative care labor and overhead costs indicate that this pattern will continue.

Dozens of government programs are sources of funding for long-term health and palliative care services, including Medicaid, the Veterans Health Administration, Social Security's Title XX for social services, and the Older Americans Act.[24] Yet, each source reg-ulates the availability of funds through rules regarding eligibility and breadth of service coverage and changes its rules frequently. Consequently, persons needing long-term health and palliative care and their caregiv-ers often find themselves ineligible for finan-cial help from these programs and unable to pay out of pocket for needed services. In one study, about 75% of the informal, unpaid caregivers of dementia patients reported that their patients did not use formal, paid services because they were unable to pay for them.[25] In addition, it is difficult for providers to con-tinue justifying resources for palliative care initiatives when data for value-added services are difficult to generate. When a patient is not readmitted to the hospital, federal programs save money, but there is little impact on the hospital's bottom line.

Recent data on Medicare and Medicaid spending affirm the trends mentioned here. In 2006, these programs cost over $3 billion

per day to run. In light of the fact that the first of the baby boomers (a cohort of 77 million) became eligible for Medicare in 2008, the cry for reform is becoming even louder. However, even the 2003 prescription drug benefit has not slowed down the increase in costs. Health-care reform will not solve all of these issues: challenges lie ahead.[26]

The Caregiving Role of Families

A number of research efforts have docu-mented that about 80% of the long-term care provided to older persons outside of nursing homes is presently provided on an in-kind basis by family members—spouses, siblings, adult children, and broader kin networks. About 74% of dependent community-based older persons receive all their care from fam-ily members or other unpaid sources, about 21% receive both formal and informal ser-vices, and about 5% use just formal services.[27] The vast majority of family caregivers are women.[28] The family also plays an important role in obtaining and managing services from paid service providers.

The capacities and willingness of family members to care for disabled older persons may decline, however, because of a broad social trend. The family, as a fundamental unit of social organization, has been under-going profound transformations that will more fully manifest over the next few decades as baby boomers reach old age. The strik-ing growth of single-parent households, the growing participation of women in the labor force, and the high incidence of divorce and remarriage (differentially higher for men) all entail complicated changes in the structure of the household and kinship roles and relation-ships. There will be an increasing number of blended families, reflecting multiple lines of descent through multiple marriages and the birth of children outside wedlock through other partners. This growth in the incidence of step- and half-relatives will make for a dramatic new turn in the family structure in the coming decades. Already, such blended families constitute about half of all households with children.[29]

One possible implication of these changes is that kinship networks in the near future will become more complex, attenuated, and diffuse,[30] perhaps with a weakened sense of filial obligation. If changes in the intensity of kinship relations significantly erode the capacity and sense of obligation to care for older family members when the baby boomer cohort is in the ranks of old age and disability, demands for governmental support to pay for long-term care may increase accordingly.

The Role of Private Insurance

Private, long-term care insurance, a relatively new product, is expensive for the majority of older persons, and its benefits are limited in scope and duration. The best-quality policies, which provide substantial benefits over a reasonable period, charged premiums in 1991 that averaged $2525 for persons aged 65 and $7675 for those aged 79.[31] Only about 4%–5% of older persons have adequate private long-term healthcare insurance, and only about 1% of nursing home costs are paid for by private insurance.[32] A number of analyses have suggested that even when the product becomes more refined, no more than 20% of older Americans will be able to afford adequate private health insurance.[33]

A variation on the private insurance policy approach to financing long-term care is continuing care retirement communities (CCRCs) that promise comprehensive healthcare services, including long-term care, to all members.[34] CCRC customers tend to be middle- and upper-income persons who are relatively healthy when they become residents and pay a substantial entrance charge and monthly fee in return for a promise of "care for life." It has been estimated that about 10% of older people could afford to join such communities.[35] Most

of the 1000 CCRCs in the United States, however, do not provide complete benefit coverage in their contracts, and those that do have faced financial difficulties.[36] Because most older people prefer to remain in their own homes, an alternative product termed "life care at home" (LCAH) was developed in the late 1980s and marketed to middle-income customers with lower entry and monthly fees than those of CCRCs.[37] However, only about 500 LCAH policies are in effect.[38]

Another approach for providing long-term health care in a residential setting is the assisted-living facility. It has been created for moderately disabled persons, including those with dementia, who are not ready for a nursing home and provides them with limited forms of personal care, supervision of medications and other daily routines, and congregate meal and housekeeping services.[39] Assisted living has yet to be tried with a private insurance approach. The monthly rent in a first-class non-profit facility averages about $2400 or higher for a one-bedroom apartment; the rent is even higher in for-profit facilities.

The Role of Medicaid

For those who cannot pay for long-term health care out of pocket or through various insurance arrangements and are not eligible for care through programs of the Department of Veterans Affairs, the available sources of payment are Medicaid and other means-tested government programs funded by the Older Americans Act, Social Service block grants (Title XX of the Social Security Act), and state and local governments. The bulk of such financing is through Medicaid, the federal-state program for the poor, which finances the care—at least in part—of about three-fifths of nursing home patients[40] and 28% of home- and community-based services.[41] The program does not pay for the full range of home care services that are needed for most clients who are functionally dependent.

Most state Medicaid programs provide reimbursement only for the most "medicalized" services that are necessary to maintain a long-term care patient in a home environment. Rarely reimbursed are essential supports such as chore services, assistance with food shopping and meal preparation, transportation, companionship, periodic monitoring, and respite programs for family and other unpaid caregivers.

Medicaid does include a special waiver program that allows states to offer a wider range of non-medical home care services, if limited to those patients whose services will be no more costly than Medicaid-financed nursing home care. However, the volume of services in these waiver programs—which in some states combine Medicaid with funds from the Older Americans Act, the Social Services block grant program, and other state and local government sources—is small in relation to the overall demand.[42] Although many patients are not poor enough to qualify for Medicaid when they enter a nursing home, a substantial number become poor after they are institutionalized.[43] Persons in this latter group deplete their assets in order to meet their bills and eventually "spend down" and become poor enough to qualify for Medicaid.

Still others become eligible for Medicaid by sheltering their assets—illegally or legally—with the assistance of attorneys who specialize in so-called Medicaid estate planning. Because sheltered assets are not counted in Medicaid eligibility determinations, such persons are able to take advantage of a program for the poor without being poor. Asset sheltering has become a source of considerable concern to the federal and state governments as Medicaid expenditures on nursing homes and home care have been increasing rapidly, nearly doubling from 1990 to 1995. Healthcare reform includes the establishment of a new office under the Centers for Medicare and Medicaid to address this issue and improve access and coordination of services for those who qualify for Medicare and Medicaid. This office is so new that there is no information about how well it is working.[44]

An analysis in Virginia estimated that the aggregate of assets sheltered through the use of legal loopholes in 1991 was equal to more than 10% of what the state spent on nursing home care through Medicaid in that year.[45] A study drawing on interviews with state government staff for Medicaid eligibility determination in four states (California, Florida, Massachusetts, and New York) found a strong relationship between a high level of financial wealth in a geographic area and a high level of Medicaid estate-planning activity. Most of these workers estimated that the range of asset sheltering among single applicants for Medicaid was between 5% and 10% and for married applicants between 20% and 25%.[46] Laws enacted in 1996 made it a federal crime to shelter assets in order to become eligible for Medicaid. However, the law is so vague that, practically speaking, it has been unenforceable. In 2012, these loopholes remain difficult to understand, and changes resulting from healthcare reform do not appear to provide increased clarity for this issue.

▶ Forces for Improving Access

From the mid-1980s until the mid-1990s, a number of national policy makers were sympathetic to these various dilemmas: the inability of individuals and their families to pay for services, the limitations of private insurance, and the anxieties of spending down. Since then, however, the main concern in Washington, DC, as well as in the states, has been to limit Medicaid expenditures. In this new context, the most likely prospect is that public resources for long-term care or palliative care services will be even less available, in relation to the need, than they have been to date.

Public recognition of a need to improve access to long-term healthcare and palliative care services for the elderly has been building over the past two decades. The major initial impetus for this increased awareness has been successful advocacy efforts on behalf of older people. An example of this action is the efforts undertaken by a political coalition formed in the mid-1970s concerned about AD.[47] This coalition was successful in getting Congress to earmark appropriations for AD research at the National Institute on Aging in the 1980s, and the amount of these funds has been increasing ever since.[48]

Advocates for patients of AD formally coalesced in 1988, with the broader constituency concerned about chronically ill and disabled older persons. The Alzheimer's Association, the American Association for Retired Persons (AARP), and the Families U.S.A. Foundation (a small organization originally established to improve the plight of poor older people) allied during the presidential campaign to undertake a lobbying effort organized under the name "Long-Term Care '88."[49] The following year, an explicit link was forged between advocates for the disabled and the elderly when congressman Claude Pepper introduced a bill to provide comprehensive long-term home care coverage for disabled persons of any age who were dependent in at least two ADLs.[50] Although this bill was not voted on by Congress, it was a milestone in that it was the first major legislative effort to programmatically combine the long-term care needs of younger disabled adults with those of elderly people.

Following the Pepper bill, several dozen long-term care bills were introduced in Congress. The lobbying efforts for long-term care that were launched during the 1988 presidential campaign have broadened to encompass the needs of younger disabled people and have been carried forward by a coalition named the Long-Term Care Campaign. This Washington-based interest group claims to represent nearly 140 national organizations (with more than 60 million members), including religious denominations, organized labor and business groups, nurses, veterans, youth and women's groups, consumer organizations, and racial and ethnic groups, as well as older and younger disabled persons.[51]

In the early 1990s, advocates for the elderly and younger disabled persons were optimistic that the federal government would establish a new program for funding long-term care that would not be means-tested, as is Medicaid. A number of bills introduced from 1989 to 1994 included some version of such a program, including President Clinton's failed proposal for healthcare reform.[52] None of these proposals became law. The major reason was that any substantial version of such a program would cost tens of billions of dollars each year just at the outset and far more as the baby boomers reach old age.

By the mid-1990s, there was a squashing of optimism regarding expanded governmental funding for long-term care. A new Republican majority in the 104th Congress reversed the focus on long-term care from expansion to retraction. It proposed to limit federal spending on Medicaid. Advocates for long-term care programs switched from offense to defense.

By 1995, Medicaid's expenditures on long-term care were growing at an annualized rate of 13.2% since 1989.[53] As part of its overall effort to achieve a balanced budget, Congress initially proposed in that year to cap the rate of growth in Medicaid expenditures in order to achieve savings of $182 billion by 2002, to eliminate federal requirements for determining individual eligibility for Medicaid (as an entitlement), and to turn over control of the program to state governments through capped block grants. Such changes were vetoed by

President Clinton. They resurfaced in 1996 with proposed reductions totaling $72 billion, but there was no legislation that year. However, in 2005, a report presented as testimony before the Subcommittee on Health and the Committee on Energy and Commerce in the U.S. House of Representatives again addressed reforming long-term care financing, referring to Medicare and Medicaid as entitlement programs.

Reduction in Medicare and Medicaid programs remains on the policy agenda at the present, strongly supported by the National Governors Association. According to one analysis, the congressional proposals for limiting Medicaid's growth would have trimmed long-term care funding by as much as 11.4% and meant that 1.74 million Medicaid beneficiaries would have lost or been unable to secure coverage.[54]

In addition, this analysis assumed that states would make their initial reductions in home- and community-based care services (because nursing home residents have nowhere else to go) and concluded that such services would be substantially reduced from their current levels. There was a projection that 5 states would eliminate home- and community-based services by the end of 1999 and that another 19 would cut services by more than half. If provisions to cap and block Medicaid do become law, they will almost certainly engender conflict within states regarding the distribution of limited resources for the care of older and younger poor constituencies.

▶ What Are the Prospects for Improved Access?

Prospects for older people having better access to general long-term health care or palliative care seem dim. With the emphasis of Congress to repeal and replace the Affordable Healthcare Act and privatizing Medicare and Medicaid, the future of treatment for chronic illnesses and long-term healthcare management appears costly at best. Currently, out-of-pocket payments for care are becoming larger and increasingly unaffordable for many. Only a minority of older persons—now about 5% and perhaps 20% in the decades ahead—might be able to afford premiums for private long-term care insurance. Broad societal trends suggest that informal, unpaid care by family members might become less feasible in the future than it is today. Moreover, contemporary federal and state budgetary politics pose a serious threat to the safety net that government programs provide by financing long-term health care for the poor.

How might the outlook improve in the future? The most promising seeds for change lie in the enormous projected growth in the number of older persons needing long-term health care, outlined at the outset of this chapter. Moreover, leaders of the American Coalition of Citizens with Disabilities, representing 8 million disabled persons, have expressed for some years the hope that they might form a powerful political alliance with organizations representing over 33 million older people to pursue this issue of mutual concern.[55]

As the demand for long-term health care increases, while the means for access remain limited or become more restricted, a widespread and deeply felt demand for expanded government funding of long-term care as well as palliative care initiatives could emerge. The entrance of the baby boomers into the ranks of old age may precipitate a grassroots movement that will revitalize political awareness of the issue as a major problem in U.S. society. This movement could learn much from the efforts of advocates for public policy from the late 1980s and early 1990s.

However, even if a grassroots movement is able to elevate the principle of expanded government funding for long-term healthcare or palliative care initiatives to the top of the agenda, that general principle masks some basic value questions that, so far, have just begun to surface in public discussion. Widespread debate on and resolution of these questions will be required for a substantial proportion of Americans to understand and support the implications of any law that is to be enacted. Even if enacted, such legislation could be quickly repealed, as was the poorly understood Medicare Catastrophic Coverage Act of 1988.[56] Yet, depending on the identity of the primary constituency, seeking support for long-term health care (a broader coalition of the aged, the disabled, and perhaps others), the configurations and primacy of the values involved might be different, and the likelihood of generating widespread support might vary substantially.

From the perspective of older persons, the view is that long-term health care is a problem besetting elderly people, categorically. Economic concern generates the predominant, though not exclusive, element of interest in additional public insurance. That concern is the possibility of becoming poor through spending down—depleting one's assets to pay for long-term chronic illness and then becoming dependent on a welfare program, Medicaid, to pay nursing home or hospital bills. There is a distinct fear, both economic and psychological, of using savings and selling a home to finance one's own health care. This anxiety reflects a desire to protect estates, as well as the psychological intertwining of personal self-esteem with one's material worth and independence.

The political weight of this type of concern, however, is not substantial in today's climate of public policy discourse and change. The spirit of the late 1970s, the political era in which categorical old-age entitlement programs were created and sustained with relative ease, appears to be gone. The aged have become a scapegoat for a variety of the United States' problems, and many domestic policy concerns have been framed as issues of intergenerational equity.[57]

If expanded public long-term healthcare insurance is to be enacted as an old-age entitlement to serve older persons as a buffer against spending down, the U.S. public will need to confront and resolve some fundamental moral and political issues. These issues include the following: Can we improve laws for protecting spouses of long-term chronically ill patients from impoverishment? Should older people have to spend their assets and income on their health care? Why should the government foot the bill? Why should it be the government's responsibility to preserve estates for inheritance?

In addition, there are concerns such as the following: Should the government take a more active role than at present in preserving economic status inequalities from generation to generation? What is the basis for taxing some persons to preserve the inheritances of others? Should the government's taxing power be used to preserve the psychological sense of self-esteem that for so many persons is bound up in their lifetime accumulation of assets—their material worth? Widespread public debate on such issues might very well fail to resolve them in a fashion that supports a major initiative in long-term health care to protect older people and the chronically ill.

Even if such questions were satisfactorily resolved, the challenge of bringing together the different perspectives of the elderly and the younger disabled population would remain. In contrast to older persons, younger disabled persons do not perceive long-term healthcare funding as mostly an issue of whether the government or the individual patient or family pays for the care. Their main concern is the issue of whether such funding covers basic access to services, technologies, and environments that will make it feasible to carry forward an active life.

They argue that they should have assistance to do much of what they would be able to do if they were not disabled. This is understandable, given their strong desires for autonomy, independence, and as much "normalization" of daily life as possible. Similarly, disabled people and the chronically ill have traditionally eschewed symbolic and political identification with the elderly because of traditional stereotypes of older people as frail, chronically ill, declining, and "marginal" to society.

For most of this century, long-term health care for the elderly and chronically ill has been a comparatively neglected backwater in the overall U.S. healthcare scene. Except for occasional nursing home scandals, fires, and subsequent ad hoc activities in response to these events, long-term health care has received little attention from the medical profession and society. The glamour and prestige of hospital-based medical care—which is inherently dramatic because it deals with acute episodes of illnesses and trauma—and its relatively high-tech and quick-fix dimensions of diagnosis and intervention eclipse long-term health care for the elderly and chronically ill.

In effect, there is a perception that long-term health care is not part of health care or is the same as health care in the general population, although long-term health care has been covered through traditional health insurance mechanisms, such as employee benefit plans. An attempt to address this issue was made through the Community Living Assistance Services and Supports (CLASS) Act that was signed into law as part of the ACA 2010 on March 23, 2010. Employees would have paid a monthly premium, through payroll deduction, and received benefits after paying for 5 years.[58] The federal government would have administered the program beginning in January 2014.

On July 19, 2011, the so-called Gang of Six in the U.S. Senate, a bipartisan group of senators, proposed to repeal the CLASS Act as part of the proposition to balance the budget. On October 14, 2011, the Health and Human Services Secretary announced that the Obama administration was taking the CLASS Act off the table for consideration because they could not "see a viable path forward for CLASS implementation."[59] Thus, when apprehensions are expressed about the fact that 40 million Americans are not covered by health insurance, remember that coverage for the elderly and disabled for long-term healthcare services has ceased to be part of the discussion.

Yet, there are good reasons to believe that long-term health and palliative care will come to be perceived more widely as part of the continuum of health care that is needed by all of us. As the baby boomer cohort begins to approach the ranks of old age, the importance of long-term health and palliative care, the formidable volume of the need for it, the difficulties of financing it, and the challenges of delivering it effectively are likely to become increasingly accepted throughout U.S. society. Such acceptance could bring with it a widespread understanding that long-term health and palliative care is health care by another name. This perception may enfold long-term health and palliative care into the shared understanding of justice in health care that dictates that access to long-term care is as much of a fundamental right as is access to other kinds of health care.

▶ Update from a Practitioner's View

In retrospect, although the numbers and percentages may have changed, the trends and issues have not. Long-term health care for the elderly and disabled continues to be problematic, and the outlook for the future is bleak. The political climate that controls funding, particularly for minority groups, creates barriers to adequate long-term care, including cultural, social, and economic issues. More specifically, because the elderly and disabled have higher-than-normal healthcare needs, a questionable healthcare status, and an anticipated need for increasing palliative care services, funding is either capped or so costly that they cannot afford the insurance to cover services. In addition, demand for long-term health care will undoubtedly increase as the baby boomers age, but it is questionable whether the relationship between cost and accessibility will maintain its status quo; budget cuts and revisions have been proposed for the ACA 2010, Medicare, and Medicaid programs.

Although there was much effort to stall the cuts in Medicare and Medicaid in the 1990s, a rebirth in cost-cutting measures has proliferated since 1998 and significantly escalated throughout the past decade because there has been a shift in the responsibility for cost containment from the federal government to the states. The effects of this shift created a push for alternative delivery methods in elder and disability care. Not surprisingly, alternative multiple methods of care are generally not government-funded. In general, funding for palliative care programs has not occurred, except for the Medicare and Medicaid payment systems that are, for the most part, inadequate in dealing with older adults who have multiple illnesses. This deficit in funding has created a disparity in a multitude of populations, including ethnic and racial groups, the poor, and those with mental illnesses.[60]

If history judges a culture by how it treats its elderly and disabled, then what legacy do we wish to leave behind? From an ethics standpoint, can we afford to be a society that values some human lives more than other lives? If so, where do we draw the line: do we stop at age 75 or 80 or what age? Do we make this determination by level and degree of infirmity? Who will make the determination, and what will be their criteria? Ultimately, from an ethics view, is limiting or denying access equivalent to selective genocide? If healthcare providers must acquiesce to the political and societal views defined by law and practice, how do they reconcile their internal need for justice within an unjust framework?

Perhaps providers should consider the words of Pope Francis when advocating for this valuable and underserved population. He wrote, "Education, work, and access to health care for all are key elements for development and the just distribution of goods, for the attainment of social justice, and for free and responsible participation in political life."[61] Is the United States a nation that meets this standard of social justice and political engagement? If so, it cannot ignore the health needs of a population that contributed to its existence.

Healthcare providers at every level are committed to a wide range of prima facie obligations. The very premise of beneficence is so contrary to the public opinions of the day that nary a healthcare provider will escape unscathed during his or her professional life while attempting to balance beneficence and nonmaleficence to produce net benefit over harm. Finally, one must consider autonomy and equal respect, sometimes described in Kantian terms as valuing others and providing them with the kind of care that you would, in turn, expect from them. In this position, all people are viewed as equal and worthy.[62] Thus, rationing or denying access to health care for the elderly or disabled denies them equal respect and autonomy.

Ultimately, the single-most important question should be, how do healthcare providers and administrators address these moral and ethical issues in a society driven by the idea of cost containment and make peace with those decisions? The implications are many, and the debate continues. What will public policy dictate, and what will society tolerate? These are just a few of the ethical challenges in dealing with the issue of older people and long-term care. The prospect of healthcare reform and cost controls on healthcare spending will only add to these profound challenges.

▶ Summary

With the aging of the baby boomers and the increasing shortage of healthcare professionals, access to long-term health and palliative care promises to continue to be a significant issue for the 21st century. This chapter identifies the populations needing care and the type of services that they will need in the future. It presents the issues surrounding access, including cost, the role of insurance, the role of the family, and methods of improving access. Finally, there was a practitioner's view that included challenges to meet in order to address the ethical issues concerning access to long-term health and palliative care.

▶ Questions for Discussion

1. Access to long-term health and palliative care seems to be a problem for the elderly in general. However, it is even more difficult for minorities. Why do you think this is true?
2. Why do you think that long-term health and palliative care insurance lacks popularity among older Americans?
3. How do you think the baby boomer generation will change access to and delivery of long-term health and palliative care services?
4. What ethical arguments can you make to answer the challenges posed by Gardner-Ray and Contreraz in the last section of this chapter?

▶ Additional Resources

1. AARP Research Center, http://www.aarp.org/research.
2. Alliance for Aging Research, *Ageism: How Healthcare Fails the Elderly* (Washington, DC: Alliance for Aging Research, 2011),

http://www.agingresearch.org/content/article/detail/694/.
3. Consumers for Affordable Healthcare, http://www.mainecahc.org/health-care/healthcareforelderly.htm.
4. National Long-Term Care Ombudsman Resource Center, http://www.ltcombudsman.org.
5. U.S. Department of Health and Human Services, *CMS Financial Report: Fiscal Year 2006* (Baltimore, MD: Centers for Medicare & Medicaid Services, 2006), http://www.cms.hhs.gov/CFOReport/Downloads/2006_CMS_Financial_Report.pdf.

▶ Notes

1. S. McConnell, "Who Cares about Long-Term Care?" *Generations* 14, no. (1990): 15–18.
2. "Trends in Aging—United States and Worldwide," *Morbidity and Mortality Weekly Report* 52, no. 6 (2003): 101–6.
3. R. Stone and P. Kemper, "Spouses and Children of Disabled Elders: How Large a Constituency for Long-Term Care Reform?" *The Milbank Quarterly* 67 (1989): 485–506.
4. "MetLife Mature Market Institute Releases Financial Planning Tips for Working Caregivers," *Bloomberg News*, July 12, 2011.
5. Center to Advance Palliative Care, "Palliative Care Definitions and Delivery Methods," 2017, https://www.capc.org/payers/palliative-care- definitions. M. P. Lawton and E. M. Brody, "Assessment of Older People: Self-Maintaining and Instrumental Activities of Daily Living," *Gerontologist* 9 (1969): 179–86.
6. National Hospice and Palliative Care Organization, *NHOCO'S Facts and Figures on Hospice Care*, 2013 ed.

(Alexandria, VA; National Hospice and Palliative Care Organization, 2013).

7. Ibid.

8. National Hospice and Palliative Care Organization, *NHOCO'S Facts and Figures on Hospice Care*.

9. S. Crystal, "Economic Status of the Elderly," in *Handbook of Aging and the Social Sciences*, 4th ed., eds. R. H. Binstock and L. K. George (San Diego, CA: Academic Press, 1996), 388–409.

10. G. K. Vincent and V. A. Velkoff, *The Next Four Decades: The Older Population in the United States: 2010 to 2050*, Current Population Reports P25–1138 (Washington, DC: U.S. Census Bureau, May 2010), 1–16.

11. W. He et al., *65+ in the United States*, Reports PPoep23–209 (Washington, DC: U.S. Census Bureau, December 2005).

12. The Healthy States Initiative, *Keeping the Aging Population Healthy: Legislator Policy Brief* (Washington, DC: U.S. Department of Health and Human Services, August, 2007), 1–12, http://www.healthystates.csg.org. Accessed December 1, 2011.

13. A. L. Jones et al., *National Nursing Home Survey: 2004 Overview*, Vital Health Statistics 13, no. 167 (Washington, DC: U.S. Government Printing Office, 2009), http://www.cdc.gov/nchs/data/series/sr_13/srl3_167.pdf. Accessed January 16, 2012. See also J. F. Fries, "The Compression of Morbidity: Near or Far?" *The Milbank Quarterly* 67 (1989): 208–32; K. G. Manton et al., "Estimates of Change in Chronic Disability and Institutional Incidence and Prevalence Rates in the U.S. Elderly Population from the 1982, 1984, and 1989 National Long Term Care Survey," *Journal of Gerontology: Social Sciences* 48 (1993): S153–66; E. L. Schneider and J. M. Guralnik, "The Aging of America: Impact on Health Care Costs," *Journal of the American Medical Association* 263 (1991): 2335–40; and L. M. Verbrugge, "Recent, Present, and Future Health of American Adults," in *Annual Review of Public Health 10*, eds. L. Breslow et al. (Palo Alto, CA: Annual Reviews, 1989), 333–61.

14. United States Census Bureau, *2009 American Community Survey*, http://www.census.gov/acs/www/. Accessed January 16, 2012. See also "The Healthy States Initiative," *Keeping the Aging Population Healthy*.

15. He et al., *65+ in the United States*.

16. U.S. Congress, Congressional Budget Office, *Policy Choices for Long-Term Care* (Washington, DC: U.S. Government Printing Office, 1991).

17. National Institute on Disability and Rehabilitation Research, *Disability Statistics Report 16* (Washington, DC: U.S. Department of Education, Office of Special Education and Rehabilitative Services, 2001).

18. J. L. Ross, *Long-Term Care: Demography, Dollars, and Dissatisfaction Drive Reform*, U.S. GAO/T-HEHS-94–140 (Washington, DC: Government Printing Office, April 12, 1994).

19. U.S. Congress, Office of Technology Assessment, *Confused Minds, Burdened Families: Finding Help for People with Alzheimer's and Other Dementias* (Washington, DC: U.S. Government Printing Office, 1990).

20. H. R. Levit et al., "National Health Expenditures," *Health Care Financing Review* 7, no. 2 (1996): 175–214.

21. U.S. Census Bureau, *Health Care Utilization and National Health Expenditures*, Statistical Abstract Addendums (Washington, DC: U.S. Government Printing Office, 2012), 134–59.

22. K. G. Allen, *Long-Term Care Financing: Growing Demand and Cost of Services Are Straining Federal and State Budgets*,

GAO-05–564T (Washington, DC: U.S. Government Printing Office, April 27, 2005).

23. Ibid.

24. C. DeNavas-Walt et al., *Income, Poverty and Health Insurance Coverage in the United States: 2005*, Current Population Reports, P60–231 (Washington, DC: U.S. Government Printing Office, 2005), 60–194.

25. C. DeNavas-Walt et al., *Income, Poverty, and Health Insurance Coverage in the United States: 2009*, Current Population Reports P60–238 (Washington, DC: U.S. Government Printing Office, 2010), 61.

26. S. K. Eckert and K. Smyth, *A Case Study of Methods of Locating and Arranging Health and Long-Term Care for Persons with Dementia* (Washington, DC: Office of Technology Assessment, Congress of the United States, 1988).

27. J. Calmes, "Elephant in the Room: Budget Wish Lists Come and Go, but 'Entitlements' Outweigh All," *Wall Street Journal* (February 3, 2006): A-l.

28. K. Liu et al., "Home Care Expenses for the Disabled Elderly," *Health Care Financing Review* 7, no. 2 (1985): 51–58.

29. E. M. Brody, *Women in the Middle: Their Parent-Care Years* (New York: Springer, 1990); R. Stone, G. L. Cafferta, and J. Sangl, "Caregivers of the Frail Elderly: A National Profile," *Gerontologist* 27 (1989): 616–26.

30. National Academy on Aging, *The State of Aging and Health in America* (Washington, DC: Syracuse University, 2010), 1–46.

31. V. L. Bengston et al., "Families and Aging: Diversity and Heterogeneity," in *Handbook of Aging and the Social Sciences*, 3rd ed., eds. R. H. Binstock and L. K. George (San Diego, CA: Academic Press, 1990), 263–87.

32. J. M. Wiener et al., *Sharing the Burden: Strategies for Public and Private Long-Term Care Insurance* (Washington, DC: Brookings Institution, 1994).

33. U.S. Congressional Budget Office, *Financing Long-Term Care for the Elderly* (Washington, DC: U.S. Government Printing Office, April 2006).

34. W. H. Crown et al., "Economic Rationality, the Affordability of Private Long-Term Care Insurance, and the Role for Public Policy," *Gerontologist* 32 (1992): 478–85; R. Friedland, *Facing the Costs of Long-Term Care: An EBRI-ERF Policy Study* (Washington, DC: Employee Benefits Research Institute, 1990); A. M. Rivlin and J. M. Wiener, *Caring for the Elderly: Who Will Pay?* (Washington, DC: Brookings Institution, 1988); Wiener, Illston, and Hanley, *Sharing the Burden*.

35. R. D. Chellis and P. J. Grayson, *Life Care: A Long-Term Solution?* (Lexington, MA: Lexington Books, 1990).

36. M. A. Cohen, "Life Care: New Options for Financing and Delivering Long-Term Care," in *Health Care Financing Review: Annual Supplement* (Thousand Oaks, CA: Sage, 1988), 139–43.

37. T. F. Williams and H. Temkin-Greener, "Older People, Dependency, and Trends in Supportive Care," in *The Future of Long-Term Care: Social and Policy Issues*, eds. R. H. Binstock et al. (Baltimore: Johns Hopkins University Press, 1996), 51–74. For an excellent review of the potential changes in health care proposed through the ACA 2010, see Henry J. Kaiser Family Foundation, *Focus on Health Reform: Summary of New Health Reform Law* (Menlo Park, CA: Henry J. Kaiser Family Foundation, 2011), http://www.kff.org.

38. E. J. Tell et al., "New Directions in Life Care: Industry in Transit," *The Milbank Quarterly* 65 (1987): 551–74.

39. Williams and Temkin-Greener, "Older People, Dependency, and Trends in Supportive Care."

40. R. A. Kane, and K. B. Wilson, *Assisted Living in the United States: A New Paradigm for Residential Care for Older People?* (Washington, DC: American Association for Retired Persons, 1993); V. Regnier et al., *Assisted Living for the Aged and Frail: Innovations in Design, Management, and Financing* (New York: Columbia University Press, 1995).

41. Wiener, Illston, and Hanley, *Sharing the Burden.*

42. American Association of Retired Persons, Public Policy Institute, *The Costs of Long-Term Care* (Washington, DC: American Association of Retired Persons, 1994).

43. R. B. Hudson, "Social Protection and Services," in *Handbook of Aging and the Social Sciences*, 7th ed., eds. R. H. Binstock and L. K. George (San Diego, CA: Academic Press, 2010).

44. E. K. Adams et al., "Asset Spend-Down in Nursing Homes: Methods and Insights," *Medical Care* 31 (1993): 1–23.

45. Levit et al., op. cit.

46. B. Burwell, *State Responses to Medicaid Estate Planning* (Cambridge, MA: SysteMetrics, 1993). For information on healthcare reform and Medicare/Medicaid, see Henry J. Kaiser Family Foundation, *Focus on Health Reform.*

47. B. Burwell and W. H. Crown, *Medicaid Estate Planning in the Aftermath of OBRA '93* (Cambridge, MA: MEDSTAT Group, 1995).

48. P. Fox, "From Senility to Alzheimer's Disease: The Rise of the Alzheimer's Disease Movement," *The Milbank Quarterly* 67 (1989): 58–102.

49. G. D. Cohen, "Alzheimer's Disease: Current Policy Initiatives," in *Dementia and Aging: Ethics, Values, and Policy Choices*, eds. R. H. Binstock, S. G. Post, and P. J. Whitehouse (Baltimore: Johns Hopkins University Press, 1992).

50. McConnell, "Who Cares about Long-Term Care?"

51. U.S. House of Representatives, Long-Term Care Act of 1989, H.R. 2263, 101st Congress (1989).

52. Long-Term Care Campaign, "Pepper Commission Recommendations Released March 2," *Insiders Update* (January–February 1990): 1.

53. Centers for Disease Control and Prevention and Merck Company Foundation, *The State of Aging and Health in America 2007* (Whitehouse Station, NJ: Merck Company Foundation, 2007), http://www.cdc.gov/aging/pdf/saha_2007.pdf.

54. U.S. General Accounting Office, *Long-Term Care: Current Issues and Future Directions* (Washington, DC: U.S. Government Printing Office, 1995).

55. E. Kassner, *Long-Term Care: Measuring the Impact of a Medicaid Cap* (Washington, DC: Public Policy Institute, American Association of Retired Persons, 1995).

56. Allen, *Long-Term Care Financing.*

57. R. Himelfarb, *Catastrophic Politics: The Rise and Fall of the Medicare Catastrophic Coverage Act of 1988* (University Park, PA: Pennsylvania State University Press, 1995).

58. R. H. Binstock et al., eds., *The Future of Long-Term Care: Social and Policy Issues* (Baltimore: Johns Hopkins University Press, 1996).

59. California Health Advocates, "Community Living Assistance Services and Supports (CLASS ACT) Summary," March 23, 2010, http://www

.cahealthadvocates.org/advocacy/2010 /class.html. Accessed January 16, 2012.

60. T. E. Quill, and F. G. Miller, eds., *Palliative Care and Ethics* (New York: Oxford University Press, 2014).

61. Pope Francis, Address of Pope Francis to Participants in the Plenary of the Pontifical Counsel for Justice and Peace (The Vatican: The Holy See, October 2014): para.3, https://w2.vatican.va /content/francesco/en/speeches/2014 /october/...

62. E. Morrison, *Ethics in Health Administration: A Practical Approach for Decision Makers*, 3rd ed. (Burlington, MA: Jones & Bartlett Learning, 2016), 11–13.

PART III

Critical Issues for Healthcare Organizations

Part III of the fourth edition reflects examples of the changes occurring in the healthcare system and their ethical challenges. This section includes major revisions to earlier chapters and new chapters that suggest the need for health care to be ethically aware as it seeks to provide quality patient services in an environment of fast-moving, multifaceted change. This chapter summarizes the functions, membership, and preparation of ethics committees. In the current area of health care, these committees provide a mechanism for hospitals and other healthcare organizations to prevent ethics situations and address those that occur. There is also a discussion of the organizational commitment to ethics committees and the committees' commitment to patients and staff. The chapter includes new concepts such as moral distress, moral residue, and moral courage. In addition, Dr. West's update provides examples of challenges faced by ethics committees in the evolving Patient Protection and Affordable Care Act of 2010 (ACA 2010) era.

Chapter 7   The chapter "Ethics in the Management of Health Information Systems" is new for this edition and features ethics as related to health information management. After clarifying definitions, the author addresses serious threats to the security of health information. He includes content about the ethics rationale of hackers, smart phones and privacy, the cloud, and ransomware. In addition, the reader is provided with three ethics decision-making models that relate to health information and its security.

Chapter 8   The chapter "Technological Advances in Health Care: Blessing or Ethics Nightmare?" features a discussion of the ethical obligations created by new and emerging technologies. These discussions include areas such as the exploitation of research subjects, synthetic biology, robotic-assisted surgery, and IBM Watson. There is also a section on the application of ethics principles to legislative requirements such as the Medicare Access and CHIP Reauthorization Act of 2015 (MACRA) and the Merit-based Incentive Payment System (MIPS). Dr. Lieneck also continues the discussion on the ethics of health information by presenting a discussion of the reasons practices do not want electronic health records (EHRs) and examples of privacy issues.

The reader is challenged to consider both the benefits of these advances and the ethics challenges that technology creates.

Chapter 9   New for this edition, the chapter "Ethics and Safe Patient Handling and Mobility" introduces the ethics dilemmas associated with patient safety in healthcare settings. Because safety is a factor for patients and staff members, the chapter provides research on the causes of patient injuries. It offers a suggestion for best practices to prevent staff injuries and discusses the barriers to implementing those practices. In addition, ethics concerns related to patient safety and the application of ethics principles to these concerns are featured in this chapter.

Chapter 10   The chapter "Spirituality and Healthcare Organizations" centers on the deeper meaning of practicing health care and the place of spirituality in healthcare organizations. After defining terms and providing empirical evidence, Freeman presents a case study that illustrates the power of spirituality and of nurturing the whole person. Morrison applies the concept of spirituality to the healthcare workplace and emphasizes the need for spiritual leadership practices. She supports ideas with research and regulation and connects ethics theories and principles to the application of spirituality in the healthcare workplace.

Chapter 11   The chapter "A New Era of Health Care: The Ethics of Healthcare Reform" deals with an ethics challenge that affects the entire structure and delivery of health care. It begins with a discussion of the history of healthcare reform and its ethical foundations. Next, the authors present the features of ACA 2010 and assess its effect on coverage, quality, and the practice of health care. In addition, the authors use extensive research to support ethics assumptions related to healthcare reform. They also provide information about differing ethical positions that influence continuing reform efforts beyond ACA 2010.

CHAPTER 6

Healthcare Ethics Committees: Roles, Memberships, Structure, and Difficulties

Michael P. West and Eileen E. Morrison

▶ Introduction

In this new era of intense change that includes the uncertainty of the ACA 2010, hospitals face issues related to balancing fiscal responsibility and quality patient care. The ACA 2010 posed the most significant changes in the system since the enactment of Medicare and Medicaid.[1,2] However, recent political changes have caused great concern among hospital systems, insurers, and others.[3] While it is too early to know all of the ramifications of this change, patients, providers, payers, and legislators expect hospitals to be able to provide compassionate, patient-centered care, while practicing distributive justice and compliance with regulation.

Changes to the ACA 2010 are not the only challenge that hospitals face. The growth and demand for technology and changing demographics also pose service, fiscal, and ethical challenges. In addition, hospitals must hire and support competent and compassionate healthcare staff on all organizational levels. How can hospitals successfully meet these demands and maintain a level ethical excellence? One answer to this question relies on engagement of ethics committees in both clinical and policy roles within the organization. The traditional ethics committee's roles of case consultation, policy development assistance, and education will need to expand to accommodate challenges to the missions and values of organizations. This chapter provides an overview of the history, roles, membership, challenges, and changes for healthcare ethics committees (HECs) in an era of change for health care.

▶ Why an Ethics Committee?

A brief overview of the history of ethics committees helps us understand their existence and expansion in health care. Ethics committees in the United States began as a response to difficult patient issues. For example, in the 1970s, when there were restrictions on hemodialysis caused by a shortage of dialysis machines, ethics committees (sometimes called "God squads") were convened to determine which patients would receive treatment. Advanced technology and the ability to prolong life increased the need for consultation on complex ethics issues. Consequently, ethics consultation and committees became more important in the practice of health care.[4,5]

In recent years, there has been an increased emphasis on the role of case consulting and policy development as part of hospital practice. In 1992, The Joint Commission (TJC) determined that there was a need for hospitals to have a formal mechanism to deal with ethical conflicts, but it did not mandate that this mechanism be an ethics committee. However, TJC required healthcare organizations to be responsible for how they conduct their business and serve patients. Therefore, most hospitals have some form of ethics consultation capabilities and ethics committees.[6] In addition, nonacute settings such as nursing facilities group practices, managed care organizations, and other healthcare organizations use ethics committees for assistance with a growing number of patient-centered and financial issues.[7]

In addition to recommendations by TJC, some of the states now mandate that healthcare facilities have ethics committees. State law can provide guidelines for structures and memberships for these committees and their practice standards. Ethics committee members are also required to be educated on the appropriate state laws. For example, in some states, there are laws and regulations concerning withholding of life support, neonatal intensive care, and long-term care. Examples of states that mandate ethics committees include Maryland, New Jersey, and Tennessee.[8]

▶ The Function and Roles of Ethics Committees

Because of the complexity of decision-making required in a busy hospital system, Darr suggests that an HEC include two subcommittees. One of the subcommittees would concentrate on issues related to administration, such as policy development, staff education, and community issues. The second subcommittee would address issues related to clinical practice and patient issues. To avoid overlapping functions, the roles and responsibilities of each subcommittee need to be clearly defined.[9]

Developing Standards and Policies

Given the future of healthcare reform, technology, and fiscal policy, hospitals need to review their standards to provide both patient-centered and fiscally responsible care.[10] This review requires an examination of policies related to areas such as informed consent, advance directives, and other patient-related ethics issues. In addition, organizational issues connected with funding, the use of resources, cultural competency, and personnel issues need review with respect to ethics and mission.

For it to be effective, the charge of HECs requires a commitment to creating clearly written policies that engage interdisciplinary teams. These teams should include staff members affected by the policy to be developed. In addition, this function also sets the tone for day-to-day operations, including an emphasis on workplace ethics, hiring and termination policies, funding, and allocation of resources. Of course, the HECs must consider the mission of each organization as they revise or create policies and procedures.

HECs are also involved in creating policies that affect patient care and difficult ethical decisions such as withdrawing life support, informed consent, and advanced directives. When assuming this role, HECs have additional responsibilities, including defining the goal of the policies using both ethics theory and principles and strategic thinking. Committee members must also work within a model that includes an assessment of stakeholders, implications of the policies, and potential legal and ethical challenges. In addition to creating policies for review, HECs must be able to explain and justify the policies in a way that facilitates their use.[11]

Education

With the potential changes in the healthcare system, HECs will be increasingly more involved in the education function of ethics for organizations, professionals, and communities. This education role includes providing staff members with information about their roles and relevance in today's healthcare environment. The education function should be concerned with "integrating ethics throughout the healthcare system from the bedside to the board room."[12]

This HEC educational function may also include setting appropriate goals for ethics education, including who should receive ethics education, how to deliver that education, and what content it should have.[13] In the role of educators, HEC members must be aware of how to provide effective consultation and share information. They must also overcome objections from the staff about the need to receive training on ethics, and be able to substantiate the benefit of such training. In addition, they need to coordinate with specialists in the area of ethics so that they can provide effective and efficient training opportunities. Finally, they are also responsible for serving as role models for the ethics they espouse. These challenging

responsibilities will continue as changes occur during the evolution of healthcare reform.[14]

Clinical Consultation

The role of HECs also includes the ability to address patient and staff concerns about ethics related to patient care. HECs address this function through the formation of subcommittees or the use of ethics consultants. Each model has its strengths and weaknesses, but the ability to provide case consultation enhances patient care and the ability to resolve issues related to patients' decision-making. The ethics subcommittee or ethical consultant will use various tools for analyzing the case and applying ethics principles.[15]

The increasing concern of patients' rights, increased regulation, and innovation in both treatment and technology result in an increase in the frequency and intensity of ethics issues that require consultation. Examples of such issues include informed consent, competency, patient surrogacy, and confidentiality, including patient records and their storage in the cloud.[16] In addition, ethics issues frequently occur at the end of life and issues related to respect for the newly dead.

HECs use several models to address the need for consultation on patient situations. According to Ashcroft, Dawson, Draper, and McMillan (2007),[16] HECs may use ethics consultants or ethicists who have the ability to apply ethics principles to difficult situations. HECs may also use subcommittees for addressing biomedical issues. Regardless of the mechanism for clinical consultation, HECs need to have access to resources such as social workers and attorneys who assist in the decision-making process.

To provide appropriate consultation on often difficult-to-solve patient issues, an HEC needs to have both goals and processes. The goal of the committee should be centered on resolving the issue at hand in a way that is respectful to the patient and based on ethics principles and the mission of the organization.

In addition, the committee must use a protocol that allows it to make the best-possible decision and justify its actions. Hester and Schonfeld (2012)[17] suggest a process that includes a format for getting a request and conducting a chart review. They also suggest that there be face-to-face meetings with the healthcare team, including caregiving nurses and other parties. This interaction should also include the patient, his or her family, and friends, when necessary. The steps are followed by information gathering and analysis based on ethics principles and the mission of the organization that provides support for the decision.

In addition, the ethics committee or consultant should document the decision in the patient's chart and conduct a follow-up to assess the impact of the decision. Ashcroft, Dawson, Draper, and McMillan (2007)[18] also suggest that the model used for decision-making include knowledge of the moral position of the patient, family, and clinicians. They also advise that HECs evaluate the quality of consultations on the basis of the number of requests, outcomes, and other criteria.

Resource Allocation

Given the recent and potential changes for the healthcare system, the ethics of resource allocation has become more significant for organizations, communities, and patients. Hoffman (2011)[19] suggested that hospitals do not have sufficient funds to meet all the demands that they face. Therefore, hospital administrators and others must make difficult decisions with respect to allocation of resources, and these decisions have ethical implications. Hoffman cites seven areas that administrators and others need to consider when making decisions about who receives what resources. These areas include funds, opinions, time, conflicts of interest, uncertainty of outcomes, competing values, and impact on job security.

Hoffman also suggests guidelines to facilitate decisions that are organizationally and ethically sound. HECs have a role in creating these guidelines and providing frameworks for evaluation. In addition, "The ethical principles of beneficence, nonmaleficence, fidelity, and justice should also be considered in making a sound decision."[20]

In a classic article on this issue, Lantos (1994)[21] discusses both the reluctance of HECs to address resource allocation and the necessity for this action. He includes the need for committee members to consider areas beyond ethics theory and principle. These areas include community values, legal requirements, and scarcity of services. He also cautions HECs to avoid politics as they make their decisions. This advice remains important in today's ethics considerations of allocation of resources because of the need to balance patient-centered care with the obligation of cost control and meeting organizational goals. In addition, the type of regulation and the funding are not certain in the post–ACA 2010 era. Therefore, HECs need to be even more vigilant to protect the mission of health care as organizations meet their fiscal responsibilities.

Addressing issues involving the microallocation of resources is also part of the duties of HECs. The center of these issues is often the individual patient and the use of scarce resources needed by that individual. For example, decisions may be required concerning who gets the only available bed in an intensive care unit, intervention in near-futile cases, and conflicts between patient desires (expressed in advanced directives and do-not-resuscitate orders) and those of family members. These microallocation issues involve both policy development and clinical consultations. Changes in health-related laws, increase in the number of patients, and diversity of patient needs will also add to the complexity and intensity of decision-making for microallocation issues.[22]

In addition to complying with changes in the healthcare system, HECs will need to be aware of advancing medical and technology. For example, television and the Internet make patients more aware of the potential for medical advancements and care. This knowledge increases the demand for services. Technology promises outcomes that may be miraculous, but these outcomes also present concerns about the balance between life-saving treatments and the cost of providing those treatments. There are often concerns about the ethics of prolonging life at the expense of the patient's level of suffering. Although no one wants to go back to the era of "God squads," cost will continue to be an essential consideration in making ethical decisions with respect to ethical decisions and the allocation of scarce resources. However, cost-effectiveness must never be the sole area for consideration for HECs. Committees must remain true to the mission of the organization as it attempts to balance its costs and the best-possible care for the patient.

A Specialized Ethics Committee: IRBs

In addition to examining the roles and functions of HECs, it is necessary to briefly review a specialized ethics committee that is found in teaching hospitals and large hospital systems. This committee is called the institutional review board (IRB) and serves a role that is important to the integrity research in the protection of patients as research subjects. An IRB is required to review research protocols to be administered in the hospital setting. This committee also has the responsibility of protecting the rights of patients who consent to be research subjects. Hospitals that participate in research use IRBs to provide oversight and consultation regarding the ethics of research conducted in their facilities. Of particular interest to this committee is elements provided by informed consent and the patient understanding of this consent.[23]

The Office for Human Research Protection[24] provides guidance for protocols and ethics decision-making within IRBs. In general, IRBs in hospitals and other settings have a membership that represents both scientific and nonscientific interests. According to Darr (2011), in addition to reviewing protocols for research and ensuring informed consent, IRBs are also concerned with equity among research subjects and reasonable risk as related to benefit. In addition, ethics issues such as falsification of research data and issues related to children and infants should be considered.[25]

▶ Ethics Committee Membership

Hester and Schonfeld (2016)[26] stressed that HECs need to reflect different views and perspectives. They suggested that these committees be multidisciplinary and that they represent a variety of expertise within the facility. In addition, the committee members should be familiar with both the ethics issues within the facility and the policies that govern the daily operations. The following are categories of membership in HECs:

- *Medical staff.* Physicians are the most common members of an HEC. Given their role in patient care and the ethics decisions that they face on a daily basis, they constitute an important presence in the committee. Physicians from specialty areas such as obstetrics, neurosurgery, neurology, nephrology, oncology, and psychiatry may also be on the committee on an ad hoc basis.[27]
- *Nursing staff.* According to Darr,[28] there is a significant representation of nurses on an HEC. Since they are involved in the daily treatment of patients, and have interest in ethics issues, the representation is not surprising. In addition, nurses often are part of case consultation as individuals or team members.
- *An administrator.* An HEC is also likely to have a high-level, qualified administrative person as a member. Because the HEC is also involved in allocation decisions, expertise insight into appropriate resource allocation is essential when making these

decisions. An ethics committee representative from administration should also be interested in organizational and patient ethics issues and consider ethics related to medical staff responsibilities, patient and employee rights, financial realities, and community concerns.[29]

■ *A social services representative.* The importance of considering the patient in making ethics decisions requires a member or members who understand the patient's view of the situation. Therefore, an HEC includes a representative from the social services. This representative also needs to balance patient care with the mission of the facility. Therefore, hospitals often include a patient representative or ombudsman who can add information from the patient or family perspective. Since cultural competence is expected in healthcare facilities, HECs are better served when they have representatives who understand patient-centered issues involving cultural or religious issues.

■ *Clergy or ethicist.* In faith-based institutions, clergy are members of the HECs. Clergy can also be members of HECs in other nonprofit and for-profit hospital settings. In addition, hospitals are also hiring and including ethicists to serve on committees and as consultants. Having at least one person with a sound background in ethics theory and principles is essential for multidisciplinary discussions about difficult ethics decisions. These members should have training not only in moral theology but also in the formal discipline of philosophical ethics in order to present the ethics theories and principles for application to individual cases.[30]

■ *A community member.* Because the hospital board represents the community, the person selected should be knowledgeable about the larger community's concerns as to the kinds of medical procedures and treatments that are needed in the demographic area that the hospital serves. In

addition, the selection of this representative is important, and there should not be a direct connection to the institution in order to avoid any perception of conflict of interest. Because the issues that come before an HEC often involve the community, it is important to have representation and understand community impact.

This interdisciplinary approach to the makeup of HECs is essential for several reasons. In the current era, ethical dilemmas are increasingly complex and are not confined to the physician–patient relationship. They include policy decision-making in an uncertain environment, balance of profit with quality patient care, the purchase and use of technology, and many other areas. The current level of change and uncertainty can contribute to issues related to interprofessional communication, patient error, and challenging patient care demands. Therefore, HECs need to consider the ethics of policies and procedures, cost control, compliance with regulation, and other nonclinical areas that are also necessary for a mission-centered organization.

HECs also must use multidisciplinary discussion and decision-making when addressing concerns of regulatory and funding organizations. For example, Medicare or Medicaid and other federal programs provide guidelines for both quality and funding of services. The federal government is also involved in providing guidelines on many areas from research to the care of newborns with defects. In addition, state and local governments provide regulation and oversight, including licensure of professionals that affect patient care. All these regulations must be addressed and compliance proven without compromising the quality of patient care. With the implementation of the ACA 2010 and the potential changes that may occur with this implementation, HECs must be more involved in the review of policies related to cost control and the protection of patients' rights.[31]

According to Weber, "The success of health reform efforts requires a recognition of the ethical responsibility to control costs. It also requires carefully considered criteria for understanding the differences between appropriate and inappropriate cost-control measures."[32]

HECs will need to develop guidelines that balance the cost of treatment with patient care decisions. This means that they must address issues such as patients' rights, informed decision-making, and standards of care. Discussions about patient justice will be necessary to clarify the difference between what patients want and what is medically appropriate and cost-effective. These discussions are particularly important, not only in the ACA 2010 era, but also in light of the growth of Medicare spending. The interdisciplinary approach of well-educated HECs is even more necessary to make sure that healthcare spending is appropriate and provides quality care for patients.[33]

Nelson[34] recognizes the need to review the roles and functions of HECs in light of today's challenging healthcare environment. In his view, HECs should go beyond clinical orientation to consider the relationship between clinical ethics and organizational ethics concerns. Examining the relationship between the two areas, administrators should apply their policies and procedures more effectively and make changes, as needed. However, increasing the role of the ethics committee with respect to organizational ethics will require additional orientation and training. In light of the challenges in the future of health care, this would be a sound investment for patient-centered care.

▶ **The Healthcare Ethics Committee's Background and Education**

Hospital and other organizations should choose HEC members carefully because of their responsibility for decisions that affect lives, care, and utilization of resources. Although there is some discussion about what "expertise in ethics" means, moral reasoning, understanding of the organization, commitment to continuing education, and decision-making ability are considered essential skills for committee members and consultants.[35] Lachman suggests that committee members:

- Be competent in their areas of expertise
- Commit to preparing for meetings (including perusing materials)
- Be up to date on the organization's ethical position, including its mission, vision, and code of conduct statements
- Be known for their high moral principles[36]

Because decisions in consultations are often emotional, HEC members need training in the process of decision-making to provide a rational and consistent process. The first step in the training process for HECs should be to select a model based on agreed-upon criteria. This model must be concise and easily understood so that it does not become an obstacle to decision-making. Once this model is chosen, current HEC members should be trained in its use so that it becomes a well-used part of the decision process. As the committee adds new members, the hospital must provide in-service education to maintain consistency and efficiency.

Nelson discusses the need for HECs to have a procedural justice approach that involves the use of a clearly understood model to increase the fairness of decisions. His multi-step model helps clarify the conflict and move to resolution with efficiency. Here is a summary of the steps in this model:

1. Be clear about the conflict and its ethical question.
2. Determine those affected by the conflict.
3. Research the facts of the conflict, including its implications.
4. Decide what ethics principles and theories apply.
5. Discuss possible alternatives to address the conflict.

6. Evaluate each of the identified alternatives.

7. Select the best alternative and communicate it appropriately.

8. Evaluate the decision to determine whether it resolved the issue.[37]

▸ Institutional Commitment

TJC has been concerned with ethics of healthcare organizations since the 1990s, and mechanisms for addressing ethics issues ethics are part of the assurance that healthcare organizations are ethically sound. Since the committees are interdisciplinary, they also serve as a vehicle for identifying and addressing emerging ethics issues that can arise as changes occur in policy, the population served, and technology. For these HECs to be effective, the institutions that employ them must also support them.

As part of their support, HECs need to be recognized by all levels of administration and staff. In addition, the chair must be well respected and have expertise in ethics. This person needs to understand and be able to communicate well with both the clinical and the administrative side of the hospital. It is also essential for the committee chair to demonstrate good judgment, practical political knowledge, and solid mediation skills.[38]

The HEC's effectiveness and accountability is often reflected in its reporting structure within the facility. Ideally, the committee should report directly to senior management, such as the chief executive officer or chief operating officer. The reporting mechanism not only demonstrates institutional commitment to the committee but also gives a source of support and finances. However, the committee's position on the organizational chart is not sufficient in itself. Members must also work to obtain commitment from department directors and clinical staff.

An HEC can also support a climate of ethics throughout the organization through active participation. The committee members can serve as consultants and educators to move the institution toward an environment where ethical concerns are part of all aspects of the organization, from the budget to vendor negotiations. In addition, an HEC that is an integral part of the organization can serve to educate the community and, above all, work for the interest of patients.[39]

An Ethics Commitment to Staff Members

The recent literature in the field of nursing addresses the phenomena of moral distress and moral courage in health care. A discussion of these areas includes their effect on employee productivity, retention, and patient care. As a response to this research and its findings, HECs are providing consultation services beyond patient care issues. They are also providing support for staff members, including nurses, social workers, physicians, and administrators, through education, counseling, and support efforts.[40] This section discusses the issues related to moral distress and moral courage. It also introduces efforts that HECs make to address these issues.

To understand the implications of moral distress, moral residue, and moral courage, one needs to define the phenomenon and its related terms. Andrew Jameton coined the term "moral distress" in 1984, and it involves the response to the inability to take action that one believes is morally right. In some cases, this inability leads to both physical and emotional responses that are termed "moral distress." This phenomenon may occur when healthcare staff wants to provide the best-quality care for patients but financial limitations or staffing issues prevent this action from happening.[41]. Other examples include situations in which patient care staff is not competent, the patients are not given appropriate pain relief, or communication is poor between patients and staff members.[42] Moral distress also has organizational implications because it affects staff satisfaction and retention. Because healthcare professionals practice within a code of ethics, they find it challenging to stay within the code that they support when it appears that the organization does not put patients first. In addition, when staff members repeatedly experience moral distress that is not resolved, it can lead to the feeling that they have compromised who they are as persons and professionals. They become indifferent to the ethics of the situation and fail to voice their concerns. Epstein and Delgado define this as "moral residue."[43] When the situation is prevalent among healthcare providers, it can lead to burnout, excessive turnover, and a decision to leave health care as a career.

Healthcare organizations are beginning to address the issue of moral distress through HECs and education. One of the suggested ways to reduce moral distress is to support moral courage among professionals. "Moral courage" involves having adequate ethical reasoning, knowing when to respond to a situation, and overcoming fear to take appropriate action. Organizations can support moral courage by practicing their mission statements and empowering staff members to raise ethical concerns. This means that leadership provides a structure and a chain of command that allow communication and resolution of ethical concerns. In addition, the culture of the organization should be proactive in addressing potential ethical concerns through frequent assessment and training efforts.[44]

In addition to addressing moral courage, organizations are beginning to be proactive in their approach to preventing moral distress. In addition to providing ethics education opportunities throughout the facility, hospitals are engaging in moral distress prevention. The option of prevention that engages HECs is a version of a clinical consult, often called "moral distress consulting" or "ethics triage." Instead of consulting about a specific patient

situation, consultation is available hospital-wide to address moral distress situations. When a health professional requests for a consult, the ethics committee member goes to the unit, meets with the healthcare professional, discusses the situation, and suggests an action plan. The consultant may also provide a gap analysis and an examination of root causes of the problem. This moral discussion also allows the HEC and the organization have a better understanding of ethics issues as they occur.[45] In addition, it encourages the organization to remain true to its mission and concern for patients and staff members.

▶ Challenges for Healthcare Ethics Committees

To remain true to the mission of providing health care, HECs or their representatives need to be part of the response to the changes that will occur with respect to the ACA 2010 and its future implementation. No matter what change occurs in healthcare delivery and reimbursement, there should always be a voice in the organization that asks, "What about the patients?" That voice can come from HEC members and professionals who have moral courage.

Complex change will be part of a healthcare organization's planning and operations. This complexity will be present because all aspects of patient care and service delivery will be involved in making change happen. In addition, current changes, such as the 10th revision of the International Statistical Classification of Diseases and Related Health Problems (ICD-10), advanced technology, and healthcare needs of baby boomers, will still exist. This cascade of change requires healthcare administrators (HCAs) and providers to avoid the "we've always done it this way" thinking and move to the "how can we do it better" thinking. There will always be a need to balance fiscal responsibility with the mission of providing quality care for patients. In addition, HECs will need to increase their involvement in policy development, resource allocation decisions, patient advocacy, and emerging issues. Taking a proactive role in this time of complex change should enable the HEC to be a force for moral reasoning and ethical decision-making.

Does Barton[46] provide any practical wisdom for the challenges of balancing ethics, organizational change, and crisis survival? Does history give any guidance for responding to chaotic change in an ethical way? While an HEC must make decisions that comply with its organization's mission, structure, and patient needs, the following ideas provide a place to start this work:

- Get the full picture. The committee should conduct research using multiple sources to maximize knowledge and accuracy of information. Accurate information adds to the power and effectiveness of recommendations.
- Be aware of rumors. Rumors can be powerful, but do not jump into the rumor mill. See the previous point.
- Communicate. A crisis can create the need for care in patients, staff members, and the community. Silence is not your friend in a crisis. Remember that the message, audience, delivery, and feedback process are all important for successful crisis management.
- Be part of the solution. Use your internal expertise and community resources (ethicist, academics, experts, etc.) to assist you in offering suggestions that will meet your organization's needs. Be sure to become members of organizational teams involved in strategic planning for and implementation of change.
- Think beyond today. Health care has been serving patients for many years and will continue to do so. Remember to be a voice for a positive future and not one for disaster. HECs can provide moral guidance and hope in times of difficult change.

Given the environment of change in 2017 and beyond, HECs will play an important role in ensuring ethics-based organizations and patient care. Therefore, it is important that committee members continue to review the organizational mission and ethics theories and principles as they apply to their organizations. In addition, they must be engaged in proactive learning so that they can address the ethics challenges in a time of overarching change for healthcare organizations.

▶ Update from a Practitioner's View

This section provides a discussion of Dr. West's observation of the current issues for HECs. Because of the constant challenges brought about by legislative uncertainty, changes in patient census, and fiscal challenges, there is an increased expectation for HECs to address policy, personnel, and patient issues that require a multidisciplinary and model-based approach to find a solution.

In this update, Dr. West discusses four examples of new or anticipated issues that HECs will face. This section centers on the issue of an HEC's reluctance to discuss its work outside of the organization. It also includes the concern about providing quality care for the aging baby boomer population who may or may not be adequately insured. As part of this issue, Dr. West also makes recommendations about the role of the HCA in HEC decision-making. Finally, he presents information about the ethics of the newly dead. This section deals with issues such as the need for respect for persons and families and a consistent policy that respects the newly dead, families, and organizational needs.

Communication with Healthcare Ethics Committees

In conducting his research among the chairs of HECs in hospitals, Dr. West found them reluctant to address current ethics issues. He explored the possibilities for this reluctance. According to Pozgar,[47] HECs must address ever-expanding issues that go beyond patient care. They are now involved with external areas related to insurance, finance, policy, and education. All of these issues affect a hospital's ability to provide care. HECs must expand their considerations to include external areas that affect care delivery.

New issues for HECs also include the change in orientation from treating the sick to engaging in prevention and population health. In addition, they must provide advice on the ethics of evidence-based medicine and the future use of technology, such as IBM Watson. With these challenges, HECs are expected to be competent in ethics theory and principles and their application to increasingly difficult decisions for both practitioners and the organizations. HECs are also still advocates for patients and a source of advice on difficult patient-centered care, such as beginning and end-of-life treatment decisions. Perhaps, a reluctance to speak about current ethics issues is not just about protecting confidentiality but also about the roles and complexity of decisions to be made.

In the current environment of health care, HECs may also feel insecure about their current knowledge and preparation. They may not be prepared analyze the ethics issues for the complexities that represent today's hospital operations. This potential insecurity makes a case for increased HEC training on the compelling issues and in ethics analysis.

What Is the Role of the HCA in a Healthcare Ethics Committee?

The information in the previous section led Dr. West to consider the need for increased involvement of HCAs in HECs. While most HECs include representation of management in some way, there is an increasing demand to provide cost-effective, quality care that is patient-centered. This responsibility requires

balancing mission and margin in a time of great demand on both. HCAs see the system differently than clinical staff members because their mission is to provide the best-possible care, while meeting payroll, operating expense, and profitability goals. They also understand the workings of hospital systems, including staffing, maintenance, regulation, and other obligations. Their knowledge and involvement provide great insight into the application of ethics within a hospital setting.

With the use of a decision-making model, the input from the HCA could provide information that makes decisions more viable for the organization. However, caution must be taken to ensure that issues in balancing costs and organizational concerns are made with a thorough discussion of ethics principles and the mission of the organization. This deliberation could prevent situations in which costs and resources overwhelm the concern for patients.

Strech, Hurst, and Danes[48] introduced an ethics situation that illustrates the need for a balance of ethics, costs, and organizational concerns. They included evidence that rationing of both input and output services is a worldwide practice and ethics concern. While no evidence was presented for the ethics of bedside rationing in the United States, the authors posited that this action will be unavoidable in the future. They offered a four-stage approach to address the ethics of rationing. This approach includes clarifying justice with economic analysis as well as ethical criteria. HCAs, with their backgrounds in finance and organizational factors, will play an essential role in providing care that is both financially and ethically just.

Quality Care for the Baby Boomer Population

The ability to provide adequate and ethics-based care for the aging baby boomer population was also a concern for Dr. West. A study by Knickman and Snell[49] assessed the upcoming challenges in addressing the health needs of baby boomers as they age. They coined the term "the 2030 problem"[50] to describe the challenge of making sure that care will be available to this population now and in the next 30 years. They also described the economic burden that has implications for policy, healthcare systems, and the community.

Their study supported the idea that caring for aging baby boomers will create a care delivery and economic burden for society. The trend toward the increasing use of the healthcare system as the baby boomers age may challenge and overwhelm the system. In addition, they presented information about the financial challenges for both individuals and systems when providing this care. For example, even baby boomers who have Medicare and private insurance must be prepared to address unknown cost areas such as uncovered costs, supplementary insurance copays, and costs related to long-term care.[51] Baby boomers who are not married face additional issues related to health care and support. They tend to have lower household incomes and are more likely to live by themselves without support from their children or others.[52]

The aging of the baby boomer generation also contributes to shortages of healthcare providers to meet the needs of current and future populations. While the population needing care will increase, the retirement of the baby boomers could lead to shortages in physicians, nurses, and other members of the labor force. A reduction in the number of qualified healthcare professionals could present major issues in both quality care and profitability. Even with the advent of greater technology, hospital systems will need to address the issue of providing care for current patients with less staff.

While issues relating to the care of baby boomers and the payment for that care are important for the entire healthcare system, hospitals must become proactive in addressing these issues. Planning for the future of caring for the needs of aging baby boomers requires consideration for innovation, population

health efforts, and expanding services that might include keeping aging baby boomers as healthy as possible. For example, the healthcare system must consider the potential for increasing its viability through developing markets that include community-based services.[53,54] This change in hospital care delivery will require active involvement of HECs in terms of both policy review and protections for vulnerable aging populations. In addition, HECs must also be aware of the financial strains that can be placed upon a system when its census increases and its workforce decreases. Additionally, HECs may need more training to fully understand the issues so that they can make recommendations that are just and compassionate.

What Are the Rights of the Newly Dead?

The ethics of care for the newly dead is an issue that is ever present but often ignored. The practice of medicine in hospital settings tends to regard death as a loss rather than part of the human experience. Phrases like "Your husband lost his fight with cancer" or "We did not save the patient" create an ideology where the newly dead are not always honored. In addition, using dark humor protects the healthcare professionals from an emotional response to the death of the patient. While professionals are trained not to be overly emotional or to cause additional distress to the families, their training can also create a lack of respect for the autonomy of the newly dead.

Hospitals also need to be concerned about their higher duty to respect all patients, even the newly dead. For example, the end of life can be viewed as a math problem versus a higher duty. In situations in which beds are needed for living patients, hospitals may move the newly dead to the morgue as quickly as possible. While this makes economic sense because it frees up beds, it does not demonstrate compassion and beneficence. Because family members are not allowed in the morgue, this decision may cause deeper grief for a family that wants to say goodbye. In addition, hospitals need to be aware of the location of their morgues. For example, the entrance to the morgue needs to be in a place of dignity and not near the hospital dumpsters. This placement would indicate that the newly dead are simply human garbage.

A larger concern with respect to the newly dead is the problem of final disposition of the remains. In medical examiner cases, where family members are not available or have refused to provide services for the newly dead, the county is responsible for interment or cremation. Cremation, because of its reduced cost to taxpayers, is often the method of choice for dealing with these newly dead individuals. Even though these individuals may have been less than well-respected citizens, their value as human beings needs to be considered as part of the ethics responsibility to the newly dead.

Dr. West's informal research and discussion with funeral directors revealed an ethics issue related to inconsistency in hospital policies regarding the newly dead. For example, inconsistency exists in the procedures for retrieving the newly dead. In addition, the policies for release times vary, which causes delay and additional costs for the funeral directors.

Funeral directors are part of the total healthcare system, but they are not always respected as part of it. As licensed professionals, funeral directors provide a service for the newly dead and their families. For example, funeral directors have an ethics duty to protect the community from hazards from inappropriate care for the newly dead. Because they do not know the cause of death or do not have immediate access to the medical records and death certificates, they are at risk. To protect themselves and the community, they must assume that every person is contagious and take precautions in the final preparation of the body. By using these precautions, the funeral directors fulfill an ethical duty to the community.

HECs need to include the newly dead in their discussions of patient-centered care. In addition, they should review policies related to the care of the newly dead to ensure that the policies are respectful as well as cost-effective. Policy development for the needs of the newly dead needs to address issues for the hospitals, including the healthcare professionals' attitudes toward the newly dead and access to these patients. HECs also need to review policies for retrieving the newly dead to make sure that they balance the hospitals' cost-effectiveness with the concerns of families and funeral directors.

▶ Summary

HECs are the primary way in which healthcare institutions address increasingly difficult ethics issues related to institutions and patients. This chapter reviews the roles of these committees and details the duties of ethics subcommittees. In addition, it presents the current and future issues for HECs. Finally, through his research on practicing HECs, Dr. West suggests that they may face difficult issues in the future related to distributive justice and the ethics of patient care. He also suggests that the ethics of the newly dead be considered in policy development. Clearly, the HECs face challenges, but they will continue to serve to address ethics issues related to cost-effective, compassionate, and responsible patient care.

▶ Questions for Discussion

1. How do you think an HEC can contribute to an organization's commitment to ethics-based practice?
2. What effect does the uncertainty of national healthcare policy have on the work of an HEC?
3. Do hospitals show respect for the newly dead in their policies and practices?

▶ Notes

1. American College of Emergency Physicians, "The Ethics of Healthcare Reform: Issues in Emergency Medicine; An Information Paper," American College of Emergency Physicians Resources (2014), https://www.ena.org/docs/default-source/resource-library/practice-resources/position-statements/interfacemihandcp.pdf?sfvrsn=16bec1ae_12

2. For a concise summary of health reform law, see The Henry Kaiser Family Foundation, *Focus on Health Reform: Summary of the New Affordable Care Act* (Menlo Park, CA: Henry Kaiser Family Foundation, 2013). It is also available on the Kaiser Family Foundation's website: http://www.kff.org.

3. T. Jost, "Day One and Beyond: What Trump's Election Means for the ACA," *Health Affairs Blog*, 2016, http://healthaffairs.org/blog/2016/1/day-one-and-beyond-what-trumps-election-means-to-aca.

4. E. B. Tapper, "Consults for Conflict: The History of Ethics Consultation," *Baylor University Medical Center Proceedings* 26, no. 4 (October, 2013): 417–22.

5. M. P. Aulisio, "Why Did Hospital Ethics Committees Emerge in the US?" *American Journal of Ethics* 18, no. 5 (May 2016): 546–53.

6. D. M. Hester and T. Schonfeld, eds., *Guidance for Healthcare Ethics Committees* (New York, NY: Cambridge University Press, 2016).

7. K. Darr, *Ethics in Health Services Management*, 5th ed. (Baltimore, MD: Health Professions Press, 2011).

8. Hester and Schonfeld, eds., *Guidance for Healthcare Ethics Committees*, 2016.

9. Darr, *Ethics in Health Services Management*, 5th ed., 2011.

10. E. E. Morrison, *Ethics in Health Administration: A Practical Approach for Decision Makers*, 3rd ed. (Burlington, MA: Jones & Bartlett Learning, 2016).

11. Hester and Schonfeld, eds., *Guidance for Healthcare Ethics Committees*, 2016.

12. R. A. Pearlman, *Ethics Committees, Programs and Consultation* (Seattle, WA: University of Washington School of Medicine).

13. L. F. Post et al., *Handbook for Health Care Ethics Committees* (Baltimore, MD: Johns Hopkins University Press, 2007).

14. Hester and Schonfeld, eds., *Guidance for Healthcare Ethics Committees*, 2016.

15. Pearlman, *Ethics Committees, Programs and Consultation*, 2016.

16. R. E. Ashcroft et al., eds., *Principles of Healthcare Ethics* (Hoboken, NJ: John Wiley & Sons, 2007).

17. Hester and Schonfeld, eds., *Guidance for Healthcare Ethics Committees*, 2016.

18. Ashcroft et al., eds., *Principles of Healthcare Ethics*, 2007.

19. P. B. Hofmann, "7 Factors Complicate Ethical Resource Allocation Decisions," *Healthcare Executive* (May/June 2011): 62–63.

20. Ibid., 63.

21. J. D. Lantos, "Ethics Committees and Resource Allocation," *Bioethics Forum* (Fall 1994): 27–29.

22. Darr, *Ethics in Health Services Management*, 5th ed., 2011.

23. Ibid.

24. Office for Human Research Protections (OHRP), *Human Subjects Regulation Decision Charts* (February, 2016), https://www.hhs.gov/ohrp/regulations-and-policy/decision-charts/index.html.

25. Darr, *Ethics in Health Services Management*, 5th ed., 2011.

26. Hester and Schonfeld, eds., *Guidance for Healthcare Ethics Committees*, 2016.

27. Ibid.

28. Darr, *Ethics in Health Services Management*, 5th ed., 2011.

29. J. F. Monagle, "Blueprints for Hospital Ethics Committees," *CHA Insight* 8, no.20 (1984): 1–4.

30. Darr, *Ethics in Health Services Management*, 5th ed., 2011.

31. Post, Blustein, and Bubler, *Handbook for Health Care Ethics Committees*, 2007.

32. L. J. Weber, "The Ethics of Cost Control: Wasteful Treatments Undermine Healthcare for All," *Ethics Progress* (November–December 2011): 69.

33. Ibid., 68–74.

34. W. A. Nelson, "Rethinking the Traditional Ethics Committee," *Healthcare Executive* 32, no. 1 (January–February 2017): 46.

35. Hester and Schonfeld, eds., *Guidance for Healthcare Ethics Committees*, 2016.

36. Lachman, *Ethical Challenges in Health Care*, 202.

37. W. A. Nelson, "An Organizational Ethics Decision-Making Process," *Healthcare Executive* 20, no. 4 (July/August 2005): 8–14.

38. Post, Blustein, and Bubler, *Handbook for Health Care Ethics Committees*, 2007.

39. Hester and Schonfeld, eds., *Guidance for Healthcare Ethics Committees*, 2016.

40. C. A. LaSala and D. Biarnason, "Creating Workplace Environments that Support Moral Courage," *OJIN: The Online Journal of Issues in Nursing* 15, no.3 (September 2010): Manuscript 4.

41. Ibid.

42. E. G. Epstein and S. Delgado, "Understanding and Addressing Moral Distress," *OJIN: The Online Journal of Issues in Nursing* 15, no.3 (September 2010): Manuscript 1.

43. Ibid.

44. Ibid.

45. Ibid.

46. L. Barton, *Crisis in Organizations: Managing and Communicating in the Heat of Chaos* (Cincinnati, OH: South-Western, 1993): i.

47. G. D. Pozgar, "Chapter 4: Health Care Ethics Committees," in *Legal and Ethical Issues for Health Professionals*, 4th ed. (Burlington, MA: Jones & Bartlett Learning, 2016), 159–72.

48. D. Strech et al., "The Role of Ethics Committees and Ethics Consultation in Allocation Decisions: A 4-Stage Process," *Medical Care 2010* 48, no. 9 (2010): 821–26.

49. J. R. Knickman, and E. K. Snell, "The 2030 Problem: Caring for Aging Baby Boomers," *Health Service Research* 37, no. 4 (2002): 849–84.

50. Ibid.

51. J. R. Knickman and E. K. Snell, "The 2030 Problem: Caring for Aging Baby Boomers."

52. L. M. Hunter, "Unmarried Baby Boomers Face Disadvantages As They Grow Older," *Population Reference Bureau* (2014), http://www.prb.org/Publications/Articles/2014/baby-boomers-and-disability.aspx.

53. S. A. Cohen, "A Review of Demographic and Infrastructural Factors and Potential Solutions to the Physician and Nursing Shortage Predicted to Impact the Growing US Elderly Population," *Journal of Public Health Management and Practice* 15, no. 4 (2009): 352–62.

54. J. R. Knickman and E. K. Snell, "The 2030 Problem: Caring for Aging Baby Boomers."

CHAPTER 7

Ethics in the Management of Health Information Systems

C. Scott Kruse

▶ Introduction

Health information management (HIM) and health information systems (HISs) are an essential part of the efficient and effective management of healthcare systems and operations. In addition, they provide information that is essential to accurate diagnoses and treatment of patients and evaluation of the system itself. This chapter begins with operational definitions of HIM and HIS to clarify the terms and how they are used. With this foundation, the author will introduce the reader to the ethical dilemmas existing within HISs. The chapter will also include models for effective decision-making when facing ethics issues.

▶ Operational Definitions

Before the exploration of the potentially deep water of the ethics in healthcare information technology, it is important to define a few key terms and abbreviations. There are subtle differences between some commonly used acronyms, and these titles could point to entirely different industries. For example, one often hears others refer to the HIM industry and the health information technology (HIT) industry as the same. While there are some significant overlaps between the two, there are other clearly defining characteristics that distinguish one from the other.

The American Health Information Management Association (AHIMA) defines health information as the data related to a person's medical history, including symptoms, diagnoses, procedures, and outcomes. Health information records include patient histories, lab results, X-rays, clinical information, and notes. One can view a patient's health information individually, to see how a patient's health has changed. One can also view this information as a part of a larger data set to understand how a population's health has changed, and how medical interventions can change health outcomes.[1]

To differentiate the terms, AHIMA defines HIM as "the practice of acquiring, analyzing, and protecting digital and traditional medical information vital to providing quality patient care. It is a combination of business, science, and information technology."[2] Professionals in this field manage patient records (physical and electronic) and quality initiatives in the healthcare organization. They also often have a hand in accreditation and utilization management. The senior managers in this field typically hold an MBA and have a certification in Six Sigma. Professionals in this field typically also have some limited access to protected health information (PHI).

The U.S. Department of Health and Human Services defines HIT broadly as a "concept that encompasses an array of technologies to store, share, and analyze health information."[3] It also states that HIT involves the exchange of health information in an electronic environment. Widespread use of HIT within the healthcare industry will improve the quality of health care, prevent medical errors, reduce healthcare costs, increase administrative efficiencies, decrease paperwork, and expand access to affordable health care. Given the extent of its use in health care, it is imperative that the privacy and security of electronic health information be ensured as this information is maintained and transmitted electronically.[4]

Professionals in HIT often focus on the technology and architecture necessary to deliver quality care in a digital environment. They are intimately involved in the day-to-day operation and support of the network infrastructure. In addition, they may manage the IT help desk for the healthcare organization. These professionals are also heavily involved in the system selection and system acquisition processes. The senior manager in this field has a master of science in information technology (MSIT) and certifications in network or system administration. Professionals in the field typically do not have access to PHI.

The World Health Organization defines the health information system (HIS) a bit more broadly. In their definition, the HIS provides the underpinnings for decision-making and has four key functions: data generation, compilation, analysis and synthesis, and communication and use. It collects data from the health sector and other relevant sectors, analyses the data and ensures their overall quality, relevance, and timeliness, and converts data into information for health-related decision-making.[5] One could view the HIS as the bridge between HIM and HIT. Both industries have a hand in the selection, implementation, and management of the HIS.

▶ Ethical Dilemmas Involving Data on HISs

Those who work with technology could be viewed as the guardians and custodians of the money in an armored truck . . . a very large armored truck. If the guards come with character flaws, then their work, and the safety of the money, will be in question. The author has a fairly diverse background: psychology, engineering, computer science, bioethics, and business. Despite his studies, the author cannot help but be constantly amazed at the audacity of some hackers to violate the privacy, sanctity, and money of others.

The author has also taught the management of healthcare information technology and healthcare information systems for almost 10 years and addressed topics such as the need for privacy and the laws that are in place to protect it. In his research and teaching, he is concerned about why society needs laws to safeguard the expectation of privacy of medical information. Shouldn't this be an area that one avoids out of respect for others' privacy? There are few things as personal details of our own health.

As the author ages, he is more acutely aware of the need for protection of privacy.

Using his military background as an example, he observed a person that he, as a non-health professional, would consider a malingerer. However, he did not have access to the subject's health information to know if that is true. The author's background in IT and position of authority in the military might have enabled him to obtain a soldier's PHI and pursue the case of malingering. However, he did not think that it was appropriate to use his power to confirm his suspicions. Accessing medical records is an issue of equity among soldiers (everyone works), but it was also a balance between privacy and equity. In addition, the author has his own moral compass that he wanted to maintain. However, the psychology of the hacker does not have the same ethos of protecting privacy, honoring the individual, and maintaining a correctly directed moral compass. The next section explores the psychology and ethics of hackers.

The Psychology of a Hacker

Just Because It Can Be Done, Does It Mean That We Should?

The U.S. Department of Justice is replete with examples of egregious violations of privacy (for personal gain), since the passage of Health Insurance Portability and Accountability Act (HIPAA) in 1996 and its compliance required by 2003. For example, in the Southern District of New York and four other Districts, indictments detailed a healthcare fraud scheme involving more than $163 million. At least 118 clinics in 25 states defrauded Medicare beneficiaries and providers of their identities and submitted fraudulent claims to Centers for Medicare and Medicaid Services (CMS) for reimbursement. In 2008 and 2009, individuals used medical records as material for blackmail to disparage the reputation or credibility of patients, some of whom were celebrities. In another case in 2010, the perpetrators

used the information from medical records in phony credit card schemes using 50,000 records from Johns Hopkins Hospital. HIPAA and other non-HIPAA statutes were used to prosecute these cases, depending on the defendants' standing as a covered entity under HIPAA or in its expanded form under the Health Information Technology for Economic and Clinical (HITECH) Act.[6]

Conspiracy to commit PHI fraud, with intent for personal gain and malicious harm is also a legal and ethical issue. For example, the U.S. Department of Justice published a report in 2008 concerning the actions of a licensed practical nurse LPN in Arkansas. The LPN, Andrea Smith (25), accessed the PHI of a patient of the clinic where she was employed. Andrea provided the PHI to her husband, who then contacted the patient and attempted to extort money to keep the information private.[7] The U.S. Department of Justice also published a report of indictment in 2014 of Joshua Hippler (30), for wrongful disclosure of individually identifiable health information with the intent of personal gain. Hippler was an employee of a covered entity, an East Texas hospital, and as such he was subject to prosecution under HIPAA.[8]

These are not victimless crimes, they harm individuals. They violate an individual's privacy and erode society's expectation of the same. When CMS pays a fraudulent claim, the U.S. government goes after the fraud once it is detected and costs rack up at an alarming rate. Fraudulent claims against private insurance are not any different because they harm taxpayers as well. These actions suggest an ethics question. Why must society as a whole fund the misgivings of the morally bankrupt?

Most of the author's moral fabric (like many others) comes from family, Boy Scouts, and West Point. At West Point, the United States Military Academy teaches its cadets three rules of thumb to help indoctrinate those with a more looser definition of moral infractions. These rules are useful in considering ethics concerns in HIM. They are as follows:

1. Does this action attempt to deceive anyone or allow anyone to be deceived?
2. Does this action gain or allow the gain of privilege or advantage to which I, or someone else would not otherwise be entitled?
3. Would I be dissatisfied by the outcome if I were on the receiving end of this action?[9]

These rules are not complicated nor they stand beyond the comprehension of anyone who resides in or does business with the United States. Despite rules like these, we still read about egregious violations of personal trust and privacy related to health information.

For example, the U.S. Department of Justice published a report in 2012 detailing several examples of moral miscreants in the area of HIM. Examples from this report demonstrate that making decisions that violate ethics can also lead to consequences that cause harm to organizations, patients, and those who make the decision. For example, a resident of Ashville N.C. submitted more than $64 million in fraudulent claims to CMS. She was a licensed psychological associate. In Miami, the three owners of a healthcare agency were sentenced to a total of 294 months in prison for a $60-million CMS fraud scheme. The chief conspirator of a home health Medicare program defrauded CMS of $42 million. Part of his scheme was to pay kickbacks and bribes to patient recruiters in return for fraudulent documentation or medically unnecessary therapy. However, the largest in Miami in 2012 was a $205-million fraud scheme.[10]

The Computer ID, Ego, and Superego and Ethics

Communication failures can often be due to differences in generations, especially in cases of how each approaches computers. While a Generation X member might be perfectly comfortable calling the power indicator on the computer by its name, a Baby Boomer member might call it "the flashy thing on the box." There are many computer terminologies that are either foreign to the Boomer or the other generations, or the terminologies are similar to words that are completely different than the computer industry uses them.

The author experiences failures in communication based on generational differences with respect to the approach to computers. For example, his father was a Boomer. His experience with computers began after his retirement, and his interest in them includes learning texts, e-mails, and eBay. The author, in contrast, is a Generation X person. His generation pioneered personal computers and the Internet's use around the world. In contrast to his father, he has won awards from the United States Army for his efforts to automate inventory to database systems. The author also holds certifications in systems engineering, security, and degrees in information technology. He has comfort and experience with technology and is quite different from his father's experience.

Some of the texts from his father like "The flashy thing on your mother's computer stopped working" create a mystery that runs the gamut from simple to complex. The issues revolve around clarification of terms, including the definition of "the flashy thing." It creates a situation for effective troubleshooting of the problem, without being insulting or forgetting about beneficence when addressing the problem. This story is included as an introduction to the concept of "computer ID."

Dr. Sigmund Freud introduced the concepts of the id, the ego, and the superego in the 1920s.[11] The id represents our most basic instincts, or the little devil on our shoulder. The superego is the angel on our other shoulder, while the ego is the negotiator between the two and ultimately determines our actions. (Note: This relationship is paraphrased.) Freud did not use the words devil or angel, nor did he intimate that they sit on our shoulders. The id invades our thoughts, but it does not always dictate our behavior; however, social and cultural norms often dictate our behavior. In addition, ethicists also theorize about the morality of behavior. For example, deontology theorizes that the categorical imperative influences our actions, our duty or our obligations to act in a certain way. This theory, however, does not mention the intent of the action.[12]

Computers can enable a person to assume a different personality. They can offer a world with apparently different rules than society. For example, a person can enter a chat room anonymously while online to academically debate a topic that would otherwise have socially negative connotations. These topics could include areas such as homosexuality, HIV/AIDS, illegal immigration, despotic or dogmatic policies in a workplace or a community, or the dangers of allowing any one leader to assume too much power. However, anonymity can also enable money laundering, theft, and damage of electronic property. There is a duality of terms between the computer world and the writings of Freud. Each day, users of a computer log into the computer using a computer identification called an ID. This grants access to resources for which the user has paid. This ID can easily unlock Freud's concept of the id, but somehow the ego and superego are not always invited to the party.

Donn Parker observed in the 1960s that when people use computers they tend to "leave their ethics at the door."[13] This observation sounds as if any filters introduced by societal, cultural, or familial norms have stopped once the user logs in with a user ID. Theft, invasion of privacy, cyber bullying, extortion, racketeering, poor decisions, and just plain unacceptable behavior occurs on the Internet continuously and ubiquitously. It is as if the ego and superego no longer exist beyond the user's ID.

This is not necessarily a new observation, although the author is unable to find the close correlation between Freud's id and the computer ID in the literature. In the 1970s, some academicians introduced basic ethics into computer courses to remind students that the social and societal expectations should not stop once an ID has been established.[14] In the 1980s, at least one book was published on computer ethics.[15] In the 1990s, an organization was established called Computer Professionals for Social Responsibility. In addition, movements to encourage social responsibility in the digital environment were noted in the United States, Australia, and Europe. During the Clinton Presidential administration, Congress passed the HIPAA in 1996, with enforcement available in 2003.

Professional societies in the computer industry were encouraged to adopt a code of ethics. The Association of Computing Machinery was one of the first, with many that followed. These associations and groups included various fields like Software Engineering, IT Professionals in New Zealand, Computer Society of South Africa, and Association of Information Technology Professionals (US). In addition, the Institute of Electrical and Electronics Engineers, Computer Society of India, System Administrators Guild, and many others developed ethics codes. In addition, the computer industry developed several peer-reviewed journals along the lines of computer ethics. Examples include *Ethics and Information Technology*, *Computer and Information Ethics*, and *International Journal of Information Ethics*.

Despite the efforts of the world community, those without a moral compass use their ID to feed their Freudian id. As a seventh grader, the author remembers debating sophomoric topics like, "If you could be invisible, and nobody would know you were there, would you sneak into the girl's locker room?" Would that not be a victimless infraction against societal norms or privacy? Nobody would know I was there because I would be invisible. I would not embarrass the girl by my presence because nobody would know I am there. Would the girl feel like there was a violation of her privacy because I was invisible? Interestingly enough, this is the exact behavior of many on the Internet with malicious intent.

Hackers sneak into the back doors of servers and lurk while other users hold an expectation of privacy. A hacker in an electronic healthcare record is able to stomp, invade, and otherwise violate the most private and delicate episodes of care. For example, is Sally pregnant? Did Sally discuss abortion with her doctor? Did the doctor recommend abortion? Such information must not become public. It is as salacious and tests the hacker's moral high ground. However, did the hacker bother to read that the pregnancy was due to rape? Did the hacker bother to read about the violence that Sally experienced, unsuspectingly and against her will? Is he/she aware of the damages that the episode caused both physically and mentally? There are ethical reasons why such information is private. Yes, even if the hacker was "invisible" his/her actions were morally corrupt from the very start.

At some point when individuals sit at a computer or mobile device, they make a decision about their conduct in the cyber community. The moment a person logs into a system, his/her identity can be determined, and others can track actions of that person. Do individuals choose how they will act the moment they log in with their ID, or does their unconscious id creep up on them while they are online? It may be a combination of the two, and it may vary depending on the background and experiences of the user.

One also needs to consider other factors that may influence individuals' actions on the Internet. For example, does a person's socioeconomic status justify bad behavior on the Internet? In daily life, there is some confusion about the effects of status and actions. "Do not steal."[16] This commandment is part of the law handed down to Moses, and it has permeated law in most countries. However, what if the person is stealing to feed his/her family? Or does not the potential thief think that he/she is stealing because the action is online?

One legend relating to the nature of theft tells of the famous Mayor La Guardia of New York during the Great Depression. He sat as judge in court one cold day in January, a rarely used privilege of that office. A store owner brought an old tattered woman to court for stealing a loaf of bread. According to the proprietor, the store was located in a rough neighborhood, and he wanted the court to fine the woman $10 or send her to jail for 10 days to set an example to the neighborhood.

The mayor asked for the woman's side of the story. She explained that she was a grandmother whose single-mother daughter had taken ill, whose husband had left her, and whose grandchildren were starving. According to legend, Mayor LaGuardia agreed with the shopkeeper that the woman should be an example concerning her actions. He fined the woman $10, paid the fine himself, then passed a hat around the courtroom and fined everyone 50 cents for allowing a grandmother to live in such conditions in their neighborhood (the money went to the grandmother).[17]

In another example, when faced with the subject of stealing to feed one's family, the Italian Supreme Court in 2016 ruled that "stealing to stave off hunger is not a crime." This case was that of a homeless man, Mr. Ostriakov, who was caught stealing sausage and cheese back in 2011. He was initially convicted of stealing, but the ruling was challenged over the course of 4 years and ended up in the hands of the highest court of that land.[18] This author does not entirely disagree, but one must agree that this can become a slippery slope.

How do these cases relate to theft and ethics via the Internet? The year 2016 saw many instances of access to HIM held for ransom. The U.S. Federal Bureau of Investigation (FBI) calls this access a ransomware. It is "a type of malware that infects computers, networks, and servers using encryption to make files unreadable. Cyber attackers then demand a ransom to return the files."[19] This is the latest in a series of cyber extortion tools that the cyber crime branch of the FBI has investigated and tracked down. While all sectors of business in the United States experience some variant of ransomware, health care has received about 88% of it, because it is time-sensitive about its day and is most likely to pay quickly.[20]

How does such an action play out in the minds of the cybercriminal? Is data held ransom for food? Is there some large "food for healthcare data cause" that reins on the dark web? The author doubts the cause is so noble. Ransomware, as well as most cybercrime, is traced to organized crime that emanates from Eastern Europe.[21] These criminals pay for cybercrime, and there do not seem to be any ethical dilemmas about the matter. Be it an organized crime or not, the computer should not provide an environment for criminal activity. Each act is initiated by one person, and each person has an account on the computer with an ID. Users should not allow their Freudian id to permeate their user ID.

The computer ID does not free the user from a social responsibility and respect to our fellow human beings. Do not allow the ID to feed your id. Encourage your ego to negotiate and regulate behavior with the ID as well as the id. The Superego knows what is morally right. Remember the principles of ethics including confidentiality, nonmaleficence, beneficence, and justice apply to computers too. In addition, do not forget those West Point "rules of thumb" as they serve as a great guide.

Privacy Versus Security

Immediately following the attack on 9/11, the U.S. House and Senate passed the Patriot Act in record time. This act gave the federal government much greater reach to seek out the sleeper cells in our country to avoid an additional attack. Our nation has endured smaller attacks under the same flag as Muslim extremism, but none on the scale of 9/11. The Patriot Act expired in 2011, 10 years after its passage. When the Patriot Act was drafted, the author remembers President Bush justifying an expiration date on the act along with a caution that

we should be very careful to whom we grant so much power.

Some believe that to protect against a wolf, you need a more powerful wolf. But that might just invite the danger into your house. To help prevent this from occurring in the management of HISs, we subject hiring candidates to a background investigation. That is good ethics, business, and risk management practice. For example, if a candidate has a mark on his/her record for identity theft, then that person can be identified as a fox and it should be very unlikely that anyone will give him/her the keys to the hen-house.

It is not enough to hire someone and say, "Protect me." Instead, one needs to provide specifics and priorities. This author once had an employer who asked if our network was hacker proof. The response was, admittedly a bit flippant, "Sir, you have not given me the budget for a hacker proof system, and if I were to create a hacker proof system, then legitimate users would not be able to access it either (because it would be secured against the insider threat as well)." Review the examples from the previous section for reminders of this insider threat. Those prosecuted under HIPAA must have been either covered entities or employees of covered entities, which means they were insiders. Non-covered entities must be prosecuted under non-HIPAA charges.

Protecting an information system is about the management of specific risk and it may also involve a bit of deflection. One should evaluate each portion of the infrastructure and each information asset and determine a priority of protection and implement reasonable safeguards for them all. You should have no intention of making your network impenetrable, but instead, make it difficult enough for a hacker to seek a softer target. If a hacker targets an organization, there are a million ways to breach the data; the easiest of which is to give a legitimate user a $1000 to walk out with an unencrypted laptop. Some might even do it for less. So encrypt the data on all computers (laptops and desktops).

In addition, you could tell the person in charge of the network that you want completely (physically) separate networks for providers doing their jobs and patients accessing free Wi-Fi. That makes it unlikely that a morally bankrupt user will be able to access patient data. Regularly provide a short security tip for users at any hospital-wide meeting. Insert yourself at every opportunity to remind users that our social responsibilities extend into cyberspace as well as the rest of our lives. Safeguarding organizational systems not only makes good business sense, but it also honors the principle of autonomy as confidentiality for both patient and organizational data. Although there must be some trade-off between privacy and security, it does not have to be unreasonable. Best practices such as background checks and slightly better-than-average network security can go far to encourage a would-be hacker to seek a softer target. It does not hurt an organization's security profile to distribute the network authority, and to audit the security of the system regularly. In fact, it shows that the ethics of confidentiality is important to the organization. As goes the cowboy proverb, "Trust everyone, but count your cows."

▶ Smartphone Network of Healthcare Awareness—Good Idea or Violation of Privacy?

Protecting the privacy of both patients and users becomes a difficult task, but by providing an umbrella of risk management over many specific risks, you provide a balance of security. For example, many smartphones today regularly collect information on individuals. This capability is enabled by faster processing chips in newer phones, and the phones can store and exchange large amounts of personal data. From an ethical view, users have agreed to this feature in one of the many long and complex user agreements. For example, they agree to the use of the feature to enable them to use Google Maps, for instance. Google Maps does an incredible job of showing traffic patterns ahead. It does this by collecting data on all the phones on the road. What a great tool, but what else is being tracked?

About one in five smartphone users have a mobile health application that is being used at any one time.[21] Apps have been developed to help users manage chronic disease like diabetes, and with weight control through activity monitors and daily activity journals. But all apps do not interface with humans well, and the information provided may not always be helpful.[18] Does a government-sponsored health app exist in the United States that will notify citizens of a health threat? There is in the United Kingdom has its own app called the Health Apps Library and is run by the country's National Health System.[22] In the United States, however, the government is not vetting health applications. There is a private venture that is entirely voluntary called "Happtique Health Apps Certification Program" (HACP).[22-24]

Can legislation to protect a user's privacy in the United States possibly keep up with the pace of the development of health applications? There are many questions that our nation needs to ask developers of applications as a medical device. How is all of this health information captured and transmitted? How is the data vetted for accuracy? Is the collection of that data a violation of privacy or a protection against public peril? These are all great questions that we should continue to ask. The convenience of some apps may not be worth the invasion of privacy that they require, which raises more questions.

Are there ethical limitations that we should impart on the applications that involve medical information? Does the fine print on a user agreement for a medical application for a smartphone walk over the user's autonomy? This author thinks that is perfectly arguable. Medical applications need to be mindful of the medical and technological literacy of its users. Commensurate with consent forms for medical procedures, the user agreements for technological applications is most likely far beyond what the average user's understanding of technology.

Health insurers at some companies are rewarding healthy behavior, and they are verifying this behavior through voluntary monitoring of wearable devices such as "Fitbits." Does this monitoring place the user at risk later when the employee moves to a different employer? Does this information become part of the medical record, medical insurance record, or any other record? For how long is the data maintained?

Smartphones and other wearable devices that collect, maintain, and transmit personal medical information can pose a risk to the user's PHI, and the complexity of the user agreements could infringe on a user's autonomy if the user does not completely understand its contents. Our nation needs to ask some difficult questions, and it needs to keep asking questions in order to keep up with the pace of technology and application development. We also need to have some sort of vetting process that would help reassure users that their information is kept and remains confidential. Only then will apps as a medical device provide a valuable service to the users while maintaining an acceptable level of privacy.

▶ Is Health Care a Right or a Benefit? What Data Protection Should Be Provided to PHI?

In all classes that the author teaches, he asks a question about how the students view health care. Is it a right of citizenship, as it is in every western nation in the world, or is it simply a benefit of employment? America is a market-based economy, and its system of government attempts to limit the influence of government in its citizens' daily lives. Many Americans consider Medicare to be a right of citizenship. Many Americans consider eligibility for Medicaid to be a right of citizenship. In addition, many Americans consider Social Security to be a right of citizenship. To support this idea, the Preamble to the United States Constitution states, "We the People of the United States, . . . establish Justice, insure domestic Tranquility, . . . promote the general Welfare . . ."[25] Is it just for one citizen to have access to health care but not all? How can there be tranquility without equality? How can there be general welfare without health? These are some fundamental questions that America must debate and resolve, but so far it has not been able to vote into law any sweeping healthcare reform that would ensure universal access. However, laws have already determined that healthcare information is protected information, which is a major portion of HIPAA. If the protection of the health information is a right of citizenship, should the case that generates the data be far behind?

Data are stored in the "cloud" as a regular course of business today. What was once a scary proposition to store PHI in an Internet resource is today becoming common practice. It makes good business sense because it shifts much of the risk to those who secure the data both at rest and in transit. However, does the potential increased access to the data create an ethical problem with storing it there? Perhaps what the healthcare industry needs is a set of ethical decision-making models to use when faced with ethical dilemmas.

▶ Ethical Decision-Making Models for the Management of HIM

While many programs teach courses in ethics in their IT programs, it might also be helpful to introduce some decision-making models for

HIM. The "Three Rules of Thumb" from West Point, introduced earlier in the chapter, serve as a good foundation. In addition, an adaptation of Weber's Individual Decision-Making Method might also be valuable to use. A third model to consider is called the "grandmother test" and will be explained below.

The "Three Rules of Thumb" applied to ransomware would posit the following ethics questions: Does the use of this ransomware attempt to deceive anyone or allow anyone to be deceived? The answer may not be definitive. Does the programming, marketing, deployment, or use of this ransomware gain or allow the gain of privilege or advantage to which I, or someone else, would not otherwise be entitled? The answer to this question is undeniably yes. One would not ordinarily have access to the PHI contained in the medical records. One would not ordinarily have unfettered access to funds that are used in the transaction to reclaim access to the records. The final question could be, would I be dissatisfied with the outcome if I were on the receiving end of this action? Once again, the answer is undeniably yes. If you were a part of the organization that lost access to the data that it owned and maintained, you would not be pleased. If it was your personal information being held hostage, and you experienced a life-threatening event, you would not be happy with the outcome. For example, if you are not able to speak for yourself because of a healthcare emergency, and your medical history could not be accessed, your treatment could be compromised. You would face unnecessary harm. The three rules of thumb could serve as a powerful instrument to help those without or with an uncalibrated moral compass to make ethics-based decisions about the management of health information.

Weber published a book on business ethics in health care and proposed a decision-making method. This author made some minor modifications to his 2001 edition in 2004 and presented these changes at several professional conferences. Weber defined a set of priorities that one should consider when faced with an ethical crossroads. He stated that individual rights should take preeminent priority, followed by community good then community interests. This is followed by organizational good than organizational interests. Lastly, one should consider individual good followed by individual interests.[26] Ransomware would serve as a good example in the use of the Weber model.

Individuals who program, develop, market, or unleash ransomware need to consider whether their interests, good, or rights are more important than those of the community. In the case of ransomware against a healthcare organization, whose individual rights are considered? This ultimately depends on how the question above is answered, "Is health care a right, and if so, is privacy of healthcare information also a right?" If the answer is yes, then this decision is resolved. Ransomware infringes on an individual's right to privacy of medical information.

If, however, the person answers negatively to this question, then perhaps he/she mentions a universal right to distribute income equitably. The author has not discussed natural law in this chapter, but there are many who believe that income should be redistributed in an equitable manner. The inherent problem with this belief is who is the one who decides what is equitable? Who determines the amount of money taken from one that is distributed to the others, and does the transaction itself have a cost? One might even say that the money gained from a ransomware event could become a community good. Once gain, who decides? What is it that Lord Acton said? "Power tends to corrupt, and absolute power corrupts absolutely."[27] It is easy to see how Weber's method could prioritize rights, goods, and interests, but it is also susceptible to interpretation on several levels.

Finally, does the decision pass the "grandmother" test?[28] At the end of the day, can you sit down with your grandmother and tell her about your actions online; assuming she understands what it is that you do? Would grandmother approve and say, "That's a good boy/girl?" or would she frown and begin to shake her head? Imagine, sitting down with her and explaining the ransomware that you developed over the last several months and released today that seizes, encrypts, and holds hostage time-sensitive medical information. Tell her how much of a great event it is for you and your friends because of how seriously healthcare organizations take their privacy policies, and how quickly they will pay, despite the urging of the U.S. FBI to not give in to such cyber exploits.

You can tell her, "Well, we don't look at the information ourselves, so we are not really breaking any rules of privacy." Perhaps you can say, "Grandma, this is so important because it will help you pay off debt, feed your family, put children through college, etc." You can tell her, "Grandmother, this is a victimless crime because the information is never violated, and the healthcare organizations are insured for such things." No matter how you tried to spin your actions, this author predicts that your grandmother would adopt the frown and shake her head left and right. Certainly, your explanation would not pass the grandmother test.

These three ethical decision-making models/methods could be taught as part of the curriculum for all industries, all certifications, and all educational programs. They serve as a grounding point and assessment for decision-making in HIT situations. Perhaps, they could also serve as a guide for those without a moral compass, or those whose moral compass is sorely out of calibration. For example, suppose that a programmer has somehow lost his/her way (morally) and has become the employer or employee of an organized crime syndicate. At some point, one would hope that conscience and a formally taught curriculum on ethical computing would help direct his/her actions in a more positive direction. Whether it is the three rules of thumb, Weber's ethical-decision-making method, or something as simple as the grandmother test, it is important to have a way of considering the ethical ramifications of actions taken in the cyber world and especially in HIT. Given that these models are not perfect, something would be better than nothing would when it comes to ethical conduct in the cyber world. When a person logs in with a computer ID, he/she should not leave social responsibility behind to allow Freud's id to reign supreme. Patients, healthcare organizations, and the community need a higher moral standard that includes the superego and its influence.

▶ Acknowledgment

The author would like to thank Karin W. Zucker for her initial edits on this chapter.

▶ Questions for Discussion

1. When thinking about health information and HIT, autonomy is often an ethics issue. What concerns would patients have about their privacy with electronic health records?

2. How is beneficence and nonmaleficence violated with ransomware?

3. Why would Weber put individual rights first when making ethics decisions about HIM?

4. How would the "Grandmother Test" assist a HIM manager in making decisions about the protection of patient health information?

▶ Notes

1. American Health Information Management Association, *Health Information 101: What Is Health Information* (Chicago, IL: American Health Information Management Association, 2016):

para 1. http://www.ahima.org/careers /healthinfo.

2. Ibid. para 2

3. HealthIT.gov., *Basics of Health IT* (Washington, DC: Office of the National Coordinator for HIT, 2013): para. 1. https:// www.healthit.gov/patients-families /basics-health-it.

    HHS.gov., *Health Information Privacy: Health Information Technology* (Washington, DC: U. S. Department of Health and Human Services, 2017): para 1. http://www.hhs.gov/hipaa/for -professionals/special-topics/health -information-technology/index.html.

4. Ibid. para 1.

5. World Health Organization, *Health Metrics Network Framework and Standards for Country Health Information Systems*, 2nd ed. (Geneva: World Health Organization, 2008), 18–20. http://apps.who.int/iris/bitstream/10665/43872/1/9789241595940 _eng.pdf.

6. United States Senate. "Statement of Loretta Lynch, US Attorney, Eastern District of New York, before the Subcommittee on Privacy, Technology, and the Law Committee on the Judiciary, US Senate" (November 9, 2011). https://www.justice.gov/sites/default /files/testimonies/witnesses/attachments/11/09/11/11-09-11-usa-lynch -testimony-re-examination-of-the -enforcement-of-federal-health-information-privacy-laws.pdf.

7. US Department of Justice, United States Attorney Eastern District of Arkansas, *Nurse pleads guilty to HIPAA violation* (April 15, 2008). https://www.justice. gov/archive/usao/are/news/2008/April /SmithLPNplea%20HIPAA%20041508. pdf.

8. The United States Attorney's Office, Eastern District of Texas, *Former hospital employee indicted for criminal HIPAA violations* (July 3, 2014). https://www.justice.gov/usao-edtx/pr

/former-hospital-employee-indicted-criminal-hipaa-violations.

9. Department of the United States Army, *United States Corp of Cadets Circular 351-2* (Washington, DC: Department of the Army, no date), 187. http://www .usma.edu/cfd/siteassets/sitepages/fdw /cadet%20required%20knowledge.pdf.

10. Department of Health and Human Services and Department of Justice, *Healthcare Fraud and Abuse Control Program: Annual Report FY 2012* (Washington, DC: Department of Health and Human Services, 2013).

11. R. Sheppard, *Explorer of the Mind: The Illustrated Biography of Sigmund Freud* (London: Carlton Books Ltd., 2012).

12. J. Summers, "Theory of Healthcare Ethics," in *Healthcare Ethics Critical Issues for the 21st Century*, eds. E. E. Morrison and B. Furlong, 3rd ed. (Burlington, MA: Jones & Bartlett Learning, 2014).

13. D. Parker. "Rules of Ethics in Information Processing," *Communications of the ACM* 11, no. 3 (1968): 198–201.

14. W. Maner, *Starter Kit in Computer Ethics* (Hyde Park, NY: Helvetia Press and The National Information and Resource Center for Teaching Philosophy, 1980).

15. J. H. Moor, "What Is Computer Ethics?" in *Computers and Ethics*, ed. T. W. Bynum (Hoboken, NJ: Blackwell, 1985), 266–275.

16. *The Holy Bible New American Standard Version* (The Lockman Foundation: La Habra, CA, 1995), Exodus 20:15.

17. D. W. McCullough, *Say Please, Say Thank You: The Respect We Owe One Another* (Boston: G. K. Hall and Company, 1999).

18. BBC News, "Italian Court Rules Food Theft 'Not a Crime' if Hungry," *BBC News*, May 2016. Retrieved from www.bbc.com/news/world-europe -36190557.

19. US Federal Bureau of Investigation, "Ransomware Is on the Rise" (Washington, DC: U.S. Federal Bureau of Investigation, 2016). www.fbi.gov/audio -repository/news-podcasts-thisweek -ransomware-on-the-rise.mp3/view.

20. H. Landi, "Report: 88 Percent of All Ransomware Is Detected in Healthcare Industry," *Health Care Informatics*, 2016. www.healthcare-informatics.com /news-item/cybersecurity/report -88-percent-all-ransomware-detected -healthcare-industry.

21. T. Armerding, "Cybercrime: Much More Organized," *CSO*, 2015. www.csoonline .com/article/298529/cyber-attacks -espionage/cybercrime-much-more -organized.html.

22. M. N Boulos, A.C. Brewer, C. Karimkhani, D. B. Buller, and R. P. Dellavalle, "Mobile Medical and Health Apps: State of the Art, Concerns, Regulatory Control and Certification," *Online Journal of Public Health Informatics* 5, no. 3 (2014): 229. doi: 10.5210./ojphi. v5i5.4814.

23. Ibid.

24. Ibid.

25. Shallus, J. (Transcription), *Constitution of the United States: Preamble* (Washington, DC: National Archives, 1787). https://www.archives.gov/founding -docs/constitution-transcript.

26. Weber, J. W. *Business Ethics in Healthcare: Beyond Compliance* (Bloomington, IN: Indiana University Press, 2001).

27. A. W. Ward, A. J. Dalberg, and A. D. Acton, 1st Baron. *The Cambridge Modern History* (Cambridge: Cambridge University Press. United Kingdom Ward, 1907).

28. Nash, L. L. *The Business of Ethics and Business: Ethics without the Sermon* (Cambridge: Harvard Business Review, 1986).

CHAPTER 8

Technological Advances in Health Care: Blessing or Ethics Nightmare?

Cristian H. Lieneck

▶ Introduction

Currently, there is a strong emphasis on increasing the prevalence and effective utilization of medical technology and health information technology (HIT) within all types of healthcare organizations. Hospitals and ambulatory care facilities are facing extreme marketing and economic pressures to employ technology in their current clinical and administrative processes in an attempt to meet quality demands as well as prescribed regulatory requirements and associated financial incentives. These attempts at technology implementation leave several basic questions unanswered: What is the overall benefit? Will quality of care improve? What potential harm may result? Is it possible to sustain equity and efficiency of care across all patient populations?

As a result of the ongoing and forthcoming ramifications of healthcare reform in the United States, it would appear that healthcare organizations must do more with fewer resources. This includes experiencing cuts in government and private payer reimbursements, increased shortages in several types of healthcare providers, as well as an ever-increasing Medicare and Medicaid population. These changes will continue to inflict strain on the system as they progress. Consequently, organizations are turning to medical technology and HIT in an attempt to increase productivity and the quality of care provided. It is hoped that the result will be a positive influence on overall patient outcomes. However, serious ethics implications may arise throughout the concurrent advances in medical technology and HIT as these outcome-based reimbursement models and related healthcare reform ideals become reality.

The field of health care encompasses many complex processes and protocols, which are in a state of constant fluctuation. Healthcare organizational leaders experience internal and external organizational influences that affect the decisions that, in turn, affect the well-being of all stakeholders involved, most importantly the external customer in health care: the patient. Often these decisions involve the procurement and implementation of technology in an attempt to further organizational productivity, process improvement, and quality of care. The discussion in this chapter focuses on several aspects of the healthcare technology front with regard to critical issues and ethics challenges, presented from an overall industry level. It also presents a distinctive view of the medical group practice perspective. The goals of the chapter are to accomplish the following:

1. Define medical technology and HIT and discuss their close relationship with advances in medical science and accountable care. This section segregates and defines the types of technology utilized in the healthcare context to set the framework for further discussion.

2. *Assess ethics challenges related to recent advances in medical technology and medical science.* This section presents a selection of complex medical innovations in which technology facilitates advancement of the medical field and quality patient care, while simultaneously questioning several ethics principles.

3. Assess HIT developments within the medical group practice, including ethics challenges related to recent and upcoming healthcare reform requirements. This section provides a realistic view of several ethics challenges as medical group practices undergo pressure regarding the implementation and meaningful use of medical technology and HIT in order to meet legislative mandates, economic goals, and market pressures.

to advance patient care, while simultaneously working to increase both the efficiency and the effectiveness of the healthcare organization, its medical providers, and medical staff. This chapter addresses these advances using the two following classifications for healthcare technology:

- *Medical technology* is defined as that which is intended to assist with proper diagnosis and further the quality of medical care by offering less invasive treatment options through the technological advancement of medical products, equipment, processes, and procedures.

- *HIT* includes a series of computer hardware, software, administrative databases, and network systems designed to assist medical providers in providing quality care using the electronic health record (EHR). The associated interoperability of peripheral electronic medical support systems is also part of this definition. Examples of these additional support systems may include computerized physician order entry; data warehousing and cloud computing; database backup, mining, and reporting platforms; and other computer-assisted management-of-care products such as clinical decision support systems (CDSS).

Although both categories define several aspects of technological resources, this chapter focuses on these two classifications and their contributions to the medical field from several ethics perspectives. A challenge exists for healthcare leaders, providers, and administrators to continue to research ethics implications as technological resources are implemented into current, everyday healthcare processes. This ongoing awareness will help ensure effective implementation and utilization of such innovations for all stakeholders involved.

▶ Medical and HIT Defined

The field of medical technology, broadly defined, relates to a series of products designed

▶ The Ethical Obligation

Developments in medical technology often aid or mediate advancements in both medical science and healthcare administrative processes.

As a result, the healthcare field is becoming increasingly dependent on technological developments to ensure organizational success as quality outcomes and reimbursement for medical services become further concomitant with continuous advancements in the technological realm. Almost overnight, the healthcare industry's primary purpose has been altered to not only involve the constant provision of safe, quality medical services but also involve the need to become highly proficient in the accumulation and communication of patient data and related patient care outcomes.

Given a new assembly of healthcare terminology dedicated to increasing the quality of care provided (and identified by a multitude of acronyms), the healthcare leader's challenge is to make sense of it all as this movement influences his or her medical organization. Examples of these acronyms include many utilized within the Medicare Access and CHIP Reauthorization ACT (MACRA) of 2015. These acronyms are encompassed within either the Merit-based Payment Incentive System (MIPS) track or the Alternate Payment Models (APMs) track and include accountable care organizations (ACOs), pay for performance (P4P), and value-based purchasing (VBP).

Healthcare systems and their internal processes are being adapted to include technology at various levels in an attempt to meet this challenge. This almost overwhelming reliance on medical technology and HIT must be continuously evaluated by healthcare leaders for its potential ethics implications from all healthcare stakeholder perspectives to ensure that the legal and fiduciary duties of the medical researchers, providers, and healthcare executives hold to the highest standards of our industry.

▶ Science and Technology Innovations and Ethics Concerns

The development of new technological resources in the field of medicine requires thorough due diligence with regard to the quality, efficiency, efficacy, and safety of the research and implementation process for an innovation. Thorough research with documented outcomes is necessary to establish the value of new procedures, treatments, and medical equipment prior to market-wide adoption of the innovation as an established industry best practice. Although several regulatory and licensing agencies exist to evaluate these continuous technological advances, the focus remains primarily on patient safety and the overall effectiveness of the technology and equipment in treatment of a disease or condition. Subsequently, a disregard for overall healthcare equity and other unintentional, yet important, ethics implications continues to exist, even before a new innovation is approved and accepted into patient care protocols. The use of medical technology and its contribution toward the research and development of medical innovations in the United States demonstrate a disassociation and lack of attentiveness regarding medical ethics and intended innovation outcomes or benefits.

Exploitation of Research Subjects During Research and Development

Prior to the actual approval and implementation of technological advances in medicine, several ethics principles come into question from the genesis and development of the innovation itself. Additionally, as new diseases and disabling conditions continue to surface, civilization becomes more dependent on advances in medical science and technology to assist in the control of these conditions' unpleasant side effects or in the cure of life-threatening conditions altogether. This dependence on technology often allows for a false sense of plausible deniability to occur, particularly as a disassociation between researchers and the research itself. This particular mind-set enables the researcher to focus directly on the study results for only those who may receive direct benefit from the study outcomes. The public thinks that this situation, enabled by technological advances in science and medicine, has happened only in remote instances throughout the history of U.S. medical research and development processes. Recently, however, researchers and historians have discovered that these ethical blemishes, once believed to be isolated incidents in our country's medical research history, existed much more frequently than originally thought.

The Tuskegee Syphilis Study and the Willowbrook Hepatitis Study are two primary, well-documented incidents of unethical medical research on human subjects, characterized by a lack of informed consent and complete disregard for the ethics principle of patient autonomy. To assist in the evaluation of these studies' methodologies and their disregard for ethics principles, Morrison[1] discusses the following elements, which we must consider to avoid the negation of autonomy as demonstrated by informed consent:

- *Competence*: Patients must understand the treatment involved with the research study. Do patients understand potential side effects, as well as the probability of receiving possible outcomes, properly?

- *Voluntariness*: Patients must get an opportunity to decide whether to participate in the study on the basis of their own terms, beliefs, and feelings. Do they get an opportunity to say no to those individuals conducting the study without remorse or follow-on judgment if such declination occurs?

- *Disclosure*: Potential study participants must have knowledge of all legal and ethical aspects of the research so that they may use this information to aid in the decision whether to participate. Are the study and all of its details transparent to all stakeholders involved?

- *Authorization*: Patients must agree with the study's treatment plan and agree to proceed as research participants. Does the subject actually know he or she is part of a research study, and if so, has he or she signed a written (informed) consent form documenting agreement to participate?

The Tuskegee study (1932–1972) involved 200 African American males serving as study control subjects, while another 200 African American males were used as the experimental group.[2] Researchers conducting the study purposely inoculated the experimental, noncontrol group with active syphilis. The individuals exposed to syphilis were told they were receiving the medical interventions as treatment for a rare and deadly blood disease. In return for their participation in the study, all the men received compensation with food, medical care, and burial insurance.

Although an individual's actions often imply autonomous consent,[3] this was certainly not the case for the Tuskegee study. On several levels, the competence, voluntariness, disclosure, and authorization requirements for consent failed to be addressed or adhered to prior to these study participants entering into the study. Moreover, there was further corruption of patient autonomy when the researchers manipulated the potential study participants and influenced them into participating in the study by offering compensation methods that were highly attractive to this disadvantaged population of potential subjects.

Researchers conducted the Willowbrook study (1963–1966) in an attempt to understand further the progression of the hepatitis virus and the effects of treatment for the disease using gamma globulin.[4] A similar research and control group methodology as in the Tuskegee study existed, except that the subjects in the Willowbrook study were all children attending the Willowbrook State School, an institution for adolescents with mental disabilities. When compared to the Tuskegee study, there were similar autonomy issue challenges, yet the Willowbrook methodology also failed to address the study participants' competency on two additional and unembellished levels.

We are often unable to deem adolescents (minors) competent when presented with medical decisions regarding their personal health. It was this acknowledgment of the inability for an adolescent patient to provide proper informed consent that eventually led to the establishment of the patient-centered medical home (PCMH) concept. This concept was born out of the pediatric specialty and is now being utilized in several other medical specialties today.[5] Furthermore, these children were mentally challenged and not able to make regular decisions by themselves in everyday situations, much less regarding the question of whether to participate in a research study that included the potential to become selected into an experimental group that was to be purposely infected with the deadly hepatitis virus.

Collective review of the Tuskegee and Willowbrook studies demonstrated the ability of researchers to become intellectually intrigued and personally invested in the methodology and potential outcome of their studies, with complete disregard of the ethics implications that continued throughout the research. More specifically, this lack of transparency failed to afford the study participants their individual autonomy by failing to disclose methodology related to the potential side effects and permanent treatment outcomes, which included the possible contraction of syphilis and hepatitis. Although these two occurrences in U.S. medical research history are both concerning and horrific, it has been recently determined that instances involving similar flawed research methodology with regard to ethics principles were more prevalent in U.S. history than originally identified.

In August 2010, Susan Reverby, a professor of history and women's and gender studies at Wellesley College, announced further evidence of unethical medical research. Her efforts of diving through the dusty coffers of medical archives in Pittsburgh resulted in the discovery and confirmation that the U.S. Public Health Service funded and conducted a syphilis inoculation program on over 5500 Guatemalan prisoners, mentally ill patients, and soldiers between 1946 and 1948.[6] Although similar to the Tuskegee and Willowbrook studies in that these study participants also did not provide consent, in this case, the Guatemalan authorities supposedly authorized the experiment on their own citizens, even though the United States funded the study and it occurred outside U.S. territory. Reverby's research findings spread like wildfire, gaining political attention in both countries. On September 30, 2010, President Barack Obama personally contacted President Alvaro Colom of Guatemala to apologize for the ethically unacceptable event and to offer his regrets for all those affected.[7] Further apologetic efforts were conducted by Secretary of State Hillary Clinton and by Health and Human Services head Kathleen Sebelius.[8]

Advancements in science and medicine are not possible without technology resources, and this technology requires thorough research and development initiatives. Moreover, new advancements in medicine often require approval by several regulatory or licensing authorities or both prior to acceptance and use in the U.S. healthcare industry. Researchers must complete these research and development steps in an ethical manner with complete transparency among all stakeholders involved, especially the research subjects. Ethics committees and review boards are necessary to offer third-party evaluation of proposed research studies, the subjects involved, and overall research methodologies. It is not just for a few uninformed or disadvantaged individuals to participate in an innovation's research and development process, even if a large population of beneficiaries may exist upon successful completion of such a study.

▶ Recent Innovations Involving Technology and Their Ethics Concerns

As new technological advances develop in the field of medicine, their availability, method of implementation, and even their existence itself often motivate questions regarding ethics and societal concerns. The initial research and development phases, as well as controlled implementation, require attentive healthcare leaders and ethics committees to ensure there is no violation of ethics principles. To demonstrate the potential ethics issues, selected advances in health care are discussed in this section. Although several ethics principles are addressed for each innovation, the author challenges the reader to identify additional principles that may apply to various situations involving these technological innovations.

Example #1: Synthetic Biology

One of the most recent and prominent fields that continues to develop from advances in both science and technology is that of synthetic biology. Posited from research studies involving molecular biology, this new genetic science builds on the initial discovery of the configuration of recombinant DNA molecules. It now allows scientists to replace the natural genetic material within a simple bacterial cell with synthetic (human-made), genetically copied material that is capable of self-replicating.[9] In other words, scientists have created non-genetic raw materials as a substitute for genetic material within a living organism (synthesized organism genes).

Since the May 20, 2010, announcement from the J. Craig Venter Institute, mixed opinions of this advance have surfaced, entailing both excitement and concern. The field of synthetic biology holds the promise of future advances in products related to several industries, including environmental pollution control, agriculture and food engineering, and the field of medicine.[10] On the other hand, because the fabrication of genetic materials from natural resources is a field still in its infancy, speculations and criticisms continue to surface, primarily as a result of the unknown future applications and consequences associated with this form of bioengineering. As a result, several ethics-based questions challenge the hastily growing science. These include the following:

- What agencies will be trusted with the oversight and regulation of this advancing science?

- Will unsupervised or non-affiliated organizations begin to replicate various organisms with synthetic genetic material for purposes that may pose harm to others?

- How does one regulate such an advanced, yet specialized, industry to ensure its purposeful use, while maintaining ethical research standards?

- As a more outrageous perspective, what will prevent the household biologist/chemist from fabricating his or her own genetic material in the secrecy of his or her private residence solely for individual motivations that do not match those of current regulatory standards?

Since the successful materialization of synthesized genetic biology, President Barack Obama requested that the Presidential Commission for the Study of Bioethical Issues investigate the field of synthetic biology and identify any ethics implications of the advancing science. A broad panel of experts, including science and engineering professionals, as well as faith-based and other secular ethicists, conducted a wide range of reviews.[11] Working to serve in a proactive manner by evaluating the ethics ramifications of the field while it is still in the developmental stages, the commission successfully identified and used five ethics principles to guide its investigation into the potential social implication of the emerging science. These principles were public beneficence, responsible stewardship, intellectual freedom, democratic deliberation, and justice and fairness.[12] The following is a brief explanation of each identified principle.

Public beneficence calls for the capitalization of overall public benefits from the science, while continuing to focus efforts on minimizing harm to the public. Similar to the main ethics principle of beneficence, public beneficence concerns the overall masses or the public populations who stand a chance to experience the gains or losses from the emerging science. These gains or losses may result from either a direct or an indirect nature. Therefore, the presidential commission has urged governments and scientific organizations to further the research and development of synthetic biology, while continuing to be increasingly aware of unintended consequences and potential harm to the public. The commission also recommended reviewing techniques for reducing research risks and the ethics implications of the science and publication of the results.[13] Support of future research and collaboration among professional organizations (e.g., the National Institutes of Health, the Department of Energy, academia, and other industrial groups) were deemed mandatory to help support public beneficence.[14] As a result, there is an intention of cooperation and transparency among all stakeholders involved to assist with protection of the masses.

Responsible stewardship directs ethics efforts toward ensuring that there is consideration of those unable to represent themselves throughout the emergence of future research studies and utilization of synthetically generated cellular material. Focusing specifically on future generations for both global and domestic communities, requirements of clarity, coordination, and accountability across governmental authorities were determined necessary to fulfill this ethics principle.[15] Therefore, all advances of the field must be clearly communicated to oversight committees and other invested stakeholders.

Furthermore, the coordinated effort should not include isolated, or lone-wolf, scientific efforts but, rather, a more collaborative and mission-centered effort. This will allow for continuous monitoring of the field's hurdles and achievements, as well as containment and prevention of ethics quandaries. In conclusion, the presidential commission also described strong recommendations related to ongoing ethics education for scientists and student

researchers in synthetic biology, as well as ongoing evaluation and reassessment of objections to the field itself.[16]

To assist in furthering the field of synthetic biology, the presidential commission called for *freedom of intellectual efforts,* while also ensuring the responsibility of all parties involved.[17] Specifically describing a moratorium on synthetic biology research as an inappropriate action, a compromise was suggested by the commission, therefore ensuring ongoing accountability through the use of periodic assessments and oversight controls.[18] As a result, the presidential commission called for a cautious freedom of study, to neither limit research efforts nor allow for unmonitored, uncontrolled research agendas. Allowing for debate among differing views, it suggested that *democratic deliberation* ensures representation from all societal groups and that they should be heard so that monitoring practices and policy-making may reflect the support of the public majority.

Finally, the commission addressed the promotion *of justice* and *fairness* with regard to those exposed to risks in synthetic biology research, as well as regarding commercial production and distribution efforts.[19] Following the main ethics principle of justice, certain individuals, groups, or communities are not to be subjected to research risks in an unfair manner. The same concept applies for the production or commercialization of synthetic products necessary to promote research in the field of synthetic biology.

Computer-Assisted and Robotic-Assisted Surgery

An area of medicine that continues to grow exponentially involves the use of technology, specifically computers and specialized peripherals, to assist medical providers during certain types of advanced surgical procedures. Computer-assisted technology, in addition to a central computer, may also include image-guided systems to allow the provider increased visibility and access to difficult procedural sites. Additionally, robotic surgery employs actual robotic equipment that functions as surgical assistants to the medical provider during surgical interventions. Virtually every field of medicine is implementing technological advances with varying levels of utilization. The following are examples of surgical specialties now performing procedures with heightened levels of computer-assisted or robotic-assisted surgeries:

- Stereotactic *radiosurgery*. Within the field of neurology/neurosurgery, physicians conduct an image-guided surgical procedure using various radiotherapy devices that strategically guide various levels of radiation at precise measurements into the brain to target both malignant and benign brain metastases.[20] Real-time radiography is typically used throughout the procedure to accurately position the instrument delivering the radiation. A device named the gamma knife delivers over 200 radiation beams into deep levels of the brain that are often inaccessible and unfeasible using conventional surgery techniques.[21]

- *Computer-aided maxillofacial surgery*. Medical providers are now realizing the increased benefits of computer-aided navigation systems, including three-dimensional (3D) systems, which allow for more accurate diagnosis and virtual planning. These systems provide increased intraoperative surgical navigation for orthognathic and temporomandibular joint surgeries.[22] This technology enables dental surgical providers to better visualize oral characteristics to ensure proper implant technique and ultimately enhanced patient outcomes. Recently, this technology created 3D images of the limited-view sinus cavities within the nasal cavity and nerves and vessels within the cavity to assist providers during complicated sinus surgeries.[23]

- *Robotic-assisted visceral surgery*. Researchers describe surgical laparoscopy of the abdomen as a more difficult procedure for the surgeon with regard to instrument

maneuverability, as well as the limited, two-dimensional vision.[24] Robot-assisted abdominal surgery, also known as tele-manipulation, has allowed surgeons to overcome these disadvantages of conventional laparoscopy. Additionally, these types of surgeries are often physically demanding for the medical providers involved. The use of robotics during surgery improves the surgeon's ergonomics during the procedure, as well as relieving other physical demands on the surgical staff members.[25]

Whereas the benefits of computer-assisted and robotic-assisted surgeries are evident, access to these highly technological devices remains quite limited. Often, healthcare facilities face challenges regarding the capital required to procure such equipment. Organizations may not be able to meet this cost and are therefore unable to provide such advanced procedures to their surrounding populations, affecting the potential for beneficent treatment for the community they serve.

The ethics principle of justice also becomes important when evaluating access to these potentially scarce health resources. Is it fair that only those patients capable of affording time away from work and of traveling to a remote site that offers such technology will benefit from its advantages over conventional surgical procedures? Furthermore, each procedure using computer-assisted or robotic-assisted surgery technology carries higher costs for the organization in an attempt to recover initial capital investment costs. Often, organizations pass this extravagant cost through to the patient, the patient's medical insurance carrier, or both. The result is inequality, because only those patients with ample financial resources or sufficient medical coverage may be able to afford these advanced surgical resources.

Continuous Advancements in Magnetic Resonance Imaging

Discoveries in diagnostic radiology have allowed physicians to identify disease and anatomic abnormalities within the body at a much more effective rate and accuracy than previously possible. One continuous drive for technological innovation to assist clinical diagnoses and medical outcomes persists within the field of magnetic resonance imaging (MRI). MRI innovations have consistently centered on the device's magnetic field strength, often termed *signal* and measured in tesla (T) units. Over the years, MRI equipment has progressed in signal strengths from 0.3T devices to 1.5T and 3T devices. Emerging research is striving to increase the signal strength to 7T and even to as much as 9.4T.[26] As signal strength increases, the image quality is enhanced and there is a possibility for shorter exam times. Although this increased signal strength may seem advantageous to the patient and assist the diagnostic effectiveness of the physician, several ethics concerns regarding the significantly expensive capital investment required for these devices remain present for both hospitals and ambulatory radiology facilities. As a result, the decision to acquire such an advanced imaging device, as well as the ethical use of the enhanced technology, requires assessment at multiple levels.

The decision for a healthcare organization to invest in an advanced MRI machine is not a simple one. It involves extensive due diligence and market research by organizational leadership to ensure that the capital investment fits directly into the organization's strategic plan. Currently, a 3T MRI machine is the most advanced MRI equipment approved for the medical treatment of humans. Higher-tesla MRI machines do exist, demonstrating faster, increased-quality images, but these devices are still in the testing and research phases and are not yet available for routine use in the medical treatment of patients. However, the 3T MRI machine does possess advantages over its predecessor and medical imaging workhorse, the 1.5T MRI machine.

Enter "3T MRI" into any Internet search engine, and the results will include several healthcare organizations advertising the advanced imaging capabilities now available with their newly procured 3T MRI machines. These boasted advantages are often compared with competitors' 1.5 MRI machines, which remain the current industry standard in MRI procedures. Comments such as "better-quality images" and "faster, more accurate diagnoses" are the most often displayed comments. As a result, the decision to acquire a 3T MRI machine may be highly influenced by an organization's marketing strategy, primarily to elevate the organization's medical technology and promote its increased diagnostic capabilities over local market competition.

Although market position is a vital component in the strategic plan of most organizations, should the decision to invest in new medical equipment rely so heavily on the desire of an organization to stand out as a more technologically advanced institution? Given continually shrinking operational revenue margins for both profit and not-for-profit sectors, would this capital investment (often $1 to $1.5 million more expensive than the standard 1.5T MRI machine) truly benefit the surrounding community? Many medical providers will base such decisions on the premise of deontology, believing that there is an obligation or duty for medical providers to be able to provide the best medical care possible, even if it is only benefiting patients with a specific diagnosis. Conversely, many healthcare administrators will assess this situation from a utilitarian viewpoint, deciding whether to invest in the new MRI technology on the basis of the overall benefit to the community and which decision would help provide ample imaging services to the most patients.[27]

The 3T MRI machine is capable of generating lower, 1.5T-quality images but in less time than the regular 1.5T machine. As a result, the possibility of increased patient throughput exists when the 3T MRI machine is used to generate images at the 1.5T signal strength.[28] The actual time difference in image generation between the 3T and 1.5T MRI machines is marginal in an individual instance. However, over time, the increased patient throughput will ultimately result in increased operational revenue for the organization, which will aid in covering the additional expense of the advanced 3T technology.[29] The decision regarding whether to use 1.5T or 3T imaging capability rests with the medical provider ordering the MRI for the patient, as well as the radiologist's expertise.

However, one must question the motivations of medical providers when using this new imaging technology in such a manner. For example, the decision to generate a reduced-quality image on the 3T MRI machine for purposes of increasing patient throughput creates ethics dilemmas with regard to quality of care, especially if the patient or referring medical provider picked that facility to perform the original MRI because of its advertised 3T advanced imaging capability (therefore potentially becoming a bait-and-switch technique). Furthermore, those patients who receive a 1.5T MRI exam that does not provide an image capable of diagnosis may then require a second, duplicate MRI procedure at the 3T image quality level. Questions of cost-effectiveness and the efficient use of medical resources arise when the same medical organization conducts repeat exams.

Currently, most healthcare payers, including Medicare and commercial insurance, are contemplating reimbursement for MRI procedures on the basis of the signal strength utilized. Some commercial healthcare payers may provide slightly higher reimbursement for a 3T MRI versus the standard 1.5T MRI procedure. This reimbursement difference depends on the medical provider's individual contract with any specific managed care organization, as well as the state in which the procedure was performed.[30] However, with no specific medical coding method to document the signal strength used for an MRI procedure, the possibility exists for a medical provider to perform a 1.5T exam and inadvertently receive the 3T image reimbursement. This occurrence will result in an overpayment to the provider, which still experiences increased patient throughput by performing the lower-level 1.5T MRI procedure.

Finally, those payers who do not reimburse more for the 3T MRI may influence medical providers to perform more 1.5T images on the 3T MRI machine to take advantage of the quicker exam time and increased patient throughput.[31] This technique was often used in order to make up the lost radiology revenue that resulted from the Deficit Reduction Act of 2005, which included strict cuts to radiology procedures.[32] In this instance, it is highly unethical for the 1.5T MRI exam to be used if the 3T MRI was initially deemed necessary to properly diagnose the patient and the lower-quality exam was simply used to increase patient throughput to enhance overall operational revenue from the 3T MRI machine. As demonstrated, one must question ethics when one makes clinical decisions such as which MRI processes to use solely on the basis of operational and financial incentives.

IBM Watson: Cognitive Health Care

Named after IBM's founder and not Sherlock Holmes's trusted friend, the IBM Watson supercomputer is offering groundbreaking innovations within the field of healthcare decision-making. Utilizing both structured and unstructured data, this computer is capable of reviewing not only millions of pages of text from medical school and research laboratory coffers within seconds, but it also continues to learn from interacting with the natural languages of humans. This supercomputer also offers ongoing algorithms to provide potential diagnoses for the patient and probabilities for each recommendation.

While some early research suggests that IBM Watson's capabilities can replace the medical physician in the clinic or hospital, other literature suggests that this supercomputer is simply a beneficial treatment aid or assistant in the diagnosing process and the individual physician can never be truly replaced. One thing is for sure—the cognitive computer continues to make large strides in advancement daily, while certainly questioning the autonomy of the individual medical provider.[33–35]

▶ HIT and the Medical Group Practice

It is an understatement to say that the field of HIT is growing at a rapid pace. With medical hardware and software becoming outdated or obsolete in months, or even days, after their clinical procurement and implementation, the HIT industry continues to focus on adapting computers and associated technology for increasing productivity, ease of reporting mechanisms, and improvement of quality outcomes for patients at an unimaginable rate. To further this rush toward technological implementation in our hospitals, clinics, and other healthcare organizations, recent legislation has added an increased pressure to establish appropriate HIT use within the organization.

The MACRA of 2015

Seen as an update to the previous Patient Protection and Affordable Care Act (ACA 2010), the MACRA possesses many unique healthcare provider and organization initiatives for payment reform that continue to identify questionable ethics principles as ongoing implementation continues.[36,37] In an attempt to provide more of a pay-for-performance (P4P) reimbursement methodology, the Medicare program has established a unique financial environment for healthcare leaders to manage within, and for healthcare providers to care for patients within, all in an attempt to provide higher quality care for the patient in the end.

While explanation of all specific details of the updated MACRA is beyond the scope of this chapter, the following ethics principles come into question (many initially unforeseen) as implementation continues:

- *Respect for autonomy of medical providers.* Medical provider profiling is greatly

enhanced as a result of this legislation. Medical providers, and also the organizations for which they work, are evaluated against each other with regard to both efficiency and effectiveness of medical care rendered to patients. Ongoing provider performance evaluation and adherence to the organization's (or external) best-practice protocols for any specific diagnosed medical condition often question the individual autonomy of the medical provider when otherwise recommended treatment goes "off script."[38,39]

- *Neutral budget legislation and the question of justice.* While MACRA MIPS reimbursement track simply provides a potential Medicare payment bonus for participating providers, it may make sense for the provider (or organization) to enter into an alternate reimbursement track with Medicare: APMs. However, MACRA was passed as budget-neutral, meaning that it must fund itself and not create any additional expense for the Medicare program. Therefore, when organizations decide to enter into the APM reimbursement track, they will be competing against other healthcare organizations across the country on various healthcare quality measures.[40,41] As a result, this program immediately creates two groups of participating organizations, questioning the overall fairness (justice) of the system: winners and losers.[42] The winners are those organizations that Medicare has deemed exceptional in performance metrics, while the losers are those who end up in the bottom rung of the performance output (when adjusted for organization type/size/other demographics).

- *Individual provider intent and nonmaleficence.* After all of the details of MACRA are sorted out by the healthcare organization and participating providers, the questions of practice treatment patterns and individual medical provider actions become important to healthcare stakeholders—as to what is driving the underlying motivation for effective and efficient performance in medicine? With most ACOs (one type of APM) failing to demonstrate shared savings in the Medicare program in 2015–2016,[43] the incorporation of reimbursement (or lack thereof) allows one to question, what is the basis for provider decisions during the treatment process? Do decisions contribute to nonmaleficence, or are they part of a complicated reimbursement program based on specific measures that may or may not be aligned with any current patient's treatment needs?

As MACRA continues to be implemented and the 2017 reporting period's data is captured to assess reimbursement penalties (or rewards), ongoing scrutiny of the program's intent continues to surface among healthcare leaders and medical providers. Its complicated reimbursement methodology does not help with implementation, while the underlying ethics principles mentioned above certainly come into question.

The Decision to Forego Electronic Health Records

The legislative and financial pressures to implement the use of EHR technology within the medical group practice are often enough to allow this process to become a line item on the agenda for organizational strategic planning meetings. However, as important and necessary as EHRs are, as the Centers for Medicare and Medicaid Services (CMS) has established, some medical providers have made the decision to opt out of the Medicare EHR incentive program, foregoing incentive payments and making plans to accept the upcoming payment reductions as a normal business expense. In other words, they have chosen not to invest in an EHR, thus remaining with paper medical records throughout their tenure as medical professionals. This decision is often made by medical providers concerned with their individual

competencies regarding computers and technology. Their concerns include the overwhelming capital expense of EHR purchase, follow-on training, and implementation expenses and the potential retirement perspective of the physician owner. These concerns mean that some medical practices have yet to implement EHR technology into their patient care processes and do not intend to do so, regardless of the financial disincentives to come.

Quality-of-care concerns have surfaced, questioning medical providers' ability to access, organize, successfully document, and report on patient care quality without an EHR system.[44] Additional advantages of an EHR system are also sacrificed, such as CDSS and e-prescribing (e-Rx). The following are examples of issues that may occur in the medical practice when it does not implement an EHR:[45]

- Patient allergy information is less accessible, and lack of e-Rx capability may result in prescribing of incorrect medications, as well as contradictory medications.
- There can be illegible physician orders, leading to dosing errors or other medical errors.
- It is possible to overlook important information within a large paper medical record that an appropriately utilized EHR will not miss.

Whereas the rush to EHR implementation primarily involves a question of the principle of beneficence, the decision to forego EHR implementation in its entirety may contradict the principle of nonmaleficence. There may be harm to those patients receiving care from a medical provider utilizing paper medical records, committing one of the example errors previously mentioned. Additionally, this omission of technology closely relates to negligence on behalf of the medical provider and organizational leadership. Regardless of the reasons for deciding against EHR adoption and implementation soon, or at all, the medical provider must consider the ethics principles of beneficence and nonmaleficence when choosing to disregard the proven quality-of-care benefits received from this technology.

Privacy Implications of HIT

Coincidentally, one of the primary benefits of HIT and EHRs can actually be a severe disadvantage and legal liability for the healthcare organization. Since the inception of the EHR, several data breaches have occurred, allowing inappropriate individuals to access individual, confidential, private health information (PHI). In some cases, there was purposeful leaking of this information into the public's view. Instead of being a single and tangible paper medical record that can be physically secured via lock and key, an EHR often allows access through several information technology (IT) resources, including desktops, laptops, tablet computers, and smartphone devices. This increased accessibility of PHI has allowed the following Health Information Portability and Accountability Act (HIPAA) violations to occur:

- A theft of a password-protected, but non-encrypted, desktop computer containing the PHI for over 4.24 million patients from a Sutter Health medical office occurred in Sacramento, California, in November 2011.[46] As a result, a suit was filed against the organization for over $1000 per patient record leaked, primarily because Sutter failed to notify the patients of the occurrence.[47]
- University of California–Los Angeles (UCLA) hospitals were sued and required to pay close to $1 million in penalties for the breach of over six celebrity medical record files, including those of the late Farrah Fawcett and Michael Jackson.[48] This case did not involve a missing computer but rather forensic IT research within the EHR system, providing documentation that UCLA Medical Center employees with no medical reason to access these specific patients' medical records did so without proper authorization.

- Kaiser Permanente fired 15 employees, and 8 others underwent disciplinary and training actions when the medical records of Nadya Suleman (the "Octomom") were accessed without medical need or authorization.[49] Afterward, it was claimed that the media frenzy that resulted was highly influenced by these employees sneaking peeks at this patient's medical records and relaying this PHI to unauthorized parties.

Regardless of whether an EHR system exists or the medical organization continues to rely on paper medical records, patients should not have to worry about the proper security and access of their PHI by the appropriate medical providers and administrative staff. It is the organization's fiduciary duty to uphold the highest security precautions, while also providing continuous education for all employees regarding the protection and limited access of patients' PHI.

An individual's medical history is a highly sensitive area and should be limited to only those who need to know. Most EHR systems will allow records to be locked from all employees, minus a select few. This option can help protect privacy by limiting access to those medical records of high interest, such as the "Octomom's," but this does not fully prevent the abuse of privacy if those leaders with continuous access abuse the system in an unethical manner. Confidentiality has been a huge criticism, even a black eye, of HIT developments and implementations over the past couple of years. Further security innovations are required as more electronic devices allow providers the capability to access such information through remote networks. Additionally, ethical leadership and ongoing training of providers and staff continues to remain a mandatory requirement during the use of this technological resource.

▶ Summary

Technological resources have allowed the medical industry to treat more medical diseases and ailments at a much more effective level, while also ensuring earlier diagnoses and less complicated treatment processes with quicker recovery periods. The overall benefits of implementing technology into medicine have easily outweighed any disadvantages, although it has not been without the negation of various ethics principles along the way. Learning from these previous, failed methodologies will allow the medical researcher to establish beneficial technological resources and also to do so in an appropriate manner, respecting individual autonomy.

Questions immediately arise regarding ethics and medical-related technology: Where does the common ground exist between the medical provider's deontological viewpoints and the healthcare administrator's utilitarian beliefs? What communities, and even individuals within each community, are to benefit from such technology? How are those individuals whose providers use new technology protected from privacy breaches and other PHI implications? It is the ethics committee's responsibility to evaluate all of these processes and potential outcomes to ensure that future ethics ramifications are not on tomorrow's front page. Although healthcare revenues are currently incapable of covering additional liability expenses related to ethics implications, the organization cannot afford to fail to uphold its fiduciary duty to address ethics before, during, and throughout all technology implementations. Simply laying technological advances over existing healthcare processes will not work, and process redesign must involve a fresh look at ethics to ensure the highest respect for all stakeholders involved.

▶ Questions for Review

1.   Healthcare technology shows promise for great benefit for patients and providers. However, there are also ethics concerns that need to be developed as these advances become part of the system. Choose an example of a new technology from this chapter or from your research. Discuss two ethics concerns that adapters of this technology must consider. Think about the investment costs of advanced healthcare technology. What ethics theories can administrators use to defend the investment required to implement new technologies?

2.   Use your imagination and describe a healthcare technology that you would like to see invented. Assume your dream technology is developed. What ethics issues would you face to implement your technology? Who should be able to use it, and why should they have access to it?

▶ Notes

1.   E. E. Morrison, *Ethics in Health Administration*, 2nd ed. (Sudbury, MA: Jones & Bartlett Learning, 2011).

2.   Centers for Disease Control and Prevention, "U.S. Public Health Service Syphilis Study at Tuskegee," June 15, 2011, http://www.cdc.gov/tuskegee/timeline.htm.

3.   Morrison, *Ethics in Health Administration*.

4.   Education Development Center, "Willowbrook Hepatitis Experiments," in *Exploring Bioethics* (Richmond, VA: Educational Development Center, 2009), http://science.education.nih.gov/supplements/nih9/bioethics/guide/pdf/Master_5-4.pdf.

5.   C. Sia et al., "History of the Medical Home Concept," *Pediatrics* 113, no. 4 (2004): 1473–78.

6.   L. Kasdon, "Presidential Panel Slams 1940s Guatemalan STD Study: Alum's Research Leads to International Condemnation of Experiments," *BU Today*, August 31, 2011, http://www.bu.edu/today/2011/presidential-panel-slams-guatemalan-sdt-study.

7.   Ibid.

8. Ibid.

9. J. Craig Venter Institute, "First Self-Replicating Synthetic Bacterial Cell," http://www.jcvi.org/cms/research/projects/first-self-replicating-synthetic-bacterial-cell/overview/.

10. Presidential Commission for the Study of Bioethical Issues, *New Directions: The Ethics of Synthetic Biology and Emerging Technologies* (Washington, DC: Presidential Commission for the Study of Bioethical Issues, December 2010), http://bioethics.gov/cms/synthetic-biology-report.

11. Ibid.

12. Ibid.

13. Ibid.

14. Ibid.

15. Ibid.

16. Ibid.

17. Ibid.

18. Ibid.

19. Ibid.

20. Johns Hopkins Medicine, "Stereotactic Radiosurgery," http://www.radonc.jhmi.edu/radiosurgery/treatmentoptions/stereotacticradiosurgery.html.

21. Johns Hopkins Medicine, "What Is the Gamma Knife?," http://www.hopkins-medicine.org/neurology_neurosurgery/specialty_areas/brain_tumor/treatment/gamma-knife.html.

22. Y. Jayaratne, R. Zwahlen, L. Lo, S. Tam, and L. Cheung, "Computer-Aided Maxillofacial Surgery: An Update," *Surgical Innovation* 17, no. 3 (2010): 217–25.

23. New York University, "Sinus Surgery at NYU Otolaryngology," http://ent.med.nyu.edu/patient-services/rhinology/sinus_surgery. Accessed July 6, 2012.

24. C. N. Gutt et al., "Robot-Assisted Abdominal Surgery," *British Journal of Surgery* 91 (2004): 1390–97.

25. Ibid.

26. R. Bell, "The Quest for Improved Image Quality, the Need for Efficiency, and Declining Reimbursement Will Shape the Burgeoning MRI Market Well into the Future," *Imaging Economics*, December 2004, http://www.imagingeconomics.com/issues/articles/2004-12_02.asp.

27. A. Montagnolo, "The Imaging Question: Are Advances in MRI Technology and CT Scanners Worth the Investment?" *Trustee*, June 2011, 25–26.

28. D. Harvey, "3T: It's in the Way That You Use It," *Imaging Economics*, November 2004, http://www.imagingeconomics.com/issues/articles/MI_2004-11_06.asp.

29. D. Hinesly, "Expanding Business and Clinical Options Using 3T MRI," *Imaging Economics*, December 2006, http://www.imagingeconomics.com/issues/articles/2006-12_15.asp.

30. Harvey, "3T."

31. S. Wallask, "Higher-Quality MRIs Raise Questions about Costs and Reimbursement," *HealthLeaders Media*, July 14, 2009, http://www.healthleadersmedia.com/content/235903/topic/WS_HLM2_TEC/Higherquality-MRIs-Raise-Questions-about-Costs-and-Reimbursement.html##.

32. Hinesly, "Expanding Business and Clinical Options."

33. S. Nayak et al., "Artificial Intelligence in Clinical Research," *International Journal of Clinical Trials* 3, no. 4 (2016): 187–93.

34. K. Y. Lee and J. Kim, "Artificial Intelligence Technology Trends and IBM Watson References in the Medical Field," *Korean Medical Education Review* 6, no. 2 (2016):51–57.

35. M. A. Bauer and D. Berleant, "Usability Survey of Biomedical Question Answering Systems," *Human Genomics* 6, no. 1 (2005): 1.

36. K. S. Held, "New Medicare Payment Rule: A Trojan Horse for Government Takeover," *Journal of American Physicians and Surgeons* 2, no. 3 (2016): 87–90.

37. D. K. Bonnell, "Health Care Fraud across Time and Delivery Systems:

Assessing the Legal Impact of the Affordable Care Act," *Master's thesis* (2016), scholarworks.gvsu.edu /thesis/822.

38. Y. Xu, and P. S. Wells, "Getting (along) with the Guidelines: Reconciling the Patient Autonomy and Quality Improvement through Shared Decision-Making," *Journal of the Association of American Medical Colleges* 91, no. 7 (July 2016): 925–29.

39. M. Roland, and F. Olesen, "Can Pay for Performance Improve the Quality of Primary Care?" *British Medical Journal* 354, no. i4058 (2016): 1–4.

40. O. Avitzur, "In Practice: Five New (Ish) Acronyms That Are Changing Physician Payment: How They Will Affect You," *Neurology Today* 16, no. 5 (2016): 10–11.

41. R. J. Zall et al., "MACRA: Quality-based Payment and ItsImplications for Stakeholders," *American Bankruptcy Institute Journal* 35, no. 11 (2016): 16.

42. S. A. Farmer et al. McClellan, "Existing and Emerging Payment and Delivery Reforms in Cardiology," *Journal of the American Medical Association Cardiology* (November, 2016), doi:10.1001 /jamacardio.2016.

43. B. A. Kash, "Interview with Eric S Weaver, FACHE, FACMPE, FHIMSS, President of the Central Texas Market for Innovista Health Solutions," *Journal of Healthcare Management* 61, no. 4 (2016): 245.

44. R. Yates, "Is it Unethical Not to Use an EHR?" *MGMA Connection* 9, no. 10 (2009): 23–24.

45. Ibid.

46. K. Robertson, "Sutter Health Says Patient Data Was Stolen," *Sacramento Business Journal* (November 16, 2011), http:// www.bizjournals.com/sacramento /news/2011/11/16/sutter-heatlh-laptop -patient-data-stolen.html.

47. D. Smith, "Sutter Health Sued over Theft of Computer Containing Patient Data," *The Sacramento Bee* (November 23, 2011), http://www.mercurynews .com/breaking-news/ci_19398492.

48. C. Clark, "Six Major Patient Record Breaches Draw $675,000 in Penalties," *HealthLeaders Media* (June 11, 2010), http://www.healthleadersmedia.com /page-1/LED-252360/Six-Major-Patient -Record-Breaches-Draw-675000-In -Penalties##.

49. B. Monegain, "Breach into 'Octuplet Mom's' Medical Records Highlights Privacy Issues Again," *HealthCare IT News* (March 31, 2009), http://www .healthcareitnews.com/news/breach -octuplet-moms-medical-records -highlights-privacy-issues-again.

CHAPTER 9

Ethics and Safe Patient Handling and Mobility

Beth Furlong

▶ Introduction

A safety, professional, legal, and ethical concern for patients, family members, and interprofessional health providers is safe patient handling and mobility (SPHM) of the patient and prevention of physical injuries to all three groups. After presenting background data on the concerns of this issue, the ethics implications of this dimension of the healthcare delivery system will be presented. While this chapter applies to all interprofessional health providers, a major emphasis with examples will be on the practice of nursing because of this chapter author being a nurse. Nurses are also featured in this chapter because nursing aides, licensed practical nurses, and registered nurses have the most injuries of the interprofessionals in health care.

▶ Extent of the Problem

The following data describe the extent of some of the problems for nurses, patients, and family members when SPHM practices are not implemented. This concern is not new; in 1994, a recommendation was given by the National Institute for Occupational Safety and Health (NIOSH) regarding lifting. The equation basically meant that a 35 lb. limit was to be used in patient care lifting, repositioning, transfers, etc. That agency had previously published practice guides in 1981 and 1985.[1] In 2000, the Nurses Strategic Action Team (N-STAT) of the American Nurses Association (ANA) was educating members to advocate with their congressional representatives to have Occupational Safety and Health Act (OSHA) ergonomics standards "to compel employers, who ironically are in the business of health and often profiting from it, to prevent debilitating disease occurrence in their own employees."[2] Both OSHA and NIOSH have endorsed an ergonomics standards approach; however, the availability and use of equipment vary much across the health system.[3] The variability is not only in hospitals but also in nursing homes, home health care, clinics, etc. For example, for the nurses who participated in the ANA's Health Risk Appraisal conducted in 2013–2014, 42% evaluated being at risk in lifting or repositioning patients, 13% had a major musculoskeletal injury, and while 75% had access to SPHM technology, only about 35% used it consistently.[4]

There are many barriers to the implementation of best practices in this aspect of the healthcare system. First, many health professionals do not have the knowledge and still rely on the myth of use of "good body mechanics," gait belts, etc.[5] A second barrier to the utilization of an SPHM program and its equipment is that researched about rehabilitation personnel: they perceived use of such equipment furthers patient dependence and there will not be the same functional outcomes for the patients.[6] In a study of 94 patients who had strokes, the group of patients for whom SPHM equipment was used had equal or better functional outcomes at the time of discharge than the other group without such usage.[7] In addition, Arnold noted the importance of influencing this particular member of the health team because rehabilitation professionals are perceived as experts in mobility; if they are furthering non-evidence-based care, many suffer.[8]

A third barrier is the intersection of two factors, that is, the high injury rate to four types of caregivers (certified nurse aides, licensed practical nurses, registered nurses, and health aides) and the majority of these individuals being women. For example, in 2004, 94% of registered nurses were women; their average age was 47, and they had less back and upper-extremity strength than men.[9] Yet, they are the main caregivers engaged in transferring, lifting, repositioning, and moving patients. A fourth barrier is equipment—whether it is available, working, easy to access, and/or utilized. Relative to the discrepancy, the ANA Health Risk Appraisal reported information concerning the availability of SPHM equipment and its consistent use. ANA leaders recognize the many questions that have to be addressed regarding this. For example, have health providers been educated in the usage? Are there aspects to particular unit work cultures that decrease health providers' use of the equipment? Is there enough staffing for use of

the technology? Is the equipment easily accessible? Is the equipment working?

While 82% of nurses report that job stress is a major health concern for them, the next highest-ranked health concern at 45% is the lifting and repositioning they do.[10] Related to this self-reporting is that the average nurse is overweight, with a body mass index of 28.[11] When caregivers manually lift patients, this is an estimated 3600 lb. per shift. The ANA has recommended 10 health practices to further the health status of those in the nursing profession; one of these is to use the appropriate equipment when moving patients.[12] Data in 2003 reported that there was a 75% risk of injury for each manual lift of patients; this resulted in 52% of health professionals reporting chronic back pain, 38% having back injuries that required time off from the job, 20% of employees who transferred to non-lifting and non-repositioning jobs, and 12% of professionals who left their profession because of the injury.[13]

Of the top 10 professions that are most likely to experience work-related back injuries, 6 are within the health system.[14] This is the ranking of the 10 worker classifications having the most injuries, with the certified nursing assistant having the most. Next, in descending order, are construction workers, garbage collectors, licensed vocational nurses, truck drivers, registered nurses, health aides, machinists, radiology technicians, and physical therapists. A 2014 report demonstrated that 13% of nurses have had debilitating musculoskeletal injuries.[15] The importance of having available SPHM equipment is demonstrated by 2017 reporting data by the Centers for Medicare and Medicaid Services *Hospital Compare Report*: when such equipment was available, there were higher ratings of quality care delivered, a lower rate of missed-care events, and fewer patient falls.[16]

▶ Problem-Solving

There have been many endeavors to further an SPHM work culture. First, many interprofessional health professionals are both members of and active in the Association of Safe Patient Handling Professionals (ASPHP). For example, one indicator of their engagement is the number of nearly 300 individuals who are now certified, either as professional or as associate by this association. The association is also developing a third certification for those professionals whose job responsibilities are predominantly clinical. The value of certification is not only to patient care and the health professional but also to the healthcare system and state budgets; this value can be seen in the following example. Research done by the AON organization showed that when less than 25% of employees in organizations were certified, there was a 75% higher workman's compensation cost (Vicki Missar, personal communication, April 15, 2017). This study was conducted on 1600 facilities, which had $40 billion in payroll and $2.4 billion in losses with regard to safe patient-handling injuries (Vicki Missar, personal communication, April 15, 2017).

Another example related to costs is that reported by the ANA: hospitals that have successful programs save between $27,000 and $103,000 yearly by avoiding a nurse turnover rate.[17] A study done on two hospitals reflected cost savings when an SPHM program was implemented. In these hospitals, 1832 health professionals were studied; for the hospital that had the program, there were 32% fewer neck and shoulder injuries, 27% fewer lifting and exertion injuries, and 22% fewer pain and inflammation symptom reporting.[18] For the hospital without the program, there were no significant changes in decreasing injury rates.

Second, a 3-year study of the nationwide veterans' hospital system was done between 2008 and 2011. There were important reductions in musculoskeletal injuries that correlated with these four variables: availability of SPHM equipment, competency assessment of employees, peer leadership training and utilization, and new employee orientation.[19] Such equipment included ceiling-mounted lifts, floor-based lifts, slings, and lateral transfer devices. The Veterans Health Administration has been a leader, historically and currently, in the promotion of the use of equipment to transfer, lift, and reposition and move patients. For example, in 1998, it developed an injury prevention program in eight of its medical centers, with positive results in reduction of severe injuries.[20] Further, at the current time, the Veterans Affairs (VA) system is an important facilitator of the yearly ASPHP conference.

A third example is the number of states that have passed a variety of legislative bills, which is 11 states.[21] Texas was the first state to enact legislation, in 2006.[22] A fourth example of addressing the challenge is that of the ANA; in 2003, it launched a Handle with Care campaign.[23] Since then it has worked closely with the ASPHP and published the *Safe Patient Handling and Mobility: Inter-professional National Standards Across the Care Continuum* in 2013. It also conducted an environmental scan in 2015 to best learn current practices, designated a Culture of Safety as the National Nurses' Week theme in 2016 and launched in 2017 as a Year of the Healthy Nurse.[24-27] A fifth example is national legislation: in 2015, four representatives introduced the Nurse and Health Care Worker bill (in 2006 a bill had also been introduced).[28] Members of the ASPHP continue seeking more congressional sponsors for the 2015 bill (Colin Brigham, personal communication, April 21, 2016).

▶ Ethics Concerns

The preceding paragraphs have identified one safety, professional, legal, and ethical problem in the healthcare system. This latter part of the chapter will address some specific ethics concerns with this issue. Registered nurses have both a professional and an ethical mandate to be patient advocates—for the patient and for having an influence in changing the health system.[29] Nurses are to remove existing barriers to best practices of health care and to further other best practices for the future. Some of these best practices are to apply the science, knowledge, technology, and use of equipment for the safe handling, movement, and mobility of patients.

Because of the increasing emphasis on inter-professional healthcare teams by the Institute of Medicine, these advocacy behaviors need to extend to other health professionals, specifically physical therapists, occupational therapists, certified nursing assistants, etc., as they, too, are directly involved in the movement, transfer, and mobility of patients.[30]

In addition, registered nurses are to apply the *Code of Ethics for Nurses* of the ANA.[31] There are specific provisions that address the kinds of responsibility and accountability nurses have relative to SPHM. Provision 6 states, "The nurse participates in establishing, maintaining, and improving healthcare environments and conditions of employment conducive to the provision of quality health care and consistent with the values of the profession through individual and collective action."[32]

Several of the classic ethics concepts undergird the rationale for implementing and advocating for SPHM best practices—nonmaleficence, beneficence, and social justice.[33] Each of these will be discussed in more detail. In the medical, clinical, and health areas of life and illness, the first one (i.e., nonmaleficence, or "do no harm") is the cardinal and singular ethics concept. That practice is the first behavior that health providers need to follow when caring for patients. When interprofessional health providers do not use the now-available evidence-based research, technology, and equipment for the SPHM of patients, they are not engaged in nonmaleficence. Further, if they do not educate patients and family members in this regard, make the necessary referrals, change systems and units in which they work, etc., they have harmed not only the patient but also the patient's caregivers and themselves. As noted, in implementing provision 6 of the *Code of Ethics for Nurses*, nurses have a responsibility not only in direct individual patient care but also in creating work cultures and policies that facilitate best practices and nonmaleficence

of patients, family members, and team health providers.

The second concept (i.e., beneficence) is that of doing the best for another.[34] While it has parallels to the first ethics concept for the betterment of the patient, it goes beyond doing no harm to furthering the best interests of not only the patient but also family members and health providers. Given other ethical values of being respectful of all and demonstrating dignity to all, practicing beneficence with these three groups of individuals also reflects that one is being respectful and demonstrating dignity for the essence of each individual. Summers notes that beneficence "requires healthcare practitioners to put patients' interests before their own."[35]

While this theme is accurate in most situations, there are nuances with the concept of SPHM. One example is that patients are, at times, dependent on family members and health professionals for their healing. If the latter two groups do not take care of themselves and utilize best practices in their care of patients, the patient's care and healing can decrease. This is not ethical stewardship. Examples could be family members and health professionals who are injured in their patient care and no longer able to care for the patient. Further, health professionals may have to undergo surgery and rehabilitation, may choose or have to leave their chosen profession of direct patient care, etc.

Besides short-term staffing concerns in affected organizational units, loss of educated staff has implications for healthcare costs in the health system. This is because of increased costs for new employees and for costs of the loss of educated staff in individual professions such as registered nurses. One example in a large Midwestern city is a black male former registered nurse now working in a grocery store delicatessen because of an orthopedic injury he had during the transfer of a patient. Men only represent 10% of the nursing profession, and blacks only represent 10% of the nursing profession; thus, cultural and gender diversity for patient care has lessened even more.[36] In summary, it is to the advantage of all three groups (patients, family members, and health providers) if SPHM equipment is used in the care of patients. One would be practicing beneficence and also demonstrating the basic ethical values of being respectful and showing dignity for the uniqueness of each individual.

These two cardinal ethics concepts of nonmaleficence and beneficence then lead to a concern with social justice, as noted in the previous example. If all three groups (patients, family members, and health professionals) are not attentive to the best practices of SPHM, there are social justice ramifications.[37] As noted in this chapter, justice implications could be (1) increased costs to society and to the healthcare system because of workmen's compensation, health insurance costs, orientation for replacement of employees, etc.; (2) nondiversity of employees to best meet the needs of diverse patients; (3) individual human suffering among many within the three groups of patients, family members, and health providers; and (4) nonutilization of one's knowledge base when such evidence-based knowledge is available.

▶ Summary

In summary, this chapter describes one problem within the healthcare system: SPHM. After describing the extent of the problem and strategies for addressing the challenges, three ethics theories are applied as a rationale for why best practices need to be followed by health professionals. The chapter concludes with four examples of other current strategies to meet these ethics concerns. The first is a state nursing organization promoting many aspects of healthy living for nurses, that is, the Nebraska Nurses Association (NNA). The Director of State Affairs of the NNA has educated and encouraged members to utilize the ANA website as a resource in their advocacy efforts in their particular work settings.[38]

A second example is a 2017 regional conference initiated by the ASPHP held in a large Midwestern city in which nurses shared with one another the kinds of specific behaviors they implement in their work settings to both best apply use of SPHM equipment directly in their patient care and change the work cultures to have consistent use of the equipment. Third, in one Midwestern city and state, the local informal SPHM city and state leader is the Safe Patient Champion of a VA hospital. She furthers best practices in that VA hospital, initiates regional conferences in the state, facilitates networking among health professionals throughout the state, and has initiated contact with four baccalaureate nursing schools. She gives lectures to all of their students and provides some clinical learning for them at a VA hospital so that they can experience and work with SPHM equipment. Fourth, at a national level, NIOSH and the Veterans Health Administration have partnered to work with 26 schools of nursing to further SPHM curricula. Further, they are working to increase the number of questions on the national nursing licensure examination about SPHM.[39] Nurses, at the individual, organizational, and policy advocacy levels, are living the ethics concepts of nonmaleficence, beneficence, and social justice.

▶ Questions for Discussion

1. What are the ethics arguments for advocacy of SPHM programs and behaviors?

2. Are there ethics arguments for not promoting SPHM programs and behaviors?

3. For the professional role you have in the health system, what are the implications of this chapter for you?

▶ **Notes**

1. T. R. Waters, "When Is It Safe to Manually Lift a Patient," *American Journal of Nursing* 107, no. 8 (2007): 53–58.

2. N-STAT Action Alert, November 8, 2000.

3. G. Powell-Cope et al., "Effects of a National Safe Patient Handling Program on Nursing Injury Incidence Rates," *Journal of Nursing Administration* 44, no. 10 (2014): 525–33.

4. R. Francis and J. M. Dawson, "Safe Patient Handling and Mobility: The Journey Continues," *American Nurse Today* 11, no. 5 (2016): 38.

5. ANA/SPHM Brochure, "Safe Patient Handling and Mobility: Understanding the Benefits of a Comprehensive SPHM Program," (2015).

6. M. Arnold et al., "Changes in Functional Independence Measure Ratings Associated with a Safe Patient Handling and Movement Program," *Rehabilitation Nursing* 36, no. 4 (2011): 138–44.

7. Ibid., 138.

8. Ibid., 139.

9. Waters, "When Is It Safe?"

10. H. Carpenter, "ANA's Health Risk Appraisal: Three Years Later," *American Nurse Today* 12, no. 1 (2017): 15.

11. "Be Healthy" *American Nurse Today* 12, no. 1 (2017):19.

12. Ibid.

13. Atlas Lift Tech vendor page in the Safe Patient Handling and Mobility Conference Proceedings Book (2017).

14. Ibid.

15. American Nurses Association, *Executive Summary: American Nurses Association Health Risk Appraisal (HRA) Findings of October 2013–October 2014* (Silver Springs, MD: American Nurses Association, 2014), 1–7.

16. J. Zolot, "Nurse Perception of Workplace Safety Affects Patient Care," *American Journal of Nursing* 117, no. 2 (2017): 14.

17. "Nurse and Health Care Worker Protection Act, H.R. 4266/S. 2408," *American Nurses Association Department of Government Affairs Action Alert* (2015).

18. L. Rapaport, "Safe Patient Handling Linked to Fewer Worker Injuries," Reuters Health, 2016, http:www.reuters .com/article/us-health-safety-patient -handling-injuries.

19. Powell-Cope, "Effects of a National Safe Patient Handling Program."

20. Ibid.

21. J. W. Collins, "Guest Editorial," *American Journal of Safe Patient Handling and Mobility* 6, no. 1 (2016): 7–8.

22. Waters, "When Is It Safe?"

23. Ibid.

24. S. M. Gallagher and J.W. Dawson, "Charting a Path Forward: Results and Recommendations from ANA's SPHM Environmental Scan," *American Nurse Today* 11, no. 3 (2016): 18–19.

25. Ibid.

26. Waters, "When Is It Safe?"

27. "ANA Calls for a Culture of Safety in All Health Care Settings," *The American Nurse* 48, no. 3 (2016): 1, 13.

28. Collins, "Guest Editorial."

29. M. A. Lucartorto et al., "Registered Nurses as Caregivers: Influencing the System as Patient Advocates," *The Online Journal of Issues in Nursing* 21, no. 3 (2016): Manuscript 2, http://www.nursingworld .org/MainMenuCategories/ANA Marketplace/ANAPeriodicalsOJIN. Accessed October 6, 2016.

30. P. A. Cuff, *Inter-professional Education for Collaboration: Learning How to Improve Health from Inter-professional Models Across the Continuum of Education to Practice: Workshop Summary* (Washington, DC: National Academic Press, 2013).

31. M. D. M. Fowler, *Guide to the Code of Ethics for Nurses* (Silver Spring, MD: American Nurses Association, 2010).

32. Ibid.

33. J. Summers, "Theory of Healthcare Ethics," in *Health Care Ethics: Critical Issues for the 21st Century*, 3rd ed., E. E. Morrison and B. Furlong (Burlington, MA: Jones & Bartlett Learning, 2014), 3–63.

34. Ibid.

35. Ibid.

36. P. McMenamin, "Diversity Among Registered Nurses: Slow but Steady Progress," *American Nursing Association Community*, http://www.ananursespace.org/blogs/peter-mcmenamin/2015/08/21/rn-diversity-note?ssopc=1.

37. Summers, "Theory of Healthcare Ethics."

38. M. Florell, "Culture of Safety," *Nebraska Nurse* (March/April/May 2016): 4.

39. Collins, "Guest Editorial."

CHAPTER 10

Spirituality and Healthcare Organizations

Dexter R. Freeman and Eileen E. Morrison

▶ Introduction

The 21st century has seen a resurgence of recognition of the importance of responding to the holistic needs of patients and providers within the medical healthcare system. The interesting thing about this spiritual and religious transformation is that the same factors that moved the healthcare industry away from religion and spirituality—namely empiricism and concerns about professionalism—have brought religion and spirituality back to the forefront of the healthcare industry. The healthcare industry abandoned its connection to religion and spirituality during the 20th century in an attempt to emphasize medical care that was reliable, scientifically sound, and effective in meeting patients' needs. The emphasis on identifying clinical practices that consistently provide successful outcomes and that are scientifically sound is commonly referred to as *evidence-based practice* (EBP). EBP, a concept that was introduced to medicine and health care in 1992,[1] has become a consistent screening criterion for selecting clinical practice approaches within the healthcare industry.[2]

Prior to the current era in health care, the focus was on curing illnesses and controlling the spread of disease. Now the emphasis is on developing hospitals that promote healing, while maintaining accountability and professionalism. Erie Chapman, author of *Radical Loving Care,* put it this way:

> How would you like to be part of a hospital that: (1) is in the top one percent in patient satisfaction, (2) has outstanding employee morale, (3) has low turnover, (4) has exceptional clinical care, (5) has a high evaluation score from the Joint Commission on Accreditation of Healthcare Organizations, (6) demonstrates good financial performance, and (7) is characterized as a loving and caring environment?[3]

The supposition is that no hospital or healthcare organization will be able to experience the aforementioned accomplishments unless it is willing to incorporate EBP that also acknowledges the holistic needs of patients, providers, and other members of the healthcare team.

This chapter provides information about the role of spirituality in healthcare work settings. It provides a narrative to promote a deeper understanding of the reasons spirituality must be part of the healthcare system and of how to ensure patient-centered care. Examples of the interest in spirituality include the observation that patients are no longer satisfied with reductionist views of curing. Furthermore, professionals are desperately seeking a sense of fulfillment that is greater than their paycheck. Even The Joint Commission (TJC) has responded by mandating that healthcare institutions incorporate spiritual assessments into their medical practice.[4] Given this change in emphasis, one must question whether it is ethical to incorporate spirituality into the healthcare work environment.

The current belief is that the essence of quality health care in the 21st century is EBP, which is deemed economically beneficial and lowers the risk of litigation. Therefore, insurance companies, policy makers, government regulators, and healthcare providers are pursuing EBP as the gold standard for success in healthcare practice.[5] However, the transition to a healthcare system that emphasizes services driven by empirical data and financial success risks another danger—creating a medical system that promotes paternalistic medical care driven by research outcomes at the expense of emphasizing healing. Chapman states, "The great unfinished business of healthcare is not curing but healing."[6] Curing focuses on relieving and treating patients' symptoms, whereas healing requires acknowledging the holistic needs of healthcare customers by tapping into the yearnings of their minds, bodies, and spirits.

Prior to the 20th century, an interweaving of religion and spirituality existed within the practice of physical and mental health.[7] However, the 20th century ushered in a new perspective toward religion and spirituality in the delivery of physical and mental health care.

During this period, healthcare professionals viewed those professions that embraced religiousness and spirituality as unprofessional, irrational, and unscientific.[8]

However, the same focus on empiricism that caused many healthcare professionals to abandon religion and spirituality in the middle of the 20th century caused them to reconsider it in the late 20th century. The empirical data were clear and consistent—religion and spirituality were not just important; they were making a difference in the health and well-being of patients. As a result, many healthcare organizations called for greater sensitivity and better training of clinicians on how to integrate religious and spiritual issues in the assessment and treatment of patients.[9] Today, spirituality has been deemed an essential ingredient for helping patients in the healthcare system find meaning and purpose in their pain and suffering. However, many healthcare providers still view spiritual care as contrary to competent EBP[10] and antithetical to what a professional healthcare organization should emulate.

This conflict exists within the healthcare environment, even though Americans typically value selfless and compassionate healthcare service that evolves from spiritual care.[11] Thus, a question that one must ask is, Given the changes that have occurred in the national healthcare system, do healthcare personnel have time to address the holistic needs of patients and employees? If one believes that patients seek quality medical treatment, and that providers enter the healthcare system to learn how to alleviate the pain of those suffering, how important is it to show loving care? Finally, is meeting the nebulous spiritual needs of healthcare customers still relevant in today's transient and technology-driven society?

There is a continual struggle within the healthcare system regarding what is most important—empiricism or relationships. Wesorick and Doebbeling point out health care's desperate need for transformation when they highlight the system's resistance to change, resulting in dissatisfaction on the behalf of many customers. They state, "Large gaps exist between evidence and practice, suboptimal quality, inequitable patterns of utilization, poor safety, and unsustainable cost increases."[12] What can help revive this system that some perceive as being out of control and at risk of going under? Some view EBP as the answer to the problem for both the system and the customers who are being affected by long waits and rising costs.[13–15]

▸ Evidence-Based Practice: The Answer and the Challenge

The International Consortium of the Clinical Practice Model Resource Center (CPMRC), a conglomeration of 23 healthcare systems that meets on a regular basis to serve as a think tank and resource center for healthcare transformation, has developed six core practice models that provide a framework for healthcare transformation. These practice models are all evidence-based strategies that incorporate interdisciplinarian partnerships and reduce redundancy through each member of the healthcare team clearly articulating its scope of practice. The models stress that teams effectively use health informatics to capitalize on evidence-based clinical knowledge to affect healthcare processes for the future. In addition, they are designed to ensure that organizations promote a health and healing environment for those who give and receive care. Finally, they emphasize that patients should receive care based on the best scientific knowledge available.[16] The practice models that have been developed by the CPMRC clearly demonstrate the belief that EBP is the means to develop a credible and viable healthcare system that will be equipped to meet the challenges of the 21st century.

Fineout-Overholt and Melnyk defined EBP as "[a] problem-solving approach to clinical practice that integrates a systematic search for, and critical appraisal of the most relevant evidence to answer burning clinical questions, based upon one's clinical expertise, and the patient's preferences and values."[17] This definition refutes the perception that EBP advocates and promotes inflexible paternalistic medical care that is driven by research and the needs of the healthcare system, without consideration of the needs of the client, customer, or patient. Furthermore, the basis for EBP is the belief and assumption that healthcare customers not only desire but also expect to receive medical care that has been proven effective.[18]

There is no doubt that EBP will continue to be a central part of the healthcare transformation that will occur throughout the 21st century. The need to identify health care that is cost-effective and that efficiently utilizes personnel is more important today than it has ever been. In fact, the CPMRC developed its healthcare practice models and beliefs about healthcare transformation in the expectation that EBP would be at the core of every practice model. The CPMRC believes that (1) every person has the right to safe, individualized health care, which promotes wholeness of body, mind, and spirit; (2) a healthy culture requires interaction and a partnership between all systems involved; (3) there must be continuous feedback and learning for a healthcare system to maintain and improve its effectiveness; (4) partnerships are essential to the proper coordination, delivery, and evaluation of health care across the continuum; (5) each individual must commit to being accountable to the system; and (6) quality will occur where there is a shared purpose, vision, and values.[19]

As one examines the importance of EBP in the transformation of the healthcare system, it is also evident that another factor, spirituality, can be viewed as a significant vehicle that would be able to promote healing in the 21st century healthcare system. However, what do we mean by spirituality? Is there evidence to support its incorporation into the healthcare system? Is it ethical to incorporate spirituality into health care, or would it be ethical to leave spirituality out?

▶ This Thing Called Spirituality

Carl Jung said, "Called or not called, God is present."[20] A spiritual ethos often serves as the impetus for many people entering healthcare professions. Dr. Rachel Remen, a clinical professor of family and community medicine at the University of California in the San Francisco School of Medicine, identified why countless numbers of scientifically competent students pursue careers in medicine: "Filled with gratitude, they choose this field and have an overwhelming desire to help others."[21] She goes on to explain that although these future physicians are scientifically gifted, they are spiritually inspired.

However, over the years, many physicians and healthcare administrators have stopped seeing themselves as facilitators of healing. Many entered the profession with idealistic hopes and dreams of being able to make a difference. Yet, the indoctrination they received in institutions of higher education and their work environments taught them that "real professionals" do not have time for matters as abstract and obtuse as exploring their patients' sense of existence or spirituality. As a result, there are now spiritless healthcare organizations and professionals who are seeking to help patients and customers who desire not only physical but also spiritual transformation.

Over the past three decades, a transition has been occurring in the healthcare industry; people are starting to express an interest in healing again. Of course, when one discusses *healing,* one is referring to it in its Old English sense, "to make whole," acknowledging that healing cannot occur without recognizing it as a spiritual process.[22] Because of this renewed interest, attitudes toward spirituality in the workplace appear to be changing. Although today's information age culture, with its emphasis on facts, brevity, and the security of depersonalization, continues to be prevalent, a transition to a deeper calling is becoming apparent. This is reflected in patients' desires. Research suggests that patients desire and feel more comfortable with physicians who not only are open to their own humanity but also are willing to allow patients to discuss their spiritual proclivities.[23]

The past two decades have revealed a resurrection of the need to embrace the whole patient in health care, and all types of organizations are beginning to recognize the importance of addressing their workers' spiritual needs. Books such as Briskin's *Stirring of Soul in the Workplace,* Bolman and Deal's *Leading with Soul,* and, more recently, Benefiel's *Soul at Work* affirm that the business world have recognized people's need to pursue a profession for more than a salary or prestige.[24]

Ashmos and Duchon associate this amplified interest in spirituality in the workplace with several factors.[25] First, the spread of worker demoralization, brought about by massive layoffs, downsizing, and workplace reengineering, has left employees empty and apathetic. Second, baby boomers are aging and beginning to recognize their impending mortality, generating greater interest in the meaning of life. Third, social isolation and the decline in neighborhood organizations have increased the need for workers to feel connected in their work environment. These social conditions support spirituality not just as something that makes people feel good but rather as an aspect of people's lives that is essential to acknowledge in order to promote the well-being of everyone.

A Review of Definitions

There is a universal force that compels humanity to express compassion for the helpless and to search for a more complete state of existence. This force is so multifaceted, dynamic, and unique that it is nearly impossible to completely describe, measure, or define. Our best efforts to define it, which some refer to as *spirit* or *soul,* often are feeble and inadequate; nevertheless, no one can ever doubt the reality of its existence.

Carl Jung said, "I do not hold myself responsible for the fact that man has, everywhere and always, spontaneously developed religious [spiritual] forms of expression, and the human psyche from time immemorial has been shot through with religious [spiritual] feelings and ideas."[26] No one can truly explain where this universal force originates or how to control it; however, research is beginning to show that its presence has a positive effect on recovery from illness, on organizational performance, and on the relationship between healthcare practitioners and their patients. Yet, how do we define the nebulous force that we call *spirit* or *spirituality*?

McBride et al. define spirituality as an intrinsic experience that goes beyond a belief in God or a higher power. It is an internal perspective that inspires one to believe in a force greater than one's self, and it serves as a guide for providing meaning to one's life.[27] Ashmos and Duchon describe the spiritual dimension as a universal state of human existence that involves a search for the experience of a sense of meaning and purpose.[28] Neck and Milliman define spirituality as an expression of one's desire to find meaning and purpose in life. It is a process of living out one's deeply held personal values.[29] Handzo and Koenig state that it is a personal quest for understanding answers to ultimate questions about life, its meaning, and one's relationship to the transcendent.[30] In summary, although spirituality can incorporate the practice of one's religious faith, it includes much more than religion. In fact, one can be religious and not spiritual, as well as be spiritual and not religious.

Spirit or spirituality is the force or source that inspires an individual, community, or organization to seek its meaning, purpose, and a connection with all things. When an individual or an organization is open to its spiritual potential, that individual or organization is multidimensional and capable of embracing a sense of duality. Conger defined spirituality as the source of one's values and meaning—a way of understanding the world, an awareness of one's inner self, and a means of integrating the various aspects of oneself into a whole.[31] If an individual or an organization is estranged from the spirit, that individual or organization becomes estranged from values, meaning, and a sense of humanity. Although this may seem theoretically understandable, there must be nomothetic knowledge or empirical research in order for modern-day healthcare organizations to integrate spirituality into their clinical practice.

Swinton describes nomothetic knowledge as knowledge that is gained through a scientific methodology that provides information that is objective, replicable, and generalizable.[32] The counterpart to nomothetic knowledge is what Swinton referred to as ideographic knowledge, which acknowledges that all understanding is limited and unique. This form of knowledge accepts that there is a phenomenon that is nonreplicable, nongeneralizable, and unique to each individual. For many years, the study of spirituality has been rejected because of its reliance upon ideographic knowledge. However, a number of scientific studies[33] on the relationship between health and spirituality and/or religion have produced significant nomothetic results.

Spirituality and Health Care–Related Empirical Evidence

The clinical practice guidelines promulgated by the CPMRC emphasized the importance of transforming healthcare organizations into healing hospitals. In a healing hospital, everyone plays a vital role in promoting holistic healing for patients. In addition, interventions used are based on EBP.[34] Even though there may be dispute over the research designs and the quality of the research to examine the effects that spirituality and religion have on health care, one cannot dispute the volume of encouraging findings as they relate to the impact that religion and spirituality have on patients within the healthcare system.

For example, research on religion and spirituality in health care has discovered that faith and intercessory prayer can reduce the mortality of cardiology patients.[35] Patients who had an active religious faith recovered quicker from significant burn injuries,[36] and patients who report a high sense of spiritual well-being tend to experience less end-of-life despair in relation to terminal conditions.[37] Furthermore, a great deal of literature also supports the idea that individuals who view faith or their spirituality as an active resource in their lives suffer fewer physical health problems, recover from illnesses sooner, and experience less stress during serious illnesses.[38,39] Whether an individual or healthcare organization chooses to believe that spirituality is significant or does not, it is difficult for one to refute the evidence. The following case scenario depicts the spiritual transformation that often occurs in patients when confronted with a medical crisis that compels them to connect with their own conception of spirituality.

Sharon's Story: Finding Peace Living in the In-Between

Sharon is a 53-year-old African American female who has relied on hard work and determination to combat fear, helplessness, skepticism, and social injustice. Despite the resounding complaints of those around her, she has never used her birth in poverty, the illiteracy of her parents, or the existence of racial injustice as an excuse for not achieving her goals in life. In fact, Sharon frequently used these ostensible barriers as motivations to work harder. She was the first member of her family to receive a college education and a master's degree; now people call her "Dr. Sharon" because she has a PhD. However, it was shortly after Sharon reached the ultimate goal in her life that her world came crashing down.

Sharon suffered from headaches, high blood pressure, and fluid retention in her legs while she was finishing her PhD. Visits to her doctor resulted in the use of medication to lower her blood pressure, and she was encouraged to modify her diet. Sharon attributed her symptoms to the stress of working a full-time job while trying to complete her dissertation—a feat that many of her family, friends, and so-called well-wishers said was impossible. She assumed that once she completed her studies, she would be back to normal. This did not prove to be the case; within a couple of months after she received her doctoral degree, she received a diagnosis of chronic kidney disease.

She now undergoes dialysis 3 days a week, is on a strict diet, is waiting for a suitable kidney donor, and is filled with countless questions. She asks herself, "Why did this happen to me?" "How did this happen to me?" "How can I have a quality life when I am always hooked up to this machine?" "Will I ever be free from this pain?" Each time Sharon goes into the dialysis center, she confronts the harsh, cold reality of her current condition. Her endless questions follow her everywhere she goes.

However, no one in the bastion of compassion and hope, better known as the dialysis clinic, asks her about her day. No one asks her questions about her apprehensions or what she relies on to make it through the day. She even wonders whether they would notice if she did not show up. As she observes the robotic manner in which many of the technicians, nurses, and social workers perform their duties, she wonders whether these people even believe in what they are doing. One part of Sharon would like to believe that the doctors and providers are working hard and really care about what is happening to her. Another part of her says that she is only a body, an insurance claim, and a name waiting on a list. Yet, Sharon has always been the eternal optimist, and she hates to see things this way. She has never had much patience for whiners, and her greatest fear is that people will view her as a whiner.

Sharon has worked most of her life to be free to pursue the life she desires. In most cases, every goal that she sought she has accomplished—that is, until now. The pain she feels is more than physical—it is the pain that comes from acknowledging the presence of two worlds, neither of which she can totally embrace. For years, she chose to believe in the value of hard work, commitment, and dedication. She felt that if people were willing to dedicate themselves to succeed, there was nothing that they could not overcome. She refused to believe that oppressors and social injustice could hold her down. She refused to be part of a world of oppression and victimization filled with pain, hopelessness, and feelings of personal and social inadequacy.

However, Sharon now is feeling oppressed and victimized by this disease that she cannot conquer. She desperately needs the assistance of someone or to go someplace where she can recapture her hope, joy, and passion for life again. She is living between hope and despair, fear and certainty, and anger and faithfulness.

Spirituality and Living in the In-Between

Many people and organizations are like Sharon, in the process of transformation; however, most are not even aware of it. People, organizations, and societies invariably grapple with who they really are, what is most important, and what is the best way to satisfy the mutual needs of everyone involved. Does one rely on policies and programs devised according to empirical wisdom? Does one allow one's conscious self to be his or her guide? Is it best to do that which is most expedient? Does one do that which is most cost-efficient? In the case of Sharon, does she continue to work hard and do what she has always done? Should a healthcare organization, physician, or administrator be concerned with helping Sharon answer her questions? Carol Pearson and Sharon Seivert described the transition from one paradigm,

or personal perspective, to another perspective as a time of living in the "in-between."[40]

During times of living in the in-between, individuals, organizations, and communities begin to uncover their deepest truths. For individuals who have always been in control, their moment of living in the in-between occurs when they become aware of their helplessness. Other individuals may have lived their entire lives nurturing and serving others; their time of living in the in-between occurs when they must seek the assistance of others and allow others to see their pain. Living in the in-between demands that individuals embrace the shadowy aspects of their souls. In the case of Sharon, she must learn to acknowledge her sense of helplessness as much a part of herself as her belief that she can control her fate through hard work. When she learns to acknowledge that she is weak as well as strong, initially she may feel more vulnerable. However, eventually she will develop a greater sense of completeness.

Nurturing the Whole Person

William Miller and Carl Thoresen discuss the perpetual pendulum that swings from science-based secularism to spiritually based holistic treatment in health care.[41] They describe how, long before the proliferation of subspecialties and the emergence of the medical-technological model, healthcare delivery systems used culturally defined healers who incorporated spiritualism to promote health. During this time in history, a lack of scientific knowledge about the disease process resulted in more reliance on spiritual and religious resources. It would not have been uncommon to rely on a shaman, curandero, priest, or pastor to assist, or in some cases serve as, the primary healthcare provider. However, as the healthcare system became more specialized, knowledgeable, and focused on understanding the organic origins of diseases and illnesses, it became more dichotomous. In an effort to become more scientifically grounded and medically proficient, many healthcare delivery systems have thrown out the "spiritual baby with the bathwater." As a result, we have people who work, manage, and seek services in healthcare delivery systems who only recognize part of the person.

Whether one is addressing the needs of people with cancer, AIDS, chronic kidney disease, diabetes, the death of a loved one, or a multitude of medical problems, the literature consistently confirms that illness is fraught with spiritual concerns and issues.[42] In her book *My Grandfather's Blessings,* Rachel Ramen notes the following:

> Through illness, people may come to know themselves for the first time and recognize not only who they genuinely are but also what really matters to them. As a physician, I have accompanied many people as they have discovered in themselves an unexpected strength, courage beyond what they would have thought possible, an unsuspected sense of compassion or a capacity for love deeper than they had ever dreamed. I have watched people abandon values that they have never questioned before and find the courage to live in new ways.[43]

The research, anecdotal accounts, and literature all agree that it is impossible to treat the whole person without acknowledging the spiritual aspects of the healthcare consumer. Larimore, Parker, and Crowther examined the literature pertinent to incorporating spirituality into medical practice. They discovered the following: (1) A positive relationship frequently exists between spirituality and physical and mental well-being; (2) most patients desire to discuss and be offered basic spiritual care by their healthcare provider; (3) most healthcare providers believe that spiritual interventions would help healthcare consumers, but they feel inadequately trained to deliver such care; and (4) most healthcare consumers (patients)

censure healthcare delivery systems for ignoring their spiritual needs.[44]

Moreover, a plethora of data supports the idea that individuals who are spiritually connected have fewer physical health problems, recover from illness quicker, and experience less stress during serious illness than those who are not.[45] Thus, it is clear that providing appropriate, competent, effective, and ethical care to consumers of healthcare delivery systems demands that the spiritual aspects of the healing process be incorporated. Moore and Casper conclude that caring for the whole person begins with the organization—in this case, the healthcare delivery system—recognizing that those who deliver care have an inner life that needs to be incorporated into the work they do.[46] The next section of this chapter addresses the importance of a spiritually oriented organization that enables consumers, workers, leaders, and communities to reach their ultimate goals in life. This discussion begins with a history of work in the United States and an overview of the business of health care.

▶ Is there a Place for Spirituality in the Healthcare Workplace?

In the ever-changing Patient Protection and Affordable Care Act (ACA 2010) era, there will continue to be challenges to the business model used in health care. Certainly, health care must continue to be concerned with efficiency, effectiveness, productivity, and profit. It also employs staff members with a great variety of skills and knowledge in order to both provide patient care and meet the business requirements of the industry. Its management must address business-type issues such as quality assurance, financial stability, marketing, and growth. However, the unique features of health care require a business model that also addresses a different set of criteria.

Healthcare professionals must be able to meet the needs of their unique customers—their patients. When these customers become part of the healthcare business, their concerns are not about whether they are getting a deal on a product or whether they are getting value for their money. Patients are often worried, in pain, or in fear. They are seeking answers to their concerns, the alleviation of their pain, or healing of their conditions. To achieve these goals, they are willing to experience embarrassment, pain from treatments, and loss of privacy. Patients as customers also assume that their needs are being met by competent professionals whose motivation is to heal with compassionate care.

In addition, patients expect that health care will be available to them in all aspects of their lives. Unlike other businesses, professionals who work in health care are available to patients at their worst and most embarrassing moments and in their most joyful ones. To obtain quality care, patients assume that all of the personnel that they encounter can be trusted with deeply personal and often embarrassing information. They also expect that healthcare professionals will respect their dignity and be compassionate.

What kinds of employees are included in the healthcare business? Certainly, this highly sensitive work and profound responsibility should attract and maintain employees who have a deep commitment to being present to people and practice compassionate care. However, to demonstrate this expected level of care on a consistent basis, healthcare staff members need more than incentive plans and bonuses. They need a type of intrinsic motivation found in organizations that champion and reward workplace spirituality.

However, the business of health care must also balance the ever-present reality of efficiency, effectiveness, and profitability with the needs of patients. In addition, healthcare businesses must hire, retain, and compensate highly educated healthcare personnel who are willing to provide services on a 24–7 basis in many cases. In addition, technology has become a way to increase efficiency and provide quality care, but it is often costly and can decrease the personal level of patient care.

In the changing and often stressful ACA 2010 era, the business of health care also needs to prove its merit to a plethora of regulators who oversee both the clinical and the financial aspects of its product. It must also cope with the many changes that legislation, new systems of coding, and technology advances produce. In striving to address these multilayers of change, health care must be vigilant to not overlook the purpose of its business-serving patients. The temptation will be to make patients "numbers on a form" or data in the computer. If healthcare staff members orient their practice toward "patients as products," they may find their work meaningless and devoid of the elements that called them to their professions in the first place.

Is it possible for a healthcare organization to meet its business demands and provide spiritual-centered, meaningful care to patients? Can health care be true to its mission of compassionate care and still make a profit? The following section will address issues related to this balance and provide information on workplace spirituality, including its current models. In addition, this final section will include a discussion of ethics principles as they relate to spirituality in the workplace.

A Brief History of Work

Why do people work? This seems like an unusual question. However, it is part of the research concerning efforts to increase productivity, profitability, and employee satisfaction. In the beginning, the answer was easy. People worked to survive. The workday lasted from the break of dawn until twilight, and the work itself was often difficult and dangerous. For many, work involved manual labor and provided subsistence-level compensation. For the most part, work was not spiritual or a vehicle for meaning and purpose in life. It was a way to survive.

With respect to health care's early history, if physicians were available, only the wealthy could receive their ministrations. Care provided to the everyday citizen was largely in the realm of women who had knowledge of herbal and other remedies, which were often effective. The basis of these healers' work was not compensation but the need to relieve pain and suffering and created meaning and purpose in these healers' lives.[47]

As the nature and complexity of work changed, it became important to understand ways that would increase the productivity and efficiency of workers. A brief review of some of the findings helps in understanding the more recent changes in thinking about work. The earliest research on motivation to work came from the Industrial Revolution and the development of Frederick W. Taylor's scientific management theory.[48] The need for management theory arose when work transitioned from a primarily agrarian and cottage industry culture to an industrial model. In response to this change, Taylor sought to make the workplace more efficient and profitable. In his view of efficiency, people worked the same way machines did, producing the same-quality work through standardization of the work process. Therefore, there was no difference between a person and a machine and no need to address the spirit or humanity of the person.

Managers achieved harmony in the work setting by organizing workers and enforcing their adherence to rules. If workers deviated from the prescribed best way to approach a task, there was a decrease in efficiency and productivity. Therefore, workers were paid to work according to standards and nothing else. Thinking was the role of the manager.

Taylor also believed that the ideal employee was one who conformed to instructions and submitted to regulations. He (gender selection deliberate) was an employee who could control himself and his emotions. He

acquired self-control by maintaining diligence when completing tedious work. In addition, Taylor expressed paternalistic attitudes toward the worker. He believed that those who had knowledge (management) should manage the poor for the poor's own good. Individuals should be willing to sacrifice for the corporation and accept a day's pay for a day's work, as determined by managerial formulas.

Even in the business of health care, the legacy of Taylor's work is alive and well in today's workplaces. Management often speaks of reengineering to increase the clockwork order of the work process and to remove human interference. There is an increasing need to standardize and to pay for performance, even in healthcare delivery systems. Management laments that it cannot get employees to "think right" or that employees are "not paid to think, just to get the work done." This thinking is also evident when bonuses are given to employees on the basis of the number of procedures completed in any given day.

The idea of employees as machines is alive and well in certain circumstances. Physicians, nurses, and other care providers still work to the limits of their resiliency, through 12- to 15-hour daily work schedules. In addition, the workplace has become increasingly stressful because of its requirements for high-level performance, increased pace, and the intensity of the work. In addition, the regulation of healthcare practices often adds to the stress of the work that providers do.

Taylor's idea of a day's pay for a day's work has evolved into bonuses and higher pay that will keep employees' efficiency high for tedious or even dangerous jobs. In certain aspects of health care, the human element is ignored in order to get the work accomplished, and money is used to "rent souls."[49] Employees find that their jobs are increasingly regimented, less in tune with who they are as human beings, and require that they sacrifice who they are. The organization's definition of proficiency often conflicts with the reason for the call to become part of the healthcare profession.

Taylor is not the only influence on the U.S. attitude toward work. For example, Douglas McGregor[50] formulated a theory on the basis of how managers viewed workers. This theory also included actions to make these people more productive. For example, in theory X, managers needed to watch workers, force them to work according to instructions, and provide money as a motivator. This was true because managers viewed these workers as lazy, irresponsible, and self-centered. Some workers had more independence and decision-making in their work. Managers believed that these workers were ambitious and capable. However, this theory did not address the motivation for work or one's need for meaning and purpose.

Researchers continued to examine the motivation for work, but many of the theories focused on how to increase productivity by examining the effects of organizational factors, leadership components, reward systems, and other areas. Some contemporary theories such as servant leadership stressed how leaders can develop and encourage strengths of their staff members. In addition, qualities such as empathy stewardship and integrity were part of the model. However, these models did not examine spiritual components of leadership such as vocation and meaning and purpose and work.[51]

A New Look at Spirituality and Leadership

The recent literature reveals an increased interest in the inclusion of spirituality in leadership practice and organizational structure. This research focuses on the impact of spirituality in organizational life and reflects extensive study conducted by the Centre for Excellence in Leadership and others. One of the influences for this research was the increase in organizations that are concerned with ethical leadership, their employees, and sustainability, while still achieving profit.[52] Corporations such as Procter & Gamble, Whole Foods, and Starbucks served as models of workplaces that

were seeking ways to value employees, maintain sustainability, and contribute to their communities.

In defining spirituality in the workplace, Fry and Altman[53] suggested that people at work need to be valued spiritually and not solely as producers of profit. They discussed characteristics such as the ability of workers to achieve their potential and to provide services that had social value and meaning. They also found that the employees' need to have a sense of community is also part of spirituality in the workplace.

Fry and Nisiewicz[54] developed a model for organizational leadership that emphasized spirituality. Their model stressed spiritually connected areas such as hope, vision, and altruistic love. In addition, they stressed the need for employees and leaders to have a vocation for the work that they do. This means that they each has a calling to his or her work and finds meaning through making a difference. This part of their theory also concurs with Victor Frankl's position on meaning in work.[55]

In addition, Fry and Nisiewicz[56] discuss the importance of spiritual well-being for both employees and leaders. Their definition of well-being includes joy, peace, and serenity. In their research, employees and leaders who have spiritual well-being also experience lower levels of stress and positive health. The authors explained that there are universal values such as honesty, trust, compassion, and a service orientation that affect both economic and spiritual environments in organizations.

Fry and Nisiewicz also found a link between positive psychology and spiritual wellness. Positive psychology as a link to spiritual wellness addresses one's life view, including his or her response to adversity. In addition, it deals with how individuals define a "good life" and their ability to capitalize on their strengths and weaknesses. Words like "self-acceptance," "environmental mastery," "purpose in life," and "personal growth"[57] are associated with the idea of spiritual well-being. Since healthcare employees spend much of their time at work and are involved in work that is challenging both physically and emotionally, a sense of spiritual well-being can affect the quality of patient care and the success of the organization.

The authors[58] go beyond a discussion of the components of spiritual leadership and offer a model for organizational transformation. The premise for their model is that employees want work that has meaning and purpose and want to be recognized as valued human beings. They also seek a sense of connection with coworkers. Achieving an organizational model that meets these goals requires a multistep approach involving surveys, analyses of stakeholders, development of interventions, and change management. While this process requires a major change in thinking about productivity and how it is best achieved, the authors were able to connect spiritual leadership practices to the scorecard business model and achieving a successful bottom line.

▶ Spirituality in the Business of Health Care

It appears from the discussion in the previous sections that an emphasis on incorporating the spirit as part of a business model is becoming part of the conversation for successful businesses. Given the nature of health care, one would assume that spiritual components are also an integral part of the healthcare systems. Certainly, faith-based systems and their facilities feature elements of spirituality as part of their mission and practice. However, other healthcare systems may be less likely to include elements like the spiritual well-being of employees, the calling to service in health care, and other spiritual elements as part of their business plan. Given the nature of health care and the challenge of change, one could agree that healthcare organizations must remain profitable to serve patients, but profit is not the only focus for healthcare organizations.

First, consider the nature of the healthcare business. What is its product? By its title, one can assume that it is providing health through the mechanism of care. What is care? Care may include examinations, tests, imaging, treatments, and medications. However, it also suggests that there is a caring relationship between those who find themselves in need of the product of this system and the professionals who provide it. In addition, if the product is actually health, it involves more than treatment. Therefore, the healthcare market is expanding to areas of population health, prevention, and even social health.

Since health care is a business, can we consider patients as customers? Given that they are often fearful, in pain, and uncomfortable in the somewhat alien world of health care, these customers (or patients) trust that providers are working in their best interests. Healthcare consumers also expect that their treatment is compassionate as well as effective. In addition, healthcare customers do not define healthcare providers as businesspeople who sell a product or service. Rather, those who provide health care are trusted with the most intimate secrets of patients' lives and with intrusive access to their physical bodies. Given the nature of health care and the expectations of patients, it seems providential to include the spiritual elements of leadership and organizational design in its business model. The next section will examine spirituality in the workplace as it pertains to healthcare organizations and the challenges that they face.

ACA, TJC, AHRQ, and Workplace Spirituality

With the passage of the ACA 2010, health care entered a period of the greatest change since the implementation of Medicare. This change, coupled with other changes such as the 10th revision of the International Statistical

Classification of Diseases and Related Health Problems (ICD-10) implementation, increases the emphasis on areas related to patients' experience in the healthcare system. For example, the ACA 2010 stresses patient-centered care. To be successful in the changing ACA 2010 environment, healthcare organizations must provide effective and efficient care to a wide variety of patients.

The idea of patient-centered care is not new. It began as a movement based on the work of Angelica Thieriot, founder of the Planetree Movement. She proposed a model for patient care that supported the human side of health care and the need for patients to be participants in their own care.[59] Her model stressed the need for human interaction, information, partnerships with patients, and a healing environment. Spirituality for patients and for caregivers was also a major part of her model. Spirituality is implemented in facilities and includes a spiritual diagnosis as part of the healing process. In addition, Planetree organizations emphasize the mind–body–spirit connection for patients, families, and staff members.

The ACA 2010 requires not only the provision of patient-centered care but also documentation of its provision. This documentation includes measurements of quality of care, patient satisfaction, and patient engagement. Healthcare professionals must also address issues such as patient autonomy, their perception of the healthcare experience through an instrument called the Consumer Assessment of Healthcare Providers and Systems (CAHPS). Since measurement relates to funding, there are concerns that professionals might see patients as data items rather than human beings. Recognizing patients as fully functioning human beings will require a deeper sense of empathy, compassion, and dedication to the work itself, which are part of spirituality in the workplace.[60]

In 2010, TJC published a guide titled *Advancing Effective Communication, Cultural Competence, and Patient- and Family-Centered Care: A Roadmap for Hospitals.*[61] This 102-page guide gives advice to healthcare institutions on how to provide patient-centered care throughout the total patient experience. Guidelines begin with admission and extend through assessment, treatment, and discharge. TJC also provided checklists and support materials for addressing areas such as patient communication, culture, spiritual beliefs, and other care concerns. Patient-centered care is also a requirement under several areas of TJC standards, such as human resources, patient safety, and quality of care.

In light of the importance of patient-centered care, the Agency for Health Research and Quality (AHRQ),[62] provided information on its benefit to both patients and organizations. It began with the premise that a hospital should engage in patient-centered care as part of its mission. However, practicing effective patient-centered care also reduces medication errors and falls, which can be costly to the institution. In addition, the agency noted that consistently practicing patient-centered care resulted in better compliance with TJC standards, higher CAHPS scores, and increased employee retention.

What kind of staff members are able to provide the patient-centered care expected by regulators and funders of health care? Do healthcare leaders expect employees to be called to their profession rather than seeing it as an income source alone? Do they want caregivers who are trustworthy, compassionate, and oriented toward serving patients? If the answer is yes to these questions, then spirituality in the healthcare workplace may be an essential element to patient-centered care and deserves attention in strategic planning in organizations. The next section will explore research on spirituality in healthcare organizations as a foundation for exploring ways to integrate spirituality in healthcare organizations and the ethics principles that apply to this action.

▶ Integration of Spirituality into Healthcare Workplaces

Non-healthcare organizations appear to be demonstrating increased concern about the quality of life and spirituality of their employees. This information makes one wonder why healthcare workplaces do not strongly emphasize spirituality. When one considers the unique work of health care with its connection to healing and life itself, it would seem logical that providing care would be the most spiritually centered work that anyone can do. However, integrating spirituality into healthcare facilities is not always easy. The first step would be to eliminate the confusion between spirituality and religion. Whereas religion holds a place in faith-based facilities, secular organizations are often uncomfortable with the idea of spirituality because they equate it to religion. Therefore, it is necessary to define spirituality in a clear and concise way.[63]

Researchers in the field of workplace spirituality offer definitions that can be adapted to healthcare environments. For example, Fry and Altman discuss workplace spirituality as a way to "include support of employees' inner lives and a support that nourishes a sense of transcendence through meaningful work."[64] This means that employees exhibit values such as respect for persons, self-reflection, honesty, and integrity. Another definition of spirituality that may be appropriate for healthcare work settings is based on the work of Viktor Frankl in *The Doctor and the Soul*.[65] Frankl believed that meaning and purpose in life are essential for full human function. Work, because of its ability to allow people to apply their unique talents, is one of the main ways that humans can find this meaning. Using Frankl's extensive research, one could begin to define spirituality at work as the ability to find meaning and purpose in the work that one does. This ability also serves as an intrinsic motivation for the employee to provide the services needed by the organization. In the case of health care, the services include healing care for people with different backgrounds and health experiences. The application of spirituality in the workplace is reinforced by the research in Pattakos's *Prisoners of Our Thoughts*.[66]

Spirituality and Leadership

Once organizations define spirituality in the workplace, there is a need for commitment from leadership for a change to or enhancement of this spirituality. This is true whether the change is a more meaningful workplace or meeting of the high-level challenges of the ACA 2010. Because of their influence through both title and personal example, leaders should demonstrate their own commitment to spirituality in the workplace in their words and actions.

Leaders also need to decide whether fostering spirituality is beneficial to the organization and its mission. They should consider that the mission of health care involves more than procedures and cost-effective care. From the patient's point of view, it also includes compassionate behavior that respects individual dignity. Can spirituality in terms of meaningful work assist in this mission and improve the bottom line of healthcare facilities? If so, then it is worth the effort needed to create an environment in which there is meaningful work and spirituality.

It is not enough to talk about mission and meaning and purpose in work. Leaders must also demonstrate their own commitment to the organization in their attitudes and behaviors. To begin the process, they need to conduct a self-assessment and identify why they work for their organization.[67] Once they identify their own meaning and purpose in work, they need to create a vision for how the workplace would exhibit this spirituality in compliance with its operational definition. Of course, an effective leader does not work alone; appropriate staff members would work toward this applied vision statement.

Organizational change happens through people. Therefore, healthcare leaders who seek to have spirituality in their workplaces need to develop mechanisms for achieving this goal. Teamwork and communication are essential for achieving any level of change, particularly one in which spirituality is included. Recognition that spirituality is part of the culture of health care needs reinforcement on many levels, including day-to-day interactions with patients and coworkers. Although this should be an easy change because of the nature of the industry, spirituality may not be a prime concern when the pressure for fiscal responsibility increases. Therefore, it is necessary for leaders to include the concept of spirituality in their daily interactions to keep it in the forefront of their actions. Dan Wilford, the one-time chief executive officer (CEO) of Memorial Hermann Healthcare Systems, said, "[T]he essence of trust is spiritual, and requires faith."[68] Given the current environment of uncertainty and change in health care, trust is a critical element for both employees and patients.

Practicing Spirituality in the Healthcare Workplace

The next step is integrating spirituality in the healthcare workplace. Given the current challenges facing health care, this may be the best time or the worst time to move the organization toward spirituality. It may be the best time because change is already happening and the door is open to new practices and procedures. It may be the worst time because employees do not even want to hear the word "change" again. Regardless of the position taken, there is a need to address workplace spirituality on some level because of its effects on quality patient care, staff commitment, and other areas mentioned earlier in this chapter. The following is a list of practical ways to address the issue:

1. Look *at what already exists.* Chapman discusses the need to have employees with a "servant's heart."[69] These employees find work meaningful and demonstrate their value through high performance. They also have personal values that are examples for others. Employees who have service to patients as a personal value should be honored and form the basis of a spirituality centered culture. They can also serve as coaches to assist others in finding their own sense spirit in their work.

2. *Think about the culture.* Cultural change in healthcare organizations should occur deliberately so that patients are part of the increasing spirituality. Persistence and focus on the mission, vision, and values of the organization can assist in making this change. In addition, leaders should exemplify spiritually centered behaviors and be open to criticism and suggestions for change.[70]

3. *Organizational development is essential.* It is not enough to tell employees to find meaning in their work in a healthcare setting. Organizations should take deliberate action such as an organizational assessment followed by skill training to address assessment results. Training sessions may include employee empowerment skills, conflict management, and practice of "forgiveness, acceptance, and gratitude."[71]

4. *There will be challenges.* Chapman notes that the process of creating meaningful, spirituality centered workplaces is not without challenges.[72] In an ACA 2010 era and

beyond, there will be concerns about meeting standards and doing more with less while maintaining profitability. In addition, the way in which health care is provided may increase the emphasis on profitability and efficiency over compassionate care. However, remember that the reason most employees seek a career in health care is not solely for financial gain. Although salaries and benefits are important, many employees have a vocation or calling to this work. In addition, increasing the emphasis on meaning in work and spirituality through employee focus on patient care may actually improve the bottom line. For example, if employees are engaged in work that they perceive to be meaningful, there can be an increase in morale and a decrease in absenteeism and turnover, thereby decreasing the cost of providing care. In addition, the potential for medical error, employee theft, and other systemic difficulties could decrease, which also improves the bottom line.

Ethics Theories and Spirituality

What is the relationship between spirituality in the healthcare workplace and theories of ethics? Certainly, elements of each ethics theory support this practice. For example, if one were a proponent of natural law, one could argue that ignoring spirituality could limit a person's ability to achieve his or her highest potential. This is especially true when considering that part of an employee's potential in natural law is to seek wisdom and to know God. Therefore, to diminish the spiritual component of a person or an organization could be an unethical practice.

Sheep proposed two spiritually laden questions that every healthcare administrator should consider when creating a work environment that is conducive to nurturing the whole worker:

- Would this organization be more productive, innovative, and the people feel more satisfied if the workers felt a greater sense of connection to their work?
- Does this organization have an ethical responsibility to seek to improve the quality of life of its workers as members of society?[73]

These questions could be answered by using a base in theory. For example, if administrators support Kantian deontology, they could use the categorical imperative as a tool for ethical decision-making.[74] An analysis with this tool could lead to a decision that respecting and allowing employees to pursue spiritual growth is a moral and ethical duty. Alternatively, administrators might consider that allowing people to find meaning in their work and life is a universal law. If there is a moral duty, healthcare leaders and administrators have an obligation to provide an environment in which spirituality is part of health care.

The practice of utilitarian theory could also consider the ethics of incorporating spirituality into the healthcare workplace. Unlike the deontological approach, which determines the appropriateness of an action based on duty, utilitarian theories of ethical decision-making use Bentham and Mill's constructs.[75] Utilitarian thinking suggests that an action or behavior might be justified if it yields the greatest good for the greatest number. Therefore, a utilitarian could support spirituality in the workplace if incorporating this practice results in increased worker productivity, decreased worker turnover, increased patient confidence in the provider, and a greater sense of connectedness between administrators and staff.

Studies by Lloyd,[76] Jurkiewicz and Giacalone,[77] and Mitroff and Denton,[78] among others, have confirmed that spirituality in the workplace does more than meet the existential desires of workers and patients. It positively affects worker performance, organizational growth, and creativity. For example, Mitroff and Denton conducted a study of spirituality in the workplace by interviewing managers and executives.[79] They discovered that the more spiritual an organization is, the more profitable it is. In addition, the more workers are able to include themselves in their work, the more creative, emotionally stable, and productive they are in the workplace.

Finally, one should consider the concept of Aristotle's virtue ethics.[80] Aristotle believed that ethical people are capable of working toward their highest level of excellence and desire to live virtuous lives. In accord with Aristotle's view, the community and patients expect healthcare professionals to have high moral character and practical wisdom in their daily practice. Certainly, developing this discernment comes from a work setting that allows for meaningful work and honors a calling to serve. Including spirituality in the healthcare workplace can facilitate and even honor this practice. If professionals actually demonstrate Aristotle's practical wisdom and high moral character, they should be better able to assist patients when they are experiencing moments of being in the in-between. They also add value to their organization as examples of caring professionals who find purpose in their work.

▶ Ethics Principles and Spirituality

Health care calls for the application of ethics principles in day-to-day practice at the patient and organizational levels. For example, first, one must practice nonmaleficence, or not doing harm to patients or employees. The story of Sharon comes to mind as an example. The lack of spiritual connection between her and the professionals who were supposed to be serving her needs caused her harm. Simple and cost-free acts, such as asking the appropriate questions and really listening to her responses, could have avoided this harm. In addition, small acts of kindness (beneficence) could have made her life-changing illness easier to bear.

Nonmaleficence and beneficence are not limited to patient spirituality. Think of how much more positive and less stressful a healthcare environment can be when professionals truly care about one another and the work that they do. Again, small actions and well-chosen words can provide a refurbishing of the spirit that can only lead to greater-quality health care and an increase in organizational loyalty. In addition, employees' view of work would be vastly different. Patient encounters would be more than just another procedure; they would be opportunities to find meaning and to honor the sacredness of health care.[81]

Respect for autonomy also relates to spirituality at work. It is impossible to imagine engaging in respect for persons without acknowledging that the spirit is part of who they are. It would seem incredibly disrespectful to do so (Kant would not be happy at all). The same is true for the autonomy of an organization. If one does not feel that one is part of something larger or that the work that one does is valued, then it would be easy to be disloyal to the organization. Imagine the financial and quality implications of a potential lack of commitment, low morale, and high turnover rates stemming from a lack of respect for employee autonomy.

It is impossible to ignore the relationship between ethics and spirituality in the healthcare workplace. To ensure just treatment, healthcare delivery systems must be willing to nurture the whole person, whether the patient or the worker. This includes more than just responding to the physical needs of the patient or the monetary needs of the worker; healthcare systems must acknowledge their spirit as well. Just treatment might require a few more minutes of listening, even when one is tired, or asking questions to determine hidden issues or concerns. It is helpful to think about the classic question, how would I like to be treated if I were in this situation?

Practicing justice that acknowledges an employee's spirituality can take many forms. Perhaps justice means making sure that breaks are part of the workday or respecting time for renewal. It may also be honoring the employees' need for understanding their purpose and meaning in life by providing them a quiet place to think. Again, acting with justice does not have to add to the cost of health care, but it can positively affect the bottom line.

Embracing the spirit in the workplace begins with spiritual leadership that results in the transformation of the organization and the community. Wolf identified several principles that spirit-focused healthcare leaders should use to promote transformation in their organizations.[82] First, spirit-focused leaders are primarily concerned with creating an environment that recognizes and respects the importance of strong moral and ethical values throughout the organization. Second, spirit-focused leaders recognize that healthcare providers enter the field in response to a calling; therefore, they give employees an opportunity to discover and examine their sense of purpose and meaning. Third, spirit-focused leaders recognize the importance of connectedness at both the vertical (with a divine being) and the horizontal (between workers and those outside the organization) level. As a result, spiritual leaders typically plan and encourage community involvement via joint programs and community-oriented activities. These leaders help create a work environment in which ethics and spirituality are the norm and in which work provides meaning and purpose to employees.

▶ Summary

This chapter examines the ethics of spirituality in the workplace. The process of providing patient-centered care is inherently spiritual because it recognizes the whole person. Further, spirituality will always be paramount to the services provided via healthcare delivery systems as long as the people who pursue careers in health care do so in response to a calling. Including spirituality in the workplace will also be important as long as people seek care because they desire healing (wholeness or a sense of completeness) and not just relief from physical symptoms. The ultimate role of those who work in the healthcare delivery system is to help communities reconcile the dichotomous thoughts, feelings, emotions, and experiences they encounter during the time of being in the in-between. These times often occur during physical crises; however, to help communities experience healing, a healthcare organization must recognize its spiritual calling, employ spirit-focused leadership, and value spirituality at every level of operation.

Although spirituality is multifaceted—and some may say nebulous and impossible to define—this chapter provides an overview of the importance and relevancy of spirituality to patient-centered care, particularly amid the challenges of ACA 2010 and its future iterations. The chapter offers information on how to recognize the influence of spirituality in the workplace. Even though some might still insist that spirituality is antithetical to professional medical care or the healthcare delivery system, this position is contrary to the expressed needs of those who work in health care and those who seek care in the system. It is clear that healthcare organizations that embrace spirituality tend to be ethically sound and maintain a healthy balance between the needs of the individual and those of the organization. They also tend to be efficient, effective, and patient-centered in both philosophy and action. Is this not what the goal for health care is for the 21st century?

▶ Questions for Review

1. What is the connection between spirituality in health care and EBP?

2. How do Pearson and Sievert define "living in the in-between," and how does this concept relate to spirituality in healthcare organizations?
3. What is the role of leadership in workplace spirituality?
4. How do the theories of ethics support spirituality in healthcare organizations?
5. Does spirituality in healthcare organizations have a base in ethics principles?

▶ Notes

1. Evidence-Based Medicine Working Group, "Evidence-Based Medicine: A New Approach to Teaching the Practice of Medicine," *Journal of the American Medical Association* 268 (1992): 2420–25.
2. B. Wesorick and B. Doebbeling, "Lessons from the Field: The Essential Elements for Point-of-Care Transformation," *Medical Care* 49, suppl. (December 2001): S49–58.
3. E. Chapman, *Radical Loving Care: Building the Healing Hospital* (Nashville, TN: Erie Chapman Foundation, 2011), 11.
4. Joint Commission on the Accreditation of Healthcare Organizations, *Comprehensive Accreditation Manual for Healthcare Organizations: The Official Handbook* (Chicago: Joint Commission on the Accreditation of Healthcare Organizations, 2003).
5. H. McKenzie, "What Does the Healthcare Patient Want?" *Home Healthcare Nurse* 28, no. 9 (2010): 575–76.
6. Chapman, *Radical Loving Care*, 4.
7. H. Koenig et al., *Handbook of Religion and Health* (New York: Oxford University Press, 2001).
8. W. L. Larimore et al., "Should Clinicians Incorporate Positive Spirituality into Their Practices? What Does the Evidence Say?" *Annals of Behavioral Medicine* 24, no. 1 (2002): 69–73.
9. Ibid.
10. P. Speck, "The Evidence Base for Spiritual Care," *Nursing Management* 12, no. 6 (2005): 28–31.
11. D. Garber, "Spirituality and Healthcare Organizations," *Journal of Healthcare Management* 46 (2001): 39–52.
12. Wesorick and Doebbeling, "Lessons from the Field," 49.
13. R. F. Levin et al., "Evidence-Based Practice Improvement: Merging 2 Paradigms," *Journal of Nursing Care* 25, no. 2 (2010): 117–26.
14. T. Leufer and J. Cleary-Holdforth, "Evidence-Based Practice: Improving Patient Outcomes," *Nursing Standard* 23, no. 32 (2009): 35–39.
15. McKenzie, "What Does the Healthcare Patient Want?"
16. Wesorick and Doebbeling, "Lessons from the Field."
17. E. Fineout-Overholt and B. M. Melnyk, "Transforming Healthcare from the Inside Out: Advancing Evidence-Based Practice in the 21st Century," *Journal of Professional Nursing* 21, no. 6 (2005): 335–44.
18. Leufer and Cleary-Holdforth, "Evidence-Based Practice."
19. Wesorick and Doebbeling, "Lessons from the Field."
20. C. Jung, cited in Chapman, *Radical Loving Care*, 4.
21. R. Remen, "Clueing Doctors in on the Art of Healing," *Science and Theology News*, July–August 2004, 32.
22. M. Burkhardt, "After All: Reintegrating Spirituality into Healthcare," *Alternative Therapies in Health and Medicines* 4 (1998): 2.
23. M. Donnelly, "Faith Boosts Cognitive Management of Cancer and HIV," *Science and Theology News*, June 15, 2006.
24. A. Briskin, *The Stirring of Soul in the Workplace* (San Francisco, CA: Jossey-Bass, 1996); L. G. Bolman and T. E. Deal, *Leading with Soul: An Uncommon Journey of Spirit* (San Francisco, CA:

Jossey-Bass, 1995); M. Benefiel, *Soul at Work: Spiritual Leadership in Organizations* (New York: Seabury, 2005).

25. D. Ashmos and D. Duchon, "Spirituality at Work: A Conceptualization and Measure," *Journal of Management Inquiry* 9 (2000): 134–45.

26. C. G. Jung, *Modern Man in Search of a Soul* (Orlando, FL: Harcourt Brace Jovanovich, 1933), 122.

27. J. L. McBride et al., "The Relationship Between a Patient's Spirituality and Health Experience," *Family Medicine* 30 (1998): 122.

28. Ashmos and Duchon, "Spirituality at Work."

29. C. Neck and J. Milliman, "Thought Self-Leadership: Finding Spiritual Fulfillment in Organizational Life," *Journal of Managerial Psychology* 9 (1994): 9.

30. G. Handzo and H. Koenig, "Spiritual Care: Whose Job Is It Anyway?" *Southern Medical Journal* 97 (2004): 1242.

31. J. A. Conger, *Spirit at Work: Discovering the Spirituality of Leadership* (San Francisco, CA: Jossey-Bass, 1994).

32. J. Swinton, "Healthcare Spirituality: A Question of Knowledge," in *Oxford Textbook of Spirituality in Healthcare*, eds. M. Cobb, C. M Puchalski, and B. Rumbold (New York: Oxford Press, 2012), 100–104.

33. J. Swinton et al., "Moving Inwards, Moving Outwards, Moving Upwards: The Role of Spirituality during the Early Stages of Breast Cancer," *European Journal of Cancer Care*, 20, no. 5 (2011): 640–52.

34. Wesorick and Doebbeling, "Lessons from the Field."

35. R. C. Byrd, "Positive Therapeutic Effects of Intercessory Prayer in a Coronary Care Unit Population," *Southern Medical Journal* 81 (1988): 826–29.

36. Speck, "The Evidence Base for Spiritual Care."

37. J. T. Chibnall et al., "Psychosocial-Spiritual Correlates of Death Distress in Patients with Life-Threatening Medical Conditions," *Palliative Medicine* 16, no. 4 (2002): 331–38.

38. H. G. Koenig and H. J. Cohen, *The Link Between Religion and Health: Psychoneuroimmunology and the Faith Factor* (London: Oxford University Press, 2002).

39. C. E. Thoresen, "Spirituality and Health: Is There a Relationship?" *Journal of Health Psychology* 4, no. 3 (1999): 291–300.

40. C. Pearson and S. Sievert, *Magic at Work: A Guide to Releasing Your Highest Creative Powers* (New York, NY: Doubleday, 1995).

41. W. Miller and C. Thoresen, "Spirituality and Health," in *Integrating Spirituality into Treatment*, ed. William Miller (Washington, DC: American Psychological Association, 1999), 3–18.

42. R. Dunphy, "Helping Persons with AIDS Find Meaning and Hope," *Health Progress* 68 (1987): 58–63; E. J. Taylor, "Why and Wherefores: Adult Patient Perspectives of the Meaning of Cancer," *Seminars in Oncology Nursing* 11 (1995): 32–40; Garber, "Spirituality and Healthcare Organizations," 42.

43. R. Remen, *My Grandfather's Blessings* (New York: Riverhead Books, 2000), 29.

44. Larimore et al., "Should Clinicians Incorporate Positive Spirituality into Their Practice?"

45. Koenig and Cohen, *The Link Between Religion and Health.*

46. T. Moore and W. Casper, "An Examination of Proxy Measures of Workplace Spirituality: A Profile Model of Multidimensional Constructs," *Journal of Leadership and Organizational Studies* 12 (2006): 111.

47. G. Collins, *Americans Women: 400 Years of Dolls, Dredges, Help Mates, and*

Heroines (New York: HarperCollins, 2007).

48. Briskin, *The Stirring of Soul in the Workplace.*

49. Ibid., 155.

50. N. Borkowski, *Organizational Behavior in Health Care*, 3rd ed. (Burlington, MA: Jones & Bartlett Learning, 2016).

51. Ibid.

52. L. W. Fry and Y. Altman, *Spiritual Leadership in Action* (Charlotte, NC: Information Age, 2013).

53. Ibid.

54. L. W. Fry and M. S. Nisiewicz, *Maximizing the Triple Bottom Line through Spiritual Leadership* (Stanford, CA: Stanford University Press, 2013).

55. A. Pattakos, *Prisoners of Our Thoughts: Viktor Frankl's Principles at Work* (San Francisco, CA: Berrett-Kohler, 2004).

56. L. W. Fry and M. S. Nisiewicz, *Maximizing the Triple Bottom Line through Spiritual Leadership.*

57. Ibid., 138.

58. L. W. Fry and M. S. Nisiewicz, *Maximizing the Triple Bottom Line through Spiritual Leadership.*

59. S. B. Frampton et al., eds., *Putting Patients First: Designing and Practicing Patient-Centered Care*, 2nd ed. (San Francisco, CA: John Wiley & Sons, 2009).

60. M. L. Millenson and J. Macri, "Summary: Will the Affordable Care Act Move Patient; Centeredness to Center Stage?" Robert Wood Johnson Foundation, http://www.rwjf.org/en/library /research/2012/03/will-the-affordable -care-act-move-patient-centeredness -to-center.html.

61. The Joint Commission, *Advancing Effective Communication, Cultural Competence, and Patient- and Family-Centered Care: A Roadmap for Hospitals* (Chicago, IL: Joint Commission, 2010).

62. Agency for Healthcare Research and Quality. *"Guide to Patient and Family Engagement,"* http://www.ahrq.gov /professionals/systems/hospital/engaging families/howtogetstarted/index.html.

63. R. A. Giacalone and C. L. Jurkiewicz, *Handbook of Workplace Spirituality and Organizational Performance*, 2nd ed. (New York: M. E. Sharpe, 2011).

64. Fry and Altman, *Spiritual Leadership in Action*, 5.

65. V. Frankl, *The Doctor and the Soul: From Psychotherapy to Logotherapy* (New York: Random House, 1986), 117–31.

66. A. Pattakos, *Prisoners of Our Thoughts: Viktor Frankl's Principles at Work* (San Francisco, CA: Berrett-Koehler, 2004).

67. W. A. Guillory, *The Living Organization: Spirituality in the Workplace* (Salt Lake City, UT: Innovations International, 2000).

68. M. H. Annison and D. S. Wilford, *Trust Matters: New Directions in Health Care* (San Francisco, CA: Jossey-Bass, 1998), 14.

69. Chapman, *Radical Loving Care*, 155.

70. D. R. Marques et al., eds., *The Workplace and Spirituality: New Perspectives on Research and Practice* (Woodstock, CA: Skylight Paths, 2009).

71. Fry and Nisiewicz, *Maximizing the Triple Bottom Line through Spiritual Leadership*, 200.

72. Chapman, *Radical Loving Care.*

73. M. Sheep, "Nurturing the Whole Person: The Ethics of Workplace Spirituality in Society of Organizations," *Journal of Business Ethics* 66 (2006): 357.

74. J. Summers, "Theory of Health Care Ethics," in *Health Care Ethics: Critical Issues for the 21st Century*, 4th ed., eds. E. E. Morrison and E. Furlough (Sudbury, MA: Jones & Bartlett Learning, 2018).

75. Ibid.

76. T. Lloyd, *The Nice Company* (London: Bloomsbury, 1990).

77. Giacalone and Jurkiewicz, *Handbook of Workplace Spirituality.*

78. I. Mitroff and E. Denton, "A Study of Spirituality in the Workplace," *Sloan Management Review* 40 (1999): 86.

79. Ibid.

80. J. Summers, "Theory of Health Care Ethics," in *Health Care Ethics: Critical Issues for the 21st Century.*

81. Chapman, *Radical Loving Care.*

82. E. Wolf, "Spiritual Leadership: A New Model," *Healthcare Executive*, March–April 2004, 23.

CHAPTER 11

A New Era of Health Care: The Ethics of Healthcare Reform

Robert W. Sandstrom and Richard L. O'Brien

▶ Introduction

Since 2010, the U.S. healthcare system has changed with the implementation of components of the Patient Protection and Affordable Care Act of 2010 (ACA 2010). The public response to this landmark legislation has been divided. In December 2016, the Kaiser Health Tracking Poll reported that 43% of Americans viewed the ACA 2010 favorably, while 46% of the public viewed it unfavorably.[1] The election of a Republican president and Congress in November 2016 has heightened expectations for significant reform and possible repeal of this legislation.

The same December 2016 Kaiser poll found that 47% of Americans do not believe that the ACA 2010 should be repealed, and another 28% of the public does not favor repeal until the details of a replacement plan are known.[2] This paradox in public opinion reflects the complex history of U.S. healthcare policy and the difficult challenge for policy makers to find a public consensus about how to improve the system. In part, this lack of policy consensus is reflective of a lack of consensus about the meaning of social justice for health care in the United States.

This chapter presents the history of the current legislation for healthcare reform and the ethics considerations that underlie this situation. It reviews the major features of this legislation and discusses its ability to address the expectations of making U.S. health care more just. It will assist the reader in understanding how ethics relates to health policy.

▶ Healthcare Reform in the United States

In 2010, Congress passed and President Obama signed H.R. 3590, the ACA 2010, and H.R. 4872, the Health Care and Education Reconciliation Act. Together these constitute healthcare reform legislation that represents the culmination of more than a century of efforts to ensure access to high-quality affordable health care for all or most Americans. For most of the 20th century, a desire to ensure access to care for all Americans drove efforts and proposals to reform the healthcare system in the United States. However, in recent decades the problems of quality and cost have assumed equal importance. Thus, access, quality, and cost control constitute the triumvirate mantra of healthcare reform and the intentions of the 2010 legislation, as well as many of the efforts to reform U.S. health care during the past quarter of a century.

There are essentially three ways to provide universal coverage for a population:[3]

- Private insurance coverage is required for all by individual or employer mandate (Bismarck model).
- The government owns and provides all required medical services (Beveridge or National Health Service model).
- The government provides health insurance (National Health Insurance model).

The U.S. system is a mixture of these three. Massachusetts has individual and employer mandates to have or provide health insurance; the Veterans Health Administration, military, and Indian Health Services are government-owned and government-operated; and Medicare and Medicaid constitute government-provided insurance.

▶ Health System Reform in the 20th Century[4]

Otto von Bismarck introduced universal health insurance in Germany in 1883. By the early 20th century, essentially all European democracies had "sickness insurance," either provided by government or mandated and provided by labor organizations or guilds, frequently with government subsidy. These plans were primarily intended to protect against wage loss rather than pay the costs of health care. Health care was not expensive, and if wages were protected, it was affordable. Most of these plans were not truly universal in coverage; they covered workers and, in some instances, those with incomes below a certain

level. A few countries, such as Germany, had (nearly) universal coverage.

In Britain, Germany, and Russia, the motives were less altruistic than in some other nations. In those countries, the motive of conservative governments was to co-opt political positions held by labor, socialist, and communist parties. As medical costs rose and became more difficult to manage on the incomes of most persons during the first half of the 20th century, most European nations evolved from wage protection plans to universal insurance that pays for medical and hospital costs.

Theodore Roosevelt was the first U.S. president to support the concept of universal health insurance. However, no legislation was introduced into Congress during his term (1901–1909). In 1912, he attempted to recapture the presidency as the candidate of the Progressive (Bull Moose) Party. That party's platform included a plank calling for national health insurance, and it was an important part of Roosevelt's presidential campaign. He was not elected.

In 1912, the American Association of Labor Legislation (AALL) created a committee on social welfare, which concentrated on health insurance. In 1914, it recruited physicians to help draft model legislation, which the American Medical Association (AMA) House of Delegates endorsed in 1917. Several states (and one Canadian province) introduced bills based on the model; it was defeated in all with intense opposition from the American Federation of Labor (AFL), state medical societies, the insurance industry, and business interests. Many of the opposition expressed their positions in ideological terms, characterizing the proposed legislation as socialism, socialized medicine, Bolshevism, or Prussian. For many in opposition, the real motives were the threat to income, fear of government controls, or, in the case of the AFL, fear of losing its power to control what benefits its members had. In 1920, the AMA reversed its position from support to opposition, marking the beginning of its opposition to all efforts at reform until the 1990s.

The impetus to provide universal coverage stalled during the 1920s and early 1930s. It was excluded from the Social Security Act (1935) because President Roosevelt was convinced it would cause the defeat of the pension portion of the bill. The Senate introduced a bill that would have enacted government health insurance in 1935, but it went nowhere.

In 1939, Senator Robert Wagner introduced S. 1620, the National Health Act, to create national compulsory health insurance for all employees and their dependents. Benefits were to include physician's services, hospitalization, drugs, and laboratory diagnostic services. Employer and employee contributions, deposited in a health insurance fund, covered the cost of insurance. If enacted, the plan would have been administered by the states. The bill died in committee. It did not have the full support of President Roosevelt and was strongly opposed by a conservative Congress elected in 1938. World War II also diverted attention from the issue.

The Wagner–Murray–Dingell Bill was introduced in 1943. It would have provided comprehensive medical insurance for people covered by the Social Security program, both working and retired, and needy persons. The plan would have covered doctors' visits; hospital costs; and nursing, laboratory, and dental services. This bill was introduced, with modifications, repeatedly during the next several Congresses, but it never passed.

In 1945, President Truman proposed, in a special message to Congress, a single comprehensive, universal national health insurance plan. In 1946, Senator Wagner introduced a bill to establish national health insurance, but the Republicans had gained control of Congress and the committee killed the bill.

In 1948, universal health insurance was part of the Democratic Party platform and one of the issues on which Truman campaigned most strongly. Public opinion polls at the time showed that 71% of Americans favored universal national health insurance. Truman won and proposed compulsory national health insurance for persons of all ages, financed by a federal payroll tax. Once again, a bill was introduced, but it never passed. It was opposed by the insurance industry, organized medicine, and political conservatives, the last of which used it to attack the bill's supporters with charges of fostering socialism or communism. Organized medicine compared it to the "socialized medicine" of the United Kingdom. This was misleading. Truman did *not* propose a National Health Service as in the United Kingdom.

The efforts of reformers probably also faltered because of the rapid and pervasive rise of employment-based health insurance. During and in the aftermath of World War II, as employers scrambled for workers in a labor-short market, unions made health insurance one of the most important parts of contract negotiations. At the beginning of World War II, fewer than 10% of Americans had employment-based health insurance. This rose to nearly 50% by 1952. In 1954, premiums became tax-deductible. This reduced the broad concern for expanding coverage. By 1980, employer coverage had risen to 80%.

In 1960, incremental increases in coverage of the uninsured began, supported by a new set of allies who vote: the elderly. The Kerr–Mills Act, authorizing the federal government to make grants to states to subsidize costs for the elderly "medically indigent," became law. It took another 5 years and President Johnson's formidable persuasive skills for Medicare, covering all Americans over 65, to be enacted into law. The legislation was vehemently opposed by the AMA, the insurance industry (both commercial carriers and Blue Cross), and politically conservative ideologues. The elderly, organized labor, and, interestingly, a segment of the business community that probably saw it as a way to reduce the cost of providing health care for retirees, all supported the legislation. Medicaid, designed to provide care for needy children, was passed in the same Social Security Act of 1965.

Although bitterly opposed by the AMA and the insurance industry, Medicare soon became a boon to both. Physicians were reimbursed for their "usual and customary fees" for providing care for the elderly, hospitals were reimbursed on a cost-plus basis, and insurers were contracted to be fiscal intermediaries for processing and paying provider claims for a population they would have had great difficulty in selling insurance to because of risk rating. In spite of these extensions of health coverage, significant fractions of Americans remained uninsured.

In 1971, President Nixon proposed a plan of compulsory employment-based health insurance for all workers and their dependents. It died a quick death when opposed by business and political conservatives who objected to a mandate and by liberals who believed it was not comprehensive enough. From then until the Clinton administration, the main government healthcare agenda was cost control, not access. In 1991 and 1992, Congress introduced a few bills that would have enacted a single-payer universal health insurance or an all-payer system. None received much attention, and none of the bills left the committee.

In 1993, the Clinton administration rolled out the Clinton National Health Security Plan. It mandated employer coverage through purchasing alliances, defined a standard benefits package, relied on premium price competition among private health insurers to control costs, and subsidized premiums for those under 150% of the federal poverty level. Early in the process of development, it had the support of 71% of the public. Immediately after the completed plan was announced, it was supported by about 60% of the public, but by April 1994, public support had dropped to 43%, largely because of the insurance industry's advertising against it.

It was endorsed by several physician groups, including the American Academy of Family Practice, the American College of Physicians, the American Academy of Pediatrics, the American College of Obstetrics and Gynecology, and the American Society of Internal Medicine. The AMA supported parts of the plan, objected to others, and neither endorsed nor condemned the plan as a whole. The American College of Surgeons debated and concluded that universal coverage was a good thing but neither endorsed nor opposed the plan. The American Hospital Association also endorsed it. Organized labor was supportive. Some leaders of large corporations expressed support, but the National Association of Manufacturers and the Chamber of Commerce denounced the plan. Intense opposition came from the insurance industry. The bill died in committee in August 1994.[2] In subsequent years, several representatives and senators introduced numerous reform bills, but none was successful.

By 2010, the fraction of the population lacking health insurance had reached more than 16%, a number that has increased steadily since the Census Bureau first began to gather this data in 1980.[5] Employment-based coverage had fallen from a high of 80% in 1980 to about 55% in 2010, largely because rising costs have made it less affordable for employers and employees, and the fraction of the population eligible for Medicare has increased substantially.[6]

Access to health care is compromised by shortages of professionals in many rural areas and inner cities. The Bureau of Health Professions publishes lists of health professional–short areas.[7] Costs have continued to rise at a rate far surpassing the growth of the economy and family incomes.[5] The United States has the most expensive health care of all Organization for Economic Cooperation and Development (OECD) nations, both in terms of per capita expense and as a share of the gross domestic product (GDP).[8] This high expenditure does not buy high-quality care. Numerous studies show significant lapses in the quality of care delivered.[9–12]

Rising numbers of the uninsured, quality lapses, and rising costs have given impetus to recent efforts to reform the system with three goals in mind:

- Greater access to care
- Improved quality
- Cost control

Early in 2009, the 111th Congress of the United States began to consider a number of healthcare reform bills introduced by both the House and the Senate. After a great deal of debate and a number of compromises, Congress passed H.R. 3590 (Public Law 111–148), the ACA 2010, and H.R. 4872 (Public Law 111–152), the Health Care and Education Reconciliation Act, in March 2010. The bulk of the legislation is contained in the ACA 2010, and that is the reform legislation discussed in the next section.

▶ Key Provisions of the Healthcare Reform Legislation of 2010 (ACA)

The following list provides a summary of the key provisions of the ACA 2010 as it currently exists:[13]

- There is a requirement for all Americans and legal immigrants to have health insurance coverage or pay a penalty (with some exemptions for financial hardship and religious belief). Businesses are also required to provide health insurance coverage or pay a penalty (businesses with 50 or fewer employees are exempted). Households with incomes of up to 400% of the poverty level are provided subsidies for premium support and out-of-pocket expenses. Small businesses will receive tax credits to offset the costs of employee coverage.
- There is a state option for an extension of Medicaid eligibility to all persons, including childless adults, with incomes at or below 133% of the federal poverty level.

- It improves Medicare benefits by providing preventive care with no copayments and lower drug prices for Medicare Drug Plan (Part D) participants, and there will be a gradual elimination of the Part D coverage gap.
- There is substantial insurance reform. Insurers are required to offer a federally defined benefit plan and guarantee issue and renewal with a limited risk rating; coverage cannot be denied to anyone. There can be no annual or lifetime limits on benefits. In addition, insurers must provide preventive care with no copayment. Insurers are also required to have minimum loss ratios of 80% for individual and small group coverage and 85% for large group coverage. States can receive financial assistance to set up state-based insurance exchanges where individuals and small businesses may shop for insurance offered by private insurers. If any states decline to set up exchanges, the federal government will provide one.
- There is substantial support for efforts to improve quality, including support of comparative effectiveness research, support for the integration and coordination of healthcare services, and incentive payments to providers on the basis of quality measures.
- To provide a balanced health professions workforce, to ensure adequate numbers of primary care providers, and to induce providers to practice in underserved areas, substantial incentives in the form of scholarships, loan forgiveness, bonus payments, and higher Medicare and Medicaid payments are offered.
- A combination of new taxes, savings, and penalties assessed on those who choose not to comply with the law will provide funding. There will be a tax assessment on high-cost "Cadillac" health plans. Increased Medicare taxes are assessed on individuals with incomes more than

$200,000 and families with incomes higher than $250,000. Insurers, pharmaceutical companies, and medical device companies are also assessed taxes. Savings will be achieved by special efforts to enforce laws against fraud and abuse, especially in Medicare and Medicaid; by reduction of hospital readmissions; and by administrative efficiencies in claims processing. Additional savings will come from reduction of payments to Medicare Advantage Plans to bring them more in line with the costs of regular Medicare and from reduction of disproportionate share payments because there will be fewer uninsured. Because of increased revenues and reduced expenditures, the Congressional Budget Office estimated that the ACA 2010 would reduce the deficit by $143 billion over the first 10 years after enactment.[14]

The following are the changes that were or will be phased in from 2010 to 2020. For purposes of clarity, the year of implementation is used for their presentation:

- 2010: Insurers may not deny children coverage because of preexisting conditions. In addition, young adults up to age 26 can be covered by their parents' health plans. By late 2011, this had resulted in 2.5 million newly covered young adults. Insurers may not rescind health insurance coverage except in cases of intentional fraud. There can be no annual or lifetime limits on coverage. Insurance companies cannot charge copayments for preventive care. Tax credits are available to small employers providing employee health coverage. Participants are provided with rebates of $250 in the Medicare Part D Drug Benefit program if they fall into the coverage gap. A number of incentives are provided to improve healthcare workforce makeup and location. These include scholarships and loan forgiveness programs for health professionals choosing primary care, as

well as other health professions training grants for professionals providing services to underserved populations. Grants are also established to support comparative effectiveness and prevention research and service.

- 2011: Copayments for Medicare preventive services, including an annual comprehensive risk assessment and prevention plan, are phased out. There is a 50% discount on brand name prescriptions filled during the Part D coverage gap. Primary care physicians and general surgeons practicing in health professional–short areas receive a 10% Medicare and Medicaid bonus. Funding for community health centers increases. Insurers must have minimum loss ratios of 80% (small group and nongroup) to 85% (large group). There will be an institution of increased primary care training opportunities for health professionals, including grants for nurse practitioner training. Wellness program grants are available to small employers.

- 2012: Performance- and efficiency-based Medicare payments to providers are begun. There will be bonus payments to high-quality Medicare Advantage Plans.

- 2013: Simplified and uniform insurance claims processing and payment are introduced. There is a phase-in of federal subsidies to close the Part D coverage gap. In addition, there is an increased Medicaid payment for primary care.

- 2014: All citizens and legal residents are required to have health coverage through employers, individually purchased plans, Medicaid, or Medicare or pay a penalty (phased in over several years). State-based health benefit exchanges for individuals and small businesses (fewer than 100 employees) are established. All insurers are required to offer the essential benefits package. Insurers are required to guarantee issue and renewal. Insurers' differences in premiums based on age are limited to 3:1; tobacco users may be charged 50%

higher premiums than nonusers. Deductibles are limited to $2000 per individual or $4000 per family. Subsidies for premiums are provided to those with incomes from 133% to 400% of the federal poverty level, and subsidies for out-of-pocket expenses are provided for those with incomes of up to 400% of the federal poverty level. Employers of more than 200 employees are required to enroll employees automatically in employer-provided coverage (although employees may opt out and buy coverage on the exchanges). Medicaid eligibility expands to everyone under 65 with incomes up to 133% of the federal poverty level. The size of the coverage gap in Medicare Part D is reduced (the coverage gap should be eliminated in 2020).

- 2016: States may form interstate compacts allowing insurers to sell across state lines. Employers with more than 50 employees are required to offer coverage at least equivalent to the prescribed benefit plan or to pay into a pool to help subsidize individual insurance purchases from the exchanges.
- 2018: Taxes are imposed on "Cadillac" healthcare plans with annual costs of more than $10,200 for individual coverage and $27,500 for family coverage (indexed to 2010-dollar purchasing power).
- 2020: There is a phase-out of the Medicare Part D coverage gap (donut hole).

▶ How Well Have the Reforms Met the Expectations of a Just Healthcare System?

If a just healthcare system provides access to high-quality affordable care for all in need of it, how well does the ACA 2010 fare in increasing access, improving quality, and controlling

costs? A fair assessment of the law is that the ACA 2010 has increased access to health care through improved affordability and availability of health insurance for about half of the uninsured population, created incentives to improve the quality of care in the delivery system, but struggled to maintain a choice of private plans in the health insurance marketplace.

The reforms addressed access through policy changes that increased the number of Americans who have health insurance. The ACA 2010 has been successful in significantly lowering the chronic, high rate of uninsurance in the U.S. population. The Census Bureau reported that the number of uninsured Americans fell from 43 million persons in 2013 (first year of full implementation of the insurance reforms) to 29 million persons in 2015.[15] Rates of growth in the insured population were particularly strong in minority communities and in states that expanded Medicaid. A record 11.5 million persons signed up for health insurance using the ACA 2010 exchanges after the November 2016 election.[16] The results of this positive change in affordability has been improved access to care. For example, the Commonwealth Fund reported that the percentage of people not going to their physicians because of cost has declined in 38 states and the District of Columbia since insurance reforms have been implemented.[17] However, about 20 million persons remain uninsured. This population includes undocumented immigrants, persons exempted from the requirement to buy insurance because of financial hardship, low-income adults eligible for Medicaid but not enrolled, and persons choosing to pay the penalty for lack of coverage rather than paying the premiums.[18]

The effect of ACA 2010 reforms on quality has been most evident in the Medicare program. Medicare hospital reimbursement methods have created "pay for value or performance" incentives and disincentives that reward hospitals for quality and efficiency.[19] This concept is being expanded to office-based physician and certain non-physician provider reimbursement methods in Medicare for 2017. It is more difficult to assess the effect of the ACA 2010 on the supply and professional distribution of healthcare providers. Most of the newly insured population was able to find a provider and were satisfied with the care that they received.[20] However, the effect of the ACA 2010 on the distribution of healthcare providers to underserved areas will take longer to determine.

The ACA 2010 addressed individual affordability through insurance reform (80% and 85% minimum loss ratios), subsidies for low- and middle-income persons and families, support of prevention efforts, increased system efficiencies, and enhanced efforts to reduce fraud and abuse. The Commonwealth Fund found that the law's tax credits improved affordability for low-income persons as it made health insurance premium costs about equivalent to comparable employer- sponsored insurance plans.[20] However, persons with higher incomes (without tax subsidies) participating in ACA 2010 exchanges incurred higher premiums and out-of-pocket costs. Individual affordability in the future has become more worrisome with the decision of major health insurers, for example, Aetna and United Health Care, to exit the ACA 2010 insurance marketplaces in 2017 because of high costs and losses.[21] These decisions are decreasing consumer choice of healthcare plans in the subsidized ACA 2010 marketplace.

The ACA 2010 was projected to slow the cost growth of health care, but costs were projected to continue to rise faster than the GDP and inflation in general.[22] From 2010 to 2013, national healthcare spending did increase at a much slower rate than the immediate years prior to ACA 2010 enactment.[23] In 2014–2015, national healthcare spending accelerated as more persons were insured (increasing to about a 5.5% annual growth rate). The effect of the ACA 2010 on the federal budget has been positive. The date at which the Medicare Hospital Trust fund will be depleted has been extended to 2028, in part, by ACA 2010 reimbursement changes to Medicare.[24] The Committee for a Responsible Federal Budget estimated in early 2017 that a full repeal of the ACA 2010 without a replacement plan would cost the federal budget 150–350 billion dollars over the next 10 years.[25]

▶ Ethics Considerations Underlying Healthcare Reform

What underlying ethics assumptions have driven healthcare reform efforts for the past 100 years? Internationally, most persons and societies in the industrialized world have concluded that there is a fundamental right to health care. This is declared in a number of international agreements, including the Universal Declaration of Human Rights (Article 25),[26] the Constitution of the World Health Organization (p. 1),[27] the American Declaration of the Rights and Duties of Man (Article 11),[28] the International Covenant on Economic, Social and Cultural Rights (Article 12),[29] the UNESCO Declaration on Bioethics and Human Rights (Article 14),[30] the Convention on the Rights of the Child (Article 24),[31] and the Convention on the Rights of Persons with Disabilities (Article 25).[32]

The preamble of the U.S. Declaration of Independence begins with the sentence "We hold these truths to be self-evident, that all men are created equal, that they are endowed by their Creator with certain unalienable Rights, that among these are Life, Liberty and the pursuit of Happiness."[33] The interpretation of this sentence is usually that access to health care is a right because it is necessary to attain the declared rights of "Life, Liberty and the pursuit of Happiness."[34] Further, the U.S. public generally subscribes to such a right. Public opinion polls have found that 70%–89% of Americans have supported universal health insurance coverage or health care at least since 1948. However, not everyone subscribes to the view that health care is a right.[35,36] Various religious traditions, including Roman Catholics, Anglican/Episcopalians, Baptists, Methodists, Jews, and Muslims, also hold health care as a right.[37–43]

Some argue that health and health care are social goods, that is, that the health of individuals is good for society and all of its members. This is a kind of contractarianism[44] or communitarianism.[45] A social contract binds us because we live in a communal society in which the good of individuals is beneficial for society as a whole. Healthy people contribute to a good society and a sound economy. As a nation we have made a compact with each other to strive to create an environment that is in the best interests of each of us and all of us. If we believe that health and health care are good for us, then we have a duty to provide them for all. Thus, it is reasonable to expect that a well-structured healthcare system will provide access to affordable, high-quality care for all.[46] The complex history of healthcare reform that was reviewed earlier in this chapter indicates that reform of health care in the United States has been incremental and occurring over decades.

Many reforms of the ACA 2010 are consistent with an egalitarian Rawlsian perspective on social justice, especially as further defined by Daniels.[47] The establishment of subsidized insurance plans for low- to moderate-income persons in state exchanges and the expansion of Medicaid for the poor and near-poor populations are consistent with the "difference principle," which states that policy is just only when inequalities in social policy improve the lot of the persons who are worst off in a society. This improvement in social justice from the Rawlsian/Daniels perspective is incomplete, that is, 20 million persons are without health insurance after full implementation of the reforms. Beyond categorical exclusions in participation in insurance exchanges and Medicaid, the refusal of some states to expand Medicaid and the relatively small individual penalties for violation of the individual mandate reflect a small government/libertarian

perspective of social justice.[48] From this perspective, the maintenance of these individual freedoms in the ACA 2010 are just.

This dichotomy in understanding the meaning of social justice is exhibited and heightened by a hyperpartisan political environment in the country.[49] Oberlander (2014) comprehensively describes the "uneasy balance" employed in the design and implementation of the ACA 2010 that both expands government involvement in health care (an egalitarian/ Rawlsian idea) and relies on market forces (a libertarian idea) to provide private insurance options and control costs.[50] Until the country settles on a consensus view of justice related to health care, it can be anticipated that the tension and conflict between these worldviews will animate the debate about the future of health policy in the United States.

▶ Summary

Health care has changed on many levels because of the enactment of the ACA 2010 and H.R. 4872, the Health Care and Education Reconciliation Act. Almost every part of the healthcare system is examining how it provides patient care and addresses the costs of this care. This chapter provides an important look at the history of healthcare reform so that we can better understand why there was a need for this monumental change. It also reviews the key features of the ACA 2010 (the primary legislation) to foster understanding. Finally, it begins to address the critical issue of justice and healthcare reform—an issue that will be part of health care as the ACA 2010 era continues.

▶ Questions for Discussion

1. The history of health care is different in the United States than it is in Europe. What ethics principles applied to reform efforts in the United States prior

to Medicare/Medicaid? After Medicare and Medicaid?

2. What principles of ethics are evident in the Medicare/Medicaid laws?

3. Justice is often viewed differently by different groups of people. Consider the ACA 2010. How is justice defined by the following: physicians, insurance companies, the currently uninsured, well-insured Americans, and those who are in poor health? How do differing conceptualizations of justice, for example, Rawlsian egalitarianism and libertarianism, affect reform of the healthcare system?

▶ **Notes**

1. Kaiser Family Foundation, "Kaiser Health Tracking Poll: The Public's View on the ACA," http://kff.org/interactive /kaiser-health-tracking-poll-the-publics -views-on-the-aca/#?response=Favorable --Unfavorable&aRange=twoYear on January 9, 2017.

2. Kaiser Family Foundation, "Kaiser Health Tracking Poll: Health Care Priorities for 2017," http://kff.org/health-costs /poll-finding/kaiser-health-tracking -poll-health-care-priorities-for-2017/ on January 9, 2017.

3. T. R. Reid, *The Healing of America: A Global Quest for Better, Cheaper, and Fairer Health Care* (New York: Penguin Press, 2009), 16–27.

4. The author (RLO) used the following sources to compile the history recounted in this chapter: R. A. Stevens, "History and Health Policy in the United States, 1948–2008," *Social History of Medicine* 21, no. 3 (2008): 461–83; J. S. Ross, "The Committee on the Costs of Medical Care and the History of Health Insurance in the United States," *Einstein Quarterly Journal of Biology and Medicine* 19 (2002):

129–34; and K. A. Palmer, "A Brief History: Universal Health Care Efforts in the US," *Physicians for a National Health Program* (Spring, 1999), http:// www.pnhp.org/facts/a_brief_history _universal_health_care_efforts_in _the_us.php?page=all. Accessed May 14, 2012.

5. C. DeNavas-Walt et al., *Income Poverty and Insurance Coverage in the United States: 2010,* Current Population Reports P60-239 (Washington, DC: U.S. Government Printing Office, 2011).

6. Ibid.

7. Health Resources and Service Administration, "Shortage Designation: Health Professional Shortage Areas and Medically Underserved Areas/Populations," http://bhpr.hrsa.gov/shortage/index .html.

8. E. Mossialos et al., eds., *International Profiles of Health Care Systems*, 2015 (Washington, DC: The Commonwealth Fund, 2016).

9. L. T. Kohn et al., *To Err Is Human* (Washington, DC: National Academy Press, 1999).

10. E. A. McGlynn et al., "Quality of Care Delivered to Adults in the United States," *New England Journal of Medicine* 348, no. 26 (2003): 2635–45.

11. S. C. Williams et al., "Quality of Care in U.S. Hospitals as Reflected by Standardized Measures," *New England Journal of Medicine* 353, no. 3 (2005): 255–64.

12. R. Mangione-Smith et al., "Quality of Ambulatory Care Delivered to Children in the United States," *New England Journal of Medicine* 357, no. 15 (2007): 1515–23.

13. A good, more extensive summary of the legislation can be found at the Kaiser Family Foundation Health Reform website, http://www.kff.org/health-reform/.

14. Letter to Speaker Pelosi, March 20, 2010 (Washington, DC: Congressional Budget Office), http://www.cbo

.gov/ftpdocs/113xx/doc11379/Amend ReconProp.pdf.

15. J. C. Barnet and M. Vornovitsky, "Health Insurance Coverage in the United States: 2015," *United States Census Bureau, Report* P60-257RV (Washington, DC: U. S. Printing Office, 2016).

16. M. Haberman and M. Sanger- Katz, "Trump Pushes Republicans for Immediate Repeal of Obama Health Care Law." *New York Times* (2017, January 10), https://www.nytimes.com/2017/01 /10/us/repeal-affordable-care-act -donald-trump.html?action=Click &contentCollection=BreakingNews &contentID=64777031&pgtype=article.

17. S. L. Hayes et al., "A Long Way in a Short Time: States' Progress on Health Care Coverage and Access, 2013–2015," (Washington, DC: The Commonwealth Fund, 2016, December).

18. M. Buettgens and M. A. Hall, "Who Will Be Uninsured After Health Insurance Reform?" (Washington, DC: Urban Institute: 2011, March), http://www .urban.org/UploadedPDF/1001520 -Uninsured-After-Health-Insurance -Reform.pdf.

19. D. Blumenthal et al., "The Affordable Care Act at 5 Years," *New England Journal of Medicine* 372 (2015): 2451–58.

20. M. Z. Gunza et al., "Americans' Experiences with ACA Marketplace Coverage: Findings from the Commonwealth Fund Affordable Care Act Tracking Survey, February to April 2016," *Issue Brief* (Washington, DC: Commonwealth Fund) 17: (July, 2016): 1–20.

21. S. R. Collins and D. Blumenthal, "ACA Marketplaces: Stressed but Fixable," *To the Point* (Washington, DC: Commonwealth Fund, 2016, August 24).

22. C. J. Truffer et al., "Health Spending Projections through 2019: The Recession's Impact Continues," *Health Affairs* 29, no. 3 (2010): 522–29.

23. A. A. Martin et al., "National Health Spending: Faster Growth in 2015 as Coverage Expands and Utilization Increases," *Health Affairs* 36, no. 1 (2017): 166–76.

24. Boards of Trustees of the Federal Hospital Insurance and Federal Supplemental Medical Insurance Trust Funds, *The 2016 Annual Report of the Boards of Trustees of the Federal Hospital Insurance and Federal Supplemental Medical Insurance Trust Funds* (Washington, DC: Boards of Trustees of the Federal Hospital Insurance and Federal Supplemental Medical Insurance Trust Funds), 7, https://www.cms.gov/Research-Statistics -Data-and-Systems/Statistics-Trends -and-Reports/ReportsTrustFunds /downloads/tr2016.pdf.

25. Committee for a Responsible Federal Budget. "The Cost of Full Repeal of the Affordable Care Act," (2017, January 4), http://crfb.org/papers /cost-full-repeal-affordable-care-act.

26. United Nations, "Universal Declaration of Human Rights." Adopted by the General Assembly of the United Nations, Resolution 217 A (III), 10 December 1948, http://www.un.org/en /documents/udhr/index.shtml.

27. World Health Organization, "Constitution of the World Health Organization," *American Journal of Public Health Nations Health* 36, no. 11 (1948): 1315–23.

28. Organization of American States, *American Declaration of the Rights and Duties of Man* (Bogota, Columbia: The Organization of American States, 1948), http://www.hrcr.org/docs/OAS _Declaration/oasrights.html.

29. General Assembly of the United Nations, *International Covenant on Economic, Social, and Cultural Rights* (New York: United Nations, 1966).

30. United Nations Educational, Scientific, and Cultural Organization, *Universal Declaration on Bioethics and Human*

Rights (Paris, France: United Nations Educational, Scientific, and Cultural Organization, 2005), http://unesdoc.unesco.org /images/0014/001461/146180E.pdf.

31. General Assembly of the United Nations, *Convention on the Rights of the Child* (New York: United Nations, 1989).

32. General Assembly of the United Nations, *Convention on the Rights of Persons with Disabilities* (New York: United Nations, 2006).

33. See *The Declaration of Independence: A Transcription*, http://www.archives.gov /exhibits/charters/declaration_transcript .html. Accessed May 6, 2012.

34. Ibid.

35. B. H. Baumrin, "Why There Is No Right to Health Care," in *Medicine and Social Justice*, eds. R. Rhodes, M. P. Battin, and A. Silvers (New York: Oxford University Press, 2002), 78–83.

36. B. Shapiro, "Health Care Is a Commodity, Not a Right," *National Review* (2017, January), http://www.nationalreview.com /article/443737/health-care-markets -government-commodity-human-right on January 12, 2017.

37. General Board of the Baptist Churches, "American Baptist Policy Statement on Human Rights," 1976; modified 1992, http://www.abc-usa.org/LinkClick .aspx?fileticket=8gLU4H3BXuE%3d &tabid=199. Accessed May 14, 2012.

38. United Methodist Church, "Social Principles of the United Methodist Church, 2009–2012," http://www.umcsc.org/PDF /boards/SocialPrinciples.pdf.

39. United State Catholic Conference, *Health and Health Care. A Pastoral Letter of the American Catholic Bishops* (Washington, DC: United States Catholic Conference, 1981), http://old.usccb.org /sdwp/national/HEALTH.PDF.

40. R. T. Alpert, "The Jewish Tradition and the Right to Health Care," *Reconstructionist* (April–May 1984): 15–20.

41. Union for Reform Judaism, "59th General Assembly Resolution on Health Care," 1987, http://urj.org//about/union /governance/reso//?syspage=article &item_id=2081. Accessed May 14, 2012.

42. Episcopal Church USA, "Right of All Persons to Comprehensive Health Care," General Convention (A010) and (A099) Resolution, 1991.

43. M. H. Al-Khayat, *Health as a Human Right in Islam* (Cairo, Egypt: Regional Office for the Eastern Mediterranean, World Health Organization, 2004).

44. A. Cudd, "Contractarianism," *Stanford Encyclopedia of Philosophy*, 2008, http://plato.stanford.edu/entries /contractarianism/. Accessed December 2, 2012.

45. D. Bell, "Communitarianism," *Stanford Encyclopedia of Philosophy*, 2010, http://plato.stanford.edu/entries /communitarianism/.

46. For a more detailed description of ethicists' consensus about what healthcare reform legislation should do, see M. A. Levine et al., "Improving Access to Health Care: A Consensus Ethical Framework to Guide Proposal for Reform," *Hastings Center Report* 37 (September–October, 2007): 14–19.

47. N. Daniels, *Just HealthCare in Studies in Philosophy and Health Policy*, ed., D. Wikler (Cambridge, UK: Cambridge University Press, 1985).

48. R. Nozick, *Anarchy, State and Utopia* (Philadelphia, PA: Basic Books, 1974).

49. J. Oberlander, "Implementing the Affordable Care Act: The Promise and Limits of Health Care Reform," *Journal of Health Politics Policy and Law* 41, no. 4 (2016): 803–26.

50. J. Oberlander, "Between Liberal Aspirations and Market Forces: Obamacare's Precarious Balancing Act," *Journal of Law and Medical Ethics* 42, no. 4 (2014): 431–41.

PART IV

Critical Issues for Society's Health

Part IV presents examples of issues faced by society that also have profound implications for the practice of ethics in health care. Again, there are many choices for inclusion in this section, but the authors chose to include selected examples that provide unique ethics challenges. In the final chapter of this part of the text, Morrison and Furlong address issues not contained in other chapters but that need to be considered for the future.

Chapter 12 The chapter "Health Inequalities and Health Inequities" presents a discussion of the equality and inequality of the healthcare system and their measurement. It also establishes the ethics positions on which Americans base their assessment of health inequalities and inequities. Finally, the author posed some ideas about dealing with inequalities and inequities when they occur.

Chapter 13 The chapter "The Ethics of Epidemics" is new to this edition and presents an ethics issue that affects public health both nationally and internationally. Adepoju begins the chapter with a discussion of the history of epidemics/pandemics and how these events affected society and ethics. She also includes examples of modern epidemics and the public health response to them as it relates to ethics. In addition, there is a discussion on autonomy versus paternalism and the presentation of a bioethical model for decision-making when addressing epidemics/pandemics.

Chapter 14 The chapter "Ethics of Disasters: Planning and Response" involves a topic that is an unfortunate part of our daily news. It gives an overview of government, healthcare system, professional, and individual responses to both human-caused and natural disasters. New information on planning and response to these events is included. There is also a discussion of ethics issues faced by organizations and individuals as they provide disaster response and patient care.

Chapter 15 In the chapter "Domestic Violence: Changing Theory, Changing Practice," Warshaw presents an issue that continues to affect individuals, the community, and health care— domestic violence. She includes information about changes in education of physicians and introduces the limitations of trauma models for treating this issue; ethics issues such as mental health, coercion, lack of insurance coverage, and the need for effective education for healthcare providers are part of her discussion.

Chapter 16   In the chapter "Looking toward the Future," Morrison and Furlong present emerging issues both in ethics theory and for society. Furlong discusses how thinking in the theory of ethics is evolving, through her introduction to the ethics care model and the narrative ethics model. She describes how these models can be used in healthcare decision-making. Morrison revises her discussion on complementary/alternative medicine (CAM) among Americans and includes ethics issues for both professionals and society. In addition, she enhances her section on the aging baby boomer population and its impact on society and on health care. Finally, she presents a new section to the chapter, "Ethics in the Epoch of Change." In this section, she provides a look at the impact of change on maintaining an ethics-based practice. She also offers suggestions for maintaining ethics practices during the time of great change.

CHAPTER 12

Health Inequalities and Health Inequities

Nicholas B. King

▶ Introduction

People have long recognized that some individuals lead longer and healthier lives than others and that often these differences are closely associated with social characteristics such as race, ethnicity, gender, location, and socioeconomic status. The introduction of the regular collection of vital statistics by European states in the 19th century enabled Edwin Chadwick and other social reformers to quantify and compare the health and living conditions of different social classes. More recently, epidemiologists, sociologists, geographers, and other researchers have used advanced qualitative and quantitative methods not only to identify and track a wide variety of health inequalities but also to produce increasingly sophisticated models to explain their causes and consequences.

As the knowledge and understanding of health inequalities have increased, so, too, has the political will to reduce or eliminate them. One of the two goals of the U.S. Healthy People 2020 initiative is to "achieve health equity, eliminate disparities, and improve the health of all groups."[1] In the United Kingdom, the release of successive government reports on socioeconomic inequalities in health in 1980 (the Black Report) and 1987 (the *Health Divide* report) stimulated increased scrutiny of the National Health Service. Other countries and non-governmental organizations have undertaken major initiatives to address health inequalities both within and between nations. As the World Health Organization's (WHO) Commission on Social Determinants of Health's 2008 final report notes:

> Within countries, the differences in life chances are dramatic and are seen worldwide. The poorest of the poor have high levels of illness and premature mortality. But poor health is not confined to those worst off. In countries at all levels of income, health and illness follow a social gradient: the lower the socioeconomic position, the worse the health . . . Putting right these inequities—the huge and remediable differences in health between and within countries—is a matter of social justice.[2]

This chapter reviews the central ethics issues raised by the existence of health inequalities, their study, and attempts to reduce or eliminate them. One can summarize the chapter's concepts in a series of basic questions: What are health inequalities? Why are some health inequalities also health inequities? How are health inequalities measured? What is the best way to reduce or eliminate health inequities?

▸ What Are Health Inequalities?

Understanding and assessing health inequalities requires us to answer three subsidiary questions: What is health? What is a health inequality? What is the difference between a health inequality and a health inequity?

Health

What is *health*? The answers vary considerably, from narrow definitions focusing on the absence of disease to broader ones encompassing a wide range of measures of subjective and objective characteristics. At one end of the spectrum, bioethicist Norman Daniels offers a narrow definition of health as "normal functioning, that is, the absence of pathology, mental or physical."[3] By contrast, the constitution of WHO defines it as "a state of complete physical, mental, and social well-being and not merely the absence of disease or infirmity."[4] More expansive definitions of health might include happiness, freedom from disability, quality of life, and the capacity to lead a socially meaningful and economically productive life. Narrow definitions have the benefit of being objectively measurable by biological and physiologic characteristics, but they fail to capture aspects of human experience that might be more relevant to ensuring social justice, such as happiness, well-being, or capabilities. Broader definitions rectify this limitation but often involve highly subjective judgments by researchers or patients and, thus, are more difficult to adequately measure and compare.

Researchers assess health status in many ways. Under a narrow definition of health, the most common health indicators are mortality, survival, life expectancy, disease incidence, and disease prevalence. Definitions that are more expansive might include physiologic indicators of overall health (e.g., height, weight, body mass index [BMI], and blood pressure), symptoms, self-rated health status, a sense of well-being, social connectedness, and productivity. Different kinds of health problems have different classification schemes. The *International Classification of Diseases* (ICD) *Manual* provides standard definitions of physical illness based around etiopathies that alter organ function and produce symptoms. ICD classifications are widely accepted and used in clinical diagnosis and health research. By contrast, the American Psychiatric Association's *Diagnostic and Statistical Manual of Mental Disorders* (DSM) defines mental health problems in terms of symptoms rather than etiology, which has been subject to considerable criticism.[5] For example, in 2010, the editors of the fifth edition of the DSM proposed classifying grief that lasts longer than 2 weeks as a major depressive disorder. Critics argued that grief is a normal human reaction to difficult life events, and classifying it as a disease would result in overdiagnosis and overtreatment and would interfere with individuals' ability to develop coping mechanisms.[6]

Because different populations can have radically different health belief systems, definitions of health, or subjective experience of symptoms, comparing populations to determine the levels of inequality between them can be difficult. This is particularly true when trying to compare rates of mental illness, symptoms, or self-reported health status between nations with widely disparate cultures. For this reason, authors often express international health inequalities in terms of adult or infant mortality, or life expectancy, which—although collected haphazardly in some locations—they think are the most objective indicators of health status available.

Composite measures such as the disability-adjusted life year (DALY) and the quality-adjusted life year—which combine information about mortality, number of life years lost, and life lived with a disability—are increasingly used for comparing different health conditions. These measures address one set of ethics dilemmas, while introducing additional ones. Imagine three different countries that are similar in every relevant respect, such as income. In country A, a small number of people suffer from severe conditions that kill at a young age; in country B, a larger number of people suffer from a moderately disabling condition that kills at an old age; in country C, everyone suffers from a mild disease. Comparing A, B, and C using a single metric, such as mortality, would undervalue diseases that cause disability but do not kill, as in country C. The DALY solves this dilemma by taking into account both morbidity and mortality. However, it introduces an additional dilemma regarding aggregation: should we really consider a mild disease that happens to affect many people to be worse than one that is more severe but affects fewer people?

Assessments of health inequalities might also use measures of health care, including rates of diagnosis, treatment, cost, insurance coverage, quality, survival, symptom reduction, or some other health outcome measure. Strictly speaking, one should distinguish *health inequalities* from inequalities in *health care*. Linkage can exist between the two; however, this not always the case. Some inequalities in health care do not necessarily lead to health inequalities, whereas many health inequalities occur in the context of healthcare equality.

Inequality

Health inequality is a descriptive term that can refer either to the total variation in health status across individuals within a population or to a difference in the average or total health between two or more populations. In **TABLE 12.1**, the average BMI of populations A and B are identical, but the variation within population A is clearly larger than that within population B. Thus, we may say that there is greater total inequality within population A than population B but that there is relative equality *between* the two populations. Although there is some debate over which is a more scientifically rigorous measurement,[7] most scholarly work on the topic defines health inequalities as differences in health between populations.

Because health inequalities generally involve the comparison of population averages (although one can use other measures), one must take great care in making inferences regarding individuals. In **TABLE 12.2**, the average BMI of population A is lower than that of population B. However, the two individuals with the highest BMI are in population A, and the individual with the lowest BMI is in population B. Thus, we cannot infer that any particular individual in a group with better health will be any healthier than an individual in a group with worse health. Inequality is a property of populations rather than individuals.[8]

TABLE 12.1 Average Body Mass Index: Example 1

Population A	Population B
40	30
38	29
18	27
16	26
Average 28	**28**

TABLE 12.2 Average Body Mass Index: Example 2

Population A	Population B
35	33
34	32
22	31
21	20
Average 28	**29**

▶ # Why Are Some Health Inequalities also Health Inequities?

In contrast to the descriptive term *health inequality*, *health inequity* is a normative term that refers to a difference that society judges to be morally unacceptable.[9] Although almost all health inequities are, by definition, health inequalities, not all health inequalities are health inequities. For example, because society does not consider elective cosmetic surgery a necessity for good health and functioning, society would not consider unequal access to such surgery to be an inequity. Similarly, because society considers skydiving to be a freely chosen behavior, it would not consider the fact that the mortality rate for falls from great heights is much higher among skydivers than the general population to be a health inequity.

Determining whether a particular inequality (or class of inequalities) constitutes an inequity requires a moral judgment based on a priori beliefs about justice, fairness, and the distribution of social resources and, thus, is one of the primary areas in which ethics analysis plays a role. One commonly defines *health inequities* by referring to either the populations affected by inequalities or the causes and consequences of inequalities.

One way of determining whether a health inequality qualifies as an inequity is through reference to the relative social position of different populations. If a health inequality benefits a population that is in some way already socially or economically advantaged, then we may deem that inequality unjust through its association with a prior distributive injustice. This "egalitarian liberal" perspective judges health inequalities morally wrong primarily because they suggest that some individuals' or groups' rights are being violated, thus negatively affecting their health.[10] For example, Paul Farmer argues that ill health, and health inequalities in particular, is evidence of injustice or structural inequity in the world, "even though it may be manifest in the patient."[11] More specifically, Paula Braveman argues that

> [a] health disparity between more and less advantaged population groups constitutes an inequity *not* because we know the proximate causes of that disparity and judge them to be unjust, but rather because the disparity is strongly associated with unjust social structures; those structures systematically put disadvantaged groups at generally increased risk of ill health and also generally compound the social and economic consequences of ill health.[12]

The existence of health inequalities might indicate that a given population has disproportionately suffered international military and economic exploitation,[13] inequitable distribution of economic resources,[14] or historical patterns of race-based economic and social injustice.[15] This definition of health inequity accords with John Rawls's "difference principle" of distributive justice: any inequalities in the distribution of an important resource should benefit the least advantaged members of a society.[16] It also has the benefit of using a priori judgments about social or economic inequity as the foundation for adjudicating claims of health inequity. Thus, for example, disadvantaged populations do not have to prove repeatedly that every health inequality adversely affecting them constitutes an inequity. It is also important to note that under this definition, health inequalities that benefit the socially disadvantaged would not be considered inequities.

However, this definition also suffers from significant drawbacks. First, the a priori identification of disadvantaged populations can be contentious or arbitrary in some situations. For example, would a health inequality favoring those with annual incomes of $5 million over those with annual incomes of $2 million constitute an inequity, or do both of these groups qualify as "advantaged"? Another example is that in most countries, despite their lesser social status, women enjoy a longer lifespan than men do. This is possibly because of genetic factors but also possibly because of lower rates of risky behaviors, such as smoking and alcohol use. Few observers identify this longer lifespan as a health inequity.

At the same time, many argue that the dramatically higher rates of morbidity and mortality from human immunodeficiency virus/acquired immunodeficiency syndrome (HIV/AIDS) among women in a number of countries[17] are evidence of serious health and social inequities.[18] By contrast, higher rates of HIV/AIDS among men in richer nations, such as the United States, have seldom been identified as a gendered health inequity (although the delay in devoting health resources to the disease during the 1980s was frequently cited as evidence of a sexual orientation health inequity). Simply assuming that a health inequality that benefits the socially disadvantaged is morally acceptable has clear drawbacks. In addition, how might this definition account for

novel forms of sociological categorization that may be accurate but do not lend themselves easily to judgments of relative disadvantage? An example of such a categorization might be race-county combinations that indicate that low-income rural blacks who live in the South have a lower life expectancy than low-income whites in Appalachia and the Mississippi Valley.[19]

This definition also neglects situations in which a genuinely unjust distribution of health might happen to benefit those in socially superior positions—as, for example, when a major pollutant happens to disproportionately affect a nearby wealthy community. Finally, if other social inequities exist and one deems them (rightly or wrongly) as socially acceptable, does this mean that the resultant health inequalities cannot qualify as unjust? Many U.S. cities tolerate a certain level of homelessness as socially acceptable. Are higher rates of tuberculosis and mental illness among the homeless therefore socially acceptable as well?

One way of addressing these concerns is to shift our focus to the *causes and consequences* of a given health inequality rather than the specific populations that it affects.[20] From this point of view, a health inequality is inequitable if it is systematic, avoidable, and unjust.[21] A *systematic* health inequality is one that consistently affects two or more populations and is not the result of random variation. For example, some so-called cancer clusters (elevated incidence of cancer in a community) are in fact the transient result of random variation. This has led to conflicts between community members who feel victimized by an apparent health inequity and health officials who argue that no such inequity exists, because the inequalities—even if they disproportionately occur in a low-income neighborhood—are random rather than systematic.[22]

The criterion of *avoidability* has several components.[23] Health inequities must be *technically avoidable*, that is, a successful means of reducing the inequality must exist. They must be *financially avoidable*, that is, sufficient resources should exist to rectify the inequality. Finally, they must be *morally avoidable*, that is, rectifying the inequality must not violate some other social value, such as liberty or distributive justice.

The third criterion is an *unjust cause*. M. Whitehead lists the following determinants of inequality:[24]

1. Natural, biological variation
2. Freely chosen health-damaging behavior, such as participation in certain sports and pastimes
3. The transient health advantage of one group over another when that group is first to adopt a health-promoting behavior (as long as other groups have the means to catch up fairly soon)
4. Health-damaging behavior where the degree of choice of lifestyles is severely restricted
5. Exposure to unhealthy, stressful living and working conditions
6. Inadequate access to essential health and other public services
7. Natural selection or health-related social mobility involving the tendency for sick people to move down the social scale

Whitehead argues that health inequalities resulting from the first three determinants are neither unjust nor unfair and should not be considered inequitable. By contrast, health inequalities arising from the latter four determinants are unjust and unfair and thus qualify as health inequities. Examples of inequalities that would not qualify as inequitable under this definition might include the following: Ashkenazi Jews' elevated risk of developing breast cancer because of their slightly higher rates of carrying the *BRCA1* and *BRCA2* mutations[25] and the previously mentioned example of skydivers, whose freely chosen behavior elevates their risk of death. Other examples include the higher rates of some communicable diseases among people living in temperate

climates, because the insect vectors for those diseases are more prevalent there than in colder climates, and early recipients of a new vaccine (provided that vaccine is not distributed in a way that systematically favors advantaged groups).

This definition of health inequity avoids the criticisms leveled at the first definition, and it accords with Iris Marion Young's observation that in general, it is not patterns of inequality per se that are morally wrong but rather those whose causes and consequences we deem unjust.[26] However, like the previous definition, it suffers from some significant drawbacks. First, the degree to which many high-risk health behaviors are "freely chosen" is a topic of considerable debate. Three of the top nine "actual causes of death" in the United States (consumption of tobacco, alcohol, and illegal drugs) involve the use of substances that are highly addictive,[27] which might significantly diminish the element of free choice. In addition, many freely chosen health behaviors exhibit strong socioeconomic gradients. For example, both lung cancer rates and cigarette consumption (a primary risk factor for lung cancer) increase as socioeconomic status diminishes.[28] Many argue that the existence of a socioeconomic gradient in smoking is evidence that these behaviors are not freely chosen (e.g., they may be mechanisms for coping with social or occupational stressors), and thus, the resulting health inequalities are inequitable.

A second problem with this definition is that by favoring cause overpopulation as the deciding factor, health inequalities that benefit otherwise socially advantaged populations would be deemed inequitable and thus ostensibly in need of social remedy. This contradicts most peoples' intuition that social justice, by definition, involves redistributing social resources to the disadvantaged rather than the other way around.

Perhaps the most significant problem with this definition is that many health problems have multicausal etiologies, and it is difficult or impossible to isolate a single, overriding causal factor. Diseases of the cardiovascular system result from a complex combination of "just" causes, such as genetic predisposition and health behaviors (diet, exercise, smoking, etc.), and "unjust" causes, such as stressful living and working conditions and inadequate access to preventive health care. In some cases, it might be possible to quantify the relative contribution of each determinant to a population's health through sophisticated regression analyses. Yet this leaves open the question of whether moral judgments of inequity should be entirely dependent on the outcome of statistical analyses.

Finally, we might judge a health inequality to be unacceptable for instrumental rather than intrinsic reasons, that is, because it is evidence of, or a contributing factor to, some other morally unacceptable situation. A health inequality thus "acts as a signpost—indicating that something is wrong."[29] For example, from an "objective utilitarian" perspective, a health inequality between two subpopulations might be judged bad because it indicates that the sum total of health in the entire population is not being maximized.[30] In this case, one does not see inequality per se as morally wrong, and the rectification of the health inequality would simply be a means toward the end of maximizing overall population health.

Similarly, some researchers argue that pervasive health inequalities across the entire socioeconomic spectrum are indications not of injustices directed at particular subpopulations but of fundamental social problems that adversely affect the health of all but those at the absolute top of the social hierarchy. Michael Marmot argues that socioeconomic gradients in chronic disease and life expectancy result from comparatively low levels of autonomy, social engagement, and social gradient.[31] Similarly, Richard Wilkinson argues that low social cohesion and pervasive psychosocial stress in societies with greater income inequality lead to shorter life expectancy.[32] If these authors are correct that almost every member of a society is in some way subject to health inequality,

then attempts to encourage health equity could appeal to self-interest rather than social injustice.

▶ How Can We Measure Health Inequalities?

Regardless of which definition of health inequity one uses, determining whether a specific situation is inequitable requires the measurement and comparison of the status of at least two populations. To do this, one must determine which *populations* are most appropriate to compare and which *measures* are most appropriate to use in comparing those populations. Although one bases these determinations primarily on technical judgments to ensure the most statistically valid measurement and data analysis, they also require ethical judgment regarding the appropriate focus of description and intervention.[33]

Populations

By definition, inequalities are differences between groups of people. In some cases, the definition of these groups may be morally arbitrary. For example, there is some evidence of an association between genetically determined height and the risk of coronary artery disease.[34] While this health inequality may be of interest from a medical or epidemiological standpoint, we would not consider it worthy of interest from a moral standpoint.

In most cases, however, defining populations involves important moral or ethical decisions. First, the populations chosen should differ from one another in some way that is socially or morally important. We would thus expect that health inequalities among socially important groups based on factors such as race/ethnicity, gender, education level, or socioeconomic status would deserve scrutiny, whereas health inequalities among groups with different hair or eye color—distinctions that carry little social or moral weight—would be of less interest. In general, there is significant overlap between commonly accepted social and political distinctions and populations of interest to health inequality researchers. However, the moral relevance of some distinctions (e.g., health inequalities between U.S. states, counties, or census tracts) is more ambiguous.

Second, health inequalities generally involve establishing a *comparison group* that serves explicitly as a reference against which one can compare one or more populations and implicitly as an ideal achievable target by all groups. A number of choices of comparison groups exist, any one of which is technically sound but each of which carries different ethics implications. Consider the hypothetical example shown in **TABLE 12.3**. Clearly, significant health inequalities exist among the different racial/ethnic groups. However, the *amount* of inequality depends on the choice of the comparison group. Which is the most appropriate in this case? Several answers are possible:

■ We might choose the *total population average* as the reference group. Intuitively, it seems most just to consider the average of the general population as the standard of fairness against which to judge any particular subpopulation, much as we might

consider a fair distribution of income to be one in which everyone clustered closely around the average.[35] In this example, the relative risk of the worst-off group (Hispanics) when compared with the total average is 1.75.

■ We might choose the *best-off population* as the reference group. Many argue that every group in a society should enjoy the best-possible level of health. Indeed, in some cases (e.g., life expectancy, immunization coverage, or access to lifesaving HIV medications), it is difficult to justify expecting anything less than the best-possible health status as a fair and just outcome. In this example, the relative risk of the worst-off group (Hispanics) when compared with the best-off group (American Indians/Alaskan natives) is 2.44.

■ We might choose the *most socially advantaged population* as the reference group. Under the first criterion we described, a health inequity is, by *definition*, a difference that favors a more (or most) socially advantaged population over a less socially disadvantaged one, and we would be less concerned with comparisons between relatively disadvantaged populations. In this example, the relative risk of the worst-off

TABLE 12.3 Disease Prevalence per 100,000

Subgroup	Disease Prevalence
Non-Hispanic white	7.6
Black	12.4
Hispanic	16.8
American Indian/Alaskan Native	6.9
Asian/Pacific Islander	10.2
Total	**9.6**

TABLE 12.4 Mortality Rate per 100,000				
Disease	Population A	Population B	RD	RR
Heart disease	80	60	20	1.333333
Cancer	270	230	40	1.173913

group (Hispanics) when compared with the most socially advantaged group (Non-Hispanic whites, the majority population) is 2.21.

- Finally, we might choose some *independently defined target rate* as a reference category. Many common health indicators, including blood pressure, BMI, and total cholesterol level, have widely accepted thresholds separating high and low risk. It might be most just to expect all groups to pass that threshold regardless of the relative rates of other groups. (The example in Table 12.3 is not pertinent to this choice.) Moreover, using this reference category would ensure that all groups use a medically justifiable amount of some healthcare resource, which is useful in cases where some subpopulations "overutilize" that resource.

Measurement

Many different statistical measures of inequality are available, from simple averages to sophisticated measures of total inequality. A comprehensive review of these measures is beyond the scope of this chapter. Instead, it will use the example of absolute and relative measures to illustrate the ethics issues often involved in choosing between different measurement strategies.[36]

Two of the simplest measures of health inequality are the *rate difference* (RD) and the *rate ratio* (RR). The RD is a number resulting from subtraction of the numeric measure of one group's health status from the other

group's. The RR is a ratio resulting from division of the numeric measure of one group's health status from the other group's. Consider the example shown in **TABLE 12.4**.

Clearly, inequalities exist and favor population B for both conditions. Suppose one could fund efforts to reduce only one of these inequalities. Absent other considerations, one might reasonably decide to fund the larger inequality, but which one is larger? In absolute terms, the inequality in cancer rates is twice as large as that in heart disease (40 vs. 20), but in relative terms, the inequality in heart disease rates is almost twice as large (33% vs. 17% higher for population A). There is no consistent standard for judging which measure is more appropriate in this case. One could make a reasonable case that the RD is more important because eliminating it would save more lives in absolute terms, and thus cancer should receive funding. Conversely, one might reasonably argue that the RR better represents the "true" inequity because the number of cases involved does not affect it, and thus there should be funding for heart disease.

The choice of the appropriate measure is particularly important when assessing health inequalities over time, as well as the relationship between *distributive* considerations (in this case, health inequalities) and *aggregative* ones (in this case, overall health). In some cases, interventions that improve aggregate health in an entire population and all of its subpopulations might simultaneously increase inequalities between the more and less advantaged members of the population. Consider **TABLE 12.5**.

TABLE 12.5 U.S. Infant Mortality Rate per 100,000 Live Births				
Year	**Black**	**White**	**RD**	**RR**
1950	43.9	26.8	17.1	1.6
1998	13.8	.6	7.8	2.3
Change	**30.1**	**20.8**	**−9.3**	**1.5**

Data from D. Mechanic, "Disadvantage, Inequality, and Social Policy," *Health Affairs* 21, no. 2 (2002): 48–59.

Between 1950 and 1998, overall infant mortality in the United States declined precipitously for all racial groups. The absolute reduction in infant deaths during this period was almost 50% higher among blacks than whites (30.1 vs. 20.8), and the rate difference decreased (from 17.1 to 7.8), which indicates that blacks benefited *more* than whites did from reductions in infant mortality during this time period. However, during the same period the rate ratio between the two groups increased (from 1.6 to 2.3), indicating that blacks benefited less. Were racial inequalities in infant mortality better or worse in 1998 than in 1950? Did improvements in infant mortality disproportionately benefit whites or did they not? Was there a trade-off between overall population health and health inequalities or not?

▶ What Is the Best Way to Reduce or Eliminate Health Inequalities?

Even if we can reach an agreement that a measurable health inequality exists, that it constitutes an inequity, and that we need to address it, there is no single rationale for determining the most ethically sound way to reduce or eliminate that inequity. Several ethics considerations play a role in deciding among possible interventions.

The first consideration concerns the relationship between equality of *treatment* and equality of *outcomes*, embodied in the principles of horizontal and vertical equity. *Horizontal equity* refers to the equal allocation of resources (in this case, health care) across a population. Universal health care accords with this principle because everyone needs health care and no individual or group should receive disproportionately better or worse care than another.

Vertical equity refers to the allocation of different resources for different levels of need. Healthcare or public health programs that target a disadvantaged social group accord with this principle on the grounds that unequal allocation of resources might be necessary to achieve equal health outcomes. An extreme emphasis on vertical equity is liberation theology's injunction that the poorest members of a society should always be accorded preferential treatment because they bear the greatest burden of social inequality.[37] In choosing between these two principles, it is worth asking these questions: If everyone receives the same treatment, are unequal outcomes ethically problematic? If everyone has the same outcome, are unequal treatments ethically problematic?

A second issue is the aforementioned relationship between distributive and aggregative considerations and the cases of "leveling up" or "leveling down" to achieve the goal of equity. Consider the four situations shown in **FIGURES 12.1** through **12.4**. Assume that the

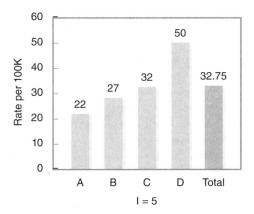

FIGURE 12.1 The Current Situation

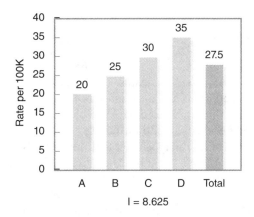

FIGURE 12.2 A Better Total Population, but Worse Total Inequity

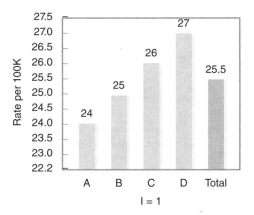

FIGURE 12.3 Changes in Sub-populations

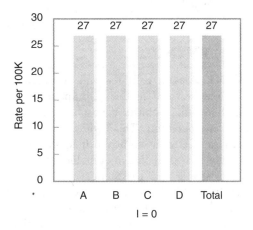

FIGURE 12.4 Sub-population Differences in Access

measured rate in these charts is something beneficial, such as access to lifesaving medications. Figure 12.1 represents the current situation, in which the total population rate is 27.5 and a simple index of total inequality[38] is 5. Suppose that we wish to *both* improve overall access to lifesaving medication *and* reduce the total inequality of access in this population. In Figure 12.2, the total population rate is better (higher), and each subpopulation has benefited, but the total inequality is worse (also higher).

In Figure 12.3, there is a great reduction in the total inequality, but there is a slight reduction in overall inequality; the access rate of the two best-off populations has decreased, but that of the worst-off has increased. Finally, in Figure 12.4, total inequality has been reduced to zero, and overall access has dropped slightly, The access of the top two populations has decreased, while that of the bottom two has increased. Which of the other three situations represents the best trade-off between reducing inequity and improving overall health?

Many other considerations regarding the appropriate distribution of social resources play a role in determining the best approach to reducing health inequities. Given a number of different subpopulations (e.g., multiple racial or ethnic groups or education levels), are some subpopulations more or less "deserving" of direct intervention to reduce health inequalities? Consider a final example. Epidemiologic evidence indicates that differences in socioeconomic status, nutrition, exposure to pathogens and toxic substances, and health care early in life can have a profound impact on health status and inequalities later in life.[39] This raises the possibility that the best way to reduce (adult) health inequalities in the long term might be to invest as heavily as possible in pre- and postnatal health care, perhaps at the expense of health care much later in life, when reducing inequalities might be prohibitively expensive. Is this an acceptable distribution of social resources?

▶ Conclusion

Despite repeated calls for and considerable resources devoted to their elimination, dramatic health inequities persist and in some cases are increasing. This review might make the task of addressing health inequities seem daunting or even insurmountable. However, the existence and persistence of significant gaps in health and longevity between the most and least advantaged populations worldwide compels us to take action, no matter how challenging the task.

▶ Summary

This chapter begins by defining the essential concepts for understanding the ethics problem posed in the chapter. It also explores the ethical difference between an inequality and an inequity. It further explains how inequalities are measured and the issues associated with defining populations and measurement standards. Finally, it presents areas to consider in reducing or eliminating health inequalities.

▶ Questions for Discussion

1. What is the difference between health (or healthcare) inequalities and inequities?
2. What ethics theories or criteria help define whether a health inequality is truly an inequity?
3. How are health inequalities indicators of larger social problems for socioeconomic groups?
4. How do researchers apply ethics to specify populations when studying health inequalities?
5. In the author's view, what is the best way to decrease health inequality?

▶ Notes

1. U.S. Department of Health and Human Services, "About Healthy People," HealthyPeople.gov, para. 5, http://www.healthypeople.gov/2020/about/default.aspx.
2. World Health Organization Commission on Social Determinants of Health, *Closing the Gap in a Generation: Health Equity through Action on the Social Determinants of Health. Final Report of the Commission on the Social Determinants of Health* (Geneva, Switzerland: World Health Organization, 2008), 1.
3. N. Daniels, "Equity and Population Health: Toward a Broader Bioethics Agenda," *Hastings Center Report* 36, no. 4 (2006): 22–35.
4. World Health Organization, "Preamble to the Constitution of the World Health Organization," *Official Records of the World Health Organization* 2 (1946).
5. P. R. McHugh, "Striving for Coherence," *Journal of the American Medical Association* 293, no. 20 (2005): 2526–28.

6. A. Frances, "Good Grief," *The New York Times* (August 14, 2010).

7. See C. J. L. Murray et al., "Health Inequalities and Social Group Differences: What Should We Measure?" *Bulletin of the World Health Organization* 77, no. 7 (1999): 537–43; P. Braveman and S. Gruskin, "Defining Equity in Health," *Journal of Epidemiology and Community Health* 57 (2003): 254–58.

8. Making inferences about the properties of individuals from aggregate group statistics is commonly referred to as the *ecological fallacy.*

9. Authors use the term *health disparity* interchangeably with *health inequities*, particularly in the United States, but it also is used interchangeably with *health inequality* in other countries. For this reason, I will use the terms *health inequality* and *health inequity* throughout this chapter.

10. M. J. Roberts and M. R. Reich, "Ethical Analysis in Public Health," *Lancet* 359, no. 9311 (2002): 1055–59.

11. P. Farmer, *Pathologies of Power: Health, Human Rights, and the New War on the Poor* (Berkeley: University of California Press, 2003), 153.

12. P. A. Braveman, "Measuring Health Inequalities: The Politics of the World Health Report 2000," in *Health and Social Justice: Politics, Ideology, and Inequity in the Distribution of Disease*, ed. Richard Hofrichter (San Francisco, CA: Jossey-Bass, 2003).

13. S. Benatar, "Global Disparities in Health and Human Rights: A Critical Commentary," *American Journal of Public Health* 88, no. 2 (1998): 295–300.

14. N. Daniels et al., *Is Inequality Bad for Our Health?* (Boston, MA: Beacon Press, 2000).

15. J. S. House and D. R. Williams, "Understanding and Reducing Socioeconomic and Racial/Ethnic Disparities in Health," in Hofrichter, *Health and Social Justice.*

16. J. Rawls, *A Theory of Justice* (Cambridge, MA: Harvard University Press, 1971).

17. T. C. Quinn and J. Overbaugh, "HIV/AIDS in Women: An Expanding Epidemic," *Science* 308 (2005): 1582–83.

18. S. Zierler and N. Krieger, "Refraining Women's Risk: Social Inequalities and HIV Infection," *Annual Review of Public Health* 18 (1997): 401–36.

19. C. J. L. Murray et al., "Eight Americas: Investigating Mortality Disparities Across Races, Counties, and Race-Counties in the United States," *PLoS Medicine* 3, no. 9 (2006): 1513–24.

20. M. Whitehead, "The Concepts and Principles of Equity and Health," *Health Promotion International* 6, no. 3 (1991): 217–28; O. Carter-Pokras and C. Baquet, "What Is a 'Health Disparity'?" *Public Health Reports* 117, no. 5 (2002): 426–34.

21. M. Whitehead, *The Concepts and Principles of Equity and Health* (Copenhagen, Denmark: World Health Organization, 2000), 5.

22. P. Brown, "Popular Epidemiology and Toxic Waste Contamination: Lay and Professional Ways of Knowing," *Journal of Health and Social Behavior* 33, no. 3 (1992): 267–81; A. Gawande, "The Cancer-Cluster Myth," *The New Yorker*, February 8, 1999, 34–37.

23. A. Bambas and J. A. Casas, "Assessing Equity in Health: Conceptual Criteria," in Hofrichter, *Health and Social Justice.*

24. Whitehead, *Concepts and Principles of Equity and Health.*

25. J. P. Struewing et al., "The Risk of Cancer Associated with Specific Mutations of BRCA1 and BRCA2 among Ashkenazi Jews," *New England Journal of Medicine* 336, no. 20 (1997): 1401–8.

26. I. Marion Young, "Equality of Whom? Social Groups and Judgments of

Injustice," *Journal of Political Philosophy* 9, no. 1 (2001): 1–18.

27. J. M. McGinnis and W. H. Foege, "Actual Causes of Death in the United States," *Journal of the American Medical Association* 270, no. 18 (1993): 2207–12; A. H. Mokdad, J. S. Marks, D. F. Stroup, and J. L. Gerberding, "Actual Causes of Death in the United States, 2000," *Journal of the American Medical Association* 291, no. 10 (2004): 1238–45.

28. C. R. Baquet et al., "Socioeconomic Factors and Cancer Incidence among Blacks and Whites," *Journal of the National Cancer Institute* 83 (1991): 551–57.

29. Carter-Pokras and Baquet, "What Is a 'Health Disparity'?," 432.

30. Roberts and Reich, "Ethical Analysis in Public Health."

31. M. Marmot, "Health in an Unequal World," *Lancet* 368 (2006): 2081–94.

32. R. Wilkinson, *Unhealthy Societies: The Afflictions of Inequality* (London: Routledge, 1996). Also note that the apparent connection between income inequality and life expectancy has been the subject of much debate; see J. P. Mackenbach, "Income Inequality and Population Health," *British Medical Journal* 324 (2002): 1–2; J. W. Lynch et al., "Income Inequality and Mortality: Importance to Health of Individual Income, Psychosocial Environment, or Material Conditions," in Hofrichter, *Health and Social Justice*; and J. Lynch et al., "Is Income Inequality a Determinant of Population Health? Part 1: A Systematic Review," *Milbank Quarterly* 82, no. 1 (2004): 5–99.

33. Material in this section draws heavily on S. Harper and J. Lynch, "Measuring Health Inequalities," in *Methods in Social Epidemiology*, eds. J. M. Oakes and J. S. Kaufman (San Francisco, CA: Jossey-Bass, 2006).

34. C. P. Nelson et al., "Genetically Determined Height and Coronary Artery Disease," *The New England Journal of Medicine* 372, no. 17 (2015): 1608–18.

35. A related problem concerns whether to include the subpopulation of interest in the total population average.

36. S. Harper et al., "Implicit Value Judgments in the Measurement of Health Inequalities," *Milbank Quarterly* 88, no. 1 (2010): 4–29.

37. Ibid.

38. Average deviation from the total population rate, $I = [|(A - T)| + |(B - T)| + |(C - T)| + |(Z>-D|)]/4$. Subtract the number in column A from the total, the number in column B from the total, the number in column C from the total, and the number in column D from the total. Divide the sum of these individual results by 4. This gives the average deviation from the total population.

39. E. D. A. Hyppbnen et al., "Prenatal Growth and Risk of Occlusive and Haemorrhagic Stroke in Swedish Men and Women Born 1915–1929: Historical Cohort Study," *British Medical Journal* 323 (2001): 10331034; A. Case et al., "The Lasting Impact of Childhood Health and Circumstance," *Journal of Health Economics* 24, no. 2 (2005): 365–89.

CHAPTER 13

The Ethics of Epidemics

Omolola E. Adepoju

▶ Introduction

While disease has always been present, significant widespread outbreaks, or epidemics, have sporadically appeared, causing significant mortality and drastic changes to humanity's understanding of health and illness. Beginning with the bubonic plague in the 14th century to the Zika virus in 2016, epidemic events have been powerful facilitators of public health change. Each epidemic brought new public health discoveries, influencing the perceptions of ethical behavior and forcing communities to view current health practices, or lack thereof, in a new light, resulting in changes to the normal behavior and understanding of ethical responsibilities for every level of society.

An understanding of the ethics of epidemics greatly informs modern-day public health ethics and its applications. Because diseases know no borders, these lessons continue to provide insights into public health policies and how societies adapted these policies to combat public health threats. Recent public health events have forced the adoption and, in some cases, the modification of long-standing ethical perspectives. This chapter discusses some of the most notable outbreaks over time and the role of public health ethics in facilitating public health improvements. At the heart of these events is the ethical determination of the decision-making responsibility, specifically balancing respect for individual freedom and liberty with the responsibility of governments to provide their citizens with some degree of protection in relation to health.

▶ Epidemics, Ethics, and Public Health

Plague

Fourteenth-century Europe, Asia, and Africa were ravished by the plague pandemic that became known as "the Black Death." The plague occurred in succession and led to as many as 50 million deaths, approximately half of them in Asia and Africa and the other half in Europe.[1] One of the oldest outbreaks known to man, the plague fed off unsanitary conditions arising from putrefaction sources, such as marshes, cesspits, and open sewers.[2] In the culture of the time, plagues were viewed with a supernatural worldview, appearing in religious literature as divine punishment for immoral actions.[3] Popular beliefs attributed illness to "bad humors," or bad air, and great effort was exerted to avoid foul smells.[4] This effort may have been misplaced, but the interest in bad air gave hope and a sense of control over the plague. It also elicited better sanitary conditions from the population.

Having lost a significant proportion of the world's population, governments began to accept a moral responsibility for the survival of their people, and the beginnings of public health systems emerged in the form of quarantines of infected persons.[5] Quarantines in these times referred to 40 days of sanitary isolation (French word *quarante*, meaning "forty"), during which interactions with the public were limited. Quarantine practices not only separate exposed individuals but also restricted their movements, creating ethics challenges from an individual freedom perspective. In modern times, the idea of quarantine has not been without contentions, with references that suggest an ultimate deprivation of liberty (Gostin, 2016).[6] Isolation of infected persons, a less dramatic alternative that "separates sick people with a contagious disease from people who are not sick,"[7] gained popularity. It was an attempt to balance the ethical dynamic of individual freedom and the public health policy goal of ensuring the conditions under which people live healthy lives.

Cholera

Like the plague, cholera outbreaks occurred at the pandemic level, ignoring traditional geographic boundaries and following human migration and trade patterns. To date, cholera has emerged in seven distinct pandemics and caused more deaths than any other epidemic in the 19th century. The first six cholera outbreaks began in Asia and followed popular travel routes, including the 19th century colonial Indian trade routes, religious pilgrimages to Mecca, and immigrant movements from Europe to North America,[8] ultimately reaching urban centers worldwide.

During 1854, the deadliest year of the third cholera pandemic, John Snow, a British physician, tracked cholera cases emerging in London and deducted that the disease originated from a well with contaminated water in the epicenter of the affected London neighborhood. Environmental public health practices in the then urban British society were subpar with historians describing overcrowded hospitals, rampant infection rates, and decaying waste in the streets. Laws at the time to address the living conditions were futile in their efforts as the laws avoided addressing the societal industrialization that produced the filth.[9]

The high death toll from these pandemics led to new public health thinking and approaches. Snow's findings influenced public perceptions of economic activities, such as increased trade and production, and the potential adverse impact on society's health and well-being. Public health efforts arose as to balance intercountry movements with the risk of disease exposure. This revelation changed how societies approached combating outbreaks, such that the fifth cholera pandemic. Cholera did not greatly affect Britain and the United States because these countries implemented as quarantine the methods based on Snow's discovery.

History has seen a shift in cholera pandemic locations away from Western nations that have developed public health systems. Regions with highly rural populations and decentralized government power, such as India and sub-Saharan Africa, remain at risk for outbreaks. Furthering the danger are the numerous refugee crises that displace people and force condensed living conditions without necessary infrastructure.

Smallpox

While public health discoveries have shown effectiveness at managing outbreaks, the upmost benefit for society would be the complete elimination of a disease. The global effort and success at eradicating smallpox is an example of this benefit. Smallpox was one of the leading causes of death, and in the 20th century, it claimed no fewer than 200 million lives.[10] An air-borne viral infection characterized by large pustules over the victim's skin, the disease was spread via coughing, sneezing, and tactile infection and flourished in dense communities. In 1980, the World Health Organization (WHO) had announced the eradication of smallpox, not having detected a naturally occurring case since 1977 in Somalia.

The time lag between the vaccine discovery by Edward Jenner in 1796[11] and disease eradication spanned almost 2 centuries. The establishment of WHO in 1948 emphasized the importance of international coordination efforts in combating infectious diseases and contributed to the worldwide eradication of the disease. Outbreak control had its benefits, but the eradication of smallpox proved that the benefits of increased international coordination, past merely controlling an outbreak, were worth the economic cost.[12]

Despite these successes, the disease has remained relevant in current events and ethical discussions because of where it may still be found. Currently two countries, the United States and Russia, maintain stocks of smallpox strains, while discussions continue about the ethics of keeping the remaining strains.[13] With escalating terrorism activities in the 21st century, there are concerns of smallpox, or similarly virulent viruses, being used in a biological warfare attack. Maintaining smallpox strains may allow for the development of more effective vaccines in the occurrence of an attack.[14] Recent storage security errors, such as the discovery of misplaced lost smallpox viruses, have cast doubt on the utilitarian purpose of keeping the strains in existence.[15]

Influenza

Despite public health's great improvements and discoveries, influenza outbreaks are examples of how epidemics take advantage of gaps in public health planning, resulting in significant morbidity and mortality. The 1918 influenza pandemic was an outbreak with massive consequences, claiming more lives than in World War II.[16] The crowded living conditions provided for soldiers and open-bay mobile medical stations facilitated the spread of the disease and exposed sick soldiers to additional infections.[17] At the war's end, the soldiers returned to their home countries, although with the influenza virus.

In 2009, there was another influenza pandemic of the H1N1, or "swine flu", strain. Over 18,500 lives were claimed by the virus, and studies have estimated that upward of 300,000 more deaths were caused by comorbid complications.[18] Coordinated efforts between national and international organizations like WHO and the U.S. Centers for Disease Control and Prevention (CDC) helped lead efforts toward combating the pandemic. National vaccination programs were implemented, and the supply of antiviral drugs was managed by the Food and Drug Administration (FDA) to ensure proper quantities of the drugs were available for at-risk populations. The CDC also provided parents and caregivers with instructions on how to prepare adult drug doses for use in children, if a shortage occurred.[19] These coordinated efforts to combat an influenza pandemic did not exist in 1918, and the contrast in severity between the two outbreaks is a testament to the effectiveness of modern public health improvements.

In the United States, response to the influenza pandemics across all 50 states involved the development of emergency policies and plans for future influenza outbreaks; however, only 6 states had written guidelines for ethical decision-making in such emergencies.[20] Scholars have noted that this low number is concerning because of the ethical responsibilities around medication rationing, isolation, and quarantine that often occur during pandemics.[21] To better prepare for future disease outbreaks, governments should have predetermined ethical decision-making procedures for public health agencies to follow in emergencies.

▶ Modern Epidemics

The reporting of infectious diseases worldwide has increased since 1980.[22] This may partially be attributed to Internet technology, which makes disease reporting easier. This significant increase has, however, created a need for reframing the definition of the word "epidemic." Some researchers have warned that overuse and overextension of the word may result in the loss of relevance, significance, and urgency.[23]

Middle East respiratory syndrome (MERS), Ebola, the seventh cholera pandemic, and H1N1 have all posed new challenges that test the effectiveness of public health emergency preparedness and disaster response. Global responses to MERS and Ebola demonstrate the changing ethics issues that result from the modern imbalance of public health resources between nations and the effect technology has as a facilitator or barrier to dissemination of current event information. **TABLE 13.1** shows notable epidemics that have occurred since 2000 by death toll and location.

Middle East Respiratory Syndrome

The outbreak of MERS in 2012 created new ethics challenges as governments implemented public health measures to control the epidemic. For example, South Korea encountered challenges in addressing the outbreak, most prominently the lack of transparency in its communication with the public regarding the epidemic. There were also concerns about the nation's purported pandemic planning procedures, which relied heavily on the quarantine of infected persons. Despite the significant constraint to individual freedom, the historical approach to quarantine is given credit for controlling the disease spread in South Korea and surrounding nations. In addition, quarantined individuals received financial compensation, and the government provided for the availability of food and necessities for these individuals.[24]

Ebola

The 2014 Ebola outbreak is the largest and most complex Ebola outbreak since the Ebola virus was first discovered in 1976. Characterized by a high case fatality rate (up to 90%) and no known treatment or vaccine,[25] stopping Ebola in its tracks was an uphill task that re-ignited the ethics discourse around public health. In only 4 months, the disease had spread to several West African countries and resulted in significant mortality. According to WHO, Ebola transmitted through[26]:

- Direct contact (through broken skin or mucous membranes) with the blood, secretions, organs, or other bodily fluids of infected people
- Direct contact with surfaces and materials (e.g., bedding, clothing) contaminated with these fluids
- Direct contact with the deceased bodies of Ebola-infected people

Caregivers and healthcare workers in close contact with exposed and infected persons often become victims of the disease themselves, especially in settings where gaps in infection control precautions still exist.[27]

Due to the rapid spread from West Africa to Europe and North America, countries developed guidance documents for epidemiologic surveillance and movement monitoring of persons with potential Ebola virus exposure. In the United States, the initial guidance document suggested self-monitoring for most exposures and controlled movement for higher-risk exposures[28] as a way of balancing autonomy and paternalism that protects the public's health. However, the guideline document was modified in response to "increased concerns related to imported Ebola cases, infections in healthcare workers, and travel by an infected healthcare worker on commercial flights during October 2014."[29] Although

TABLE 13.1 Notable Epidemics, 2000–2016

Year	Disease	Deaths*	Location
2002–2003	SARS coronavirus	774	China origin, worldwide
2008–2009	Cholera	4,282	Zimbabwe
2009–2010	Meningitis	1,100+	West Africa
2009	H1N1 "swine flu"	151,000–575,000	Worldwide
2010–2016	Cholera	6,631	Hispaniola
2010–2011	Measles	1,085	Congo
2011	Hand, foot, and mouth disease	170	Vietnam
2011–2016	Dengue fever	219	Pakistan
2012	Yellow fever	171	Darfur Sudan
2012–2016	MERS	643	Worldwide
2013–2016	Ebola	11,325	West Africa
2015–2016	Measels	400+	Congo
2016	Chikungunya	191	Americas
2015–2016	Zika virus	39,987	Worldwide
2016	Yellow fever	369 (as of 08/2016)	Angola

SARS, severe acute respiratory syndrome.
*Data from the Centers for Disease Control and Prevention and the World Health Organization (2016).

two Americans contacted the disease while in Ebola-infected counties, they survived the disease through treatment with trial medicines.

WHO also faced ethics challenges in responding to the Ebola epidemic. As part of improving its response to public health events, WHO developed a plan for expediting drug trials, while still ensuring patient safety with the experimental medications. Ethics units were established to review new vaccination research protocols and communicate with national ethics committees in affected countries (Saxena and Gomes, 2016).[30]

Zika

The Zika virus is a primarily mosquito-transmitted virus that was first detected in the Zika Forest of Uganda in 1947. Outbreaks were scarce, and up until 2007, there had only been only 14 cases documented by global health organizations.[31] However, this low trend drastically changed in 2015 with an outbreak in Brazil, which quickly spread across South and Central Americas, with later cases appearing in North America as well. By the end of 2016, 69 countries had reported cases.[32]

The Zika virus poses a unique danger in that the initial symptoms of infection are often not severe; however, the virus has been found to cause birth defects such as microcephaly and Guillain–Barré syndrome if pregnant women are exposed to it.[33] The ethics concerns created by this disease and its related complications were outlined in the *Zika Ethics Consultation Report* by the Pan American Health Organization (2016). The identified ethics issues included access to women's health services and contraceptives in societies with conflicting social norms and care for children born with birth defects.[34] As the situation continues to evolve, healthcare systems must acknowledge these ethics conflicts to ensure future efforts address the needs of all stakeholders.

▶ Determination of the Decision-Making Responsibility: Individual Autonomy Versus Paternalism

Together with the principles of beneficence, nonmaleficence, and justice, autonomy has been widely accepted as one of the four principles of medical ethics.[35] These four principles also symbolize the ethical groundwork for a variety of U.S. public health reports of lasting import.[36-38] These principles not only guide the development of public health policies but also come into play in policy modification by contributing to problem definition. They are also part of the development of possible solutions and of dealing with political circumstances that may lead to new or amended policies.

Western medicine has grappled with public health responsibility and whether it belongs with the individual or with the public health provider, which may be the government. The nature of clinical care that fosters patients' reliance on their healthcare providers' knowledge for the demand and supply of healthcare services further fosters this debate. This approach, in its extreme, can shift the decision-making responsibility to clinicians on the basis of their determination of what is in the patients' best interests,[39] even for those patients who can make the decisions for themselves. This form of paternalism has faced several criticisms, most recently with the focus on shared decision-making and patient engagement as pillars to delivering the "Triple Aim" objectives (care, health, and cost).

When public health officials hold too much decision-making power, they can endanger the human rights of patients with long-lasting negative consequences. For example, between 1932 and 1972, African American men in rural Alabama were systematically refused diagnosis and later denied treatment for syphilis in order to study the effects of the disease on an untreated population.[40] A grave bioethical error was made in placing greater importance on scientific research than on the individuals' well-being. The grave implications of this study continue to this day, affecting trust in public health officials and hampering progress in combating recent epidemics like human immunodeficiency virus/acquired immunodeficiency syndrome (HIV/AIDS).[41]

The ethics principle of respect for persons is based on the concept that individuals have the right to their own beliefs and values and to the decisions and choices that further those beliefs and values. However, when individuals do not feel a moral responsibility for the health of their society, personal behaviors may jeopardize the well-being of others. For example, Mary Mallon, better known as "Typhoid Mary," was identified as the cause of many typhoid cases in 1906 because of poor handwashing while employed as a cook. Public health officials placed her in quarantine but had to act in a way that did not infringe on her rights. Upon release, Mallon infected 25 more people with typhoid before her death.[42]

Policies guided by a preference for the individual autonomy limit paternalism.[43] An example of such a policy is the 1990 Patient Self-Determination Act (P.L. 101–508). This policy gives individuals the right to make decisions concerning their medical care, including the right to accept or refuse treatment and the right to formulate advance directives regarding their care.[44] However, according to Beauchamp and Childress (2012), no fundamental conflicts or inconsistencies exist between the autonomy of individuals and the role of the government as long as it does not go beyond the limits set by the governed.[45]

▶ International Perspectives and the Bioethics Model

International organizations and public health institutions in several industrialized countries have recognized the importance of public health ethics. Several institutions have adopted a public health ethics model called the stewardship model "as a reference point for guiding decisions about what types of intervention may be justified."[46] The stewardship model emphasizes the role of governments in ensuring the conditions under which people can lead healthy lives. It also cautions that governments should not coerce people or limit their freedom without cause.[47]

This caution has important ramifications for reducing health inequalities and protecting the health of vulnerable groups, including children, persons with disabilities, and older adults.[48] Nevertheless, the stewardship model has been questioned as a reference for ethics analysis in public health on the grounds that it overvalues the principle of autonomy. This principle occupies a central position in the model and is based on a simplistic view of John Stuart Mill's harm principle.[49]

▶ Summary

This chapter presents a discussion of the current and historical challenges faced by public health in preventing and reducing the impact of epidemics. Without a doubt, epidemics have informed the understanding of public health and promoted philosophical underpinnings that have shaped ethical responsibilities for every level of society. These lessons continue, especially with new and emerging threats to health care and public health. As long as the government's authority does not exceed the limits set by those governed, public health can be promoted, while ensuring the protection of human rights. Given the challenges of prevention and treatment of current and future epidemics, ethics-based public health policy will continue to face ethics dilemmas. Making ethics part of the consideration when developing policy should provide an ethical justification for action.

▶ Questions for Discussion

1. Why is it important for policy makers in public health to understand the principles of ethics?

2. What are some examples of violations of personal ethics with regard to public health policy?

3. Why do you think public health has an obligation to autonomy? How can public health balance the need to take action with respect for human rights?

▶ **Acknowledgment**

The author would like acknowledge the contribution made by Andrew Mask, graduate research assistant at the School of Health Administration, Texas State University.

▶ **Notes**

1. World Health Organization (WHO), "Emergency Preparedness Response, Plague," 2016.

2. A. Wear, "Making Us as Cruel as Dogs: Plague in 16th and 17th Century England," *The Lancet* 385, no. 9986 (2015): 2456–57.

3. P. Slack, "Responses to Plague in Early Modern Europe: The Implications of Public Health," *Social Research* (1988): 433–53.

4. J. Wright, "Looking at Pandemics: From Black Death to Swine Flu," *British Journal of School Nursing* 6, no. 4 (2011): 200–01.

5. J. W. Dickerson, (1998). Historical Perspectives on Health. "Aspects of Public Health up to Chadwick," *Journal of the Royal Society for the Promotion of Health* 118, no. 3 (1998): 182–85. doi:10.1177/146642409811800311.

6. L. O. Gostin, "A Very Long Journey: A Decade's Quest for Quarantine Regulations," *The Milbank Quarterly* 94, no. 4 (2016): 724–28.

7. Centers for Disease Control and Prevention (CDC), "Quaratines and Isolation," (2016): Line 3, https://www.cdc.gov/quarantine/.

8. CBC News, "Cholera's Seven Epidemics," 2008, http://www.cbc.ca/news/technology/cholera-s-seven-pandemics-1.758504.

9. J. Mackintosh, "Snow: The Man and His Times," *Proceedings of the Royal Society of Medicine* 48, no. 12 (1955): 1004.

10. J. N. Hays, *Epidemics and Pandemics: Their Impacts on Human History* (Santa Barbara: ABC-CLIO-LC, 2005).

11. S. Riedel, "Edward Jenner and the History of Smallpox and Vaccination," *Proceedings of Baylor University. Medical Center* 8, no. 1 (2005): 21–25.

12. S. Barrett, "Eradication Vs. Control: The Economics of Global Infectious Disease Policies," *Bulletin of the World Health Organization* 82, no. 9 (2004): 683–88.

13. A. Khalakdina et al., "Smallpox in the Post-Eradication Era," *Weekly Epidemiological Record* 91, no. 20 (2016): 257–64 select.

14. J. Welsh, "World Health Organization Decided to Keep Smallpox Stocks. For Now," 2011, http://www.livescience.com/14297-smallpox-decision-stocks.html.

15. J. Christensen, "CDC: Smallpox Found in NIH Storage Room Is Alive," 2014, http://www.cnn.com/2014/07/11/health/smallpox-found-nih-alive.

16. Wright, "Looking at Pandemics: From Black Death to Swine Flu," 200–01.

17. G. D. Shanks et al., "Variable Mortality from the 1918–1919 Influenza Pandemic and Military Training," *Military Medicine* 181, no. 8 (2016): 878–82. doi:10.7205/MILMED-D-15-00124.

18. F. S. Dawood et al., "Estimated Global Mortality Associated with the First 12 Months of 2009 Pandemic Influenza A H1N1 Virus Circulation: A Modeling Study," *The Lancet Infectious Diseases* 12, no. 9 (2016): 687–95. doi:10.1016/S1473-3099(12)70121-4.

19. Centers for Disease Control and Prevention (CDC), "The 2009 H1N1 Pandemic: Summary Highlights, April 2009–April 2010," (2010), http://www.cdc.gov/h1n1flu/cdcresponse.htm.

20. J. C. Thomas and S. Young, "Wake Me Up When There's a Crisis: Progress on State Pandemic Influenza Ethics Preparedness," *American Journal of Public Health* 101, no. 11 (2011): 2080–82. doi:10.2105/AJPH.2011.300293.

21. J. Y. Lin and L. Anderson-Shaw, "Rationing of Resources: Ethical Issues in Disasters and Epidemic Situations," *Prehospital & Disaster Medicine* 24, no. 3 (2009): 215–21.

22. K. F. Smith et al., "Global Rise in Human Infectious Disease Outbreaks," *Journal of the Royal Society Interface* 11, no. 101 (2014): 20140950.

23. J. Anomaly, "What Is an Epidemic?: Currents in Contemporary Bioethics," *Journal of Law, Medicine & Ethics* 42, no. 3 (2014): 389–91. doi:10.1111/jlme.12155.

24. K. Ock-Joo and O. -J. Kim, "Ethical Perspectives on the Middle East Respiratory Syndrome Coronavirus Epidemic in Korea," *Journal of Preventive Medicine & Public Health* 49, no. 1 (2016): 18–22. doi:10.3961/jpmph.16.013.

25. Centers for Disease Control (CDC), "2014 Ebola Outbreak in West Africa," 2014, https://www.cdc.gov/vhf/ebola/outbreaks/2014-west-africa/.

26. World Health Organization (WHO), "Ebola Virus Disease Fact Sheet," 2016, http://www.who.int/mediacentre/factsheets/fs103/en/.

27. Ibid.

28. Centers for Disease Control and Prevention (CDC), "Notes on the Interim U.S. Guidance for Monitoring and Movement of Persons with Potential Ebola Virus Exposure," 2016, https://www.cdc.gov/vhf/ebola/exposure/monitoring-and-movement-of-persons-with-exposure.html.

29. Centers for Disease Control and Prevention (CDC), "Notes on the Interim U.S. Guidance for Monitoring and Movement of Persons with Potential Ebola Virus Exposure," 2016: Paragraph 2, https://www.cdc.gov/vhf/ebola/exposure/monitoring-and-movement-of-persons-with-exposure.html.

30. A. Saxena and M. Gomes, "Ethical Challenges to Responding to the Ebola Epidemic: The World Health Organization Experience," *Clinical Trials* 13, no. 1 (2016): 96–100. doi:10.1177/1740774515621870.

31. Centers for Disease Control (CDC), "Zika Overview," 2016, https://www.cdc.gov/zika/about/overview.html.

32. A. Saxena and M. Gomes, "Ethical Challenges to Responding to the Ebola Epidemic: The World Health Organization Experience," *Clinical Trials* 13, no. 1 (2016): 96–100. doi:10.1177/1740774515621870.

33. World Health Organization (WHO), "Zika Virus Fact Sheet," 2016, http://www.who.int/mediacentre/factsheets/zika/en/.

34. Pan American Health Organization (PAHO), "*Zika Ethics Consultation: Ethics Guidance on Key Issues Raised by the Outbreak*," Washington, DC, 2016, http://iris.paho.org/xmlui/bitstream/handle/123456789/28425/PAHOKBR16002_eng.pdf.

35. T. L. Beauchamp and J. F. Childress, *Principles of Biomedical Ethics*, 5th ed. (New York: Oxford University Press, 2001).

36. D. M. Maloney, *Protection of Human Research Subjects: A Practical Guide to Federal Laws and Regulations* (New York: Springer Science & Business Media, 2012).

37. L. T. Kohn et al., *To Err Is Human: Building a Safer Health System* (Vol. 6), (Washington, DC: National Academies Press).

38. L. Murgic, P. C. Hébert, S. Sovic, and G. Pavlekovic, "Paternalism and Autonomy: Views of Patients and Providers in a Transitional (Post-Communist) Country," *BMC Medical Ethics* 16, no. 1 (2015): 65.

39. L. Sandman and C. Munthe, (2010). "Shared Decision Making, Paternalism and Patient Choice," *Health Care Analysis* 18, no. 1 (2010): 60–84.

40. R. C. Warren and W. L. Tarver, "A Foundation for Public Health Ethics at Tuskegee University in the 21st Century," *Journal of Health Care for the Poor & Underserved* 21, no. 3 (2010): 46–56. doi:10.1353/hpu.0.0358.

41. S. B. Thomas and S. C. Quinn, "The Tuskegee Syphilis Study, 1932 to 1972: Implications for HIV Education and AIDS Risk Education Programs in the Black Community," *American Journal of Public Health* 81, no. 11 (1991): 1498–1505. doi:10.2105/AJPH.81.11.1498.

42. Wright, "Looking at Pandemics: From Black Death to Swine Flu," 200–201.

43. B. Longest, *Health Policymaking in the United States* (2002), 6th ed. (Chicago: Health Administration Press, 2016).

44. Ibid.

45. T. L. Beauchamp and J. F. Childress, *Principles of Biomedical Ethics,* 5th ed. (New York: Oxford University Press, 2001).

46. Good Stewardship Working Group, "The" Top Five" Lists in Primary Care: Meeting the Responsibility of Professionalism," *Archives of Internal Medicine* 171, no. 15 (2011): 1385.

47. World Health Organization, *The World Health Report 2000: Health Systems: Improving Performance* (Geneva: World Health Organization, 2000).

48. J. Krebs, "The Importance of Public-Health Ethics," *Bulletin of the World Health Organization* 86, no. 8 (2008): 579.

49. A. Dawson and M. Verweij, "The Steward of the Millian State," *Public Health Ethics* 1, no. 3 (2008): 193–95.

CHAPTER 14

Ethics of Disasters: Planning and Response

Eileen E. Morrison and Karen J. Bawel-Brinkley

▶ Introduction

What is a disaster, and how do we respond to it? This chapter explores disasters and the ethics challenges they present. It begins with a definition of the concept of disaster and a discussion of the response from a national and a state level. This section includes both planning for disasters and responding to them when they occur. A discussion of the ethics implications of these national and state responses follows this information.

The next section of the chapter explores the healthcare response to disasters, beginning with the lessons learned from the Katrina experience. It stresses hospitals' disaster planning, training and preparation, and special issues related to the healthcare disaster response. This section is followed by a discussion of the ethics implications for disaster responses in healthcare systems. Finally, the chapter addresses individual responsibility for preparation in disaster situations and the ethics related to this responsibility.

Disaster Defined

The occurrence of disasters is not unique to one nation or even one continent. According to the World Health Organization (WHO),[1] disasters occur worldwide and require prevention, preparedness, response, rehabilitation, and reconstruction. Sources for disasters include natural causes such as storms, earthquakes, and floods. They also have human causes, including fire, war, and acts of terrorism.

Because disasters involve people, WHO's model for describing disasters[2] includes vulnerability, hazards, and trigger events. Vulnerability for disasters includes poverty, access to resources, and illness and disability. Pressures that affect these vulnerabilities include the lack of institutions and education opportunities. In addition, the conditions of the physical and economic environment contribute to the vulnerability for disasters. With respect to hazards, WHO includes trigger events such as earthquakes, floods, and human actions.

The International Federation of Red Cross and Red Crescent Societies[3] define a disaster in a similar way. In their definition, they stress that disasters disrupt communities and societies. Disasters cause losses that go beyond the community's resources and ability to address these losses. Loss, in this case, includes human, economic, and environmental factors. They use a formula that sums up disasters in a visual way. It is (**Vulnerability + Hazard)/Capacity = Disaster**.[4]

Like other countries in the world, the United States has experienced disasters resulting from natural events, such as fires, floods, tornados, and hurricanes. However, there are an increasing number of human-made events (anthropogenic hazards), such as mass causality situations. These disasters challenge the resources and ability of the community to response in an effective way. Examples of these situations include the release of harmful chemicals, terrorism, and explosions.[5]

It is imperative for human safety and well-being that communities, organizations, and individual prepare for all potential disasters. Communities, states, and the federal government should prepare to respond to events in a way that is both rapid and compassionate. From an ethics view, the goal of disaster response should be to limit unnecessary harm and respect the autonomy of individuals. This response planning will also require cooperation and communication between national, state, and local agencies, including healthcare institutions. The chapter continues with an examination of past responses to disasters and lessons learned from those responses.

▶ Disasters in U.S. History

Disasters occur in from two main sources, natural and human-caused. Disasters from both these causes have occurred throughout U.S. history. While they were tragic in terms of loss of life and resources, these events have added to the knowledge of prevention and preparedness. For example, the United States has experienced natural disasters such as severe hurricanes (Betsy, Camille, and Ivan), floods (Johnstown, Pennsylvania, in 1889, and the Mississippi River flood in 1993), and fires (Chicago in 1871 and San Francisco in 1906). Recent examples of disasters include Hurricane Katrina, which claimed at least 1833 lives in the states of Louisiana, Mississippi, Florida, Georgia, and Alabama. In 2016, the hurricane season featured 15 named storms and 7 hurricanes, the highest frequency since 2012. Twelve of the named storms affected land in the Atlantic states, causing property damage from both wind and flooding. Hurricane Matthew, for example, was a category 5 storm and also contributed to over 1600 deaths, with Haiti having the greatest number of fatalities.[6]

In 2011, over 300 tornados (ranking high on the tornado severity scale) rampaged through the Southeast, demolishing whole towns and killing hundreds of people. On May 22, 2011, this tornado outbreak was followed by another level 5 tornado in Joplin, Missouri, that destroyed the town and killed 158 people. The National Weather Service and emergency managers reported that this was the deadliest storm in modern times, with damage to 75% of Joplin.[7]

Human-made disasters have also caused devastation and costs in lives and property. Americans now remember where they were on September 11, 2001 (9/11 hereafter), and many must live with the loss of life caused by the choices that others made on that day. Acts of mass violence such as shootings and bombings at airports, schools, and a famous marathon race have altered the prevention and preparation tactics for public safety and event response teams. Hick et al.[8] describe the aftermath of an active shooter or bombing incident as requiring different strategies for dealing with victims. First, these incidents are often short but cause more life-threatening injuries than other disasters. Because of the nature of these events, law enforcement, emergency response teams (ERTs), and hospitals need to coordinate their responses to save as many lives as possible. Because of the severity of injuries, all responders should be prepared to apply tourniquets and other life-saving processes. The authors' report includes specific information to assist law enforcement, dispatchers, emergency medical responders, hospitals, and community agencies in the best ways to address mass violence attacks.

No matter what the nature of the disaster, preparation on all levels of response is necessary. Depending on the type and severity of a disaster, this preparation includes federal, state, and local resources. Hospitals and ERTs must be prepared for events that they hope will never happen. In addition, without adequate disaster planning, chaos can proliferate, leading to poor decision-making and unethical behaviors. To have both an ethical and an efficient response to a disaster, order needs to be reestablished and chaos eliminated through a well-planned response.[9]

▶ Disaster Planning and Response by the Federal Government

According to Redlener, the events of 9/11 spurred efforts to upgrade the United States' ability to plan for disasters.[10] However, as of 2017, we still remain vulnerable to the effects of major disasters. Although the ability to respond to human-caused and natural disasters has improved, communication, distribution of resources, and ethics are still part of the issues related to emergency response. In addition, partnerships among the government levels (federal, regional, state, and local); non-profit organizations; healthcare systems, including first responders; and individual citizens need to be strengthened. In general, the United States responds well in crises. It demonstrates

compassion for those it does not even know and tries to diminish suffering. However, the United States is also a nation based on autonomy and the rights of individuals; therefore, planning for disaster responses must consider the individual as well as the community. The federal government has several agencies that contribute to this planning.

The Department of Homeland Security

The Department of Homeland Security (DHS) was created after the attack of 9/11 and remains part of the U.S. culture. Anyone who travels on an airplane is aware of this agency's security efforts to prevent future terrorist attacks. In addition, the DHS now includes areas such as biological and chemical security and counteracts threats from domestic and international terrorists.[11] Its mission has expanded to include the prevention of terrorism, border management, cyberspace security, disaster resilience, and immigration law enforcement.[12]

However, the security of borders and airports is only one part of how the DHS uses its $41.2 billion budget.[13] The DHS now also includes the Federal Emergency Management Agency (FEMA), the U.S. Immigration and the Customs and Border Patrol Agency, and the U.S. Coast Guard. In 2016, the DHS added prevention of cyberattacks to its many responsibilities. This function of disaster preparedness includes a public awareness campaign called "Stop.Think.Connect." This purpose of this program is to assist citizens in maintaining Internet security.[14]

The Federal Emergency Management Agency

In its 39-year history, FEMA has responded to both local and national disaster situations. As part of the DHS, FEMA's mission is to assist in preparing for, responding to, and recovering from all types of disaster situations. Using regional offices, it coordinates efforts and resources to address disaster situations when they occur.[15]

FEMA currently includes a Center for Faith and Neighborhood Partnerships as part of its ability to include a broader base of support for disaster prevention and recovery efforts. The effects of Hurricanes Katrina, Rita, and Wilma provided an incentive for this expansion of community support for responding to national disasters. In addition to the center, FEMA provides training assistance to faith-based and neighborhood organizations on the issue of human trafficking and its prevention.[16]

The Centers for Disease Control and Prevention

Other federal agencies are also involved in planning and responding to natural and human-caused disasters. For example, the Centers for Disease Control and Prevention's (CDC) Office of Public Health Preparedness and Response (PHPR) takes a public health view of disasters. The CDC plans for and responds to disasters caused by biological events, natural events, and chemical/radiological incidents. The CDC's website[17] features the efforts of the PHPR for preparedness through coordination with local and state public health departments. It also advocates for well-trained professional staff to mobilize and collaborate with other organizations, when needed. In addition, the PHPR maintains a stockpile of medicines and supplies to assist with emergencies and is responsible for providing laboratory support in the event of a threat or disaster. This system of 150 laboratories can assist in identifying threats and providing information on prevention and treatment.

The American Red Cross

Although not a government agency, the American Red Cross (ARC) is a major resource for disaster response information.[18] Inspired by the Swiss International Red Cross movement, the ARC is a humanitarian organization founded in 1881. It uses the power of trained volunteers from both medical and non-medical communities to respond a variety of disasters that include floods, earthquakes, wild fires, tornados, and superstorms, and assist in the relief efforts.

The ARC disaster relief programs provide for the *immediate* needs of individuals and families affected by a disaster. When a disaster strikes, the ARC provides shelter and food and assists with healthcare issues and mental health services. It also offers support services for those who are part of the disaster relief efforts, including emergency workers. The organization also addresses the aftermath of a disaster by providing cleanup support, comfort kits, shelters, and food.[19]

The ARC is active in preparedness efforts through education. Its website includes information for individuals and families and their readiness for an emergency. It offers specific information on preparation of an emergency kit, details for creating a response plan, and other important information.[20] In addition, the ARC provides training opportunities for individuals and professionals, including first-aid courses, volunteer training, and certified nursing assistant training and testing. While no agency can address all the needs for national preparedness for disasters, the ARC seeks to be present when disasters occur and to support professionals, volunteers, and those affected by these events.

Ethic Issues and National Disaster Response

Government and other agencies contribute information, plans, and funding to assist in disaster planning and response. However, these contributions are not always effective and can present ethics concerns, including social justice. Planning for disasters can be extensive, but the actual implementation of plans is challenging in terms of resources and ethics. In addition, the postrecovery situation is at best complicated and complex, often resulting in chaos. In these situations, there is a probability of ethics principles being violated.

Roberts and DeRenzo suggest that ethical responsibility begins with the plan itself.[21] Because there is a need to make serious ethical decisions once a disaster happens, it is necessary to be prepared *ethically* as well as *logistically* in the event of a disaster. This means that planners need to make ethics part of the plan's guiding principles and foundation. For example, the very nature of a disaster presents conflicts of interest that will require discussion and the formulation of standards that account for the community's interest as well as of those who respond to the disaster.

A consistent theme in Roberts and DeRenzo's work is the necessity of balancing utilitarian and deontological views. In a disaster situation, many feel that the "greatest good for the greatest number" is the most logical approach, maximizing the benefits for as many people as possible. Typically, the definition of this benefit is the number of lives saved. When healthcare providers are presented with the challenge of caring for the acutely sick and injured and managing those with chronic illnesses and special needs, they may use the utilitarian approach. In this case, triage provides a strategy for healthcare providers to offer the greatest good for the greatest number of disaster victims. The goal is to minimize risks, maximize resources, and simplify administrative processes to facilitate aid to survivors, especially the most vulnerable ones.[22]

Triage also provides a tool for disaster responders to assist in bringing order in a chaotic situation. It allows decisions about intervention and treatment when limitations in treatment exist. Reilly and Markenson[23] also note that there are many systems for triage, including one specifically for children and CareFlight. Common categories used in this coding system include the *immediate*, which refers to people who have a threat to their lives and must be treated as a top priority.

The second category of *delayed* indicates those who need care but whose situation is not life-threatening. *Minimal* is used as a category for those who have minor injuries that need attention, but treatment can be delayed. *Expectant* is a category for those who have little or no chance of survival, and *dead* is a category for those who are not breathing.

Whatever the system for triage, its base in utilitarianism has a number of limitations when one considers the viewpoint of the individual and the community.[24] For example, after Hurricane Katrina and other disasters, much effort and money were expended on recovery of the remains of the dead. Although strict utilitarianism would find this to be unacceptable because the dead do not offer much benefit to the living, the families and the community involved found this action and expense to be appropriate. Even though the dead could no longer create benefit, the moral obligation to honor their lives justified the recovery efforts.

In the case of response to a disaster, utilitarianism needs to be balanced with concerns for Kantian, or duty-based, ethics. In this approach to ethics, all humans have worth. Therefore, it would be inappropriate to sacrifice some individuals over others, even if it means ignoring the rule of the greatest good for the greatest number. For example, duty explains the use of the greater resources needed to assist those who are elderly, ill, or otherwise vulnerable. The duty to fellow human beings would not allow us to leave these people behind because they lack resources to respond to a disaster.[25] This situation was one of the recurring issues in the disaster response of Memorial Hospital.[26]

Another ethics issue that might emerge during a disaster is respect for autonomy. Individual freedom, which is part of the principle of autonomy, can often come into question when a disaster occurs. For example, should an individual have the right to build a home on a flood plain and not have flood insurance? If an individual decides to ignore disaster warnings or cannot take action when a disaster occurs, what is the government's responsibility? What if there is evidence of exposure to a highly infectious disease? Does the community have the right to quarantine an individual against his or her will in an effort to protect itself? Where does autonomy stop and community protection begin?

Meyer and Kunreuther,[27] in their thought-provoking book, *The Ostrich Paradox*, provide information about how brain physiology and factors affect individuals' decisions with respect to preparation for potential disasters. These factors, including the ostrich paradox and core biases, help explain the rationale for those who do not pay attention to warnings and protective actions. However, the issues of autonomy versus common good will remain unless there is a better system for informing and influencing individual behaviors.

The concept of social justice is also a major ethics consideration with respect to the response to disasters. When a disaster occurs, Americans expect that the government will do whatever it can to respond to the situation and to relieve the suffering of its citizens. Historically, Americans have been both compassionate and generous when disasters have occurred. They expect coordinated action that protects both individual lives and community property. When communication and coordination between government entities are lacking, there can be tragic consequences. Communities react with moral outrage and demand investigation.

An example of this expectation and lack of coordination occurred during the response to Hurricane Katrina, which led to an investigation and the publication of *A Failure of Initiative: Final Report of the Select Bipartisan Committee to Investigate the Preparation for and Response to Hurricane Katrina*.[28] This report provides an extensive review of the human and ethical impact of disaster responses. It also includes detailed recommendations that can improve disaster response on both a government and a community level.

▶ Disaster Preparedness and Response for Healthcare Institutions

Disaster Preparation and Response from Hospitals

When a disaster occurs, the community seeks a response from professionals (doctors, nurses, paramedics, emergency medical technicians, firefighters, the police, and the military) and from healthcare institutions. Therefore, professionals and respective organizations have an ethics duty to be ready for natural and human-made events that lead to disaster situations. To be effective in this response, institutions and professionals need to have a plan of action that can adapt to the situation at hand. Since hospitals are often the main response to disasters, they have a particular obligation for developing a plan and practicing it and to be always ready.

Riley and Markenson[29] provide extensive information concerning the field of hospital emergency management. They suggest that hospitals invest in a plan that will address all hazards and engage the community in the planning process. They also suggest the use of The Joint Commission (TJC) standards. Effective emergency management includes the ability to address issues related to communication, capacity, coordination of volunteers, equipment and supplies, and education and training.

In addition to an ethics duty to communities, hospitals must maintain their accreditation for credibility and funding. TJC, the accrediting body for hospitals, includes emergency management as part of its standards and offers a framework for planning and evaluating those standards.[30] TJC provides many resources for hospitals and other agencies, including an all-hazards approach and step-by-step guidance for plan design with practical advice on budgets, design, and command systems. In addition, there are disaster-specific resources related to storms, floods, and security issues. TJC's library also addresses meeting the mental health needs of physicians, first responders, and receivers of care. In response to current issues for disaster planning, TJC includes information on ransomware attacks and networking portals.

Ethics and Hospital Disaster Preparation

While hospitals have a duty to the community and to patients to be disaster-ready, there are a number of ethics considerations that must be addressed in fulfilling this responsibility. The burden of providing the service may also be different for hospitals with respect to setting and size. For example, a small hospital in a rural area must still maintain readiness for disasters but may not have the capacity to serve patients if an event occurs. However, the obligation to do so is much more demanding on this kind of facility than it would be on a multihospital system that has greater resources and capacity.

One of the ethics issues faced by hospitals in their obligation for preparedness is that of justice. Specifically, there can be a conflict between social justice and market or distributive justice.[31] Those who support market justice support the idea that fairness and service will be handled through the marketplace. However, those who argue that social justice is needed for truly equal allocation support the concept of using the best care available to prevent or reduce the effects of disasters. Because there are economic ramifications of justice when dealing with disaster situations, it is important for hospitals to review their ethics position on what is appropriate in a disaster situation with their ethics committees and include ethics in their standards and planning.

In addition, hospitals may choose to address the ethics of beneficence by providing education and support for communities so that individuals have an emergency plan.

Redlener[32] offers a brief history of an individual's response to preparedness efforts and a discussion of making individuals safer. Among his suggestions is a list of criteria for population preparedness. These criteria include being able to respond appropriately in a situation, maintaining cardiopulmonary resuscitation (CPR) credentials, having a personal network and communication plan, and building family resiliency. Hospitals and other healthcare facilities could use this information and other sources to engage in community outreach and education about disaster planning.

Attention to another area of ethics was highlighted in the events that occurred at Memorial Hospital during Hurricane Katrina.[33] This hospital and its employees faced unthinkable challenges and heartbreaking decisions in their efforts to deal with a disaster situation that exceeded their capacity and required extraordinary ethical decisions. A new area of ethics decision-making is called "altered standards of care"[34] on the basis of a directive from the DHS; these standards provide guidance for addressing policy development and activation for situations where a hospital's capacity is not able to adequately address the disaster. For example, a rural hospital might need to use altered standards of care when dealing with a mass shooting event.

The altered standards of care address areas such as staffing, patient ratios, scope of practice, and supplies. In addition, there are sections on admissions, transport, and other areas for consideration. For example, when a disease outbreak occurs, staff members may be reluctant to serve patients because of concerns for their families and themselves. The plan suggests ways to temporarily change patient ratios, shifts, and credentialed staff members who do not normally have a clinical role. Addressing these and the many other issues related to large-scale disasters provides guidance for action and the ability to be prepared through scenarios in other practices.

Of course, these standards also have ethics implications for staff members and hospital systems. The CDC[35] offers guidelines that apply to disaster situations where systems can be overwhelmed. Among its suggestions are establishing a priority for transparency, including the hospital board, community members of all types, and staff members. In addition, each guideline should be reviewed using an ethics perspective, and procedural justice must be included in the guidelines. This means that there is training on these procedures and that it is carried out consistently for everyone. The guidelines also address the importance of autonomy versus the general good and offer a rationale for decisions that appear to restrict the individual's freedom.

▶ Professional Readiness for Disasters

Society entrusts certain professionals (doctors, nurses, paramedics, emergency medical technicians, firefighters, the police, and the military) with the responsibility to act in ways that facilitate the whole society's ability to overcome or recover from a disaster. Given the nature of the situations that these professionals encounter, they and their respective organizations have the responsibility to be logistically and ethically prepared. This preparedness requires practicing for what might never happen, being ethically ready for adverse situations, and having an adequate support system for their coping with what they face.

Application of the ethics principles of nonmaleficence, justice, autonomy, and beneficence should also be part of disaster planning and training. This preparation is necessary because emergency care professionals deal with unpredictable and often dangerous situations where ethics must be applied in a situation requiring quick action. Erbay[36] provides a survey of ethics issues that this group of healthcare professionals may face. These issues are

divided into the following categories: before intervention, treatment, and end-of-life care. For example, the issue of appropriate application of justice when dealing with situations of scarcity affects emergency providers and also the dispatch center. In addition, there could be a violation of beneficence when the responders cannot locate the address or are faced with personal risk.

With respect to treatment, there is a constant dialogue between beneficence and nonmaleficence with respect to the patient. Triage is an example of the application of the limitations of benefit and how to provide "maximum beneficence."[37] Examples of other treatment issues are dealing with difficult patients, conflicts between emergency personnel, and informed consent. Often, first responders are challenged to make decisions when a do-not-resuscitate document does not exist or when a patient is not competent to express his or her desires. In addition, there are particular ethics issues related to the end of life. These include the need to decide when and how long to provide CPR. In general, protocols assist with responses to these dilemmas.

While this discussion includes highlights of ethics issues faced by emergency care professionals, it should be noted that personal ethics may also be challenged in this work. For example, if a professional must deliver care to individuals with whom he or she does not feel comfortable because of his or her personal beliefs, it may cause conflict within that person. The ability to discuss the situation with others may be useful to advance an individual's ethics reasoning and practice when personal norms are challenged.

▶ Individual Response to Disasters

Despite the extensive media coverage of disasters and mass casualty events, most people think that these events will never happen to them. Perhaps it is part of human nature not to want to prepare for the worst, but it is necessary. Studies indicate that some of the most vulnerable people, such as low-income families, are the least prepared to deal with emergencies. Others simply feel that because these events are rare, there is no need to be concerned.[38, 39]

According to the ARC, people should be "Red Cross Ready" in the event of an emergency.[40] This readiness includes preparing an emergency first-aid kit that will enable people to care for their own emergencies. In the event of a major disaster, government assistance might not be immediate, so preparedness is essential. It also includes having at least three days' worth of supplies for survival. This includes having at least 1 gal. of water and 1600 calories of food that does not require cooking per person per day. These survival materials should be stored in containers that are easily accessible. The ARC also asks individuals to include money, a flashlight, a battery-operated radio, and prescription medicines in the emergency kit.

Preparedness requires that individuals develop a disaster plan. This plan should contain information about what they would do in an emergency. It should identify where they would go and who they would need to contact. The ARC encourages individuals to communicate their plan to family members and friends and even to conduct practice sessions so that they are prepared in an emergency. Finally, individuals should know about the types of disasters that could occur in their area and how to get accurate information pertaining to them. The ARC also encourages everyone to learn first aid and CPR because it may take time for emergency medical staff to reach everyone in a major disaster.

The CDC notes that individuals might have to shelter in a place when a disaster occurs.[41] This means that people must be able to prevent contamination if a chemical or radiological disaster occurs. The CDC suggests choosing a room in the home to prepare

as a shelter. This room would contain a disaster supply kit, food, and sufficient water supply for the family. Businesses should have an emergency plan to get employees to a designated shelter. This shelter should have first-aid kits, food, and water. The police or fire departments should have the ability to issue warnings whenever a shelter-in-place policy is necessary.

Redlener[42] also suggested that citizens receive CPR and first-aid training through either the ARC or another entity. It also is important to be aware of one's situation at work, at home, or in the community. This might include knowing how to exit buildings, being aware of people in one's surroundings, and anticipating any dangers in one's environment. To be truly disaster-ready, Americans need information about their own communities and the potential for disasters. Individuals must also prepare for situations in which traditional telephone services might not be operational. In such cases, two-way communication devices such as smart phones might become lifelines because they can be battery-operated. In an age when nature and humankind can cause disasters, citizens and families need to be able to control their disaster responses by being prepared.

Ethics Implications for Individual Responses to Disasters

When a disaster strikes, fear and injury cause individuals to enter into survival mode. This mind-set may negate the ethics of respecting the rights and dignity of others. In the United States, individuals tend to expect the government to respond in a timely manner whenever any type of emergency occurs. Because of the country's history of responding to disasters, they put great faith in the ability of U.S. citizens and the government to handle emergencies. However, individuals also have an ethical responsibility to be prepared to handle emergencies on their own, because government help may not be imminent.

Autonomy is another ethics issue for individuals who are in disaster situations. As the government and organizations begin to use high-tech tools to prevent potential disasters, individuals question how much of their privacy and autonomy is being lost versus the benefits gained. For example, more and more cities are adding camera surveillance on streets to protect against potential terrorist acts or other crimes. In addition, there has been a rapid expansion of the use of drones to prevent mass shootings and fight fires. Google maps can provide individuals with a bird's-eye view of their homes and property. Although surveillance technology has benefits, some individuals question its value in light of the loss of personal freedom. Others believe that such surveillance is the beginning of a "slippery slope" on which all citizens can be a target and autonomy is nonexistent.

Beneficence also is an issue for individuals in both planning and responding to disasters. Without acts of beneficence, many individuals will not survive. The good news is that citizens often become even more altruistic and compassionate in times of disaster and widespread suffering. However, in planning for disasters, individuals have to consider how far their responsibility goes. Are they going to be responsible for all the elderly in their neighborhood or just for their immediate family members? Who will be responsible for those in the community who might require extra relief during a disaster? What is the gap between individual beneficence and the government's responsibility? These questions pose a challenge to an individual's concept of duty (deontology) and make for deep levels of discussions around family dinner tables.

▸ Update from a Practitioner's Point of View

As a clinician and educator in nursing, Dr. Karen Bawel-Brinkley has expertise that includes educating professionals in the field of nursing using clinical simulation. In her section, Dr. Bawel-Brinkley addresses the need for planning for adequate response and recovery functions during disasters. Using Bandura's and others theories, she also explains how individuals respond to disasters from a theoretical base. As an educator, Dr. Bawel-Brinkley also provides insights into the preparation needed for effective responses to disasters.

Disaster Planning and Ethics

In the United States, the evolution of emergency management, response, and recovery functions was accelerated with the tragic events of 9/11. Because disasters include people, responders, the community, and the government, the application of emergency management is complex and leads to many logistics and ethics concerns. For example, who is responsible for disaster preparation? Is there an ethical duty for the citizens of this country to be proactive and self-sufficient in a variety of disasters? How can individuals learn to respond to disasters and make quality decisions that will benefit the most individuals affected?

Effective responses to natural and human-made disasters require that different components and participants act in appropriate ways. For example, leadership, communication, and teamwork must be present and involve multiple types of professionals. The disaster plan itself must mean the needs of the environment and the community. One plan will not fit all. In addition, the training of responders may also vary from one situation to the next.[43] Plans for disasters must also be in place for all levels from nations to individuals so that responses are rapid, effective, and life-saving.

Disaster Planning and Individuals

Vulnerability is a concern in disaster planning from a professional and ethical view. In all situations, people are involved, and the goal is to limit unnecessary harm and to respect the autonomy of individuals. Therefore, it is prudent to remember that we look at a theoretical model that supports dynamic and interactive cognitive processes of an individual and his or her human thinking. Bandura's[44] social cognitive theory provides a triadic reciprocal causation perspective that involves the person, the environment, and the task present. For example, we have the individual (responder or vulnerable person), the environment (the location where the disaster is occurring: restaurant, airport, or apartment), and the task of being prepared and/or surviving the disaster in planning.[45, 46] Each of these internal personal factors interact bidirectionally.

Even though individuals come with a variety of knowledge, skill sets, and experience, the one variable in all disasters is the person, so the main task in disaster planning is ensuring the person's survival in changing environments. Therefore, if the task is to survive or respond to a disaster, the person becomes the focal point and then can transfer knowledge to a variety of situations.

How do individuals plan for disasters? The process of adopting a disaster plan and putting that plan into action involves the transaction and interaction of the person, behavior, and environment. Bandura[47, 48] suggested that individuals have the ability to alter and adapt to circumstances, situations, and activities on the basis of their ability to be active participants within their environment. For people to alter and adapt to changes introduced into their lives, they must have the ability to use their self-referent and self-regulatory skills.

Self-referent and self-regulatory skills include cognitive, motivational, and affective processes that transform knowledge into action. These skills include the ability to think and reason, solve problems, critically analyze, evaluate experiences, and then apply that knowledge to alter and adapt to a behavior. Therefore, an individual has the ability to think ahead and formulate future plan on the basis of past knowledge and experience to

ever-changing and future activities. So with the necessary knowledge, skills, experience, deliberate practice, and feedback in similar situations, the individual can learn and then translate that knowledge and skills to a variety of disasters situations.

However, during a disaster, individuals may make inappropriate decisions. For example, Meyer and Kunreuther[49] suggested that during situations involving danger, our brain tends to resort to two cognitive systems: (1) automated and instinctive thoughts that are fast, reflexive, and usually unconscious, and (2) more controlled thoughts such as emotions and instincts, making critical-thinking decisions rather than reacting to the situation.[50] While both of these systems are connected, a person with experience and knowledge can learn to make decisions rather than reacting to the situation.[51] Bandura[52] suggested that when people have little control over a disaster situation, they have the ability to translate it and react to a variety of situations. If a person comes prepared with knowledge, skills, and confidence, he or she is better able to adapt and respond appropriately to a situation.

Cognitive, motivational, and affective processes are primarily influenced by an individual's belief about his or her ability. This belief will influence the action to make a disaster part of a person's lifestyle and prepare for its possibility. Therefore, individuals will use their self-referent and self-regulatory skills within the framework of the belief in their ability to perform specific tasks. These skills include developing a disaster plan for the home and within the community. Therefore, an individual's beliefs in his or her ability or self-efficacy affects the knowledge, skills, and resources needed to change from a lifestyle that does not include a disaster plan to one that includes a disaster plan and prepares to practice that plan.

By enhancing the self-efficacy about planning, preparing, and practicing disaster plans, an individual can learn to exercise some control in times of disasters and when responding to disasters.[53] In addition, initiating a disaster plan involves a process of change. Change typically involves a process of deciding that one has the ability to engage in the exercise. This decision is followed by planning to take action and then taking action. The transtheoretical model of behavioral change helps explain the process of change by older adults,[54] but it may also be useful for addressing the specific stages of behavioral changes that predict whether a person will engage in planning, preparing, and practicing a disaster plan.

The transtheoretical model is a stage model and consists of three basic components: (1) stages of change, (2) processes people use to change, and (3) levels of change.[55, 56] Research findings suggest that when people change from a high-risk behavior (no disaster plan) to a healthier alternative (disaster plan), they tend to use covert and overt activities to progress through each of the stages. Being able to identify the stage of behavioral change in an individual may provide information about the usability of the model in the vulnerable population. Identifying the stage of behavior change then provides insight into the processes used by individuals in a particular stage. Understanding the process of adoption in older adults can also provide information for developing and implementing individualized interventions for people who are especially vulnerable to disasters.

Stages of Change Behavior

In their research findings, Prochaska and DiClemente[57] identified six stages of behavior change that a person progresses through when confronted with change in his or her lifestyle: (1) precontemplation, (2) contemplation, (3) preparation, (4) action, (5) maintenance, and (6) relapse. They conceptualized each stage in terms of time, as well as achieving a set of tasks that would equip the person for the next stage of change. As a result, the length of time a person spends in each stage is unique and advancement to the next stage depends on mastery of the set of tasks within that stage.[58, 59]

The first stage of change behavior is precontemplation. In this stage, the individual does not intend to plan for a disaster within the next 6 months. The characteristics of individuals in the precontemplation stage can be grouped into two major categories: (1) they spend less time cognitively processing the problem, and (2) they may have been unsuccessful in past attempts to change. Individuals in this stage spend less time processing information about the problem of experiencing a disaster and tend to be unaware of the detrimental outcomes of a disaster. They may also spend less time and energy on self-evaluating and reevaluating themselves as being sedentary. One reason for this lack of processing is that they may be unacquainted with or have limited information about survival strategies and even experience less emotional reaction to the negative aspects of a disaster.

In the contemplation stage, the individual may be intending to change within the next 6 months. He or she is aware of the negative consequences of a disaster and the benefits of preparing for a disaster. However, there is a balance between the pros and cons of preparing for a disaster. Therefore, the individual may begin the development of a disaster plan but will lack clarity to change and action may not occur. As a result, he or she may remain in this stage for some time.[60]

The third stage is known as the preparation stage. A plan for action is formulated to take place in the immediate future, typically within the next month. Individuals become aware that planning and preparing for human-made or natural disasters can reduce negative outcomes. They also have taken some type of action within the prior year. For example, they may have participated in a disaster training course at the local ARC and begun a decision tree for keeping themselves safe. In the action stage, the individuals will demonstrate obvious changes in their lifestyles within the past 6 months. They decide to plan, implement, and practice a disaster plan on a regular basis.[61]

Individuals who have a disaster plan for at least 6 months to 5 years are identified as being in the maintenance stage. In this stage, people focus on working to maintain their plans by review and practice drills. However, relapse can occur during the action or maintenance stage of behavioral change. Recently, Prochaska and DiClemente[62] added another stage, termination. In this stage, individuals do not experience a temptation to quit or forget their disaster plan and do not practice the plan.

The stages of this model provide the health provider with a temporal dimension for understanding individuals' change in attitude, intentions, or behavior. Prochaska and DiClemente[63] also identified 10 overt and covert activities and experiences that adults use to modify their behaviors: (1) consciousness raising, (2) dramatic relief, (3) self-reevaluation, (4) environmental reevaluation, (5) self-liberation, (6) social liberation, (7) counterconditioning, (8) stimulus control, (9) contingency management, and (10) a helping relationship.

In addition to the constructs of stages, processes, and levels of changes, Prochaska and DiClemente[64] also integrated two other constructs into the transtheoretical model of behavioral change: decisional balance and self-efficacy. Self-efficacy is situation-specific and influences an individual's self-regulatory skills and motivation. Therefore, an individual's self-efficacy influences his or her behavior and the outcome of that behavior.[65, 66]

Preparation of Responders

Mass causality found at disaster sites requires rapid critical-thinking and decision-making.[67] The ability to triage victims in a safe and ethical manner becomes essential. However, mass casualty training is time-consuming, labor-intensive, and costly, so training tends to be infrequent. Interestingly, nursing and medical students have relatively little experience during their education in disaster training. In addition, responders generally get their training in classrooms, lectures, and skills labs, which are far removed from authentic settings.

Deliberative Practice

It is critical that those who respond to disasters have expertise in both motor and procedural skills. Practice over time allows responders to master these skills. According to Ericsson, improvement of performance is affected both by how much learners practice and by how they practice.[68, 69]

The learning strategy of deliberate practice enhances the ability to become competent in the skills needed for disaster response. The characteristics of deliberative practice are that it is highly structured, is adapted to the learner's level, and requires a commitment to long hours of practice. In addition, deliberate practice involves a high level of motivation and concentration. Feedback is also important in this learning process.[70, 71]

Feedback in deliberate practice requires analysis of performance gaps and a specific learning plan. Planning is also needed to ensure the effective use of time and resources for responder training. When this learning technique is used successfully, it results in the ability to adapt physically and cognitively to the demands of a situation. In a disaster, this means that responders can make critical decisions that are safe, professional, and ethical.

In addition, training using simulation technology has led to a reduction in medical errors in emergency department, operating room, and delivery room contexts. This finding is especially important when one considers the potential for medical errors during a disaster response. Research findings also suggest that the overall benefit of clinical simulation is the immersive qualities of the participant in a safe learning environment. Despite the benefits of simulation, the challenges of using high-fidelity clinical simulation in nursing or other education are expense, space, computer literacy, and technical support.[72] In addition, the participants and facilitators must be in the same place at the same time. Other industries already make use of formal training. For example, to better prepare pilots and their crew for potential airline disasters, the airline industry developed supplemental training in crew resource management using flight simulators.[73]

To better prepare professionals to manage patients in rapidly changing and complex disaster environments, many organizations are using technology to create more realistic learning experiences and opportunities to practice. For example, nursing, medical, and other schools have incorporated the use of "midfidelity" patient simulators (mannequins) into their skills labs to improve clinical skills. Medical and nursing schools are expanding the scope of their current skills lab simulations with virtual world simulations to create more robust learning experiences.[74–76] Clinical simulation also provides healthcare providers with a safe learning environment to develop critical-thinking skills with jeopardizing the safety of an actual patient.[77, 78] Research studies that assessed learning using the strategy of clinical simulation suggested that learning in the cognitive, affective, and psychomotor domains was reflected in the learner. In addition, clinical simulation has been shown to change participants' learning from simulation activities and results in behavior change in the actual environment.[79]

By combining human patient simulators with immersive learning environments in 3D virtual worlds, there is a potential to increase the professional responders' ability to transfer knowledge gained in skills labs or during mock disaster drills. With enhanced deliberate practice, interprofessional responder teams can also be better prepared to assess and manage actual victims in a hospital situation and/or in the field. Virtual worlds offer new opportunities to create a more realistic skills lab environment that helps students acquire specific competencies through frequent practice and feedback.[80] The synergy of these technologies represents one of the first efforts to incorporate virtual world technology in an immersive environment

that allows learners to participate in a variety of realistic, yet simulated, disaster situations. Participants will be able to safely learn and practice basic rescue skills, and acquire the skills and confidence they need to transition from the skills lab to safe practice in a clinical setting.[81, 82]

▶ Summary

Human behavior is complicated and complex in normal times, but when individuals must deal with life-altering changes, chaos tends to prevail. Therefore, understanding how people respond to a disaster situation is important in developing strategies to help vulnerable individuals and responders. While it is important that education reaches all people, it also becomes an issue of attempting to change an individual's behavior into acknowledging there will be disasters and to become prepared for them. This situation leads us back to the issue of individual autonomy. Therefore, it is important to develop strategies to assist individuals in understanding that the benefits of disaster preparedness outweigh its barriers when it comes to surviving a disaster and that being proactive is in their best interest.

In disaster training, providing responders with a more holistic approach to engage in representative tasks found in a disaster setting enables the responders to respond with confidence and logical thinking. Therefore, we need to advocate and use the latest resources in this approach and promote increased opportunities for deliberate practice. Using virtual world simulations, disaster teams and/or responders can learn and fill knowledge and skill gaps. In addition, they can reflect upon their observed performance and standards with the intent to improve their performance. Being proactive and creating individual engagement in disaster preparedness, while costly, save lives, reduce the amount of disaster recovery time, and benefit the community. They also honor health care's ethical duty for beneficence, nonmaleficence, and social justice.

▸ Questions for Discussion

1. What ethics theories apply to the use of scarce resources in a disaster situation?
2. Who should be responsible for what happens during a disaster: the individual or the government?
3. What is the role of the hospital in disaster preparedness?
4. How can hospitals justify the cost of their involvement in disaster preparedness from an ethics standpoint?

▸ Notes

1. World Health Organization/Emergency Humanitarian Action, "*Disasters & Emergencies: Training Package*," 2002, http://apps.who.int/disasters/repo/7656.pdf.
2. Ibid.
3. International Federation of Red Cross and Red Crescent Societies, "What is a disaster?," http://www.ifrc.org/en/what-we-do/disaster-management/about-disasters/what-is-a-disaster/.
4. Ibid., para. 2.
5. M. J. Reilly and D. S. Markenson, *Health Care Emergency Management: Principles and Practice* (Burlington, MA: Jones & Barlett Learning, 2011).
6. J. Belles et al., "2016 Hurricane Season Recap: Ten Things We Will Remember," *The Weather Channel*, November 29, 2016, https://weather.com/storms/hurricane/news/hurricane-season-2016-atlantic-recap.
7. National Weather Service, "Joplin Tornado Event Summary: May 2, 2011," http://www.crh.Noaa.gov/sgf/?m=event_2011may22_summary.
8. J. L. Hicks et al., *Health and Medical Response to Active Shooter and Bombing Events* (Washington, DC: National Academy of Medicine, 2016).
9. M. Baker, "Creating Order from Chaos, Part I: Triage, Initial Care, and Tactical Considerations in Mass Casualty and Disaster Response," *Military Medicine* 172 (2007): 232–36.
10. I. Redlener, *Americans at Risk* (New York: Albert A. Knopf, 2006).
11. Department of Homeland Security, "Prevent Terrorism," https://www.dhs.gov/preventing-terrorism.
12. Department of Homeland Security, "Our Mission," https://www.dhs.gov/our-mission.
13. See the Department of Homeland Security website, http://www.dhs.gov/.
14. Department of Homeland Security, "Stop.Think.Connect," https://www.dhs.gov/stopthinkconnect.
15. Federal Emergency Management Agency, "About us," https://www.fema.gov/about-agency.
16. Federal Emergency Management Agency, "Center for Faith-Based and Neighborhood Partnerships," https://www.fema.gov/faith.
17. Centers for Disease Control, "What We Do."
18. See the American Red Cross website, http//www.redcross.org/about-us/our-work/disaster-relief, general information.
19. Ibid.
20. American Red Cross, "Who We Are," http://www.redcross.org/get-help/how-to-prepare-for-emergencies/make-a-plan.
21. M. Roberts and E. G. DeRenzo, "Ethical Considerations in Community Disaster Planning," in *Mass Medical Care with Scarce Resources: A Community Planning Guide*, eds. S. J. Phillips and A. Knebel (Rockville, MD: Agency for Health Research and Quality, 2007), 9–23.
22. Ibid.

23. Reilly and Markenson, *Health Care Emergency Management: Principles and Practice*.

24. P. Mallia, "Toward an Ethical Theory in Disaster Situations," *Medicine, Health Care and Philosophy* 18, no.1 (2015): 3–11.

25. Ibid.

26. S. Fink, *Five Days at Memorial Hospital* (New York: Crown Publishers, 2013).

27. R. Meyer and H. Kunreuther, *The Ostrich Paradox: Why We Underprepare for Disasters* (Philadelphia, PA: Wharton Digital Press, 2017).

28. Select Bipartisan Committee to Investigate the Preparation for and Response to Hurricane Katrina, *A Failure of Initiative: Final Report of the Select Bipartisan Committee to Investigate the Preparation for and Response to Hurricane Katrina*, House Report 109–377 (Washington, DC: U.S. Government Printing Office, 2006), http://biotech.law.lsu.edu/katrina/govdocs/109–377/katrina.html.

29. Reilly and Markenson, *Health Care Emergency Management: Principles and Practice*.

30. The Joint Commission, *Emergency Management Resources,* https://www.jointcommission.org/emergency_management.aspx.

31. R. A. Culbertson, "Trauma Care: Economic Versus Social Justice," *Healthcare Executive* 32, no. 4 (2017 July/August): 48–49.

32. Redlener, *Americans at Risk*.

33. Fink, *Five Days at Memorial Hospital*.

34. Reilly and Markenson, *Health Care Emergency Management: Principles and Practice*, 406.

35. K. Kinlaw and R. Levine, *Ethical Guidelines in Pandemic Influenza: Recommendations for the Ethics Subcommittee of the Advisory Committee to the Director* (Atlanta, GA: Centers for Disease Control and Prevention, 2007).

36. H. Erbay, "Some Ethical Issues in Prehospital Emergency Medicine," *Turkish Journal of Emergency Medicine* 14, no. 4 (2014): 193–8. doi:10.5505/1304.7361.2014.32656.

37. Erbay, "Some Ethical Issues in Prehospital Emergency Medicine," 195.

38. American Red Cross and Wirthlin Worldwide, "U.S. Public Unprepared," *The Wirthlin Report* 13, no. 5 (2004) Http://www.redcross.org/images/pffs/WirthlinReport.pdf

39. Meyer and Kunreuther, *The Ostrich Paradox: Why We Underprepare for Disasters*.

40. American Red Cross, "Prepare your Home and Family," http://www.redcross.org/prepare/location/home-family.

41. Centers for Disease Control, "Learn How to Shelter in Place," http://emergency.cdc.gov/preparedness/shelter/.

42. Redlener, *Americans at Risk*.

43. Ibid.

44. A. Bandura, *Social Foundations of Thought and Action: A Social Cognitive Theory* (Princeton, NJ: Prentice-Hall, 1986).

45. Ibid.

46. A. Bandura, "Social Cognitive Theory: An Agenetic Perspective," *Asian Journal of Social Psychology* 2 (1999): 21–41.

47. A. Bandera, *Social Learning Theory* (Englewood Cliffs, NJ: Prentice-Hall, 1997).

48. Bandura, "Social Cognitive Theory: An Agenetic Perspective."

49. Meyer and Kunreuther, *The Ostrich Paradox: Why We Underprepare for Disasters*.

50. Ibid., 8–9.

51. Meyer and Kunreuther, *The Ostrich Paradox: Why We Underprepare for Disasters*.

52. Bandura, "Social Cognitive Theory: An Agenetic Perspective."

53. Bandura, *Social Learning Theory*.

54. J. O. Prochaska and A. DiClemente, *The Transtheoretical Approach: A Handbook of Integrative Psychotherapy* (New York: Brunner/Mazel, 1996).

55. J. O. Prochaska and A. DiClemente, "Stages and Processes of Self Change of Smokers: Toward an Integrated Model of Change," *Journal of Consulting and Clinical Psychology* 51 (1983): 390–95.

56. Prochaska and DiClemente, *The Transtheoretical Approach: A Handbook of Integrative Psychotherapy.*

57. Ibid.

58. Ibid.

59. J. O. Prochaska and W. F. Velier, "The Trans-Theoretical Model of Health Behavior Change," *American Journal of Health Promotion* 12, no. 1 (1997): 38–48.

60. J. O. Prochaska and A. DiClemente, *The Transtheoretical Approach: A Handbook of Integrative Psychotherapy.*

61. Ibid.

62. Ibid.

63. Ibid.

64. Ibid.

65. Bandura, *Social Foundations of Thought and Action: A Social Cognitive Theory.*

66. Bandura, "Social Cognitive Theory: An Agenetic Perspective."

67. D. S. Vincent et al., "Teaching Mass Casualty Triage Skills Using Iterative Multimanikin Simulations," *Prehospital Emergency Care* 13, no. 2 (2007): 241–46.

68. K. A. Ericsson, "An Expert—Performance Perspective of Research on Medical Expertise: The Study of Clinical Performance," *Medical Education* 41 (2007): 1124–30.

69. V. Moulaert et al., "The Effects of Deliberate Practice in Undergraduate Medical Education," *Medical Education* 38 (2004): 1044–52.

70. Ericsson, "An Expert—Performance Perspective of Research on Medical Expertise: The Study of Clinical Performance."

71. Moulaert et al., "The Effects of Deliberate Practice in Undergraduate Medical Education."

72. P. Jeffries, *Clinical Simulations in Nursing Education: Advanced Concepts, Trends and Opportunities* (Washington, DC: National League for Nursing, 2014).

73. P. Youngblood et al., "Design, Development and Evaluation of an Online Virtual Emergency Department for Training Trauma Teams," *Simulation Healthcare* 3, no. 3 (2008): 146–53.

74. M. H. Oermann, "Guest Editorial," *Journal of Nursing Education* 50, no. 2 (2011): 63–64.

75. D. Z. Hambrick et al., "Deliberate Practice: Is That What It Takes to Become an Expert?" *Intelligence* 45 (2013): 34–45.

76. Jeffries, *Clinical Simulations in Nursing Education: Advanced Concepts, Trends and Opportunities.*

77. Hambrick et al., "Deliberate Practice: Is That What It Takes to Become an Expert?"

78. Jeffries, *Clinical Simulations in Nursing Education: Advanced Concepts, Trends and Opportunities.*

79. Ibid.

80. S. L. Farra et al., "Virtual Reality. Disaster Training: Translation to Practice," *Nursing Education in Practice* 15 (2015): 53–57.

81. Jeffries, *Clinical Simulations in Nursing Education: Advanced Concepts, Trends and Opportunities.*

82. J. Whyte IV and E. Cormier, "A Deliberative-based Practice Training Protocol for Nursing Students," *Clinical Stimulation in Nursing* 10, no. 12 (2014): 617–25.

CHAPTER 15

Domestic Violence: Changing Theory, Changing Practice

Carole Warshaw

▶ Introduction

Despite widespread recognition of domestic violence as a public health problem, many clinicians still have difficulty integrating routine intervention into their day-to-day work with patients. This is, in part, because domestic violence raises a distinct set of challenges for both providers and the institutions that shape clinical practice. Domestic violence is a complex social problem rather than a biomedical one; addressing it means asking clinicians to step beyond a traditional medical paradigm to confront the personal feelings and social beliefs that shape their responses to patients and to work in partnership with community groups committed to ending domestic violence. In addition, addressing domestic violence raises important challenges to the healthcare system itself—to its theoretical models, to the nature of medical training, and to the structure of funding and service delivery. If, as healthcare providers, we truly want to play a role in preventing domestic violence rather than just treating its consequences, we also need to play a role in broader community efforts to transform the social conditions that create and support this kind of violence in the first place.[1]

Over the past 35 years, it has become increasingly clear that domestic violence carries not only serious health consequences for women but also many hidden social costs as well. As clinicians, we see the profound effects of this violence on a daily basis.[2] We often are deeply affected when we allow ourselves to listen, understand, and grapple with issues that require far more than our medical expertise.

However, over time, the healthcare field has made considerable strides in its efforts to address domestic violence. For example, standard guidelines now exist because of the combined efforts of the domestic violence advocacy community, individual practitioners, and numerous professional societies. Major initiatives have been launched to increase provider awareness, establish and distribute clinical guidelines, and offer strategies for improving institutional responses to domestic violence, including recommendations for screening.[3] Innovative hospital-based advocacy programs have increased in number, and over 60% of medical schools, over 80% of family practice residencies, and approximately 70% of obstetrics/gynecology residencies have incorporated training on family violence into their standard curricula.[4] Furthermore, under the Patient Protection and Affordable Care Act of 2010 (ACA 2010), all new and non-grandfathered health plans are required to cover screening and brief counseling for domestic violence, and plans cannot require cost sharing or deductibles for these services. Yet despite widespread recognition of domestic violence as a public health problem, many clinicians still have difficulty in integrating routine inquiry about domestic violence into their day-to-day clinical work.[5] Understanding the difficulties faced by healthcare providers as they attempt to address this issue can help not only improve the practice of medicine but also develop more realistic strategies for prevention and social change.[6]

Addressing domestic violence requires more than simply adding new diagnostic categories to differential diagnoses or new technical skills to clinical repertoires. As noted previously, it means asking clinicians to step beyond a traditional medical paradigm to confront the personal feelings and social beliefs that shape their responses to patients, which presents a difficult barrier. In addition, the healthcare system itself, through its theoretical framework, the nature of its training process, and the changing structure of clinical practice, presents another set of barriers that profoundly affect the ability of individual providers to respond to people who have been abused by an intimate partner.[7]

▶ Personal and Social Barriers

As Holtz et al. have reported, the majority of healthcare providers have not learned about domestic violence during their training. Although more recent trainees have been exposed to the topic during their graduate and postgraduate years, the amount of time devoted to it is limited.[8] As a result, "clinical" responses often are shaped by an interplay of a physician's own personal experiences and social, cultural, and religious beliefs.[9] Many factors combine to shape the ways we interpret and respond to life events, including our individual experiences and the social contexts in which they take place.

Koss et al.,[10] Johnson,[11] Brown,[12] Rieker and Carmen,[13] and Miller[14] have described the psychological impact of gender socialization, the traumatic effects of social disenfranchisement, and the ways in which the denial of intolerable feelings can shape our perceptions and lead to protectively rationalized ways of viewing ourselves, other people, and the world. For instance, the psychological need to protect ourselves from certain feelings in order to ensure psychic survival combined with social or cultural explanations of our experiences can solidify into beliefs and values that may then appear to us as givens.[15] Clinicians absorb a range of societal views regarding gender and power, around which their own identities are constructed. Assumptions about gender, race, and class so permeate our culture that they often provide an unconscious backdrop through which we come to understand our own experiences and interpret those of others.

In addition, listening to people describe the violence in their lives can have a significant psychological impact on providers.[16] When physicians are not specifically trained to deal with psychological trauma, they are forced to rely on their own capacities to address painful and potentially overwhelming issues. In addition, given the prevalence of gender-based violence in this society, a significant number of physicians will have experienced or witnessed abuse in their own lives.[17] These issues touch too close to home for many healthcare providers, who may be understandably reluctant to have their own painful experiences evoked while trying to function in a professional capacity.[18]

▶ Systemic Barriers

Impact of Medical Training

Once they enter the healthcare arena, clinicians are faced with a new set of forces that shape their perceptions and responses.[19] A number of authors have described the gaps in medical education that influence the psychosocial aspects of care.[20] Not only is medical training often lax in equipping physicians to deal with difficult social and personal issues, but also, more insidiously, the process of professional socialization can actually diminish the capacities individuals already have. Pain, anger, frustration, and sadness are common responses to hearing about abuse. Without specific training and support, many clinicians find themselves dealing with these situations through a variety of techniques designed to protect and distance themselves from potentially distressing encounters.

In a field where competence and mastery are highly valued, it is difficult to risk venturing into areas that make clinicians feel less competent. They may find it easier to focus on problems for which interventions lead to outcomes that are more predictable or for which it is possible to retain a greater sense of control. Time-pressured working conditions only magnify these difficulties.[21]

Professional Socialization and the Intergenerational Transmission of Abuse

Extrapolating from the works of Richman et al.,[22] Baldwin et al.,[23] and others,[24] we can see how abusive training environments might also affect clinicians' abilities to deal with abuse among the women they see as patients. Medical training can be physically punishing, emotionally draining, and socially isolating. Trainees often report feeling humiliated and controlled as well as anxious, exhausted, depressed, overwhelmed, and traumatized.[25] Over time, both students and house staff begin to reorient their identities in terms of medicine's values, to internalize its constructs and judge themselves by its terms. Thus, medical training itself can create some of the same dynamics as abuse. In addition, the structure of medicine is hierarchical and, as such, reflects the gendered power arrangements of the larger society.

In their review of the sexual harassment literature, Schiffman and Frank found that sexual harassment and gender discrimination were common experiences among women physicians, adding yet another layer of abuse for women working within that system.[26] Clinicians' inabilities to recognize abuse in their own lives, whether personal, social, or professional, or to tolerate acknowledging their own vulnerability, make it more difficult for them to empathize with a person who is struggling in an abusive relationship. The need to maintain a sense of power and control in order to be recognized as competent within that system and the pressure to avoid feelings that might arise when one cannot do so reinforce this dynamic on both individual and systemic levels. Although there has been much discussion about how abuse is transmitted intergenerationally within families, the process of professional socialization within the current structure of medicine can also serve as a vehicle for the intergenerational transmission of abuse.[27]

▶ Impact of Theory on Clinical Practice

The theoretical foundations of medical education also affect a physician's ability to treat patients affected by domestic violence. For example, there is often a connection between social problems and clinical diagnoses, even though they are much more complex than any clinical label. In addition, traditional mental health models may be limited as clinical models in providing a framework for recognizing and treating domestic violence. In fact, the mental health system may actually be retraumatizing to patients. The healthcare system is beginning to recognize that a trauma-informed approach may be necessary for addressing this critical problem.

It is now well-documented that childhood adversity, interpersonal violence, ongoing legacies of historical trauma and structural violence, and other social determinants of health, including social isolation and food, housing, and economic insecurity, play a significant role in the development and exacerbation of health and mental health conditions. Yet, traditional medical paradigms are not designed to address many of the non-physiological factors that jeopardize health and well-being, including ongoing domestic violence.[28]

Medicalization of Social Problems

One aspect of medicalization involves the reduction of complex social problems into distinct clinical diagnoses.[29] One of the clearest illustrations of the need to shift from a standard problem-oriented framework to a more comprehensive model involves our evolving understanding of the role domestic violence plays in the lives of women with human immunodeficiency virus (HIV). Several studies have reported that many HIV-positive women either are or have been abused by partners.[30] Many "discrete" medical problems are, in fact, intimately connected to domestic violence, but because we think of them as separate issues, their interrelationships are more likely to be missed. For instance, one might easily generate a problem list that includes HIV infection, substance abuse, pregnancy, depression, post-traumatic stress disorder (PTSD), and domestic violence without necessarily seeing the connections among them.

Initial recognition of domestic violence among HIV-positive women led to appropriate concerns about reducing the risk for further violence, particularly regarding partner notification.[31] It took longer for the incorporation of domestic violence education and intervention into risk reduction counseling for HIV, pregnancy, and substance abuse. The fact that sexual coercion, birth control sabotage, and the inability to use barrier protection within the context of an abusive relationship are risk factors for HIV transmission and other consequences of unprotected sex has important implications for funding, education, treatment, and prevention. Similarly, substance use, another major risk factor for HIV among women, increases in the context of domestic violence. While some women use substances to manage the traumatic effects of abuse, many are coerced into using substances by abusive partners who may also try to sabotage their recovery efforts.[32] In fact, recognition of these connections has led a number of comprehensive HIV programs to integrate screening and counseling for domestic violence and other lifetime trauma into the prevention and treatment services they provide.[33] In addition, reproductive coercion is now considered a key issue to be addressed in obstetrics/gynecology and family planning settings, and efforts are under way to increase recognition of substance use coercion in primary care, HIV, and behavioral health settings.[34]

Limitations of Mental Health Models

The process of stripping away context and transforming lived experience into disorders also occurs within the major mental health models and affects the nature of both diagnosis and intervention. For example, clinicians who work within a purely biological or disorder-specific framework run risks similar to their medical and surgical colleagues of failing to recognize and respond to the ongoing violence in a patient's life. They may also see the abuse as being caused by a particular woman's increased vulnerability or as only a secondary problem—a social stressor affecting the course of her primary biological or developmental disorder.

Traditional psychoanalytic theory historically has presented a different set of limitations. The context of ongoing violence and danger that creates and perpetuates a woman's symptoms might not be addressed or might be regarded as symptomatic rather than etiologic. In addition, a clinician bound by the constraints of remaining true to the neutrality of a psychodynamic framework might find it difficult to play a more active role in advocating for safety and in helping women gain access to community resources. Of course, other models— both feminist and psychodynamic—do recognize the importance of social and intersubjective contexts.[35]

When domestic violence is framed solely under the rubric of "family violence," the gendered aspects of this problem are obscured and are more likely to be seen in terms of dysfunctional couple or family dynamics. In doing so, clinicians can lose sight of the larger social dynamics that shape gendered behaviors in families, and are thus less able to help women gain perspective or mobilize necessary resources. A family systems approach can present even greater dangers to domestic violence survivors. Assuming equal power within and responsibility for relationship dynamics, it inadvertently holds survivors of domestic violence responsible for their partners' criminal behavior and keeps them engaged in the countertherapeutic task of trying to change themselves in order to get their partners to change. In addition, counseling sessions often precipitate further threats or violence.

Andersen et al.[36] and Walker[37] described the dynamics of battering in terms of ongoing domestic terrorism, akin to hostage situations. In that kind of setting, particularly when their partners continue to engage in violence, controlling behavior, or threats, it is not safe for individuals to be honest or to assert themselves, nor are they likely to be free to make their own choices.[38] Again, newer models of family and couples therapy are being developed that

specifically address domestic violence.[39] However, limited data are available on the effectiveness or safety of these treatment modalities, and they have been studied in couples where the level of violence is low.[40]

The emergence of trauma theory over the past three decades has created a significant shift in the conceptualization of mental health symptoms and in our understanding of the role abuse and violence play in the development of psychological distress and mental health conditions. Arising out of the experiences of survivors of civilian and combat trauma, it views symptoms as survival strategies and as adaptations to potentially life-shattering situations that one makes when real protection is unavailable and normal coping mechanisms are overwhelmed. Trauma models, although immensely helpful in understanding the impact of domestic violence and other types of victimization, also have limitations in the context of ongoing domestic violence. These models typically focus on trauma that occurred in the past. Yet for many survivors of domestic violence, the trauma is unremitting and symptoms may reflect responses to ongoing danger and coercive control, including coercive tactics specifically designed to compromise their mental health and well-being. In addition, therapies that focus on helping survivors understand why they unconsciously "chose" abusive partners, that label them as "codependent" or "enabling," or that hold them responsible for their partners' abusive behavior and for stopping it can also be undermining and potentially endangering to someone who is currently entrapped or unsafe.[41]

These models are limited precisely because they are clinical models. They do not provide a framework for recognizing that it is the combination of the abuser's use of violence, threats, and intimidation with the social conditions that reinforce stigma associated with mental health and substance use conditions, support gender inequality, and limit options for safety that keeps survivors trapped in abusive situations and restricts their possibilities for change.[42] These same gender biases also contribute to the reduced likelihood that the small percentage of men abused by female partners will receive services and to the transphobia and homophobia that impede recognition of domestic violence in lesbian, gay, bisexual, transgender, queer, questioning, and intersex relationships.

Inadvertent Retraumatization

Inadvertent retraumatization of patients through disempowering interactions within the health and mental health system is another crucial issue. The pressure under current practice arrangements, particularly in managed care or under resourced public sector environments, to make rapid assessments, diagnoses, and treatment recommendations can push clinicians into taking a more controlling stance in their clinical encounters. For someone whose life is already controlled by another person, the subtly disempowering quality of many clinical interactions can serve to reinforce the idea that adapting to another's controlling behavior is both expected and necessary for survival. Guidelines for implementing trauma-informed services have begun to address some of these concerns.[43]

Changing Theory and Incorporating Context

Clearly, a purely clinical framework limits our ability to respond to abuse. In fact, maintaining such a stance would require that we "diagnose" and find ways to "treat" a pervasive, long-standing form of normative social pathology characterized by a gender socialization process that, in its most polarized form, has taught women to focus their identities on meeting men's needs and on maintaining relationships at all costs. It also teaches men that it is both necessary and legitimate to sustain their sense of self at the expense of those with less power, often women and children.[44]

This belief is produced within the context of a socioeconomic system that frequently leaves women, particularly those with small children, more limited options for living independent lives[45] and a criminal justice system that often fails to protect or does so in discriminatory ways.

Although the healthcare system is finally beginning to face the consequences of a problem rooted in centuries of social and legal tradition, it is important for us to address the more difficult task of transforming gender socialization patterns and to recognize that gender equality is an essential component of primary prevention.[46]

We also stretch the boundaries of the healthcare system when we work with the domestic violence advocacy and criminal justice systems. For example, many survivors of domestic violence are in danger at the time they seek health care, yet the danger itself is not something amenable to medical intervention. By becoming informed of options available in their communities for increasing survivor safety, clinicians can help survivors access the range of services they may need. Developing relationships with domestic violence service providers can also help clinicians gain a better understanding of the complex issues survivors often face. Will a woman risk losing her children in a custody battle? Will she risk losing her means of providing for them? Will she risk deportation if she seeks help? Does she qualify for immigration remedies under the Violence Against Women Act? Will a survivor risk losing someone he or she loves and who might act lovingly toward him or her much of the time? Will the survivor risk the possibility of being killed if he or she leaves? A more comprehensive model provides a framework for understanding responses to not only trauma but also, more significantly, ongoing danger and mobilization of the social and legal resources that can increase safety, expand options, and ultimately prevent further violence.[47]

▶ Structural Constraints

Healthcare providers face a number of structural constraints that affect their ability to provide appropriate care to individuals who are dealing with ongoing abuse. In the current healthcare climate, cost containment is often achieved at the expense of care, and clinicians' needs are placed in conflict with those of patients for access to diminishing resources.[48] This is a problem, particularly for primary care providers, who often are penalized for spending too much time with patients and for making too many referrals. This is even more problematic for patients, however, at a time when reimbursement for social and mental health services may be at risk.

Micromanagement strategies devised by insurance companies to reduce "unnecessary" mental healthcare utilization (e.g., continuous intrusive demands to justify treatment) can be disruptive and traumatic in themselves. They create an environment in which short-term medication management or potentially retraumatizing directive treatments focused on symptom reduction rather than healing have become the standard of care, making the consistency and safety required for long-term trauma recovery less likely to be reimbursed.

It is unfortunate that just when an expanding body of research is clearly delineating the impact of trauma on the human psyche and the need for more intensive treatment for many survivors,[49] market forces decrease the likelihood that these kinds of services will be available. This becomes increasingly true as the changing healthcare landscape further erodes the possibility of choosing one's provider and type of treatment, removing even the consumer-based economic power from individuals seeking care. For low-income women whose only access to services has been through the public mental health system, this lack of choice has been the norm.[50]

Although providing short-term cost reductions, these policies do not address the long-term personal, financial, and, ultimately, social costs of failing to provide appropriate intervention.[51] In this type of setup, cost containment is seen only in terms of direct individual costs to a given insurance company, employer, or government-sponsored health plan, whereas the exponential, but indirect, personal and social costs that could be prevented by early intervention are not considered part of the relevant financial equation.

A diagnosis-driven reimbursement system poses yet another set of problems for survivors of domestic violence. For a person to use mental health services, he or she must be given a diagnosis. But for domestic violence survivors, the very diagnosis itself can create new dangers. In addition to deliberately engaging in behaviors designed to undermine a partner's sanity and control her access to treatment, the abuser often uses his partner's psychiatric diagnosis to "prove" that she is right, that the problems are her fault, that she is crazy, or that she is an unfit mother. In seeking treatment, a survivor of domestic violence potentially risks losing her children in a custody battle and losing her credibility in court. Stigma associated with substance use and mental illness contributes to the effectiveness of these abusive tactics and can create additional barriers for survivors and their children when they try to seek help.[52] However, appropriate documentation of the mental health impact of domestic violence, including documentation of this type of abuse (mental health coercion), can help a survivor build her legal case. For some women, "psychiatric" symptoms disappear once they are out of danger, but many women continue to be threatened and stalked long after they have left the relationship.[53] For others, symptoms of PTSD may not emerge until they are relatively safe.[54]

In the past, women were refused health insurance for having the preexisting condition of being battered and were refused disability or life insurance because they were considered at higher risk for injury and death.[55] In addition, if a woman was insured on her husband's policy and the bills were sent to him, she was likely to be placed in further jeopardy when he discovered she was seeking outside help. There have been strides in both these areas. Since 1994, 41 states have enacted legislation prohibiting discrimination against victims of domestic violence, and starting in 2014, the ACA 2010 has prohibited insurance companies, healthcare providers, and health programs that receive federal financial assistance from denying coverage to women on the basis of being a survivor of domestic violence. In addition, Health Information Portability and Accountability Act regulations allow the sending of bills to a safe address at a patient's request.[56]

In some states, laws that require mandatory reporting of domestic violence can again place the clinician's legal obligations in conflict with the wishes and the safety of the patient. Not only do these policies potentially destroy the ability of clinicians to provide a safe place for survivors to discuss their most pressing concerns, they also violate survivors' rights to choose what they feel will be safest and most helpful to them and their children. Under these conditions, both clinicians and patients may avoid raising concerns about abuse, thus losing important opportunities for intervention.[57]

Listening to patients, learning about the repercussions of our interventions, and working to prevent revictimization within the system's survivors are important components of our roles as healthcare professionals practicing preventive medicine. Without a clear institutional commitment to address these issues, however, the pressures to continue practice as usual may be greater than the ability to change.

▶ Implications for Training and Practice

Experience has led many clinician-educators to realize that new training strategies must be developed in order to change attitudes and behavior on the scale that is required to address domestic violence.[58] Standard didactic formats, for example, do not provide sufficient opportunity to address the attitudes and feelings that might interfere with a clinician's ability to provide appropriate care, nor do they offer room to acquire the interviewing skills necessary for an optimal response. Training environments that offer the emotional safety to explore personal and cultural responses to abuse and the opportunities to discuss individual, professional, and institutional obstacles can provide a vehicle for generating change within the healthcare community. Although one-time training might raise awareness, ongoing feedback and support are necessary to sustain provider response.[59]

Providing quality health care involves integrating routine inquiry about domestic violence into ongoing clinical practice. This means asking all patients about abuse and violence in their lives. Whether a person chooses to use services or leave his or her partner, our intervention is important. People often return to violent partners many times before they feel safe enough to leave, feel that they can survive on their own, or can accept that the persons they love will not change. When we fail to ask about abuse, we inadvertently isolate people who are living in danger.[60] Just by inquiring and expressing concern, we begin to build bridges, decrease isolation, and create hope.

For persons who live in an atmosphere of ongoing threats, intimidation, and violence, being treated with respect, being taken seriously, and feeling free to make their own choices let them know that supportive experiences are possible. By asking survivors to describe the pattern of their abuse and level of danger and to discuss their options for safety, we provide a place for them to reflect on their situations and consider their choices. By providing access to resources and by facilitating the survivors' own decision-making process rather than attempting to direct them to change, we help them shift the balance of power in their lives. When we work collaboratively with other members of our communities, we not only help individual survivors rebuild their lives but also help change the conditions that allow domestic violence to exist.

For clinicians to develop and sustain appropriate responses to domestic violence, however, they must have the support of the institutions in which they practice. Thus, addressing this issue requires some fundamental changes in the nature of most medical training and in the culture of medical institutions. Creating practice environments and policies that model non-abusive ways of interacting, that support clinicians' efforts to address complex issues with skill and compassion, and that reimburse the more labor-intensive tasks of listening and advocating for change are important components of institutionalizing effective responses to domestic violence.[61] Refocusing our priorities is particularly important in a healthcare climate in which administrators, insurers, and those who influence healthcare policy must begin to recognize that the long-term consequences of nonintervention far exceed the costs of investing in appropriate intervention and prevention.[62]

In addition, providers acting alone, no matter how motivated, cannot meet all the needs of domestic violence survivors and their children. An optimal response requires the efforts of all members of the community. Developing interdisciplinary teams within the healthcare setting and creating collaborative partnerships among the domestic violence advocacy community, the mental health and healthcare systems, the child protective system, and the legal system serve a number of functions: They not only provide referral networks for patients but also create support networks for providers. More important, it is only by working together that we can begin to develop the kinds of intervention strategies that will be appropriate for and respectful to all victims of domestic violence, while laying the groundwork to develop effective prevention strategies as well.

▶ Conclusion

When we ask what survivors of domestic violence need from individual providers, we must also ask what providers need from their training institutions and practice environments in order to respond to those needs. When we do not address the denial of intolerable feelings at a personal level, we are in danger of recreating them not only in individual relationships but also on social and political levels. Further, when socially sanctioned abuses of power are not acknowledged, they often are internalized and reproduced through individual interactions. If we truly want to play a role in preventing domestic violence, rather than just treating its consequences, it is important to work together to address the social conditions that create and support this kind of violence in the first place.

▶ Summary

Domestic violence is widely recognized as a social problem that affects both the family and the community. Clinicians deal with the effects of this issue on an almost daily basis, but they often find it difficult to treat and beyond their medical expertise. This chapter presents a discussion of why physicians may not be prepared to address the needs of those affected by domestic violence and the need for changes in physician training and practice. In addition, it suggests strategies for institutions' and communities' engagement in better addressing the challenges of this significant social issue.

▶ Questions for Discussion

1. How does the training environment influence future physicians' position on responding to survivors of domestic violence? How does it influence how they address domestic violence?

2. What is the connection between social justice and the treatment of the traumatic effects of domestic violence?

3. What is a physician's moral duty to the victims of domestic violence? How could the changes in the healthcare system affect this duty?

4. Does a utilitarian approach help or hinder treatment for victims of domestic violence?

5. How does the principle of autonomy relate to the issue of domestic violence?

▶ Notes

1. N. A. Kapur and D. M. Windish, "Optimal Methods to Screen Men and Women for Intimate Partner Violence: Results from an Internal Medicine Residency Continuity Clinic," *Journal of Interpersonal Violence* 26, no. 2 (2011): 2335–52; K. C. Young-Wolff et al., "Transforming the Health Care Response to Intimate Partner Violence: Addressing "Wicked Problems," *JAMA* 315, no. 23 (2016, June 21): 2517–18.

2. M. A. Black et al., *National Intimate Partner and Sexual Violence Survey 2010: Executive Summary* (Atlanta, GA: National Center for Injury Prevention and Control, Centers for Disease Control, 2011), http://www.cdc.gov /ViolencePrevention/pdf/NISVS _Executive_Summary-a.pdf; E. Stark and A. Flitcraft, "Violence among Intimates: An Epidemiologic Review," in *Handbook of Family Violence*, eds. V. N. Van Hasselt et al. (New York: Plenum, 1988), 293–317; D. Drossman et al., "Sexual and Physical Abuse in Women with Functional or Organic Gastrointestinal Disorders," *Annals of Internal Medicine* 113 (1990): 828–33; J. Domino and J. Haber, "Prior Physical and Sexual Abuse in Women with Chronic Headache: Clinical Correlates," *Headache* 27 (1987): 310–14; M. Koss and I. Heise, "Somatic Consequences of Violence Against Women," *Archives of Family Medicine* 1 (1992): 53–59; M. P. Koss et al., "Deleterious Effects of Criminal Victimization on Women's Health and Medical Utilization," *Archives of Internal Medicine* 151 (1991): 342–47; J. Fildes et al., "Trauma: The Leading Cause of Maternal Death," *Journal of Trauma* 32 (1992): 43–45; L. McKibben et al., "Victimization of Mothers of Abused Children: A Controlled Study," *Pediatrics* 84 (1989): 531–35; E. Stark and A. Flitcraft, "Women and Children at Risk: A Feminist Perspective on Child Abuse," *International Journal of Health Services* 18 (1988): 97–118; E. Stark and A. Flitcraft, "Killing the Beast Within: Woman Battering and Female Suicidality," *International Journal of Health Services* 25 (1995): 43–64; A. Jacobsen and B. Richardson, "Assault Experiences of 100 Psychiatric Inpatients: Evidence of the Need for Routine Inquiry," *American Journal of Psychiatry* 144 (1987): 908–13; L. S. Brown, "The Contribution of Victimization as a Risk Factor for the Development of Depressive Symptomatology in Women" (paper presented at the 97th Annual Convention of the American Psychological Association, New Orleans, Louisiana, August 1989); J. A. Hamilton and M. Jensvold, "Personality, Psychopathology and Depression in Women," in *Personality and Psychopathology: Feminist Reappraisals*, eds. L. S. Brown and M. Ballou (New York: Guilford Press, 1992); J. Herman, *The Aftermath of Violence: From Domestic Abuse to Political Theory* (New York: Basic Books, 1992); B. M. Houskamp and D. Foy, "The Assessment of Posttraumatic Stress Disorder in Battered Women," *Journal of Interpersonal Violence* 6 (1991): 367–75; A. Kemp et al., "Post-Traumatic Stress

Disorder (PTSD) in Battered Women: A Shelter Sample," *Journal of Traumatic Stress* 4 (1991): 137–48; J. C. Campbell, "Battered Woman Syndrome: A Critical Review," *Violence Update* (December 1990), 1, 4, 10–11.

Health Impact: A. L. Coker et al., "Association of Intimate Partner Violence and Childhood Sexual Abuse with Cancer-Related Well-Being in Women," *Journal of Women's Health* 21, no. 11 (2012): 1180–88; N. M. Heath et al., "Interpersonal Violence, PTSD, and Inflammation: Potential Psychogenic Pathways to Higher C-Reactive Protein Levels," *Cytokine* 63 (2013): 172–78; S. M. Mason et al., "Intimate Partner Violence and Incidence of Type II Diabetes in Women," *Diabetes Care* 36 (2013): 1159–65; S. M. Mason et al., "Intimate Partner Violence and Incidence of Hypertension in Women," *Annals of Epidemiology* 22, no. 8 (2012): 562–67; A. M. Buller et al., "Associations between Intimate Partner Violence and Health among Men Who Have Sex with Men: A Systematic Review and Meta-Analysis," *PLoS Medicine* 11, no. 3 (2014): e1001609.

Mental Health Prevalence/Mental Health Impact of IPV: G. Dillon et al., "Mental and Physical Health and Intimate Partner Violence against Women: A Review of the Literature," *International Journal of Family Medicine* (2013): 313909; K. M. Devries et al., "Intimate Partner Violence and Incident Depressive Symptoms and Suicide Attempts: A Systematic Review of Longitudinal Studies," *PLoS Medicine* 10, no. 5 (2013): 21001439; A. M. Nathanson et al., "The Prevalence of Mental Health Disorders in a Community Sample of Female Victims of Intimate Partner Violence," *Partner Abuse* 3, no. 1 (2012): 59–75; K. Trevillion et al., "Experiences of Domestic Violence and Mental Disorders: A Systematic Review and Meta-Analysis," *PLoS One* 7, no. 12 (2012); e51740, https://doi.org/10.1371 /journal.pone.005174; M. C. Black et al., *The National Intimate Partner and Sexual Violence Survey (NISVS): 2010 Summary Report* (Atlanta, GA: National Center for Injury Prevention and Control, Centers for Disease Control and Prevention, 2010); C. Cerulli et al., "Co-Occurring Intimate Partner Violence and Mental Health Diagnoses in Perinatal Women," *Journal of Women's Health* 20, no. 12 (2011): 1797–803; V. Jaquier et al., "Posttraumatic Stress and Depression Symptoms as Correlates of Deliberate Self-Harm among Community Women Experiencing Intimate Partner Violence," *Psychiatry Research* 206, no. 1 (2013): 37–42: B. Duran et al., (2009), "Intimate Partner Violence and Alcohol, Drug, and Mental Disorders among American Indian Women in Primary Care," *American Indian and Alaska Native Mental Health Research* 16, no. 2 (2013): 11–27; T. O. Afifi et al., "Victimization and Perpetration of Intimate Partner Violence and Substance Use Disorders in a Nationally Representative Sample," *Journal of Nervous and Mental Disorders* 200, no. 8 (2012): 684–91; H. A. Beydoun et al., "Intimate Partner Violence against Adult Women and Its Association with Major Depressive Disorder, Depressive Symptoms and Postpartum Depression: A Systematic Review and Meta-Analysis," *Social Science & Medicine* 75, no. 6 (2012): 959–75; J. W. Hahn et al., (2014). "Examining the Impact of Disability Status on Intimate Partner Violence Victimization in a Population Sample," *Journal of Interpersonal Violence* 29, no. 17 (2014): 3063–85.

3. Institute of Medicine, *Clinical Services for Women: Closing the Gaps*

(Washington, DC: National Academies Press, 2011), http://www.iom.edu/Reports/2011/Clinical-Preventive-Services-for-Women-Closing-the-Gaps.aspx.; Health Resources and Services Administration, "Women's Preventive Services: Required Health Plan Coverage Guidelines," http://www.hrsa.gov/womensguidelines/; H. D. Nelson et al., "Screening Women for Intimate Partner Violence: A Systematic Review to Update the U.S. Preventive Screening Task Force Recommendation," *Annals of Internal Medicine* 156, no. 11 (2012): 796–808; American College of Obstetricians and Gynecologists, Committee on Health Care for Underserved Women, "Intimate Partner Violence," *Obstetrics and Gynecology* 119 (2012): 412–17, http://www.acog.org/Resources_And_Publications/Committee_Opinions/Committee_on_Health_Care_for_Underserved_Women/Intimate_Partner_Violence; A. Flitcraft et al., *Diagnostic and Treatment Guidelines on Domestic Violence* (Chicago, IL: American Medical Association, 1992); C. Warshaw et al., *Improving the Health Care Response to Domestic Violence: A Resource Manual for Health Care Providers* (San Francisco, CA: Family Violence Prevention Fund and Pennsylvania Coalition Against Domestic Violence, 1995); C. J. Scott and N. Matricciani, "Joint Commission on Accreditation of Health Care Organizations Standards to Improve Care for Victims of Abuse," *Maryland Medical Journal* 43 (1994): 891–98; W. K. Taylor and J. C. Campbell, "Treatment Protocols for Battered Women," *Response* (1992): 1–21; A. Flitcraft, "Physicians and Domestic Abuse: Challenges for Prevention," *Health Affairs* 12 (1993): 156–61; E. M. Miller et al., "Integrating Intimate Partner Violence Assessment and Intervention into Healthcare in the United States: A Systems Approach," *Journal of Women's Health (Larchmt)* 1 (2015): 92–99. doi:10.1089/jwh.2014.4870.

4. L. K. Hamberger, "Preparing the Next Generation of Physicians: Medical School and Residency-Based Intimate Partner Violence Curriculum and Evaluation," *Trauma, Violence, and Abuse* 8 (2007): 214–25; E. J. Alpert, "Family Violence Curricula in U.S. Medical Schools," *American Journal of Preventive Medicine* 14 (1998): 273–82; S. Rovi and C. P. Mouton, "Domestic Violence Education in Family Practice Residencies," *Family Medicine* 31 (1999): 398–403; R. A. Chez and D. L. Horan, "Response of Obstetrics and Gynecology Program Directors to a Domestic Violence Lecture Model," *American Journal of Obstetrics and Gynecology* 180 (1999): 496–98; *Curricular Principles for Addressing Family Violence: Conference Report* (Oklahoma City, OK: Robert Wood Johnson Foundation, 1995); S. Hadley, "Working with Battered Women in the Emergency Department: A Model Program," *Journal of Emergency Nursing* 18 (1992): 18–23; C. Warshaw et al., "An Advocacy-Based Medical School Elective on Domestic Violence," (class offered at the National Conference on Cultural Competence and Women's Health, Curricular in Medical Education, Washington, DC, October 1995).

5. L. R. Chambliss et al., "Domestic Violence: An Educational Imperative?" *American Journal of Obstetrics and Gynecology* 172 (1995): 1035–38; L. S. Friedman et al., "Inquiry about Victimization Experiences: A Survey of Patient Preferences and Physician Practices," *Archives of Internal Medicine* 152 (1992): 1186–90; E. Gondolf, *Psychiatric Responses to Family Violence: Identifying and Confronting Neglected*

Danger (Lexington, MA: Lexington Books, 1990); R. I. Buranosky et al., "Once Is Not Enough: Effective Strategies for Medical Student Education on Intimate Partner Violence," *Violence Against Women* 10 (2012): 1192–212; L. Gotlib Conn et al., ""I've Never Asked One Question." Understanding the Barriers among Orthopedic Surgery Residents to Screening Female Patients for Intimate Partner Violence," *Canadian Journal of Surgery* 57, no. 6 (2014): 371–78.

6. N. K. Sugg and T. Inui, "Primary Care Physician's Response to Domestic Violence: Opening Pandora's Box," *Journal of the American Medical Association* 267 (1991): 3157–60; D. H. Gremillion and G. Evins, "Why Don't Doctors Identify and Refer Victims of Domestic Violence?" *North Carolina Medical Journal* 55 (1994): 428–32; C. Warshaw, "Limitations of the Medical Model in the Care of Battered Women," *Gender and Society* 3 (1989): 506–17; C. Warshaw, "Domestic Violence: Challenges to Medical Practice," *Journal of Women's Health* 2 (1993): 73–80.

   S. L. Sprague et al., "Perceptions of Intimate Partner Violence: A Cross Sectional Survey of Surgical Residents and Medical Students," *Journal of Injury and Violence Research* 5, no. 1(2013): 1–10.

7. Warshaw, "Domestic Violence."

8. B. Gerbert et al., "Simplifying Physicians' Response to Domestic Violence," *Western Journal of Medicine* 172, no. 5 (2000): 329–31; H. A. Holtz et al., "Education about Domestic Violence in U.S. and Canadian Medical Schools: 1987–1988," *Morbidity and Mortality Weekly Report* 38 (1989): 17–19; Alpert, "Family Violence Curricula in U.S. Medical Schools," 273–82.

9. S. K. Burge, "Violence against Women as a Health Care Issue," *Family Medicine* 21 (1989): 368–73; A. Kramer, "Attitudes of Emergency Nurses and Physicians about Women and Wife Beating: Implications for Emergency Care," *Journal of Emergency Nursing* 19 (1993): 549.

   D. R. Langford, "Consortia: A Strategy for Improving the Provision of Health Care to Domestic Violence Survivors," *Response to the Victimization of Women and Children* 13 (1990): 7–18; N. S. Jecker, "Privacy Beliefs and the Violent Family: Extending the Ethical Argument for Physician Intervention," *Journal of the American Medical Association* 269 (1993): 776–80; D. Kurz and E. Stark, "Not-so-Benign Neglect," in *Feminist Perspectives on Wife Abuse*, eds. K. Yllo and M. Bograd (Newbury Park, CA: Sage, 1988), 249–66.

10. M. P. Koss et al., *No Safe Haven: Male Violence against Women at Home, at Work and in the Community* (Washington, DC: American Psychological Association, 1994).

11. K. Johnson, *Treating Ourselves: The Complete Guide to Emotional Well-Being for Women* (New York: Atlantic Monthly Press, 1990).

12. L. S. Brown, "A Feminist Critique of Personality Disorders," in *Personality and Psychopathology: Feminist Reappraisals*, eds. L. S. Brown and M. Ballou (New York: Guilford Press, 1992).

13. P. Rieker and E. Carmen, "The Victim-to-Patient Process: The Disconfirmation and Transformation of Abuse," *American Journal of Orthopsychiatry* 56 (1986): 360–70.

14. A. Miller, *Prisoners of Childhood: The Drama of the Gifted Child and the Search for the True Self* (New York: Basic Books, 1981); A. Miller, *Thou Shalt Not Be Aware: Society's Betrayal of the Child* (New York: Farrar, Straus & Giroux, 1984).

15. Rieker and Carmen, "The Victim-to-Patient Process"; Miller, *Prisoners of Childhood*; Miller, *Thou Shalt Not Be Aware*.

16. E. Arledge and R. Wolfson, "Care of the Clinician," in *Using Trauma Theory to Design Service Systems*, eds. M. Harris and R. Fallot (San Francisco, CA: Jossey-Bass, 2001), 91–98; K. Baird and A. Kracen, "Vicarious Traumatization and Secondary Traumatic Stress: A Research Synthesis," *Counseling Psychology Quarterly* 19 (2006): 181–88; I. Way et al., "Vicarious Trauma: A Comparison of Clinicians Who Treat Survivors of Sexual Abuse and Sexual Offenders," *Journal of Interpersonal Violence* 19 (2004): 49–71; L. H. Madsen et al., "Sanctuary in a Domestic Violence Shelter: A Team Approach to *Healing*," *Psychiatric Quarterly* 72 (2003): 155–71; B. Bride, "Prevalence of Secondary Traumatic Stress among Social Workers," *Social Work* 52 (2007): 63–70; C. R. Figley, "Compassion Fatigue: Toward a New Understanding of the Costs of Caring," in *Secondary Traumatic Stress: Self-Care Issues for Clinicians, Researchers, and Educators*, ed. B. H. Stamm (Lutherville, MD: Sidran Press), 3–28; S. R. Jenkins and S. Baird, "Secondary Traumatic Stress and Vicarious Trauma: A Validational Study," *Journal of Traumatic Stress* 15 (2002): 423–33; G. Iliffe, "Exploring the Counselor's Experience of Working with Perpetrators and Survivors of Domestic Violence," *Journal of Interpersonal Violence* 15 (2000): 393–413; J. L. Herman, *Trauma and Recovery*, Rev. ed. (New York, NY: Basic Books, 1997); M. A. Dutton, *Empowering and Healing the Battered Woman: A Model for Assessment and Intervention* (New York: Springer, 1992); M. P. Koss, "The Women's Mental Health Research Agenda: Violence Against Women," *American Psychologist* 45 (1990): 374–80; L. Goldman et al., *American Medical Association Diagnostic and Treatment Guidelines on Mental Health Effects of Family Violence* (Chicago, IL: American Medical Association, 1995).

17. Sugg and Inui, "Primary Care Physician's Response to Domestic Violence."

18. Warshaw, "Domestic Violence"; Koss et al., *No Safe Haven*; Johnson, *Treating Ourselves*; Brown, "A Feminist Critique of Personality Disorders."

19. Warshaw, "Domestic Violence."

20. P. D. Connor et al., "Intimate Partner Violence Education for Medical Students: Toward a Comprehensive Curriculum Revision," *Southern Medical Journal* 105, no. 4 (2012): 211–15; P. Williamson et al., "Beliefs that Foster Physician Avoidance of Psychosocial Aspects of Health Care," *Journal of Family Practice* 13 (1981): 999–1003; R. Fox, "Training in Caring Competence: The Perennial Problem in North American Medical Education," in *Education: Competent and Humane Physicians*, eds. H. C. Hendrie and C. Lloyd (Bloomington, IN: Indiana University Press, 1990), 199–216.

21. Warshaw, "Domestic Violence."

22. J. A. Richman et al., "Mental Health Consequences and Correlates of Reported Medical Student Abuse," *Journal of the American Medical Association* 167 (1992): 692–94.

23. D. Baldwin et al., "Student Perceptions of Mistreatment and Harassment during Medical School: A Survey of Ten United States Schools," *Western Journal of Medicine* 155 (1991): 140–45.

24. E. Frank et al., "Clinical and Personal Intimate Partner Violence Training Experiences of U.S. Medical Students," *Journal of Women's Health* 15 (2006): 1071–79; P. Babaria et al., "'I'm Too Used to It': A Longitudinal Qualitative Study of Third Year Female Medical Students' Experiences of Gendered Encounters in Medical School," *Social Science and Medicine* 7, no. 7 (2012): 1013–20; B. J. Tepper, "Consequences of Abusive Supervision," *Academic Management Journal*

43 (2000): 178–190; D. M. Elnicki et al., "Medical Students' Perspectives on and Responses to Abuse during the Internal Medicine Clerkship," *Teaching and Learning Medicine* 14 (2002): 92–97; T. J. Wilkinson et al., "The Impact on Students of Adverse Experiences during Medical School," *Medical Teaching* 28 (2006): 129–35; L. N. Dyrbye et al., "Systematic Review of Depression, Anxiety, and Other Indicators of Psychological Distress among U.S. and Canadian Medical Students," *Academic Medicine* 81 (2006): 354–73; L. N. Dyrbye et al., "Medical Student Distress: Causes, Consequences, and Proposed Solutions," *Mayo Clinic Proceedings* 80 (2005): 1613–22; M. Seabrook, "Intimidation in Medical Education: Students' and Teachers' Perspectives," *Studies in Higher Education* 29 (2004): 59–74; D. G. Kassebaum and E. R. Cutler, "On the Culture of Student Abuse in Medical School," *Academic Medicine* 73 (1998): 1149–58; T. M. Wolf et al., "Perceived Mistreatment and Attitude Change by Graduating Medical Students: A Retrospective Study," *Medical Education* 25 (1991): 182–89.

25. Warshaw, "Domestic Violence"; Richman et al., "Mental Health Consequences and Correlates of Reported Medical Student Abuse"; C. Moutier et al., "The Culture of Academic Medicine: Faculty Behaviors Impacting the Learning Environment," *Academic Psychiatry* 40, no. 6 (2016): 912–18.

26. D. Wear et al., "Retheorizing Sexual Harassment in Medical Education: Women Students' Perceptions at Five U.S. Medical Schools," *Teaching and Learning Medicine* 19 (2007): 20–29; F. M. Witte et al., "Stories from the Field: Students' Descriptions of Gender Discrimination and Sexual Harassment during Medical School," *Academic Medicine* 81 (2006): 648–54; T. D. Stratton et al., "Does Students' Exposure to Gender Discrimination and Sexual Harassment in Medical School Affect Specialty Choice and Residency Program Selection?" *Academic Medicine* 80 (2005): 400–08; S. A. Shinsako et al., "Training-Related Harassment and Drinking Outcomes in Medical Residents Versus Graduate Students," *Substance Use and Misuse* 36 (2001): 2043–63; J. Bickel, "Gender Equity in Undergraduate Medical Education: A Status Report," *Journal of Women's Health* Gen-B 10 (2001): 261–70; Richman et al., "Mental Health Consequences and Correlates of Reported Medical Student Abuse"; Baldwin et al., "Student Perceptions of Mistreatment and Harassment during Medical School"; Wolf et al., "Perceived Mistreatment and Attitude Change by Graduating Medical Students"; M. Schiffman and E. Frank, "Harassment of Women Physicians," *Journal of the American Medical Women's Association* 50 (1995): 207–11; D. A. Charney and R. C. Russell, "An Overview of Sexual Harassment," *American Journal of Psychiatry* 151 (1994): 10–17; M. Komaromy et al., "Sexual Harassment in Medical Training," *New England Journal of Medicine* 328 (1993): 322–36; N. Fnais et al., "Harassment and Discrimination in Medical Training: A Systematic Review and Meta-Analysis," *Academic Medicine* 89, no. 5 (2014): 817–27; R. Jagsi et al., "Sexual Harassment and Discrimination Experiences of Academic Medical Faculty Research Letter," *JAMA* 315, no. 19 (2016): 2120–21.

27. Warshaw, "Domestic Violence"; Kurz and Stark, "Not-so-Benign Neglect"; Koss et al., *No Safe Haven*; Johnson, *Treating Ourselves*; Brown, "A Feminist Critique of Personality Disorders"; Fox, "Training in Caring Competence"; C. S. Widom, "Does Violence Beget

Violence? A Critical Examination of the Literature," *Psychology Bulletin* 106 (1989): 437–47.

28. P. Braverman and L. Gottlieb, "The Social Determinants of Health: It's Time to Consider the Causes of the Causes," *Public Health Reports* 129, supplement 2 (2014, January–February): 19–31; M. A. Sotero, "Conceptual Model of Historical Trauma: Implications for Public Health Research and Practice," *Journal of Health Disparities Research and Practice* 1, no. 1 (2006): 93–98.

29. K. Johnson and E. Hoffman, "Women's Health and Curriculum Transformation: The Role of Medical Specialization," in *Reframing Women's Health: Multidisciplinary Research and Practice*, ed. A. Dan (Thousand Oaks, CA: Sage, 1994), 27–39.

30. A. C. Gielen et al., "HIV/AIDS and Intimate Partner Violence," *Trauma, Violence, and Abuse* 8 (2007): 178–98; S. Maman et al., "The Intersections of HIV and Violence: Directions for Future Research and Interventions," *Social Science and Medicine* 50 (2000): 459–78; A. Raj et al., "Perpetration of Intimate Partner Violence Associated with Sexual Risk Behaviors Among Young Adult Men," *American Journal of Public Health* 96 (2006): 1873–78; B. Lichtenstein, "Domestic Violence, Sexual Ownership, and HIV Risk in Women in the American Deep South," *Social Science and Medicine* 60 (2005): 701–14; A. J. Heintz and R. Melendez, "Intimate Partner Violence and HIV /STD Risk among Lesbian, Gay, Bisexual, and Transgender Individuals," *Journal of Interpersonal Violence* 21 (2006): 193–208; G. Wyatt et al., "Does History of Trauma Contribute to HIV Risk for Women of Color? Implications for Prevention and Policy," *American Journal of Public Health* 92 (2002): 660–65; A. Raj et al., "Abused Women Report

Greater Male Partner Risk and Gender-Based Risk for HIV: Findings from a Community-Based Study with Hispanic Women," *AIDS Care* 16 (2004): 519–29; N. El-Bassel et al., "HIV and Intimate Partner Violence among Methadone-Maintained Women in New York City," *Social Science and Medicine* 61 (2005): 171–83; J. M. Simoni and M. T. Ng, "Trauma, Coping, and Depression among Women with HIV /AIDS in New York City," *AIDS Care* 12 (2000): 567–80; S. C. Kalicharan et al., "Sexual Coercion, Domestic Violence, and Negotiating Condom Use among Low-Income African American Women," *Journal of Women's Health* 7 (1998): 371–79; M. Cohen et al., "Prevalence of Domestic Violence in Women with HIV" (paper presented at the Midwest Society of General Internal Medicine, Chicago, October 1995); K. Rothenberg et al., "Domestic Violence and Partner Notification: Implications for Treatment and Counseling of Women with HIV," *Journal of the American Medical Women's Association* 50 (1995): 87–93;

J. Sareen et al., "Is Intimate Partner Violence Associated with HIV Infection among Women in the United States?" *General Hospital Psychiatry* 31, no. 3 (2009): 274–78; A. M. Teitelman et al., "Sexual Relationship Power, Intimate Partner Violence, and Condom Use among Minority Urban Girls," *Journal of Interpersonal Violence* 23, no. 12 (2008): 1694–712; J. P Meyer et al., "Substance Abuse, Violence, and HIV in Women: A Literature Review of the Syndemic," *Journal of Women's Health* 20, no. 7 (2011): 991–1006; E. L. Machtinger et al., "Recent Trauma Is Associated with Antiretroviral Failure and HIV Transmission Risk Behavior among HIV-Positive Women and Female-Identified Transgenders,"

AIDS and Behavior 16, no. 8 (2012): 2160–170; R. A. Siemieniuk et al., "The Clinical Implications of High Rates of Intimate Partner Violence Against HIV-Positive Women," *JAIDS Journal of Acquired Immune Deficiency Syndromes* 64, no. 1 (2013): 32–38; S. Illangasekare et al., "Clinical and Mental Health Correlates and Risk Factors for Intimate Partner Violence among HIV-Positive Women in an Inner-City HIV Clinic," *Women's Health Issues* 22, no. 6 (2012): e563–69; E. Machtinger et al., "Psychological Trauma in HIV-Positive Women: A Meta-Analysis," *AIDS and Behavior* 16, no. 8 (2012): 2091–100. doi:10.1007/s10461-011-0127-4.

31. Rothenberg et al., "Domestic Violence and Partner Notification."

32. Stark and Flitcraft, "Violence among Intimates."

33. New York State Department of Health, "Guidelines for Integrating Domestic Violence Screening into HIV Counseling, Testing, Referral, and Partner Notification," http//www/health.ny.gov/nydoh/rfa/hiv/guide.htm; S. J. Klein, "Screening for Risk of Domestic Violence Within HIV Partner Notification: Evolving Practice and Emerging Issues," *Journal of Public Health Management* 7 (2001): 46–50; R. Wolfe et al., "Screening for Substance Use, Sexual Practices, Mental Illness, and Domestic Violence in HIV Primary Care," *Journal of Acquired Immune Deficiency Syndromes* 33 (2003): 548–50; Maman et al., "Intersections of HIV and Violence"; J. E. Maher et al., "Partner Violence, Partner Notification, and Women's Decisions to Have an HIV Test," *Journal of Acquired Immune Deficiency Syndromes* 25 (2000): 276–82; S. J. Klein et al., "Implementation of Domestic Violence Screening as a Component of HIV Partner Notification in New York State" (paper presented at the National HIV Prevention Conference, Atlanta, Georgia, 1999); Cohen et al., "Prevalence of Domestic Violence in Women with HIV"; Rothenberg et al., "Domestic Violence and Partner Notification"; V. Breitbert et al., "Model Programs Addressing Perinatal Drug Exposure and HIV Infection: Integrating Women's and Children's Needs," *Bulletin of the New York Academy of Medicine* 71 (1994): 236–51.

34. E. Miller et al., "A Family Planning Clinic Partner Violence Intervention to Reduce Risk Associated with Reproductive Coercion," *Contraception* 83 (2011): 274–80. Reproductive Coercion: E. Miller et al., Contraception 89, no. 2 (2014, February): 122–28. doi: 0.1016/j.contraception.2013.10.011; D. J. Tancredi et al., "Cluster Randomized Controlled Trial Protocol: Addressing Reproductive Coercion in Health Settings (ARCHES)," *BMC Women's Health* 15, no. 57 (2015, August): doi: 10.1186/s12905-015-0216-z; American College of Obstetricians and Gynecologists, "ACOG Committee Opinion No. 554: Reproductive and Sexual Coercion," *Obstetrics and Gynecology* 121, no. part 2 (2013): 411–15.

35. Miller, *Thou Shalt Not Be Aware*; G. Atwood and R. Stolorow, *Structures of Subjectivity: Explorations in Psychoanalytic Phenomenology* (Hillsdale, NJ: The Analytic Press, 1984); L. Brown, *Subversive Dialogues: Theory in Feminist Therapy* (New York: Basic Books, 1994).

36. S. Andersen et al., "Psychological Maltreatment of Spouses," in *Case Studies in Family Violence*, eds. R. Ammerman and M. Hersen (New York: Plenum, 1991): 293–328.

37. L. Walker, "The Battered Woman Syndrome," in *Family Abuse and Its Consequences*, eds. G. T. Hotaling et al. (Beverly Hills, CA: Sage, 1988), 139–48.

38. Brown, "A Feminist Critique of Personality Disorders"; M. Bograd, "Family Systems Approaches to Wife Battering: A Feminist Critique," *American Journal of Orthopsychiatry* 54 (1984): 558–68.

39. M. Hansen, "Feminism and Family Therapy: A Review of Feminist Critiques of Approaches to Family Violence," in *Battering and Family Therapy: A Feminist Perspective*, eds. M. Hansen and M. Harway (Thousand Oaks, CA: Sage, 1993); M. Harway and M. Hansen, "Treatment of Spouse Abuse," in *Spouse Abuse: Assessing and Treating Battered Women, Batterers, and their Children*, eds. M. Harway and M. Hansen (Sarasota, FL: Professional Resource Press, 1994), 57–88; V. Goldner, "Morality and Multiplicity: Perspectives on the Treatment of Violence in Intimate Life," *Journal of Marital and Family Therapy* 25, no. 3 (1999): 325–36.

40. K. O'Leary et al., "Treatment of Wife Abuse: A Comparison of Gender-Specific and Conjoint Approaches," *Behavior Therapy* 30 (1999): 475–505.

41. Focusing on how a client should change herself may reinforce a perpetrator's controlling tactics (i.e., "You are the one with the problem") and further undermine her ability to gain perspective on her situation or to take steps that would increase the safety of herself and her children. This may be of particular concern for clinicians who conduct couples or family therapy. See C. Warshaw, "Women and Violence," in *Psychological Aspects of Women's Health Care: The Interface between Psychiatry and Obstetrics and Gynecology*, eds. D. Stewart and N. Stotland (Washington, DC: American Psychiatric Association Press, 2001); C. Warshaw et al., *Mental Health and Substance Use Coercion Survey: Report on Findings from the National Center on Domestic Violence, Trauma & Mental Health and the National Domestic Violence Hotline* (Chicago, IL: National Center for Domestic Violence Trauma & Mental Health, 2014); C. Warshaw et al., *A Systematic Review of Trauma-Focused Interventions for Domestic Violence Survivors* (Chicago, IL: National Center on Domestic Violence, Trauma & Mental Health, 2013), supported through grant #90EV0417 from the U.S. Department of Health & Human Services, Administration for Children and Families, Family and Youth Services Bureau, Family Violence Prevention and Services Program, http://www.nationalcenterdvtraumamh.org/wp-content/uploads/2013/03/NCDVTMH_EBPLitReview2013.pdf.

42. A. Jones and S. Schechter, *When Love Goes Wrong: What to Do When You Can't Do Anything Right* (New York: Harper, 1993); A. Ganley, "Understanding Domestic Violence," in *Improving the Health Care Response to Domestic Violence: A Resource Manual for Health Care Providers*, eds. C. Warshaw et al. (San Francisco: Family Violence Prevention Fund and Pennsylvania Coalition Against Domestic Violence, 1995), 15–45; E. Miller et al., *Trauma-Informed Approaches for LGBQT* Survivors of Intimate Partner Violence: A Review of the Literature and a Set of Practice Observations* (Cambridge, MA: GLBTQ Domestic Violence Project, 2016), http://www.nationalcenterdvtraumamh.org/2016/09/new-resource-trauma-informed-approaches-for-lgbqt-survivors-of-intimate-partner-violence-a-review-of-literature-and-a-set-of-practice-observations/.

43. M. Harris and R. Fallot, "Envisioning a Trauma-Informed Service System: A Vital Paradigm Shift," *New Directions for Mental Health Services* 89 (2001): 3–22; C. Warshaw *Thinking about Trauma in the Context of Domestic Violence: An Integrated Framework. Synergy:*

The Newsletter of the Resource Center on Domestic Violence, Child Protection and Custody, special issues no. 2 Fall-Winter (Reno: National Council on Juvenile and Family Court Judges, 2014); *Trauma-Informed Approach and Trauma-Specific Interventions*, Substance Abuse and Mental Health Services Administration website, https://www.samhsa.gov/nctic/trauma-interventions.

44. Miller, *Prisoners of Childhood*.

45. A. Brown, "Violence, Poverty, and Minority Races in the Lives of Women and Children: Implications for Violence Prevention" (paper presented at the Centers for Disease Control Violence Prevention Conference, Des Moines, Iowa, October 1995).

46. Other forms of inequality also contribute to abusive power dynamics, and eradicating those are important aspects of primary prevention.

47. P. F. Cronholm et al., "Intimate Partner Violence," *American Family Physician* 83, no. 10 (2011): 1165–72; D. S. Morse et al., "They Told Me to Leave: How Health Care Providers Address Intimate Partner Violence," *Journal of the American Board of Family Medicine* 25, no. 3 (2012): 333–42; Jones and Schechter, *When Loves Goes Wrong*; A. Ganley, "Understanding Domestic Violence," in *Improving the Health Care Response to Domestic Violence: A Resource Manual for Health Care Providers*, eds. C. Warshaw and A. Ganley (San Francisco, CA: Family Violence Prevention Fund, 1998); "VAWA Laws for Abuse Victims," WomensLaw.org, http://www.womenslaw.org/immigrantsVAWA.htm.

48. S. Woodhandler and D. Himmelstein, "Extreme Risk: The New Corporate Proposition for Physicians," *New England Journal of Medicine* 33 (1995): 1706–08; S. Glied and S. Kofman, *Women and Mental Health Reform* (New York: Commission on Women's Health, Commonwealth Fund, 1995).

49. L. Mellman and R. Bell, "Consequences of Violence Against Women," in *Violence against Women in the United States: A Comprehensive Background Paper* (New York: Commonwealth Fund Commission on Women's Health, 1995), 33–40; L. Innes and L. Mellman, "Treatment for Victims of Violence," in *Violence Against Women in the United States*, 41–54.

50. E. Carmen, "Inner-City Community Mental Health: The Interplay of Abuse and Race in Chronically Mentally Ill Women," in *Mental Health, Racism, and Sexism*, eds. C. Willie et al. (Pittsburgh, PA: University of Pittsburgh, 1995).

51. T. Miller et al., *Crime in the United States: Victim Costs and Consequences* (Washington, DC: National Institute of Justice, 1995).

52. C. Warshaw, "Women and Violence," in *Psychosocial Aspects of Women's Health Care: The Interface between Psychiatry and Obstetrics and Gynecology*, 2nd ed., eds. N. L. Stotland and D. E. Steward (Washington, DC: American Psychiatric Press, 2001), 477–548; D. Markham, "2003 Mental Illness and Domestic Violence: Implications for Family Law Litigations," *Journal of Poverty Law and Policy* (May–June, 2003): 23–35; C. Warshaw et al., "*Mental Health and Substance Use Coercion Survey: Report on Findings from the National Center on Domestic Violence, Trauma & Mental Health and the National Domestic Violence Hotline.*"

53. Walker, "The Battered Woman Syndrome"; Jones and Schechter, *When Love Goes Wrong*; Ganley, "Understanding Domestic Violence."

54. Warshaw, "Domestic Violence"; Burge, "Violence against Women as a Health Care Issue."

55. Women's Law Project and Pennsylvania Coalition against Domestic Violence, *Insurance Discrimination Against Victims of Domestic Violence* (Harrisburg, PA: Coalition Against Domestic Violence, 1995); L. Kaiser, *Survey of Accident and Health and Life Insurance Relating to Insurance Coverage for Victims of Domestic Violence* (Harrisburg, PA: Pennsylvania Insurance Department, 1995).

56. See also the Women's Law Project website, http://www.womenslawproject.org /New-Pages/wkImpact_litigation.html. In 1994, in partnership with the Pennsylvania Coalition against Domestic Violence, the Women's Law Project began its ongoing effort to stop insurers from discriminating against victims of domestic violence. The impetus for this work was the denial of health, life, and mortgage disability insurance to a Pennsylvania woman because of medical records revealing an incident of domestic violence. The advocacy began with administrative and legislative efforts to stop such discrimination in Pennsylvania and expanded to assuming a leading role in efforts nationwide to stop discrimination against victims of domestic violence. At present, 41 states have legislation prohibiting insurance discrimination against victims of abuse, and efforts continue to ensure comprehensive legislation at the state and federal levels.

57. A. Hymes et al., "Laws Mandating Reporting of Domestic Violence: Do They Promote Patient Well-Being?" *Journal of the American Medical Association* 272 (1995): 1781–87. For more information, see the American Association of Orthopaedic Surgeon's website, http://www.aaos.org/ about/abuse/ststatut.asp. See also the National Center for Domestic and Sexual Violence's website, http:// www.ncdsv.org/, and the Health Cares about IPV. Understanding Reporting Requirements website, http://www.healthcaresaboutipv.org /getting-started/understanding -reporting-requirements/.

58. Warshaw et al., *Improving the Health Care Response to Domestic Violence*; Hadley, "Working with Battered Women in the Emergency Department"; S. V. McLeer et al., "Education Is Not Enough: A Systems Failure in Protecting Battered Women," *Annals of Emergency Medicine* 18 (1989): 651–53.

59. N. E. Allen et al., "Promoting Systems Change in the Health Care Response to Domestic Violence," *Journal of Community Psychology* 35 (2007): 103–20; D. Minsky-Kelly et al., "We've Had Training, Now What? Qualitative Analysis of Barriers to Domestic Violence Screening and Referral in a Health Care Setting," *Journal of Interpersonal Violence* 20 (2005): 1288–309; M. J. Zachary et al., "Provider Evaluation of a Multifaceted System of Care to Improve Recognition and Management of Pregnant Women Experiencing Domestic Violence," *Women's Health Issues* 12 (2002): 5–15; J. C. Campbell et al., "An Evaluation of a System-Change Training Model to Improve Emergency Department Response to Battered Women," *Academic Emergency Medicine* 8 (2001): 131–38; G. L. Larkin et al., "Effect of an Administrative Intervention on Rates of Screening for Domestic Violence in an Urban Emergency Department," *American Journal of Public Health* 90 (2000): 1444–48; Warshaw et al., *Improving the Health Care Response to Domestic Violence*; McLeer et al., "Education Is Not Enough."

60. Jones and Schechter, *When Loves Goes Wrong*.

61. Warshaw et al., *Improving the Health Care Response to Domestic Violence.*

62. S. R. Dube et al., "The Impact of Adverse Childhood Experiences on Health Problems: Evidence from Four Birth Cohorts Dating Back to 1900," *Prevention Medicine* 37 (2003): 268–77; V. J. Felitti, "The Relationship Between Adverse Childhood Experiences and Adult Health," *The Permanente Journal* 6 (2002): 44–47; C. L. Whitfield, "Adverse Childhood Experiences and Trauma," *American Journal of Preventive Medicine* 14 (1998): 245–58; V. J. Felitti et al., "The Relationship of Adult Health Status to Childhood Abuse and Household Dysfunction," *American Journal of Preventive Medicine* (1998): 245–58; Warshaw et al., *Improving the Health Care Response to Domestic Violence.*

CHAPTER 16

Looking Toward the Future

Beth Furlong and Eileen E. Morrison

▶ Introduction

This chapter looks into the future with ethics eyes and discusses additional areas of ethics theory and examples of emergent issues that affect the practice of ethics. Furlong discusses the ethic of care and the narrative models of ethics. Morrison presents ethics issues related to the aging of the baby boomer generation and new material on the ethics of change.

▶ New Considerations in Ethics Theory

Ethic-of-Care Model

Whereas some health providers have utilized and applied such ethics theories as deontology, utilitarianism, virtue ethics, and principlism (autonomy, beneficence, nonmaleficence, and justice), other health providers, notably women and nurses, have also incorporated an ethic-of-care model.[1,2] This theory, which evolved from the moral development research of feminist Carol Gilligan in the 1980s, focuses on the importance of relationships and context in decision-making. This model is attentive to the needs of all. Lachman wrote that this theory "has a focus on the context of the situation versus impartial deliberation of the ethics issue. Impartial reflection is an element of justice-based moral deliberation and does not take into consideration the level of caring or closeness in the relationship."[3]

Gilligan noted in her previous research that women never reached the highest levels of moral decision-making. Her research showed the difference between some men's and women's approaches to decision-making, namely, men are more justice-oriented, and women are more oriented to the complex of relationships, caring, and the context of a situation in arriving at an ethical decision.[4,5] Whereas men might resolve ethics dilemmas with black-and-white rules, women do not. Women are concerned about the particular situation and the current and future interpersonal connections and relationships of those involved. Because women dominate the nursing profession, nurses embrace this model more than other health provider professions.

Volker argued that using an ethic-of-care model is not unique to nurses.[6] She acknowledged that a core theme of nursing, recognized by nurses, other health providers, society, and the media, is that of the caring relationship between patients and nurses. However, such a dynamic also applies to other patient–health provider relationship. For nurses, the model's accompanying traits of empathy, compassion, and connectedness resonate in their daily care of patients and their families, 24 hours daily, 7 days weekly. Given the nurses' intensity of care of patients in vulnerable, intimate situations, the ethic-of-care model has integrated easily with their lived reality.

Edwards asserted that the history of medicine and nursing, with the differentiation of "curing" and "caring" between them as their major distinctive goals and functions, resulted in the four-principle approach being used by physicians, whereas the ethic of care seemed more appropriate to the women-dominated nursing profession.[7]

Several authors have furthered this ethical model for nursing.[8, 9] Their arguments are based on the strong assertion of the importance of the caring theme to nursing practice. These authors proposed that the ethic of care be used as the dominant model versus the principlism model. Volker noted that the former model "is intuitively attractive to many nurses" because it integrates well with how nurses have been educated, socialized, and perceived by society.[10]

However, to date, research does not demonstrate a clear picture. One can cite research showing nurses who apply a justice orientation, whereas other research shows nurses using a care orientation.[11, 12] Pinch critiqued some use of the ethic-of-care model because of concerns that it furthers oppression of nurses.[13] Edwards summarized the evolvement of Gilligan's work by categorizing her work in the early 1980s as the first version of an ethic of care. Tronto's work a decade later represented the second version, and work by Little in 1998 and Gastmans in 2006 constituted the third version.[14] Tronto differentiated between an ethics of responsibility and an ethics of obligation. Further, she proposed four elements of care (attentiveness, responsibility, competence,

and responsiveness) and four phases. Finally, the third version can be summarized by Gastmans's following words: "[C]are ethics is more a stance from which we can theorize ethically rather than a full-blown ethical theory in itself."[15]

Although the literature provides no definitive answer to the soundness of the ethic-of-care model or the extent of its usage by nurses, this author (Furlong) will end this section by citing a group of authors who advocate for this model for nurses. They note the particularity of specific situations and respectful relationships between patients and nurses and provide evidence of the value of a caring relationship to the healing process of patients.[16] They argue that an ethic of care, versus other theories, is the one needed. In particular, they directly address some conflicts between being caring and providing justice for a nurse's assigned group of patients; they conclude that "in some cases individual exceptions must be allowed."[17]

In summary, for the past 30 years, Gilligan's work, which evolved into the ethic-of-care model, has been an important model for nurses, other health providers, and those in other disciplines. The utility of this model continues to be studied and critiqued.

Narrative Ethics Model

A second emerging model is the narrative ethics model, which has gained increased proponents in the past two decades. McCarthy broadly described narrative ethics' tenets in the following way: (1) Because every moral situation is unique, no one universal law or principle applies; (2) any healthcare decision can be justified, given an individual's life story; and (3) the dialogue for justification of a decision is to be open and the tensions explored.[18] A narrative is "a first person narrative, personal story . . . for qualitative data about the unique lives of individual people."[19]

Another way of perceiving, understanding, and analyzing the difference between narrative ethics and other theories is McCarthy's statement of this difference "as one between those theorists who see principles at the heart of moral life and those who see communication at its core."[20] The former group comprises those theorists who promote principlism and the latter those who advocate the use of narrative ethics. On a personal and professional note, the author Furlong has recognized the value of the latter when assigning a narrative, "Procedures," as an assignment in a graduate healthcare ethics program. Student response is quite compelling when reading this first-person patient account of a woman's experience with the healthcare system.[21] McCarthy noted that principlism has dominated health providers' approach to bioethics for the past two decades.[22] It is the evaluation of the author Furlong that narrative ethics may better resonate with health providers at this time because the first-person patient story provides learning and reflection at a time when all health providers are concerned about the provision of safety and avoidance of errors in the health system. Concisely said, health providers need to listen to and hear from the patient. Hearing, reading, and understanding the communication gaps that are occurring among patients, family members, and health providers provide insights into how to better the health system. Analyzing narratives facilitates this reflective understanding.

Those who advance the use of narrative ethics note the importance of storytelling by the patient.[23] Further, this model honors an individual's life story and how one makes an ethical decision at a point in time. McCarthy noted that the following skills are necessary to promote narrative ethics with a patient: (1) literary skills to understand and interpret someone's story, (2) an ability to construct metaphors and recognize the bigger picture, (3) an ability to be reflective, and (4) compassionate communication skills.[24]

Adams[25] expanded on some of the analysis by McCarthy. One of his critiques of principlism is that it is a preformed set of rules that can do violence to a person's singular experience. By metaphor, in U.S. society, the colloquial phrase "Been there, done that" is not accurate, because every situation is different. An inability to reflect on and recognize this has some parallel to nonrecognition of the value of narrative ethics. This is furthered by Ellis, who noted that there are no universal principles that apply to all situations, except the general premise of doing no harm.[26] In summary, those interested in ethics analysis of individual, clinical, and population concerns can enhance their understanding by using this method. A review of its strengths and limitations is beyond the purview of this chapter.

Emergent Issues and Ethics

Change! This word seems to be the driving force of today's healthcare system. Whether it is a new coding system (the 10th revision of the International Statistical Classification of Diseases and Related Health Problems) or a technology that promises faster, better, and more accurate health care, the effect on the system is that things are different than they used to be. In addition, there are major considerations with respect to changes that govern both practice and finance, such as the evolving status of the Patient Protection and Affordable Care Act of 2010 or the implementation of the Medicare Access and CHIP Reauthorization Act of 2015. The practice of health care begins to feel more than a white water of change and more closely like a tsunami. In addition, greater emphasis is placed on patient-centered and value-based care, which would imply that revenue cannot be the only consideration in health care. Given the circumstances, it would appear that mission-centered and ethics-based healthcare practices may be more difficult to achieve but will remain essential to the success of the organization in its quest to provide services that meet the needs and expectations of patients.

Although it is not within the scope of this chapter to examine every one of the changes in health care's future, it will address three areas of interest. The first is a discussion of the interest in and application of complementary and alternative medicine (CAM) or integrative medicine (IM) among both patients and conventional medical practitioners. These areas of health care are becoming more acceptable to conventional medicine, and research in their efficacy is ongoing. For the purpose of readability, the abbreviation CAM/IM is used in this section to denote both areas. In addition, this section discusses the ethics ramifications of these practices for professionals and patients.

The second area is an update on the impact of the baby boomer generation on the delivery of health care. This discussion will focus on meeting the needs of this diverse population and the ethics issues caused by the increasing needs of this population group. In addition, there is a third area of interest that will examine the effect of the current epoch of high-impact change and its potential for serious ethics challenges for the healthcare system.

Complementary and Alternative Medicine and Ethics

What is now called CAM or IM has roots that are thousands of years old and serves as a healing practice worldwide.[27] In the United States, these practices are becoming a greater part of mainstream medicine because of patients' interest in health and prevention. For example, prestigious healthcare institutions such as the Mayo Clinic and the Cleveland Clinic now offer services and conduct research in this field. The Mayo Clinic has a Center for Integrative Medicine and Health on its Arizona and Minnesota campuses. These centers include acupuncture, massage, resilience training, and nutrition among their services. These campuses are also engaged in research in areas such as IM and fibromyalgia and the effect of massage on treatment. In addition, there is a great deal of patient information available, including podcasts on IM practices.[28]

The Cleveland Clinic's Wellness Institute includes a Center on Integrative Lifestyle and Medicine; its staff sees over 5000 patients a year. The center's services include acupuncture, hypnotherapy, massage, Chinese herbal therapy, and nutrition. It also has a unique nutrition-based program for reversing cardiovascular disease (the Esselstyne Program). Staff members are licensed and credentialed in their fields of excellence.[29]

In addition, there is a greater interest in educating healthcare professionals in CAM/IM areas. For example, Harvard Medical School[30] has the Osher Clinical Center for Integrative Medicine, which includes clinical practice, research, and education in IM. The center works in collaboration with Brigham and Women's Hospital and Harvard Medical School to provide clinical services that include acupuncture, creative arts therapy, palliative care, music therapy, and other CAM/IM services. Its 32 centers and over 110 credentialed clinicians provide patients with treatments that support healing, health, and wellness.

The Osher Clinical Center also provides ongoing research in IM through its center-without-walls model. This integration of researchers is conducting studies on a continuum that spans from cell biology to cost-effectiveness studies. For example, in its mind-body-movement lab, studies are being conducted in tai chi and massage and their effects on chronic diseases. These diseases include Parkinson disease, migraines, and cancer. More information can be found in their research map.[31] In addition to research, the Osher Clinical Center also provides educational opportunities to begin to integrate other disciplines of health care with the practices of IM. It provides publications, fellowships, and seminars in many areas of IM. It also provides monthly IM grand rounds that are open to medical students, researchers, and clinical practitioners.[32]

While not all medical and nursing schools have centers of IM, many are expanding their curriculum to include aspects of its practice.

For example, the Academic Consortium for Integrative Medicine and Health[33] includes medical schools from 30 states and the District of Columbia. Its mission is to share information in support for integrative medical medicine principles, research, and education. Members include medical schools from Vanderbilt University, Duke University, Columbia University, Boston University, and Johns Hopkins University, to cite a few examples.

Nursing schools are also adding curricula for holistic nursing that includes IM techniques. The Integrative Nursing Institute[34] provides a professional program for clinical nurses to increase their knowledge and skills through training programs and mentoring. It also features retreats sponsored by national faculty that feature mind-body healing, nutrition, and holistic nursing. Its programs are not limited to hospital-based nurses but also include nurses involved in home care, nurses in hospice, and nurse practitioners.

On a national level, IM is represented in the National Institutes of Health. The National Center for Complementary and Integrative Health (NCCIH), formally the National Center for Complementary and Alternative Medicine (NCCAM),[35] serves as a clearinghouse for information related to IM practices. It provides information for professionals and patients regarding definitions of information IM modalities and summaries of their practices. In addition, the NCCIH sponsors research and clinical trials on CAM/IM practices through grant funding. It also provides training for health professionals in these areas, including continuing medical education (CME) courses.

Conventional Medicine and CAM and IM

Although interest in CAM/IM practices is increasing among healthcare professionals and they have popularity among patients, the medical community still has concerns about their use in practice. Conventional medicine bases treatment on its definition of scientific principles, including Newtonian physics. Practitioners of conventional medicine base their values on what they consider verifiable scientific knowledge about the body and its functions. They also base their actions on the diagnostic criteria of a disease or diseases and the ability to treat those conditions.[36] This biomedical model tends to view the patient in a way that focuses on his or her physical body, and treatments address observed or verified physical problems and favor traditional treatment modalities.

The basis of CAM/IM comes from a different model. This model integrates the physical, spiritual, psychosocial, and energy aspects of humans into practice modalities. It offers treatments that combine these aspects to treat the whole person.[37] It is easy to see the paradigm conflict and the foundation of concern from conventional medicine's viewpoint. One of the arguments of conventional medicine against CAM/IM is that there is no proof of the efficacy of CAM/IM practices by research (specifically randomized, double-blind, control group studies, which are the gold standard of research). This claim ignores the current research conducted at medical schools (including Harvard University) and through research grant funding provided by the NCCIH. See the previous discussion about NCCIH research efforts.

In 2005, Shelle et al. found challenges in assessing the quality of studies involving CAM/IM practices.[38] Their concerns were that presentation of negative results of CAM/IM studies most often occurred in mainstream medical journals. In contrast, CAM/IM journals most often featured positive results. In addition, the indexing of CAM/IM journals was incomplete or improperly done. Therefore, publication biases existed. In addition, there were issues regarding the internal validity and reliability of the studies reviewed because of the need to provide replication. They also noted the lack of analogues in Western medicine, the inability to blind some of the CAM/IM practices, and the inability to mask the placebo effect. Finally, there was concern about how to assess the rare-event side effects of CAM/IM treatments through databases and other sources.

There is also concern about CAM/IM practices that has a historical base. In the early history of U.S. medicine, medical school graduates were an elite minority, and healers, midwives, and an assortment of non-medical-school-trained practitioners provided most patient care.[39] Over time, medical schools became increasingly science-based, and the medical profession extended its authority to define acceptable medical practice. This change caused increasing conflict between orthodox medicine and those who provided other ways of treatment, including the establishment of the American Medical Association's Committee on Quackery.[40] This long-standing concern with quackery and fraudulent practices has continued to affect attitudes toward CAM/IM practices in the 21st century.

However, a new dialogue has begun on the basis of a different direction in the medical community, which has become more open to examining diversity, dissatisfaction with the existing medical system, and the impersonal nature of medical technology. Given the change in education and research discussed earlier, greater opportunities for partnership with conventional practices exist. In addition, many CAM/IM practitioners hold licenses or registrations. This external validation of standards adds greater quality assurance in the eyes of conventional medicine. Although issues remain, there is certainly a movement toward cooperation between the different views on and the practice of medicine.

Research on the Use of CAM/IM

While the popularity of CAM/IM appears to be increasing among the general public, research is also being conducted to determine what services are being used and why patients choose them. Clark, Black, Stussman, Barnes, and Nahin[41] reported on a national study on trends in the use of CAM/IM. Their study included data from 2002, 2007, and 2012 and compared the increase in selected modalities and the differences in use by age, origin, and race. Their data sample included more than 88,000 adults over the age of 18 and was based on interviews through the National Health Interview Survey. The survey asked participants whether they had used any of a list of CAM/IM approaches, such as acupuncture, Ayurveda, guided imagery, tai chi, and yoga.

The results of this study were extensive and are summarized as follows:[42]

■ This landmark study estimated the prevalence of the use of CAM/IM to be 34% for the 2012 population. The study also clarified definitions of modalities so that data can be accurate in the future.

■ Dietary supplements were the most commonly used products in all three time periods. They were followed by deep-breathing exercises.

■ Yoga and tai chi use increased over the three study years, with yoga cited as the most commonly used modality in this comparison.

■ Chiropractic care and meditation were found to be the fourth and fifth most commonly used modalities, respectively.

The study also found a decrease in the use of CAM/IM modalities among Hispanics and non-Hispanic black adults, with an increase in use by non-Hispanic white adults. This information is helpful in understanding what modalities are most commonly used in current population groups and trends over time.

The American Association of Retired Persons and the NCCAM (now called the National Center for Complementary and Integrative Medicine) conducted a study to determine the use of CAM/IM modalities among patients over the age of 50.[43] They were particularly interested in the communication between patients in this age group and their healthcare providers with respect to these modalities. In this study, 47% of the respondents said that they used CAM/IM during the previous 12 months. College graduates were more likely to use CAM/IM products and services. The top four areas used were herbal products, massage and body work, mind-body practices, and acupuncture, naturopathic, and homeopathic practices. With respect to age, the highest percentage of respondents fell in the 50- to 69-year age group.

This study also revealed that respondents chose these options for wellness and pain reduction.[44] A somewhat surprising finding was that many (67%) of the study group did not discuss CAM/IM practices with their healthcare providers. The data revealed that women were more likely to discuss CAM/IM options with their physicians and that all those in the 50- to 64-year age group were more likely to have discussed these options with nurse practitioners. In addition, the study found that most often, CAM/IM is introduced by the patients rather than the providers in the discussion of care. Given the potential benefit of these modalities for this patient group, the authors conclude that providers need to offer information on CAM/IM during patient visits.

Patients, Ethics, and the Use of CAM/IM Modalities

Those who wish to make CAM part of their practice of health care seek a more holistic form of medicine. Their intent is not to avoid what they perceive as the technology- and body-part-centered system so aptly described by Geisel[45] but to enhance that care by using the many available CAM/IM options. Making this choice involves ethics issues that well-informed patients must consider. For the sake of brevity, the following discussion centers on the four principles of ethics—autonomy, beneficence, nonmaleficence, and justice— and how they relate to the use of CAM/IM.

Autonomy

Issues of autonomy, or the freedom for self-rule, would appear to be the most obvious issue for patients. In commenting on autonomy, Mertz found that the use of the practice of CAM/IM was ethical.[46] However, having the freedom to select practitioners for one's health care carries with it the responsibility for researching the practices and qualifications of those chosen. In addition, because health insurance does not always cover the costs of CAM/IM services, patients must be vigilant to understand both the treatment procedures and the cost of each visit. Patient responsibility is part of exercising one's autonomy.

Informed consent is an expression of autonomy in health care. This issue is also part of CAM/IM. Professionals who provide these services must give accurate information, including the risks involved. In addition, they must gather medical information from patients in order to formulate the best treatment plans. The patient also has an ethical obligation to provide accurate information to the CAM/IM provider.

An ethics issue also exists with respect to informed consent and CAM/IM for conventional health providers. Even with expanded use and acceptance, patients may still feel that their conventional health providers do not accept their use of these practices. The basis of the perception may be comments or even nonverbal cues. Regardless of the reason, patients often take a "don't ask and don't tell" strategy about CAM/IM use. Conventional practitioners have an ethical responsibility to take advantage of the many options for learning about CAM/IM and be able to answer the patients' questions with appropriate information. In today's practice, many conventional medicine practices include the use of CAM/IM in their consent forms and have begun to ask about this use. However, patients also need to be forthcoming about what health practices they use, without fear, so that treatment can be optimal.

Beneficence and Nonmaleficence

One should also consider the principles of beneficence and nonmaleficence when thinking about patients becoming partners in their health care through the selection of CAM/IM practices. Because of the holistic nature of these practices, beneficence, that is, acting in charity and kindness, would appear to be an integral part of their philosophy. Patients often feel that CAM/IM practitioners listen, allow them to be partners in treatment, treat them with respect, and give compassionate care. In addition, from the patients' view, CAM/IM practitioners have a broader view of healing than contemporary medical providers do and respect their experience of illness, including its spiritual aspects.[47]

From the patients' perspective, nonmaleficence is more complicated. Just like in conventional medicine, CAM/IM practices have the potential to cause harm. Although licensed or registered practitioners provide most of the commonly used CAM/IM practices, there are practitioners who do not have such credentials. In addition, some CAM/IM practices may have more risks than benefits or may even be fraudulent. Patients have the responsibility to protect themselves from harm by researching the credentials of CAM/IM practitioners and the efficacy of CAM/IM practices themselves. Although word of mouth is often the source of referral to CAM/IM practitioners, patients should be diligent in selecting a CAM/IM provider. Because of the expanding interest in and knowledge of these practices, they can seek advice from physicians, nurse practitioners, and other healthcare professionals regarding their choice to use CAM/IM modalities.[48]

Justice

The patient's right to choose CAM/IM in addition to conventional medicine includes the principle of justice. Patients have their own belief systems about their illness, spirituality, and treatment of their conditions and need to be treated fairly, even when this system is different from conventional medicine. Fairness and respect for patients translate into feeling comfortable discussing the use of CAM/IM with those who practice conventional medicine. Although physicians, nurse practitioners, dentists, and other healthcare providers may not agree, they should consider diversity of belief systems as part of the provision of patient-centered care.

Practitioner-Centered Ethics Issues

Ethics concerns are not limited to the patient. Practitioners should also consider their ethical duty where CAM/IM is concerned. Part of this duty is to be current and accurate in one's information about these practices and why patients seek their services. While maintaining currency in this area may be an additional demand on practitioners' time, there are opportunities for increasing one's knowledge in the field. For example, workshops and online courses are available as part of CME for physicians, nurses, physical therapists, and other healthcare practitioners.[49] In addition to knowledge about CAM/IM and its practices, conventional medicine practitioners should consider potential ethics issues, including those of autonomy, beneficence, nonmaleficence, and justice.

Autonomy

Most practitioners of conventional medicine entered the field because they wanted to make a difference and to assist patients to be well. They spent many difficult years learning the science and art of medicine and are appropriately proud of their accomplishments. However, in the traditional medical education process, they also learned the concept of paternalism. This means that, given their superior knowledge in the field, the authority of those who are educated in medicine is often greater than the rights of patients to make their own decisions about health issues.[50] Given this view, CAM/IM practices threaten the autonomy of practitioners because they do not fit their orientation to care for their patients. Further, CAM/IM practitioners are viewed as having knowledge and credentials that are not in any way equivalent to those of conventional medicine practitioners. In addition, despite current research, some practitioners may still view CAM/IM practices as not scientifically based and do not want to risk their autonomy by endorsing what they see as "quackery."

Beneficence and Nonmaleficence

With respect to beneficence, conventional medicine often has a concept of healing that differs from that of CAM/IM. Given this difference, conventional medicine may question whether CAM/IM provides benefit to patients. However, conventional practitioners may be changing this view on the basis of the trend toward understanding the patient experience and moving beyond disease care. If CAM/IM provides benefit to patients, should conventional medicine consider it in its lexicon of acceptable treatments?

"First do no harm" is part of the core of the ethics of conventional medical practice. Given this foundation, practitioners may question whether CAM/IM causes harm to patients by what it does and does not do. This is part of the reason for requiring evidence-based proof of effectiveness beyond the placebo effect. Of even greater concern is the fear that patients will use CAM/IM in place of conventional medicine, thereby causing themselves harm by not using verified conventional treatments. Although most Americans use both systems, there are cases where this situation does occur, and it is of concern to ethics-based conventional practitioners.[51]

Justice

The concept of justice also poses ethics issues for conventional practitioners. On the one hand, justice calls for the patient's right to choose a treatment or procedure and to be treated fairly while making this choice. Therefore, patients must have the right to choose CAM/IM options as well as those of conventional medicine. However, conventional medicine, with its emphasis on the scientific model, does not always accept CAM/IM. Therefore, the possibility of supporting these modalities, educating patients on their use, or offering them as part of healthcare insurance may not appeal to many on the conventional side of medicine. Certainly, there is a continuing need for research, education, and dialogue before conventional medicine could support the justice of including CAM/IM practices in treatment protocols.[52]

Here Come the Boomers!

The creation of the baby boomer generation was triggered by the homecoming of soldiers who served in World War II. However, the population group known as the baby boomers represents people who were born from 1946 to 1964 and represents a trend that is significant to the United States' population but also an event that occurred worldwide. When the last of the baby boomers reach the age of retirement, approximately 20% of the population in the United States will be 65 or older.[53] This means that this group will constitute a large part of the population, now and in the future. The baby boomer population also has a longer life span because of lifestyle changes and advances in treatments for diseases from diabetes to cancer.[54]

The baby boomer generation influenced each social institution that the baby boomers encountered. In addition, their numbers continue to dominate markets and influence social institutions.[55] For example, when the baby boomers entered the elementary school system, the system was not prepared for their numbers. Therefore, an expansion of classrooms and increased hiring of teachers occurred to meet the baby boomers' educational needs. The decade of the 1960s also helped to define the baby boomer generation. These turbulent times saw civil rights protests; assassinations of a president, presidential candidates, and civil rights leaders; and Woodstock's celebration of rock and roll. The Vietnam War was also a major influence on the baby boomers' attitudes toward the federal government. With all of these events, the 1960s were a roller-coaster of hope and despair for the early baby boomers (1946–1957) and influenced U.S. culture on many levels.[56]

The baby boomers' experiences influenced their outlook on life and on their futures. Although one cannot assign a specific attitude set to individuals, certain attitudes tend to be prevalent in this population. These include the desire not to get old (maintaining youthfulness), to make a difference, and to be empowered.[57] In addition, the baby boomer generation tends to have greater financial power than previous aging populations.[58] These attitudes and the baby boomers' financial power shape their vision of the aging process and can greatly influence markets.

Dychtwald devotes several chapters to the market influence of the baby boomers and to how they perceive aging.[59] Baby boomers continue to redefine the attitudes toward this process. This attitude change has opened up a large market for antiaging products, from makeup with serum included to gene therapy and bionics. In addition, baby boomer retirement is not about sitting in a rocking chair and waiting to die. For the baby boomers, it is about continuing to be productive even as they age, making a difference, and having meaningful employment and second careers.[60]

The Baby Boomers' Ethical View

According to Smith and Clurman, the baby boomers have their own moral focus that will continue to be important to them as they age.[61] They have moved from an orientation of self-expression and abundance to one dominated by concern for moral issues. The last section of Smith and Clurman's book focuses on the aging baby boomers' moral agenda, which includes continuing to have a sense of purpose, concern about maintaining health and avoiding frailty, and reconnecting with the community. In addition, baby boomers expect that they can take charge of their health and that the healthcare system will be able to provide adequate insurance coverage, fix their problems, and provide quality care.

Impact of the Baby Boomers on Future Healthcare Practice

As one can imagine, the aging baby boomers promise to continue to have an impact on the healthcare market. On the positive side, Dychtwald listed over 50 areas for new markets to meet the needs of this emerging demographic.[62] Some of these areas include business opportunities for services to maintain health and independence, such as companies that coordinate care, Internet-based medical systems, and financial services. Creativity will be needed to determine what the baby boomers want and then providing the required services. One can create profitable businesses by assisting baby boomers to remain active as long as possible.

However, there are also serious concerns about the adequacy of services to meet the needs of aging baby boomers. With the baby boomers turning 65 in record numbers, there is a major concern about the ability of current healthcare benefit plans (Medicare, Medicaid, etc.) to meet the care needs of this population and maintain its fiscal viability.[63] Many predict massive changes in these plans—changes that will not please the politically powerful baby boomers. Dychtwald stressed that healthcare systems need to be ready for the chronic diseases that will accompany the aging of the baby boomers.[64] Healthcare systems must also address the shortage of long-term care facilities, from nursing homes to adult day care centers. In addition, there will be a lack of caregivers, including professionals such as geriatricians, nurses, physical therapists, and others. There will also be a need for non-professional caregivers who can provide homemaker services, home repair services, and transportation. Since the goal of the baby boomers is to remain in their homes as long as possible, these providers are essential.

Not all of the baby boomer generation is financially ready for retirement and the aging process. Dychtwald points out that "as much as one-third (and a group disproportionally female)—has no savings, no investments, no pensions."[65] This group may not be able to survive on Social Security alone (assuming that it is continued) and face dependency on their children, charities, or other sources of survival. There is a great need for financial planning for all baby boomers, including increasing their savings, reducing credit card debt, and reviewing their current pension plans. From the healthcare standpoint, providing affordable long-term care insurance products may assist baby boomers in coping with potential reductions in Medicare services.

Ethics Issues for the Healthcare System

Given their numbers, the healthcare system needs to assess its moral position with respect to care for the baby boomers. Given the complexity of the population and the healthcare system, ethics of caring for the aging baby boomer population could be a book of its own. For brevity's sake, one could apply the four principles of ethics—autonomy, beneficence, nonmaleficence, and justice—as a focal point for discussion.

Autonomy

The issue of autonomy is an important one for the individual baby boomer in that he or she wants to be in charge of his or her health as much as possible. This means that the healthcare system must also do a better job attending to patient needs (patient-centered care) and communicating with patients. In addition, there will be a greater need to maintain high standards of quality in terms of meeting the needs of the baby boomer group and addressing patient safety. Thinking from an economic point of view, the baby boomers' need to spend money to maintain their autonomy can be a boon to healthcare businesses. For example, markets that address the needs of baby boomers as they age have the potential of being extremely profitable, but ethics must be part of the planning to avoid exploitation. These and other baby boomer-related issues will continue to be important in dealing with the baby boomers.

In addition to baby boomers as patients, healthcare facilities must also deal with the aging of their employee base. The healthcare industry must consider this issue with its labor force and the potential shortages of healthcare professionals in the near feature. The Institute of Medicine notes that it may be difficult to achieve the desired workforce because of the large number of health professionals who will choose to retire. For example, "by 2020, nearly half of all registered nurses will reach traditional retirement age. Currently, the average age of a nurse in the United States is 50."[66] Strategies to retain older workforce members need to be part of the workforce planning in health care. Examples of such strategies might include flexible schedules, short work weeks, part-time employment, and use of technology that will assist with the realities of older workers.[67]

Beneficence

Patients enter the healthcare system with the expectation of treatment based on charity and kindness. This is certainly true for the baby boomer generation. However, their numbers may cause violations of this basic premise for health care. For example, when staff members have too many patients and too little time, patients can become just another "head in a bed." This lack of compassionate care will not be acceptable to baby boomer patients. Therefore, healthcare systems must continue to evaluate processes and procedures to not only increase efficiency but also increase the emphasis on human-to-human interaction. This effort will pay off not only in terms of patient satisfaction but also in reduction of medical errors and increased organizational image and business potential.

Nonmaleficence

A key element in all health care is to "first do no harm." Because baby boomers do not want to age, they may be attracted to businesses and services that feature antiaging products and procedures. Although these services may be highly profitable, it is important to consider the benefit to the patient versus the harm. Minimally, patients need to be informed about the risks and the benefits of any antiaging procedures so that an informed decision can be made.

In addition, the healthcare system needs to practice vigilance to avoid errors and safety violations that can cause harm to the patient and to the reputation of the organization. This requires continuous evaluation, staff education, and diligence. Of course, as healthcare reform progresses, more attention will be drawn to these issues, linked not just to ethics, but also to financial repercussions.

Justice

Justice is perhaps the most difficult ethics area to address with respect to the baby boomers. One needs to ask, "What is just?" and "To whom is it just?" The baby boomers have a highly focused sense of justice, which includes fair treatment of their needs. Fairness, in their view, centers on getting what they need and what they feel they deserve. In addition, this conception of fairness is linked to effective communication. In other words, if the patient understands why something has occurred, he or she will be less likely to see it as an injustice. This need for effective communication is not limited to the baby boomer generation but would serve to enhance the understanding of patient justice.

There are also justice issues for staff members working in a high-baby-boomer-population situation. Healthcare systems may ask their employees to do more with less on a consistent basis. Although this makes economic sense, it creates feelings of being treated unfairly, which can lead to high turnover, lower staff ratios, and poor morale in an era of potential staff shortages. This situation can then lead to robotic, uncompassionate patient care and the continuation of an undesirable and unprofitable business cycle. Finding solutions to avoid this cycle requires attention to detail, creativity, training, and evaluation.

Ethics in the Epoch of Change

It appears that the one constant in today's healthcare environment is change. However, change is not new to health care; the health care industry has faced change for all of its history. For example, think about the impact of discoveries in medicine that created the ability to go beyond treatment to cure. Certainly, health care has also embraced change from technology and its variations. What is different now?

The difference is not that there is change; it is the nature of that change. The change occurring in today's health care system is both rapid and deep.

It is beginning to upturn the traditional practice of medicine, and the pressure to change or fail is eminent. The change affects the structure of health care and also challenges its professionals on many levels. In the end, despite the pressure of change, the healthcare system has an ethical, professional, and financial duty to provide quality health care that is both effective and compassionate. This goal must be met in an environment that demands greater accountability and adaptability to new and different business demands. How will this epoch of change challenge the mission and practice of ethics in health care?

Impact on Healthcare Professionals

According to Borkowski,[68] there is resistance to change when there is uncertainty, a perception of a negative impact, and an excessive amount of change. Given the current situation in health care, these variables are present in today's system. For example, there is uncertainty about organizational finance, sustainability, and many other variables. This uncertainty contributes to the feeling of insecurity about the changes that might happen and how they would affect one's job and job security. This insecurity also can contribute to "lower morale, increased absenteeism, and reductions in both quality and quantity of output."[69]

In addition, if there is no clear communication, there are also concerns about how to provide quality patient care and whether the mission of patient care is important.

When change is excessive, there are also ramifications for healthcare practice. For example, when healthcare organizations must address the multiple and simultaneous changes required in today's environment, it can be difficult to understand one's priorities. In addition, those who provide patient care and support the organization begin to experience that they have too much to do and too little time in which to do it. This perception, which might also be in actuality, increases the potential for employee burnout and lower standards of patient care.[70]

Today's healthcare environment, with its multifaceted change structure, suggests a new look at the triangle model that has defined quality. Perhaps, the triangle should now reflect a balance between finance, patient care, and change. Such a model would suggest that addressing the multiple changes required in the current healthcare environment should be part of quality. Certainly, organizations must be prepared for rapid change as the norm and make efforts to remain true to their mission of patient-centered care. The ability to do this will be both a challenge and a benefit for the future.

Maintaining Ethics-Based Practice

How does the practice of ethics relate to the current healthcare environment? First, healthcare organizations must continue to rely on all levels of their staff to practice ethics as part of realizing their mission. In times of great change and multiple pressures from multiple sources, there is a potential for an ethics disaster to occur. Bauer[71] provided an in-depth examination of disaster prevention in his book, *Better Ethics Now: Avoid the Ethics Disasters You Never Saw Coming*. He suggested that it is not enough to follow the rules of ethics given in training or the codes of ethics for professionals. Rather, healthcare organizations must understand that the practice of ethics is based on how one chooses to behave in any situation. For this reason, even staff members who believe that they are highly moral people can cause ethics problems.

It is important to understand why these staff members may be involved in ethics violations. Often, these compromises in values are affected by a loss of status, perceived loss of value, or threats to security. Bauer suggested[72] that the work environment may contribute to these impressions and that both staff and administration should be alert to what he called "red flags." Examples include ideas such as "I got away with an action that might be questionable," "someone else can cover for me on my action," "I just did it one time," and "everyone does it." This mode of thinking makes it easier to violate ethics without perceiving oneself as being unethical.

Because ethics is important to the mission and image of health care, it is important to make ethics disaster prevention a priority among organizations. Since health care is trust-based, it will be necessary for organizations to stress that ethics matters. This means going beyond stating the mission of the organization to being proactive when dealing with ethics situations. This might include providing a consistent message on the practice of ethics in the organization, taking appropriate action on ethics violations, and providing realistic training on ethics expectations. In addition, healthcare leaders on all levels should remember that "positive or negative, your behavior sets the tone for your team. You need to model appropriate values and behavior all day, every day!"[73]

Meaning in Work

Even though health care is in an epoch of profound and accelerating change, those who serve patients, care, or support that care can still find meaning in their work. Given the nature of health care, it should be a most meaning-filled occupation. How does one find meaning in health care, and how does this meaning relate to ethics?

Frankl reminds us that meaning is found "(1) by creating a work or doing a deed; (2) by experiencing something or encountering someone; and (3) by the attitude we take toward unavoidable suffering."[74] Given this definition, one can see that health care is an environment for meaning-filled work. Chapman[75] considered health care to be a "culture of sacred work."

However, in the current environment of health care, it is easy to get lost in the day-to-day challenges of providing care amid time demands and the pressure to do more and more. In this situation, it is necessary to remember that the process of providing care is also important. In fact, health care is about the relationships with patients and with one another. It is through these relationships that healthcare providers can find meaning in work. Relationships also allow healthcare providers to find meaning in the moment. For example, they are often present for the patient when a joyful occasion happens, such as the birth of a child. They are also present for the patient at the end of his or her life. These moments and many other examples provide opportunities to experience meaning in work and add to the personal commitment to serve patients.

"Few of us get through our lives unscathed."[76] While the sometimes chaotic environment of health care can be

overwhelming, all who work in health care must understand that change is the new norm and cannot be avoided. However, Frankl stresses that there is always a choice, even in the worst of circumstances.[77] This means that, although busy, healthcare professionals do not have to give up their beneficence, respect for confidentiality, autonomy, or sense of justice.

How does meaning in work relate to practicing ethics? First, if one finds that work is not just a source of a paycheck but something that adds meaning to one's life, it changes the attitude toward the work itself. When work is meaningful, it is less likely that a person will make decisions that cause ethics violations that could be harmful to patients or for the organization. Being part of something that is bigger than one's self encourages self-monitoring where ethics decisions are concerned.[78] If the culture also is one where the meaning and value of the provision of health care and its staff, from housekeepers to neurosurgeons, are honored, a culture of ethics can also exist.

Ethics Still Matters

The future of health care reminds one of the saying "May you live in interesting times." Assuredly, the current epoch of health care is a time of change and ethics challenge. However, the practice of ethics will be a necessary and expected part of this work because its true mission goes beyond financial success and workforce satisfaction. The center of health care must be the patient.

The disruption in the healthcare system through changes in financing, legal requirements, technology, and other areas can also be a positive force for innovation. This type of change can result in a fresh look at the way health care is provided and the way to best meet patients' needs. For example, Samet and Smith[79] suggested that if organizations choose an optimistic and empowering attitude toward innovation, it can lead to the development of new services, collaborations, and delivery of care. The spirit of innovation can also increase the energy among healthcare staff members and lead to solutions for existing problems.

▶ Summary

In this chapter, Furlong and Morrison provide a discussion of issues that will affect the practice of ethics in health care in the immediate and near future. They also provide new models for thinking about healthcare ethics and its practice. In addition, the authors consider issues that affect both patients and caregivers and pose ethics challenges for both. Finally, they summarize a new issue of the impact of profound and constant change on the practice of ethics in health care. It is important to note that in health care, ethics matters, even when the system and individuals are challenged by external and internal changes.

▶ Questions for Discussion

1. Does the ethic-of-care model change the way that you think about ethics?
2. How does the narrative ethics model compare with the theories presented by Summers?
3. Despite the increased acceptance of CAM/IM practices, what ethics issues still exist for the healthcare system and practitioners?
4. How will the aging of the baby boomers affect ethics in the future of health care?
5. How can healthcare professionals adapt to change and maintain their ethics and integrity?

▶ Notes

1. D. L. Volker, "Is There a Unique Nursing Ethic?" *Nursing Science Quarterly* 16, no. 207 (2003): 207–11.
2. S. D. Edwards, "Three Versions of an Ethic of Care," *Nursing Philosophy* 10 (2009): 231–40.
3. V. D. Lachman, "Applying the Ethics of Care to Your Nursing Practice," *Medsurg Nursing* 21, no. 2 (2012): 112.
4. Volker, "Unique Nursing Ethic?"
5. Edwards, "Three Versions of an Ethic of Care."
6. Volker, "Unique Nursing Ethic?"
7. Edwards, "Three Versions of an Ethic of Care."
8. D. C. Thomasma, "Toward a New Medical Ethics: Implications for Ethics in Nursing," in *Interpretative Phenomenology: Embodiment, Caring, and Ethics in Health and Illness*, ed. P. Benner (Thousand Oaks, CA: Sage, 1994).
9. A. Bishop and J. Scudder, *Nursing Ethics: Therapeutic Caring Presence* (Sudbury, MA: Jones and Bartlett Publishers, 2001).
10. Volker, "Unique Nursing Ethic?" 209.
11. M. Corley and P. Selig, "Prevalence of Principled Thinking by Critical Care Nurses," *Dimensions of Critical Care Nursing* 3 (1994): 96–103.
12. A. Gaul, "Casuistry, Care, Compassion, and Ethics Data Analysis," *Advances in Nursing Science* 17, no. 3 (1995): 47–57.
13. W. J. Pinch, "Is Caring a Moral Trap?" *Nursing Outlook* 44 (1996): 84–88.
14. Edwards, "Three Versions of an Ethic of Care."
15. C. Gastmans, "The Care Perspective in Health Care Ethics," in *Essentials of Teaching and Learning in Nursing Ethics: Perspectives and Methods*, eds. A. J. Davis et al. (London: Churchill Livingston), 146.
16. P. Nortvedt et al., "The Ethics of Care: Role Obligations and Moderate Partiality in Health Care," *Nursing Ethics* 18, no. 2 (2011): 192–200.
17. Ibid., 197.
18. J. McCarthy, "Principlism or Narrative Ethics: Must We Choose Between

Them?" *British Medical Journal* 29 (2003): 67.

19. Ibid., 67.
20. Ibid., 65.
21. K. Dayton, "Procedures," in *An Arduous Touch: Women's Voices in Health Care*, eds. A. M. Haddad and K. H. Brown (West Lafayette, IN: Purdue University Press, 1999), 12–20.
22. McCarthy, "Principlism or Narrative Ethics," 66.
23. Ibid., 65–71.
24. Ibid., 70.
25. T. E. Adams, "A Review of Narrative Ethics," *Qualitative Inquiry* 14 (2008): 179.
26. C. Ellis, "Telling Secrets, Revealing Lives: Relational Ethics in Research with Intimate Others," *Qualitative Inquiry* 13 (2007): 3–29.
27. For excellent resources on the history and practice of CAM/IM, see M. S. Micozzi, *Fundamentals of Complementary and Alternative Medicine*, 5th ed. (St. Louis, MO: Saunders, 2015).
28. The Mayo Clinic, Center for Integrative Medicine and Health, 2017, http://www.mayoclinic.org/departments-centers/integrative-medicine-health.
29. The Cleveland Clinic, *Center of Integrative and Lifestyle Medicine*, 2017, https://my.clevelandclinic.org/departments/wellness/integrative.
30. Harvard Medical School and Brigham and Women's Hospital. Osher Center for Integrative Medicine, "Home" (2017), http://oshercenter.org/.
31. Harvard Medical School and Brigham and Women's Hospital, Osher Center for Integrative Medicine, "Research" (2017), http://oshercenter.org/research/.
32. Harvard Medical School and Brigham and Women's Hospital, Osher Center for Integrative Medicine, "Education" (2017), http://oshercenter.org/educational/.
33. Academic Consortium for Integrative Medicine and Health, "Home" (2017), https://www.imconsortium.org/members/members.cfm.
34. Integrative Nursing Institute, "About Us," 2017, http://www.integrativenursinginstitute.org/.
35. National Institutes of Health, "National Center for Complementary and Integrative Health," 2016, NCCIH https://nccih.nih.gov/.
36. S. Tyremann, "Values in Complementary and Alternative Medicine," *Medical Health Care and Philosophy* 14 (2011): 209–17.
37. Micozzi, *Fundamentals of Complementary and Alternative Medicine*.
38. P. G. Shelle et al., "Challenges in Systematic Reviews of Complementary and Alternative Medicine Topic," *Annals of Internal Medicine* 142, no. 12 (2005): 1042–47.
39. T. J. Kaptchuk and D. M. Eisenberg, "Varieties of Healing, 1: Medical Pluralism in the United States," *Annals of Internal Medicine* 135, no. 3 (2001): 189–95.
40. Ibid., 1.
41. T. C. Clarke et al., "Trends in the Use of Complementary Health Approaches among Adults: United States, 2002/2012," *National Health Statistic Reports* 79 (2015, February): 1–15.
42. Ibid.
43. AARP and the National Center for Complementary and Alternative Medicine, "Complementary and Alternative Medicine: What People Age 50 and Older Discuss with Their Healthcare Providers," *National Institutes of Health* (2011, April): 1–14.
44. Ibid.
45. T. S. Geisel, *You're Only Old Once: A Book for Obsolete Children* (New York: Random House, 1986). Note: This is a "must read" to understand the patient experience.
46. M. Mertz, "Complementary and Alternative Medicine: The Challenges of

Ethical Justification," *Medicine, Health Care, and Philosophy* 10 (2007): 329–45.

47. Ibid., 334.

48. M. S. Micozzi, *Fundamentals of Complementary and Alternative Medicine*, 5th ed.

49. National Institutes of Health, "National Center for Complementary and Integrative Health," 2016, NCCIH https://nccih.nih.gov/.

50. Mertz, "Complementary and Alternative Medicine," 333–34.

51. Ibid., 337–41.

52. C. L. Ross, "Integral Healthcare: The Benefits and Challenges of Integrating Complementary and Alternative Medicine with a Conventional Medical Practice," *Integrative Medicine Insights* 4 (2009): 13–20.

53. American Hospital Association, *When I'm 64: How Boomers Will Change Health Care* (Chicago, IL: American Hospital Association, 2007).

54. Ibid.

55. The Gale Group, "Baby Boomers," Encyclopedia of Aging, 2002, http://www.encyclopedia.com/social-sciences-and-law/sociology-and-social-reform/sociology-general-terms-and-concepts/baby-boom.

56. J. W. Smith and A. Clurman, *Generation Ageless: How Baby Boomers Are Changing the Way We Live Today . . . And They're Just Getting Started* (New York: Harper Collins, 2007), xv.

57. Ibid., 30.

58. K. Dychtwald, *Age Power: How the 21st Century Will Be Ruled by the New Old* (New York: Jeremy P. Archer/Putnam, 1999), 15–19.

59. United States History, "Baby Boomer Generation," http://www.u-s-history.com/pages/h2061.html.

60. Dychtwald, *Age Power*, Chaps. 2 and 4.

61. Smith and Clurman, *Generation Ageless*, Chaps. 6–8.

62. Dychtwald, *Age Power*, 70–78.

63. R. Schwartz, "Baby Boomers, Agents, and Health Care," *Florida Underwriter*, September 2010, 14–15.

64. Dychtwald, *Age Power*, Chap. 6.

65. Ibid., 173.

66. L. Harrington and M. Heidkamp, "The Aging Workforce; Challenges for the Health Care Industry Workforce," *Issue Brief of the NTAR Leadership Center* (2013, March): 1–9, https://www.dol.gov/odep/pdf/NTAR-AgingWorkforceHealthCare.pdf.

67. Harrington and Heidkamp, "The Aging Workforce; Challenges for the Health Care Industry Workforce."

68. N. Borkowski, *Organizational Behavior in Health Care*, 3rd ed. (Burlington, MA: Jones & Bartlett Learning, 2016).

69. Ibid., 405.

70. Borkowski, *Organizational Behavior in Health Care*, 3rd ed.

71. C. Bauer, *Better Ethics Now: Avoiding the Ethics Disaster You Never Saw Coming*, 2nd ed. (Nashville, TN: Aab-Hill Business Books, 2008).

72. Ibid., 71.

73. Bauer, *Better Ethics Now: Avoiding the Ethics Disaster You Never Saw Coming*, 106.

74. V. E. Frankl, *Man's Search for Meaning* (Boston, MA: Beacon Press), 111.

75. E. Chapman, *Radical Loving Care: Building the Healing Hospital in America* (Nashville, TN: Erie Chapman Foundation), 121.

76. A. Pattakos, *Prisoners of Our Thoughts: Victor Frankl's Principles at Work* (San Francisco, CA: Barrett-Koehler Publishers, Inc.), 109.

77. Frankl, *Man's Search for Meaning*.

78. Bauer, *Better Ethics Now: Avoiding the Ethics Disaster You Never Saw Coming*.

79. K. A. Samet and M. S. Smith, "Thinking Differently: Catalyzing Innovation in Health Care and Beyond," *Frontiers of Health Services Management* 33, no. 2 (2016, Winter): 3–15.

Glossary

a priori Experience-based knowledge.

absolute difference (AD) A number obtained by subtracting the numeric measure of the health status of one group from that of another group.

accountable care organization A group of providers of coordinated care for patients. There is a link between their reimbursement for this service and their quality care goals.

act utility In utilitarianism, the tenet that one should judge each act on its own overall benefit. This version of utilitarianism is not conducive to health care.

activities of daily living (ADLs) Basic needs and activities of life, such as getting in and out of bed, toileting, bathing, dressing, and eating.

ADL-dependent A term used for individuals who have cognition issues and need support for completing the requirements for daily living.

adult protective services (APS) Agencies that have the task of assisting older adults when they are not able to meet their needs or are abused, neglected, or exploited.

advance directive A document that allows a patient to express his or her wishes about end-of-life issues and treatment. Hospitals and others also use the term *living will* for this legal document.

alternative payment model (APM) A payment system for Medicare reimbursement that rewards quality and cost-effectiveness.

altruism Act of behaving unselfishly or in the belief that one's actions benefit others.

anthropogenic hazard A harmful situation that results from the interaction of human beings with the world. The situation can be a result of intent to harm, human error, or negligence.

antinomies Two statements that appear to be correct but do not agree, creating a paradox.

assisted living facility (ALF) A recent addition to long-term care options that provides assistance with activities of daily living, greater privacy, and independence, primarily for seniors.

assisted reproduction The use of technologies, such as in vitro fertilization, artificial insemination, and cloning, to facilitate procreation.

assisted reproductive technology (ART) Any of a number of alternative ways to reproduce children. Cloning is one example of ART.

authority-based ethics Theories of ethics that use faith or ideology as the focal point for making ethical decisions.

autonomy In healthcare ethics, the ability to act independently and to make decisions about actions, treatment, and health practices.

baby boomer generation A group of people who were born in the period following World War II. Because of their numbers, this group has changed U.S. culture in many ways.

beneficence An act of charity and kindness. It applies to both professionals and organizations.

best-off population A method of computing the amount of inequality in populations. In the case of health care, those who are the best off in terms of health serve as the reference group for comparisons with the worst-off group.

biological reductionism A view that reduces human beings to the cellular level and assumes that one human can replace another.

bureaucratic parsimony An organization's unwillingness to spend money or resources on programs.

categorical imperative Emmanuel Kant's tool for making ethical decisions. It includes the ideas of a decision being able to become a universal law and of respect for humankind. If both these concepts apply, then the action can be truly moral.

CCRC: An abbreviation for continuing care retirement community. These facilities provide care for the life of their residents at appropriate levels.

clinical decision support system (CDSS) A type of health information technology that gives physicians information for making patient treatment decisions.

clinical practice guidelines Recommendations for medical practice developed by experts in the field and based on evidence-based treatment practices.

cloning The process of creating a plant or an animal that is genetically identical to its parent through asexual reproduction.

clouded genetic heritage A situation that occurs when reproductive technologies are used and the genetic identity of the produced child is unknown.

collaborative reproduction The use of surrogates, cloning, and other alternative reproductive options to produce a child.

computer-assisted maxillofacial surgery The use of computer-aided navigation systems in order to better conduct dental surgery and other procedures with fewer complications.

computer-assisted surgery The use of computers and specialized equipment to assist physicians in advanced surgical procedures.

Consumer Assessment of Healthcare Providers and Systems (CAHP®) A mechanism for collecting data on consumer perceptions of their healthcare experience. The data collected are part of consideration for Medicare payments.

consequentialism A theory in which the value of decisions is based on their consequences and not on the intent of the agent. This is part of teleological ethics theories.

curing Bringing an end to illness or injury through medical treatment.

cyber attacker An individual who deliberately attempts to damage or destroy systems or individual computer networks.

deontology A theory of ethics, largely attributed to Kant, that uses the concept of duty and respect for persons to define appropriate ethical action.

disability-adjusted life year (DALY) A measure of the burden of a disease on the basis of lost years through poor health, disability, or death.

disease experience The way patients see the disease process, which can be vastly different from the way professionals view it.

disenfranchisement A circumstance in which a person's rights to full participation in society appear to be limited; the individual does not feel that he or she has the right to benefits that others receive.

distributive justice A subset of justice that addresses the balancing of benefits and burdens and the appropriate sharing of those benefits and burdens.

domestic violence A complex social problem that carries serious healthcare consequences, especially for intimate partners and others in society.

elder health care A descriptive term for services that are provided to individuals who need support with their daily activities and health care because of their age and infirmity.

electronic medical record (EMR) A generic term for the creation, maintenance, and storage of a patient's medical record on a computer system.

elitism A practice in which a person can set his or her own standards for what is virtuous in a situation. This practice can lead to decisions that do not display virtue being viewed as virtuous.

empiricism The philosophical position that all knowledge comes from observed information and experimentation.

ensoulment Part of the beginning of moral personhood, conceptualized as the moment when a fetus gains a soul. The mother feels it as "quickening."

epidemic The widespread presence of a disease or health issue in a community that occurs at the same time.

ethical analysis The application of ethics theories and principles to concrete clinical situations.

ethical climate The overall culture of an organization with respect to ethics. The climate for the application of ethics to decision-making can be favorable or unfavorable.

ethical egoism An ethics theory that is based on individuals acting solely for their best interests when making decisions. The goal is to find benefit, pleasure, or good that only benefits the person seeking it. This term also describes an ethical position that maintains that people should act only for their own self-interest or benefit. This position does not fit well in the healthcare context, because healing requires putting the patient's interests before those of the healer.

ethical relativism The theory that because every situation is different, there is no appropriate ethics theory or set of theories. Ethical decisions would depend on the situation. Because of the nature of health care, this position is not appropriate.

ethicist A professional who typically has a doctoral degree in ethics, bioethics, and sometimes theology. He or she serves as a consultant on ethics issues for a hospital or an ethics committee.

ethics committee A group of people who serve in an advisory capacity for ethics issues in a hospital or major clinic; membership varies depending on the committee's function.

ethics toolbox The knowledge and application of ethics theories and principles to everyday issues in health care. If one has a full ethics toolbox, one can better choose appropriate ethics-based actions.

eudaimonia A term that means happiness or well-being. However, in Aristotle's philosophy, eudaimonia is different from mere pleasure in that it occurs when a person lives a rational life.

evidence-based practice (EBP) Medical care provided on the basis of scientifically sound treatments and procedures that produce successful outcomes.

family systems approach A perspective of psychotherapy that views the family as a unit and addresses problems within the system of the family.

financially avoidable health inequity An inequality that is avoidable if adequate resources exist.

formula for disasters A way to sum up the definition of disasters used by the American Red Cross. Disaster = (Vulnerability + Hazard)/Capacity.

fungible The ability to be interchanged or substitutable.

gender socialization The process by which males and females learn their identities and roles in society.

genetic mother A woman who provides the germ cells (egg) for the creation of a child; she may or may not be the gestational mother.

genetic therapy An intervention that includes gene testing and counseling of prospective parents about genetic-related diseases.

gestational mother A woman who carries a fertilized egg in her uterus; she may or may not be the genetic mother.

grandma test An informal system for judging whether a decision is ethical or unethical.

H1N1 The influenza virus that causes swine flu and has contributed to a worldwide pandemic.

hacker An individual who uses his or her expertise to break into a computer system; hacking can be done for illegal purposes or just for the hacker's own amusement.

harm In a clinical setting, something that makes the situation worse for the patient. Harm can be physical, emotional, financial, or spiritual.

harm as negligence A situation in which healthcare personnel fail to protect patients, families, or communities from injury, damage, or impairment caused by encounters with the healthcare system.

hazard vulnerability analysis A process of evaluating potential emergencies and their effect on hospitals and communities. Several areas are included in such an analysis, including mitigation, response, and recovery operations.

healing The process of treating a patient beyond his or her symptoms, using the mind, body, and spirit.

health disparity Different health statuses that exist for different groups in society. Factors such as race, ethnicity, gender, and income may influence the occurrence of higher rates of certain diseases.

health inequality Variations of health status across individuals within a population or a difference in the average or total health between two or more populations.

health inequity A difference in the health status of populations or individuals within populations that society or individuals find morally unacceptable.

health information systems Grouped technology that collects, stores, analyzes, and reports patient and health information.

health information technology (HIT) The computer hardware, software, databases, and systems that support quality care through electronic medical records.

Health Information Technology for Economic and Clinical Health (HITECH) Act Part of the American Recovery and Reinvestment Act of 2009. This law is an attempt to ensure the adoption of electronic medical records.

Health Insurance and Portability and Accountability Act (HIPAA) of 1996 A law designed to protect the confidentiality of patient records through standards for electronic exchange of this information.

Healthy People 2020 The title of a government program addressing prevention strategies for many diseases and health conditions.

horizontal equity The equal allocation of a resource across a population.

human-caused disaster A situation of loss of life, property, or sense of safety created by the actions of humans rather than by nature.

IBM Watson A supercomputer that is capable of manipulating big data with short processing times. This system shows potential for multiple applications in health care and other industries.

ideographic knowledge Knowledge that accepts that understanding is limited and unique to each person.

in vitro fertilization (IVF) A procedure that involves the fertilization of the ovum by the sperm outside the human body. In cases where conception is affected by low fertility, couples can use IVF for conception.

inerrant A person who is incapable of making a mistake or doing something that contains mistakes.

institutional review board (IRB) A committee made up of experts and concerned individuals whose mission is to ensure protection of human subjects in research.

instrumental activities of daily living (IADLs) A category of functional capabilities that includes taking medications appropriately, managing finances, using the telephone, and being able to get in and out of the home.

integrated ethics An approach to ethics whereby ethics is part of the "business as usual" workings of an organization rather than solely the responsibility of an ethics committee or the chaplaincy.

intergenerational problem A situation in which a problem or condition affects patients of two or more generations. An example of an intergenerational problem is domestic violence or alcoholism.

intergenerational transmission of abuse The process of passing the culture of abuse from one generation to another in families.

intimate partner violence (IPV) Any type of harm caused by a current or past partner of a person; this is also known as domestic violence. Remember that this issue is not limited to women.

The Joint Commission (TJC) An agency that accredits or certifies thousands of healthcare facilities in the United States. Its mission is to improve the quality of health care.

justice A principle of ethics that includes actions that provide fairness or address the perception of what a person or community deserves.

legal right The existence of legislation that grants a person an entitlement.

libertarianism The position, taken by Robert Nozick and others, that freedom or liberty is the central moral principle. Therefore, individual autonomy is critical to moral action.

life care at home (LCAH) A form of long-term care that emphasizes maintaining the individual in his or her home environment while providing required services. It includes a membership and monthly fees similar to what would occur in a long-term care facility.

long-term care The use of health care on a long-term basis, as required by an individual's physical or mental limitations.

mass-casualty event A natural or human-caused occurrence in which more than the expected number of deaths and injuries occur. Such events challenge hospitals and other healthcare systems.

mass prophylaxis Efforts for community preparedness for and prevention of natural or human-caused disasters.

maximum beneficence A term used in responding to disasters. While maximum benefit or kindness is desirable for all patients, disaster situations may not allow for this to be true. Emphasis is often placed on the greatest good or saving the most lives.

meaning in work A person's perception of the value of work on income. It includes areas such as contribution to others, accomplishments, and the community.

meaningful use As used in the HITECH act, the requirement to demonstrate the application of computer systems to patient care and quality improvement.

Medical Access and CHIP Reauthorization Act (MACRA) A new Medicare reimbursement system that focuses on quality, accountability, and better care for patients.

medical technology A general term for medical products and equipment used to provide less invasive treatment and diagnostic options.

medicalization of social problems Conversion of areas viewed as social problems into medical ones. For example, society now recognizes alcoholism as a disease and not just a social failing.

Merit-based Incentive Payment System (MIPS) A program to determine Medicare payment adjustments using performance scores. Scores determine bonuses and penalties for reimbursements.

metaethics The study of ethical concepts and definitions. Think of this as the macrostudy of ethics itself.

mitigation Organizational and individual efforts to lessen the impact of a disaster. Disaster planning is part of mitigation efforts.

moral community The group of people with whom we feel a moral affinity and for whom we assume an ethical obligation. Perceptions of who is and is not a member establish the boundaries of the moral community.

moral courage The ability to use moral reasoning and be empowered to take action when an ethics situation occurs.

moral distress The anxiety that is caused when someone knows what is the right thing to do but cannot implement this action because of conflicts between organizations, providers, or family members.

moral personhood The point at which one transitions into membership in the moral community.

moral residue When someone experiences moral distress on a long-term basis, it can affect attitudes about the profession and the organization. More residue has been linked to burnout and employee turnover.

morally avoidable inequity An imbalance or unfair situation that can be corrected. When society corrects an inequity, the correction must not violate other social values, such as liberty or distributive justice.

most socially advantaged population A method of computing the amount of inequality in a population. In this case, the most socially advantaged group serves as a reference group for comparison with other groups in the population.

National Institute for Occupational Safety and Health A federal agency that is engaged in research and prepares guidelines with regard to work-related injury or illness prevention.

natural disaster A situation in which there is loss of life, property, or sense of safety that is caused by natural events such as floods, hurricanes, fires, and tornados.

natural law theory A branch of ethics based on the tradition of St. Thomas Aquinas. It uses the rationality of God and the idea of conscience to determine ethically appropriate actions.

natural right Respect for attributes that contribute to a human being's highest good and that come from nature. An example of a natural right is the right to the pursuit of happiness.

negative right A term that means that a person has a right to do anything not defined by the law. Examples of negative rights are found in the Bill of Rights and include the rights to assembly and free speech.

nomothetic knowledge: Information gained through scientific, objective, replicable, and generalizable methods.

non-consenting third party With regard to reproductive technologies, a potential child created by these technologies. The potential child cannot give consent for the treatment that initiates its existence.

nonmaleficence The ethical principle of refraining from causing harm or preventing intentional harm from occurring.

non-marital third party With regard to reproductive technologies, individuals who contribute to the procreation of a child but who will not be the parents of the child. Examples include egg and sperm donors.

normative ethics The application of ethics in determining what is right or wrong in a certain situation, such as the provision of health care.

noumenal world For Kant, the world as it exists within itself and not as we interpret it.

original position Part of John Rawls's hypothetical model to assist in determining what is just. In this hypothetical position, all people are equal and are not aware of personal circumstances (the veil of ignorance).

palliative specialist A healthcare professional who specializes in providing care that reduces pain and suffering without eliminating the cause. Such expertise is particularly important for end-of-life care.

pandemic The presence of a disease or health issue that spreads to multiple locations.

patient-centered medical home (PCMH) A medical care delivery system with services coordinated through primary care physicians. It focuses on appropriate care and maximizing health outcomes for patients.

patient-focused care (patient-centered care) The delivery of healthcare services with the patient as the center of care. Elements of this type of care include providing information, patient-friendly environments, open medical records, and the use of care partners.

pay-for-performance (P4P) A payment system that rewards providers who meet certain predetermined standards and goals. It is also known as value-based purchasing.

person An entity who can maintain social relationships with other persons. It involves a social role and not just a biological one.

positive right A limited example of legal rights, this term means that a person has a right to a social good and the right is the basis for entitlement.

posttraumatic stress disorder (PTSD) A mental health issue experienced by people who live through a traumatic event such as a sexual assault. Symptoms may last long after the event and affect the quality of life.

PPACA An abbreviation for H.R. 3590, the Patient Protection and Affordable Care Act of 2010. Some sources use the abbreviation ACA.

practical wisdom In Aristotle's virtue ethics, the process of using one's character, education, and experience to decide on a correct action in a situation.

pre-embryo A human to be. It has the potential to become a human being but has not achieved full human status.

prima facie A legal term indicating the assumption that something exists on initial examination.

principle of double effect An ethical principle used when there is a conflict between the good and evil effects of one action.

procedural justice Due process. Violations of due process can occur with healthcare employees and the use of procedures for decision-making.

professional socialization A process by which physicians and other healthcare professionals learn the knowledge, skills, and attitudes necessary to assume their roles.

psychic survival The denial of feelings and formation of values in order to protect oneself from psychological harm.

public beneficence A principle similar to the ethical principle of beneficence. However, it involves decisions concerning the public's ability to experience gains from emerging scientific discoveries.

quality-adjusted life year (QALY) A measure of the burden of a disease using the number of years lived and the quality-of-life indicators.

radical loving care A term, coined by Chapman, that describes a way of treating patients that is effective and holistic, and respects their spirituality.

ransomware A type of software that can block access to computer data. Those who use it threaten to publish or delete the blocked data unless some form of ransom is paid.

reflective equilibrium A decision-making model for dealing with ethics concerns that involves considered judgment and ethical intuition.

relative difference (RD) A number obtained by the division of the numeric measure of the health status of one group by that of another group.

research cloning The use of cloning technology to advance the study of disease prevention and treatment.

responsible stewardship A concept dealing with the ethical efforts to ensure that those persons unable to represent themselves receive consideration in the practice of future research studies.

retraumatization Trauma created after a person suffers a trauma, such as domestic violence, by virtue of the process used to gain information required for treatment. The patient must relive the pain and psychological damage in order to obtain treatment. Retraumatization also occurs if the individual decides to press charges against the abuser.

robotic-assisted surgery Procedures that employ actual robots to provide greater visibility and accessibility in different procedural sites and to reduce fatigue for surgeons.

rule utility Part of the theory of utilitarianism; the concept that the person making a decision should consider the greatest benefit (or good) for the greatest number. Rule utility can assist with policy decisions.

safe patient handling and mobility (SPHM) Practices for lifting, moving, and positioning patients in ways that do not cause injury to healthcare workers.

scientific-based secularism An orientation to medical practice that excludes religion or spirituality as a consideration of diagnosis or treatment practice.

self-identity The process of knowing who one is and of perceiving one's uniqueness.

sex-selective abortion The termination of a pregnancy on the basis of the preference for a particular gender, usually male.

shelter in place The policy of remaining in one's home, school, or place of business until help is available in the event of an emergency or natural disaster.

sine qua non A legal term meaning an essential condition or prerequisite.

social mother A woman who cares for a child after birth; she may or may not be the genetic or gestational mother.

spiritual well-being A measure of non-physical health that reflects joy, peace, and serenity in life.

stereotactic radiosurgery An image-guided procedure using radiotherapy devices and precise measurements in the brain. Surgeons use this procedure in treating malignant and benign brain tumors.

stewardship A management philosophy whereby one recognizes that one does not own resources. The manager, instead, protects the use of these resources in trust for the community or other stakeholders. Such a philosophy implies a high level of ethical awareness and application.

stewardship model A public health ethics model that stresses autonomy and supporting health among populations.

substantive right Something that is morally appropriate, such as food, housing, or a minimum wage. Substantive rights may or may not be legal rights, depending on the government structure.

Summa Theologica The title of one of the primary works of St. Thomas Aquinas, which includes his discourse on ethics.

surrogate In healthcare situations, one who makes decision for another, such as a relative who makes decisions for a nursing home resident.

surrogate mother With respect to reproductive technology, a woman who carries another woman's child in her womb. The process is known as surrogacy.

surveillance reports In disaster planning, documents that provide information on potential natural or human-caused disasters. Planners use several methods to obtain this information, including weather reports, telephone monitoring, and tracking of suspicious individuals.

synthetic biology A new genetic science that allows scientists to replace natural genetic material with genetically copied material.

systematic health inequality A difference in health that consistently affects two or more populations and is not caused by random variation.

technically avoidable health inequity A term used to describe an issue of inequality that is avoidable because a means for reduction exists.

technology diffusion The process of a technology becoming so common in a culture that it helps to define that culture.

telemanipulation Robot-assisted surgical procedures that allow surgeons improved ergonomics during the procedure.

telemedicine A general term for the use of email, video links, computers, and other telecommunications to send information about patients to medical staff members.

teleology The collection of ethical theories based on explanations of ethics as related to a goal or result.

tesla signal strength A measurement of the magnetic field strength of a magnetic resonance imaging machine.

third-party donor A person who contributes sperm or ova in a collaborative reproduction effort.

total population average A method of computing the amount of inequality in a population; it examines the average of healthcare events in the population as a reference group to compare the same event with subpopulations.

triage A system used in disaster and other mass causality situations to assess the severity of injury and guide an appropriate response. Triage often clashes with beneficence and autonomy.

unjust cause One of the criteria for judging health inequities; health inequities that result from severe restrictions to lifestyle choices, unhealthy working conditions, and inadequate access to health services fall into this category.

utilitarianism A doctrine that means that actions are ethical when they produce the greatest happiness, or utility. The reverse is also true. Actions are good when they avoid producing the greatest harm. This term is often seen as a synonym for consequentialism.

vertical equity The allocation of different resources for different needs.

virtue ethics Part of authority-based ethics; theories of virtue ethics seek to determine the proper behavior for human beings. In other words, "How does an ethical person live his or her life?"

workplace spirituality A culture within a workplace that supports employees' ability to find meaning and purpose in their work.

Index

Tables and figures are indicated by *t* and *f*, respectively.

A

AARP. *See* American Association for Retired Persons

absoluteness, role of ethical theories in, 6

abuse, intergenerational transmission, 241. *See also* domestic violence prevention

ACA. *See* Affordable Care Act

Academic Consortium for Integrative Medicine and Health, 265

access to quality elder care, ethical prospects for improving, 87–100

accountable care organizations (ACOs), 139

ACOs. *See* accountable care organizations

act analysis, of reproductive technologies, 72

act consequentialism. *See* classical utilitarianism

act of commission, 42

act of omission, 42

action stage, of behavior change, 232

activities of daily living (ADLs), 89, 90, 95

AD. *See* Alzheimer disease

Adams, T. E., 263

Adepoju, Omolola E., 211

ADLs. *See* activities of daily living

administration model, of healthcare ethics committees, 114

administrators, 111–112, 113

adoption

    as analogous to reproductive assistance, 74

    regulations, 74

adult caregivers, 88

advance directives, 110, 217

Advancing Effective Communication, Cultural Competence, and Patient- and Family-Centered Care: A Roadmap for Hospitals (TJC), 173

affordability, 190

Affordable Care Act (ACA), 88, 96, 99, 107, 147, 240, 263. *See also* healthcare reform

    increased complexity of healthcare with, 1, 3

    key provisions of, 187–189

    passage of, 183, 187

    patient-centered care model, 172–173

    shortfalls of, 191

    spirituality and, 174

    success of, 189

Agency for Health Research and Quality (AHRQ), 173

aggregative considerations, health inequalities and, 205

aging-in-place programs, 89

AHIMA. *See* American Health Information Management Association

AHRQ. *See* Agency for Health Research and Quality

AIH. *See* artificial insemination by husband

"alien dignity," 79

allocation. *See* resource allocation

"altered standards of care," 227

Alternate Payment Models (APMs), 139

altruism, 10, 73, 77–78, 81

Alzheimer disease (AD), 89, 95

Alzheimer's Association, 95

AMA. *See* American Medical Association

American Association for Retired Persons (AARP), 95, 266

American Coalition of Citizens with Disabilities, 96

American Health Information Management Association (AHIMA), 123–124

American Medical Association (AMA)

    Committee on Quackery, 266

    position on universal healthcare, 184, 185

American Nurses Association (ANA)

    Health Risk Appraisal, 153–154

American Red Cross, 224

ANA. *See* American Nurses Association

Anarchy, State, and Utopia (book), 23

Andrea Smith case, 125

animal rights, 63

APMs. *See* Alternate Payment Models

Aquinas. *See* St. Thomas Aquinas

Argentina's Dirty War, 74

Aristotle, 5, 8, 12–14, 33*n*24,*n*29, 177

artificial insemination by husband (AIH), 75

ASPHP. *See* Association of Safe Patient Handling Professionals

asset sheltering, 94

assisted-living facility, 93

assisted reproduction, 79

Association of Computing Machinery, 127

Association of Safe Patient Handling Professionals (ASPHP), 155, 157

authority-based theories, 4, 7–8

authorization, in clinical research, 140

autonomy, 147

    for boomer generation, 271